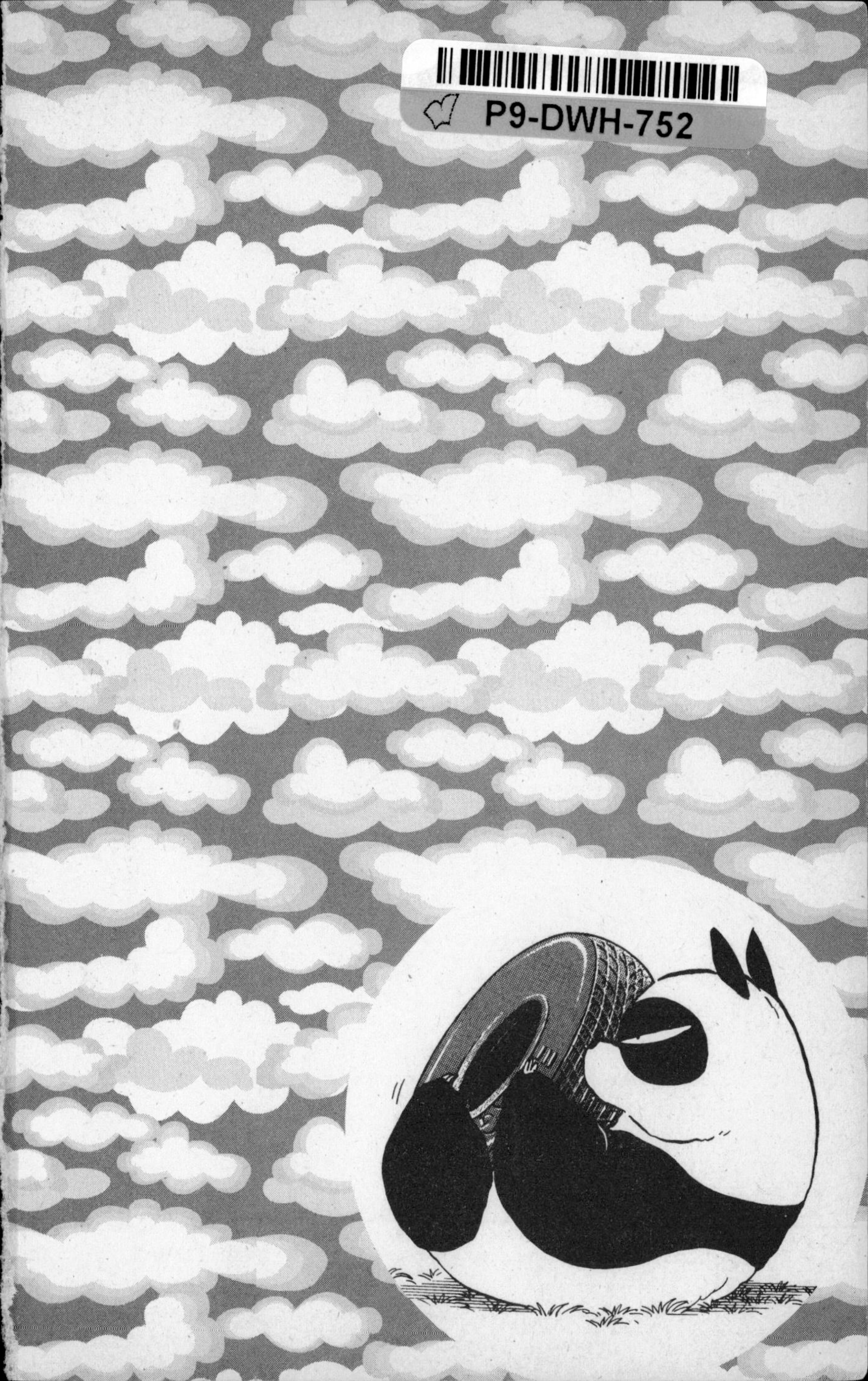

Ranma ½

VOL. 25   Action Edition

STORY & ART BY
RUMIKO TAKAHASHI

Ranma ½

VOL. 25
Action Edition

Story and Art by
RUMIKO TAKAHASHI

English Adaptation by Gerard Jones
Translation by Kaori Inoue
Touch-Up Art & Lettering/Wayne Truman
Cover and Interior Design & Graphics/Yuki Ameda
Supervising Editor/Julie Davis
Editor/Avery Gotoh

Managing Editor/Annette Roman
Director of Production/Noboru Watanabe
VP of Publishing/Alvin Lu
Sr. Director of Acquisitions/Rika Inouye
VP of Sales and Marketing/Liza Coppola
Publisher/Hyoe Narita

Published by VIZ Media, LLC
P.O. Box 77010
San Francisco, CA 94107

Action Edition
10 9 8 7 6 5 4 3 2
First printing, January 2004
Second printing, October 2005

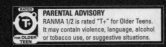
PARENTAL ADVISORY
RANMA 1/2 is rated "T+" for Older Teens.
It may contain violence, language, alcohol or tobacco use, or suggestive situations.

www.viz.com

STORY THUS FAR

The Tendos are an average, run-of-the-mill Japanese family—at least on the surface, that is. Soun Tendo is the owner and proprietor of the Tendo Dojo, where "Anything-Goes Martial Arts" is practiced. Like the name says, anything goes, and usually does.

When Soun's old friend Genma Saotome comes to visit, Soun's three lovely young daughters—Akane, Nabiki, and Kasumi—are told that it's time for one of them to become the fiancée of Genma's teenage son, as per an agreement made between the two fathers years ago. Youngest daughter Akane—who says she hates boys—is quickly nominated for bridal duty by her sisters.

Unfortunately, Ranma and his father have suffered a strange accident. While training in China, both plunged into one of many "accursed" springs at the legendary martial arts training ground of Jusenkyo. These springs transform the unlucky dunkee into whoever—or whatever—drowned there hundreds of years ago.

From now on, a splash of cold water turns Ranma's father into a giant panda, and Ranma becomes a beautiful, busty young woman. Hot water reverses the effect...but only until next time.

Ranma and Genma weren't the only ones to take the Jusenkyo plunge—it isn't long before they meet several other members of the "cursed." And although their parents are still determined to see Ranma and Akane marry and carry on the training hall, Ranma seems to have a strange talent for accumulating extra fiancées, and Akane has a few suitors of her own. Will the two ever work out their differences, get rid of all these extra people, or just call the whole thing off? And will Ranma ever get rid of his curse?

CAST OF CHARACTERS

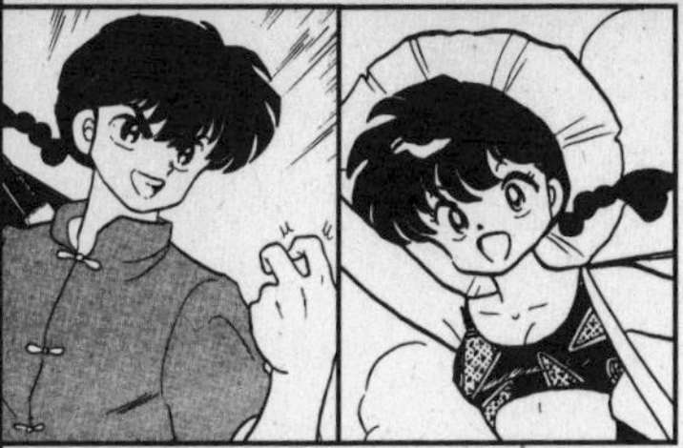

RANMA SAOTOME
Martial artist with far too many fiancées, and an ego that won't let him take defeat easily. He changes into a girl when splashed with cold water.

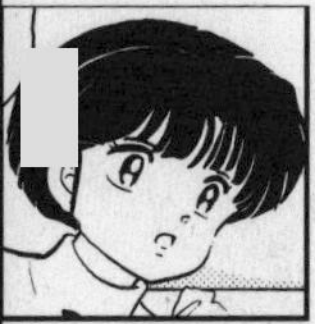

AKANE TENDO
A martial artist, tomboy, and Ranma's fiancée by parental arrangement. She has no clue how much Ryoga likes her, or what relation he has to her pet black pig, P-chan.

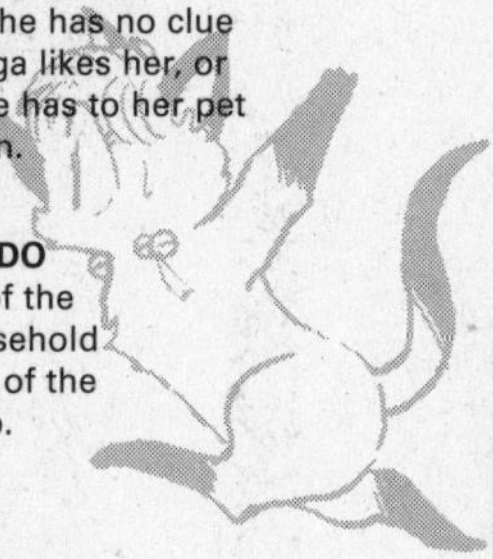

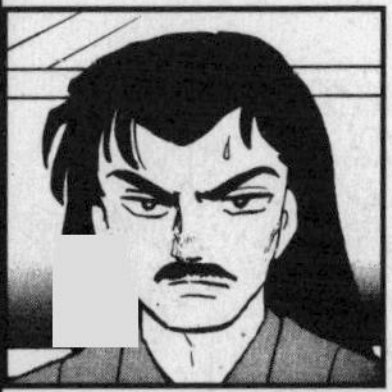

SOUN TENDO
The head of the Tendo household and owner of the Tendo Dojo.

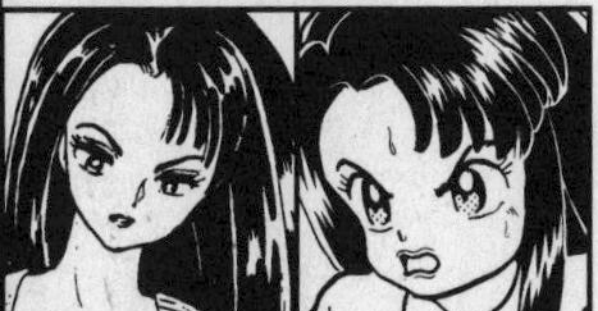

HINAKO NINOMIYA
A high school teacher with the martial arts ability to siphon energy from her opponents and change form.

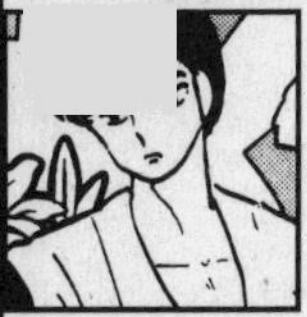

TATEWAKI KUNO
Furinkan High's *kendo* club president is smitten with both Ranma (in girl form, a.k.a. the "pigtailed girl") and Akane.

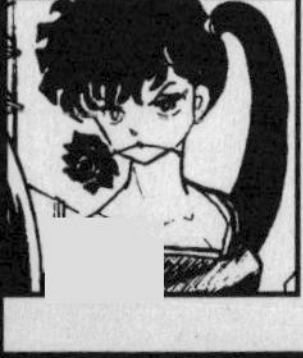

KODACHI KUNO
Kuno's demented sister is a diabolical gymnast who is determined to make Ranma her own.

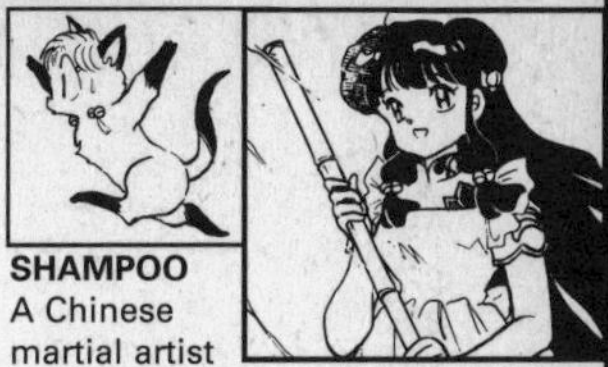

SHAMPOO
A Chinese martial artist from a village of amazons who is in love with Ranma and claims that he must marry her due to village law. She changes into a cat.

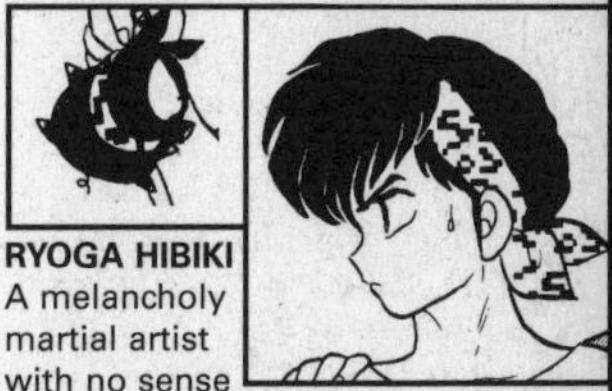

RYOGA HIBIKI
A melancholy martial artist with no sense of direction, a crush on Akane, and a grudge against Ranma. He changes into a small, black pig Akane calls "P-chan."

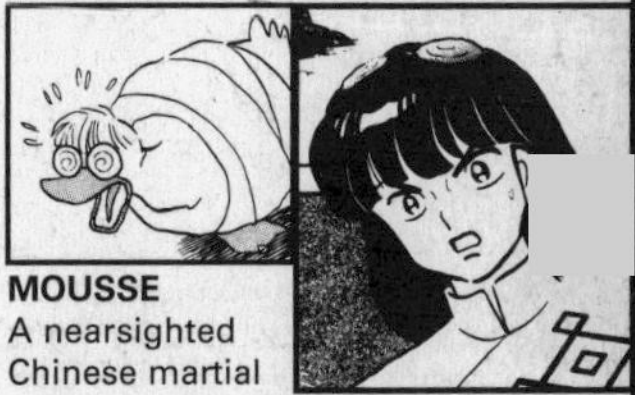

MOUSSE
A nearsighted Chinese martial artist whose specialty is hidden weapons, Mousse has been Shampoo's suitor since childhood. He changes into a duck.

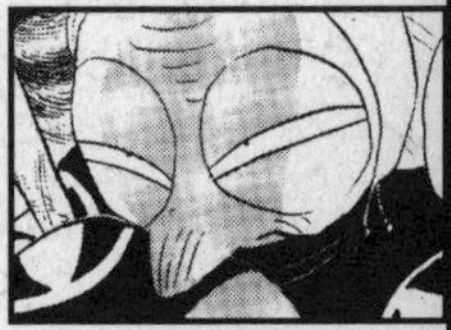

COLOGNE
Great-grandmother to Shampoo who's looking forward to getting a new grandson-in-law in Ranma.

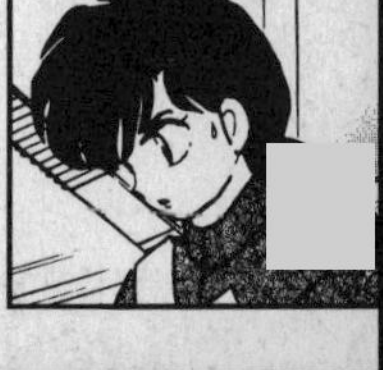

UKYO KUONJI
Another of Ranma's fianceés, Ukyo is both a martial artist and an *okonomiyaki* chef.

CONTENTS

Part 1

DANGER: HOME VISIT AHEAD!

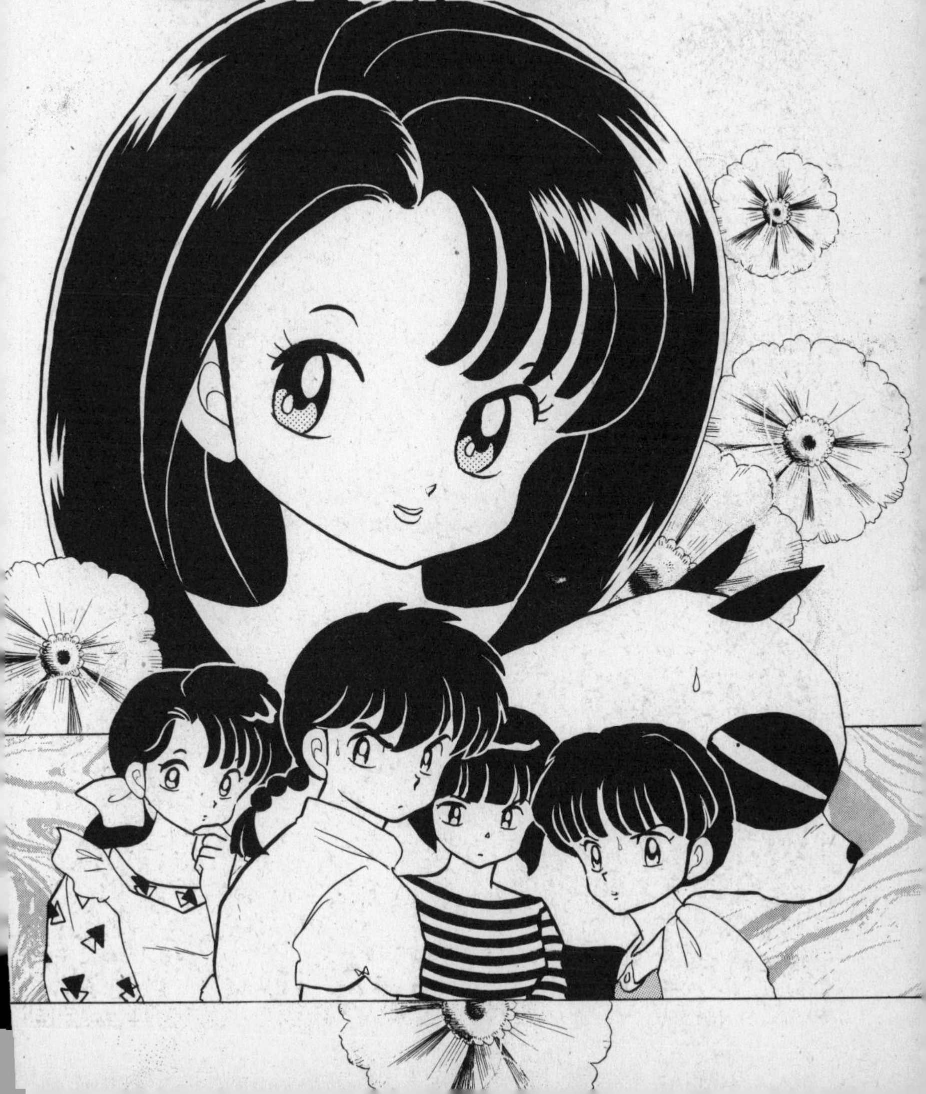

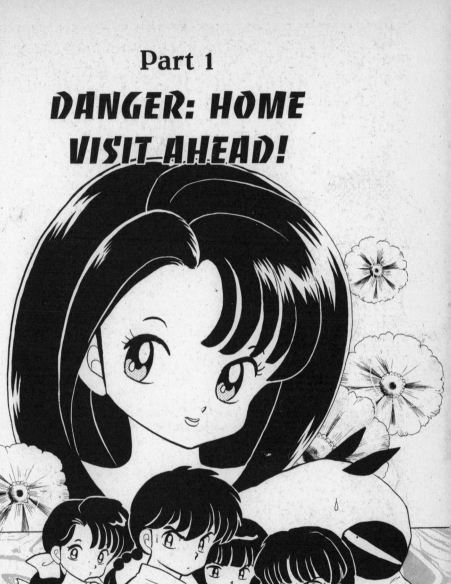

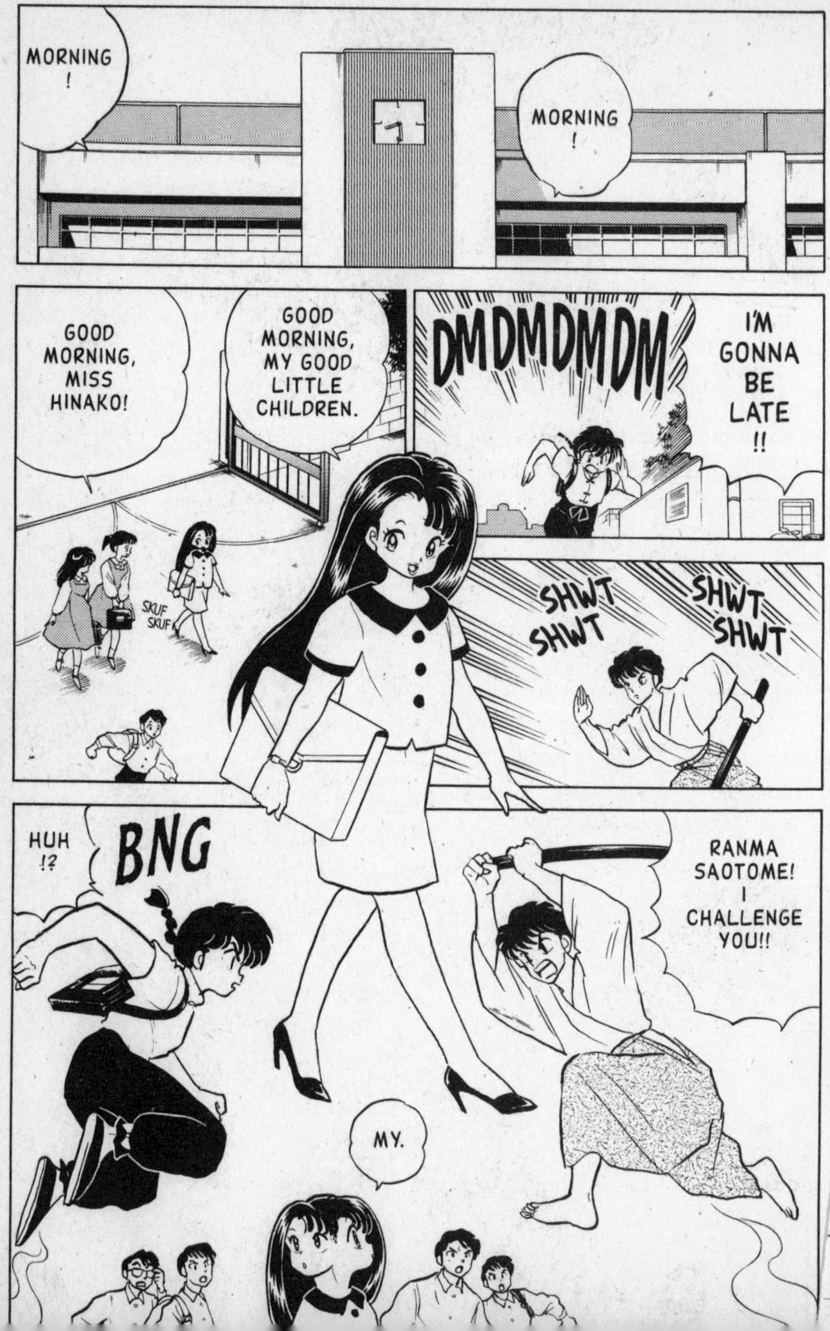
MORNING!
MORNING!
GOOD MORNING, MISS HINAKO!
GOOD MORNING, MY GOOD LITTLE CHILDREN.
SKUF SKUF
DMDMDMDM
I'M GONNA BE LATE!!
SHWT SHWT
SHWT SHWT
HUH!?
BNG
RANMA SAOTOME! I CHALLENGE YOU!!
MY.

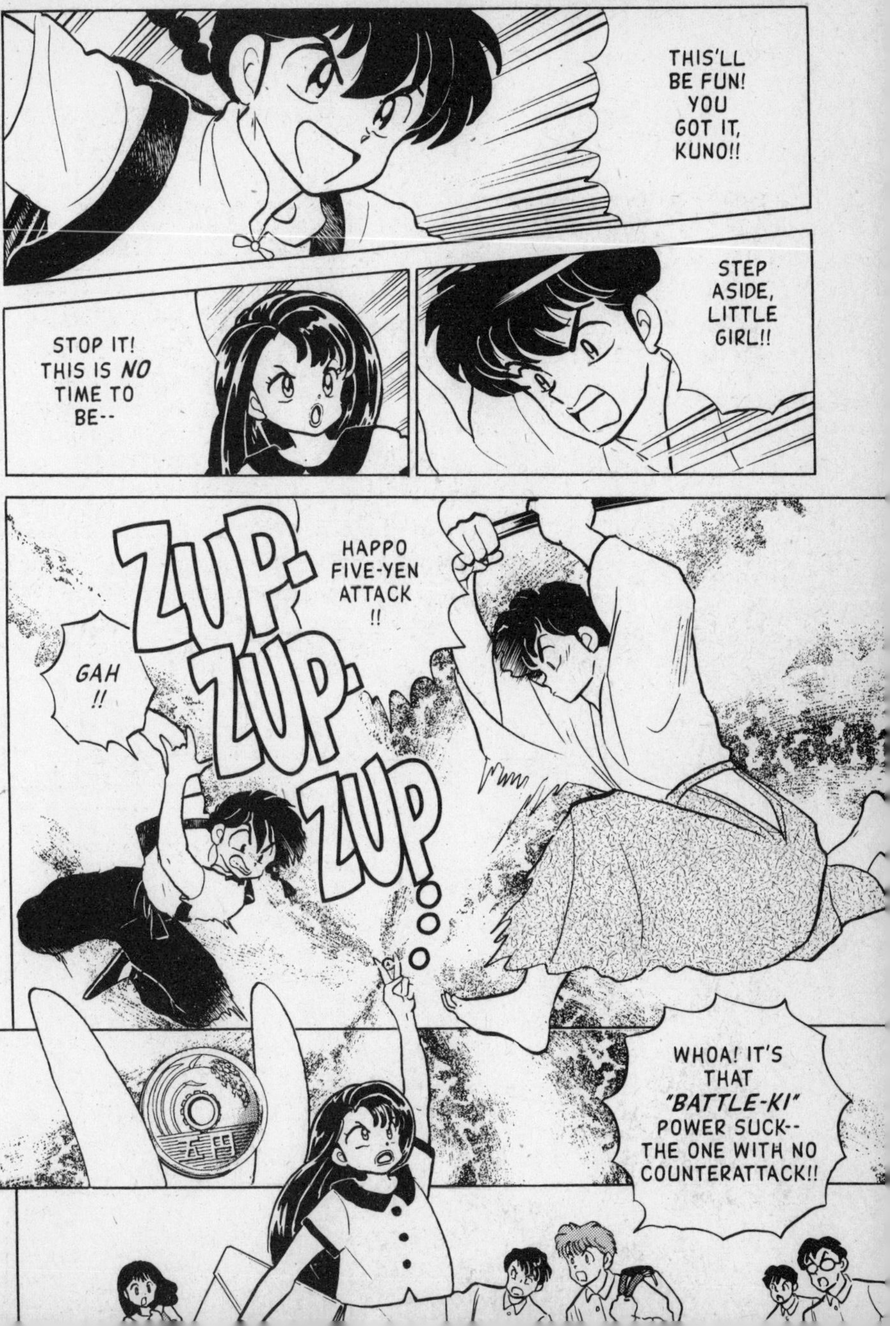
THIS'LL BE FUN! YOU GOT IT, KUNO!!
STOP IT! THIS IS *NO* TIME TO BE--
STEP ASIDE, LITTLE GIRL!!
HAPPO FIVE-YEN ATTACK !!
GAH !!
ZUP-ZUP-ZUP
WHOA! IT'S THAT *"BATTLE-KI"* POWER SUCK-- THE ONE WITH NO COUNTERATTACK!!

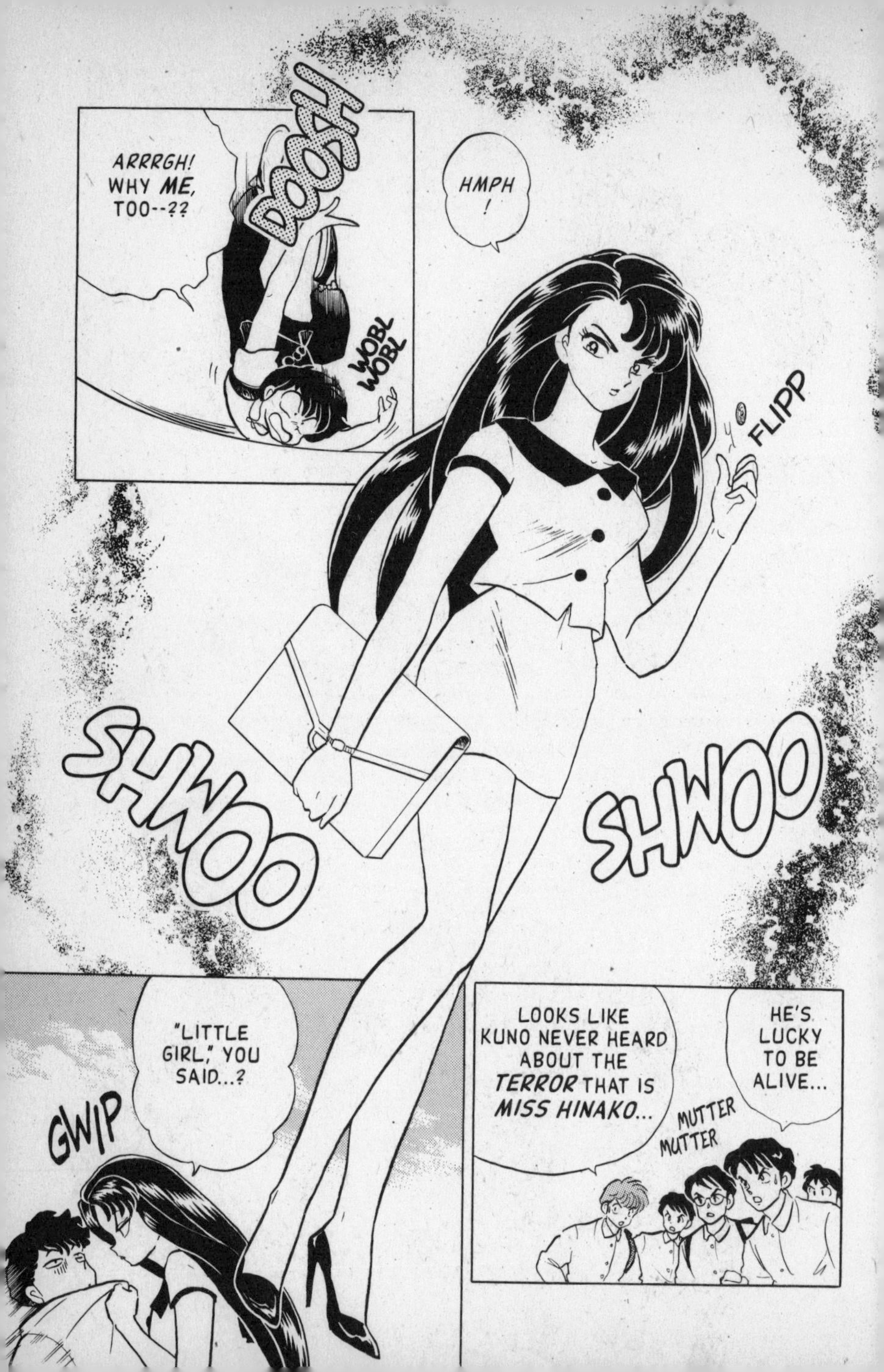
ARRRGH! WHY ME, TOO--??
DOOSH
WOBL WOBL
HMPH!
FLIPP
SHWOO
SHWOO
"LITTLE GIRL," YOU SAID...?
GWIP
LOOKS LIKE KUNO NEVER HEARD ABOUT THE TERROR THAT IS MISS HINAKO...
HE'S LUCKY TO BE ALIVE...
MUTTER MUTTER

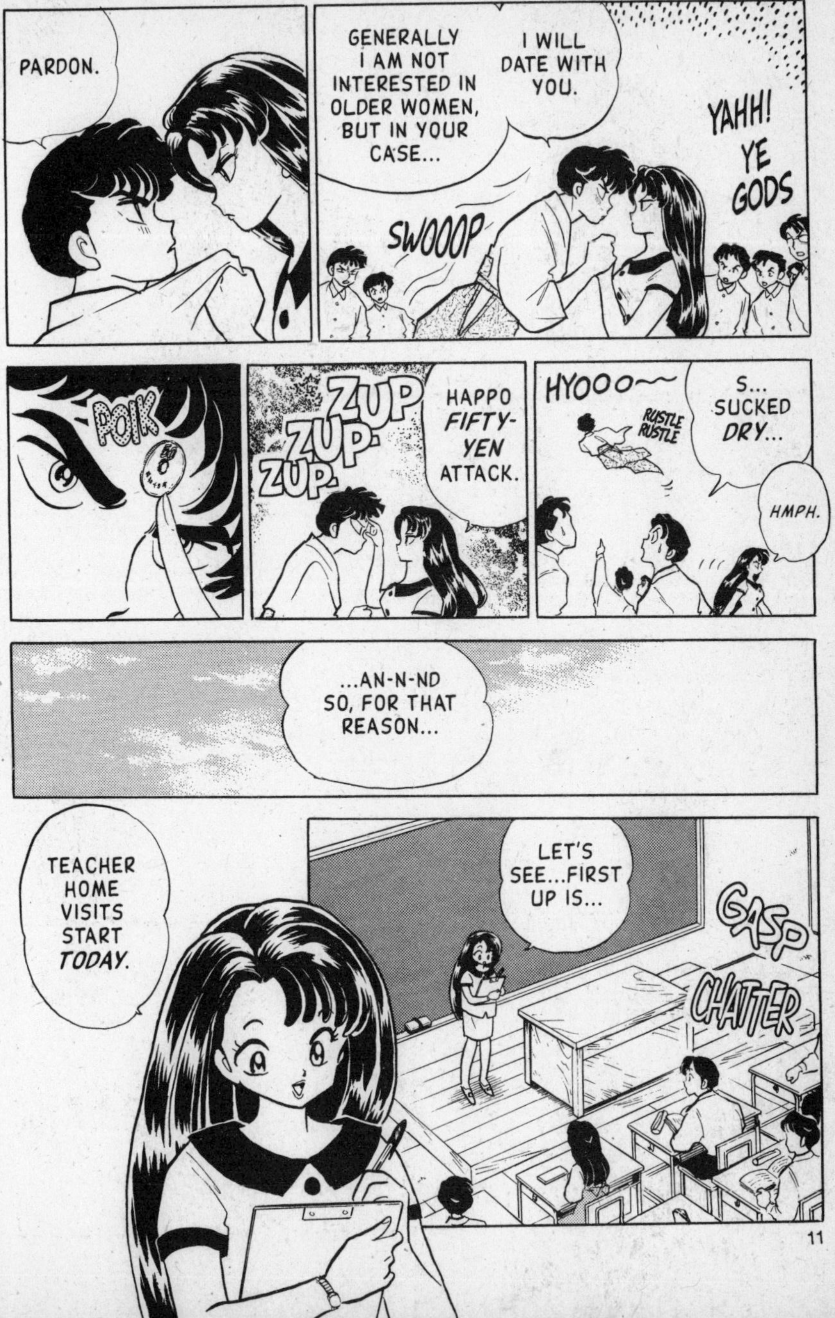
PARDON.
GENERALLY I AM NOT INTERESTED IN OLDER WOMEN, BUT IN YOUR CASE...
I WILL DATE WITH YOU.
YAHH! YE GODS
SWOOOP
POIK
ZUP ZUP ZUP
HAPPO FIFTY-YEN ATTACK.
HYOOO~~
RUSTLE RUSTLE
S... SUCKED DRY...
HMPH.
...AN-N-ND SO, FOR THAT REASON...
TEACHER HOME VISITS START TODAY.
LET'S SEE...FIRST UP IS...
GASP
CHATTER

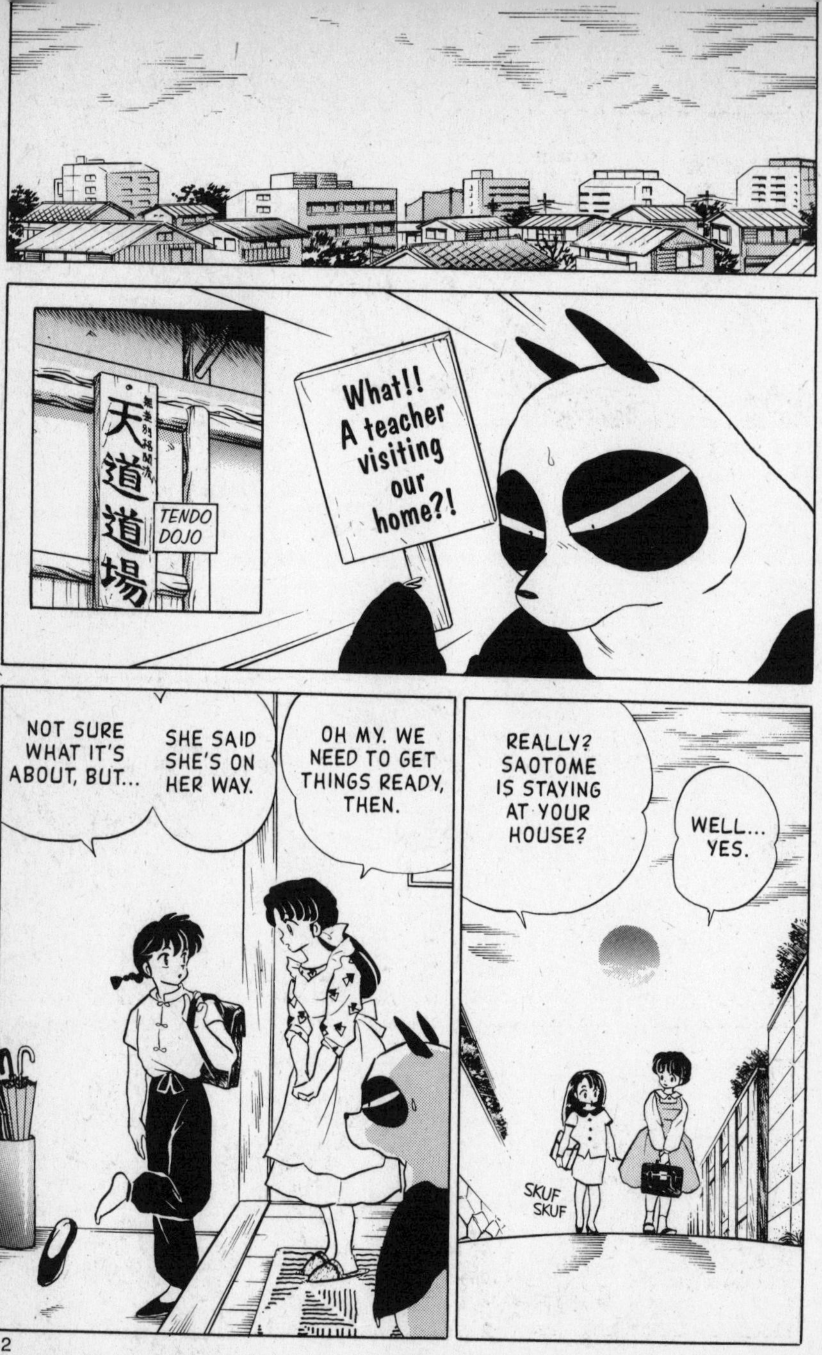
無差別格闘流
天道道場
TENDO DOJO
What!! A teacher visiting our home?!
NOT SURE WHAT IT'S ABOUT, BUT...
SHE SAID SHE'S ON HER WAY.
OH MY. WE NEED TO GET THINGS READY, THEN.
REALLY? SAOTOME IS STAYING AT YOUR HOUSE?
WELL... YES.
SKUF SKUF

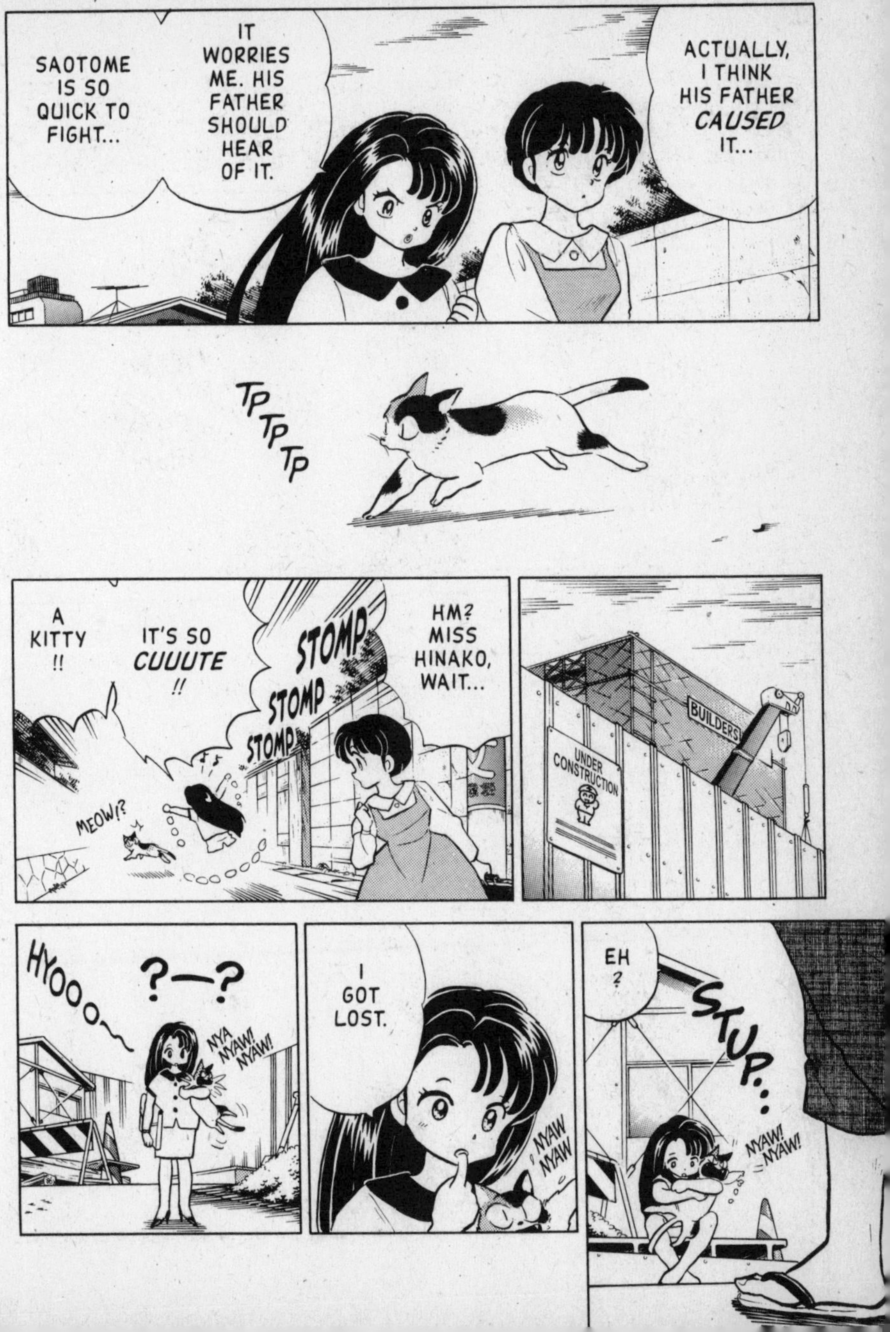
SAOTOME IS SO QUICK TO FIGHT...
IT WORRIES ME. HIS FATHER SHOULD HEAR OF IT.
ACTUALLY, I THINK HIS FATHER CAUSED IT...
TPTPTPTP
A KITTY !!
IT'S SO CUUUTE !!
STOMP
STOMP
STOMP
HM? MISS HINAKO, WAIT...
MEOW!?
UNDER CONSTRUCTION
BUILDERS
HYOOO~
?—?
NYA NYAW! NYAW!
I GOT LOST.
NYAW NYAW
EH?
STUP...
NYAW! NYAW!

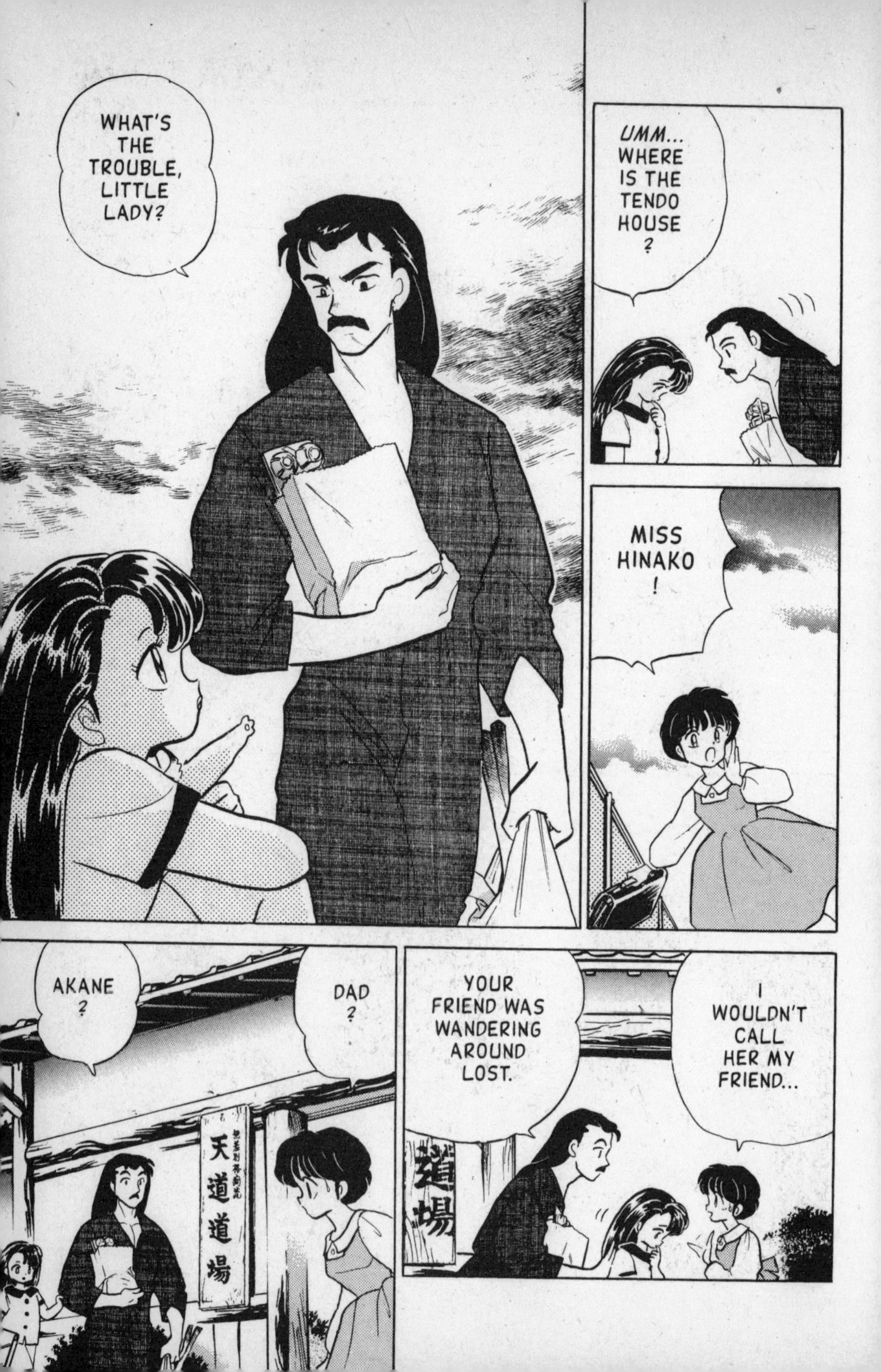
WHAT'S THE TROUBLE, LITTLE LADY?
UMM... WHERE IS THE TENDO HOUSE?
MISS HINAKO!
AKANE?
DAD?
天道道場
YOUR FRIEND WAS WANDERING AROUND LOST.
I WOULDN'T CALL HER MY FRIEND...

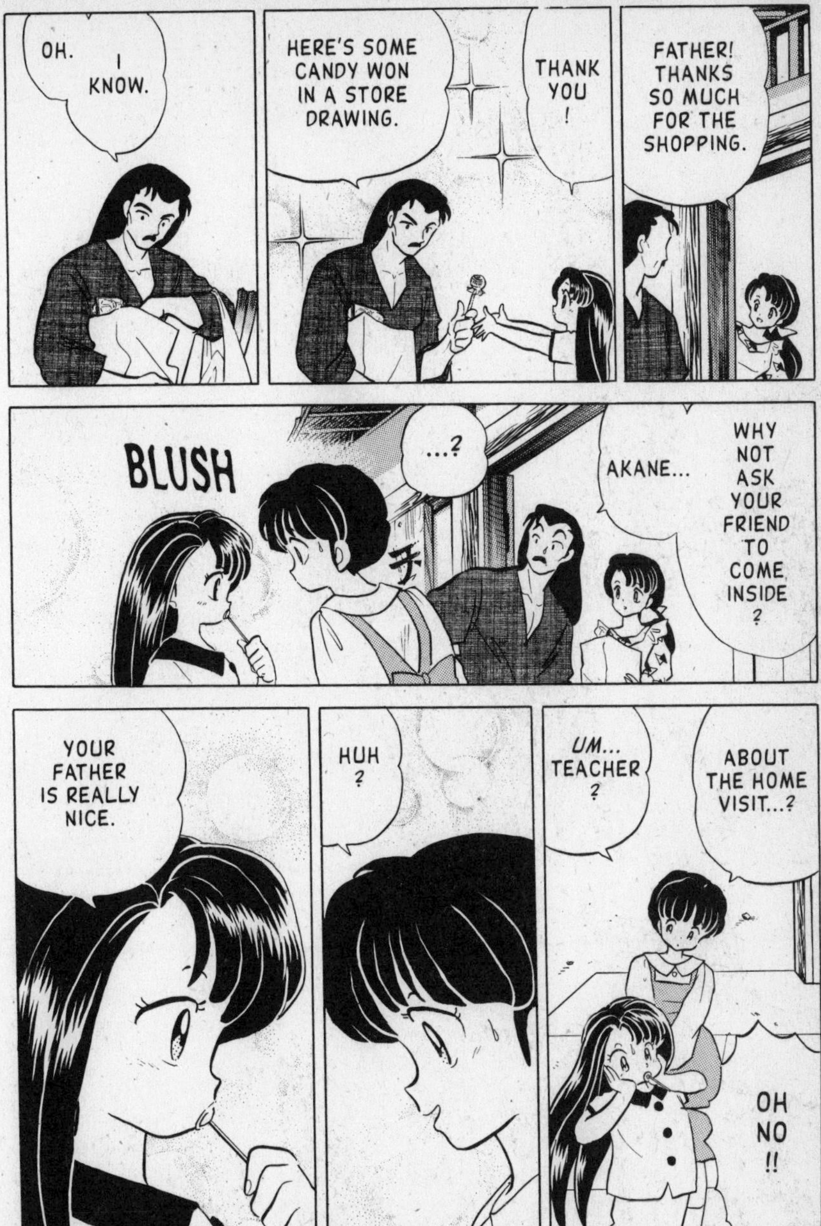
OH. I KNOW.
HERE'S SOME CANDY WON IN A STORE DRAWING.
THANK YOU!
FATHER! THANKS SO MUCH FOR THE SHOPPING.
BLUSH
...?
AKANE...
WHY NOT ASK YOUR FRIEND TO COME INSIDE?
YOUR FATHER IS REALLY NICE.
HUH?
UM... TEACHER?
ABOUT THE HOME VISIT...?
OH NO!!

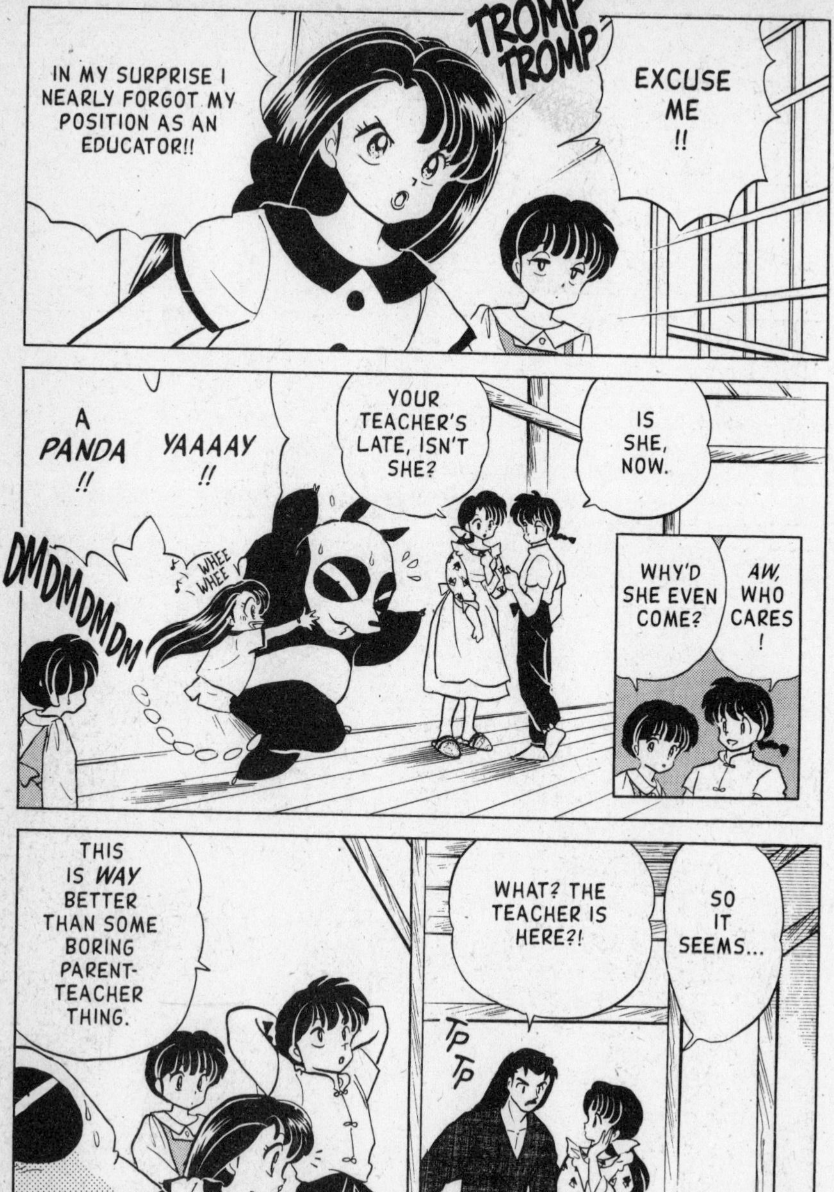
IN MY SURPRISE I NEARLY FORGOT MY POSITION AS AN EDUCATOR!!
TROMP TROMP
EXCUSE ME !!
A PANDA !!
YAAAAY !!
DMDMDMDMDM
WHEE WHEE
YOUR TEACHER'S LATE, ISN'T SHE?
IS SHE, NOW.
WHY'D SHE EVEN COME?
AW, WHO CARES !
THIS IS WAY BETTER THAN SOME BORING PARENT-TEACHER THING.
WHAT? THE TEACHER IS HERE?!
SO IT SEEMS...
TP TP

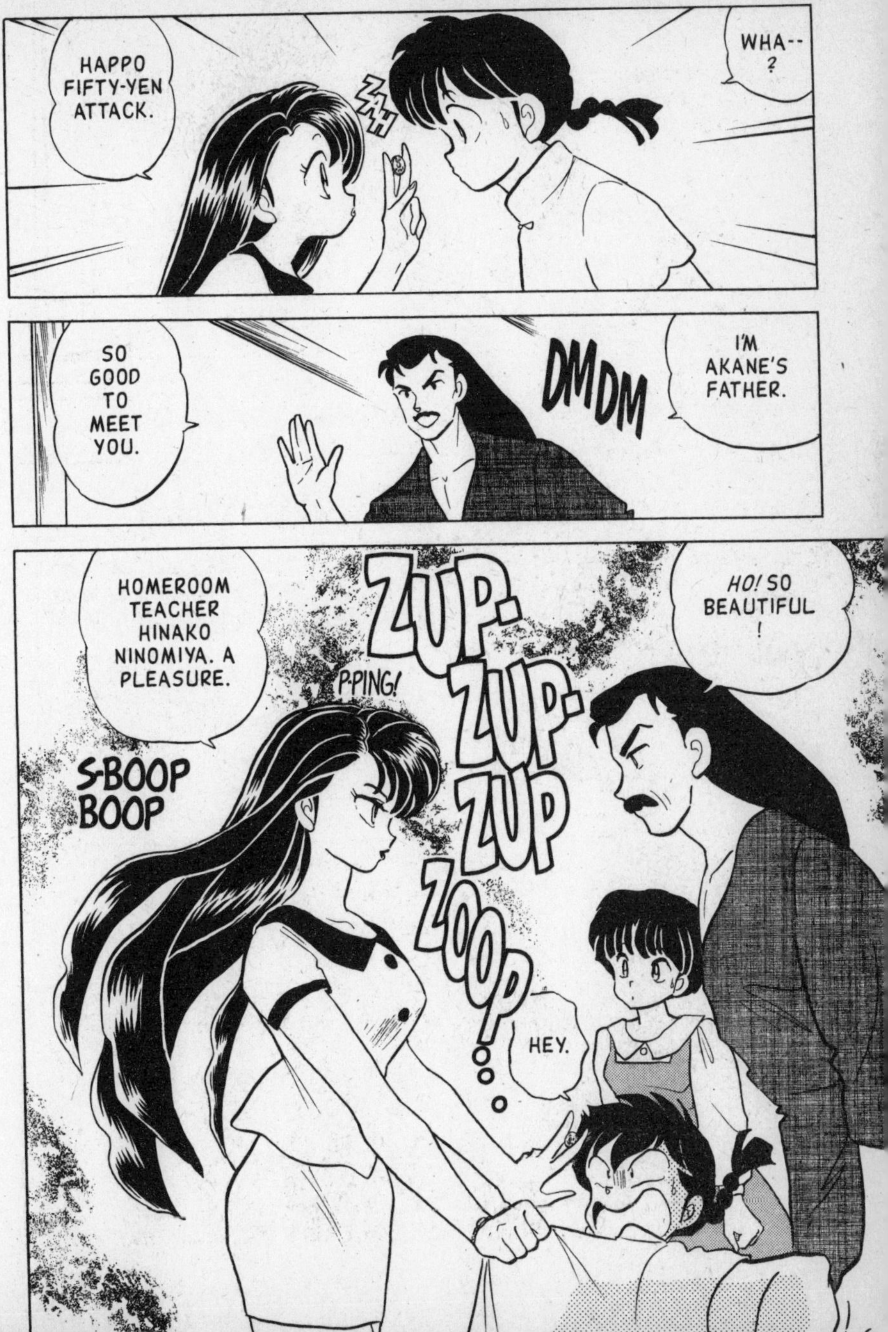
HAPPO FIFTY-YEN ATTACK.
ZAH
WHA-- ?
SO GOOD TO MEET YOU.
DMDM
I'M AKANE'S FATHER.
HOMEROOM TEACHER HINAKO NINOMIYA. A PLEASURE.
ZUP-ZUP-ZUP-ZUP ZOOP
P-PING!
HO! SO BEAUTIFUL !
S-BOOP BOOP
HEY.

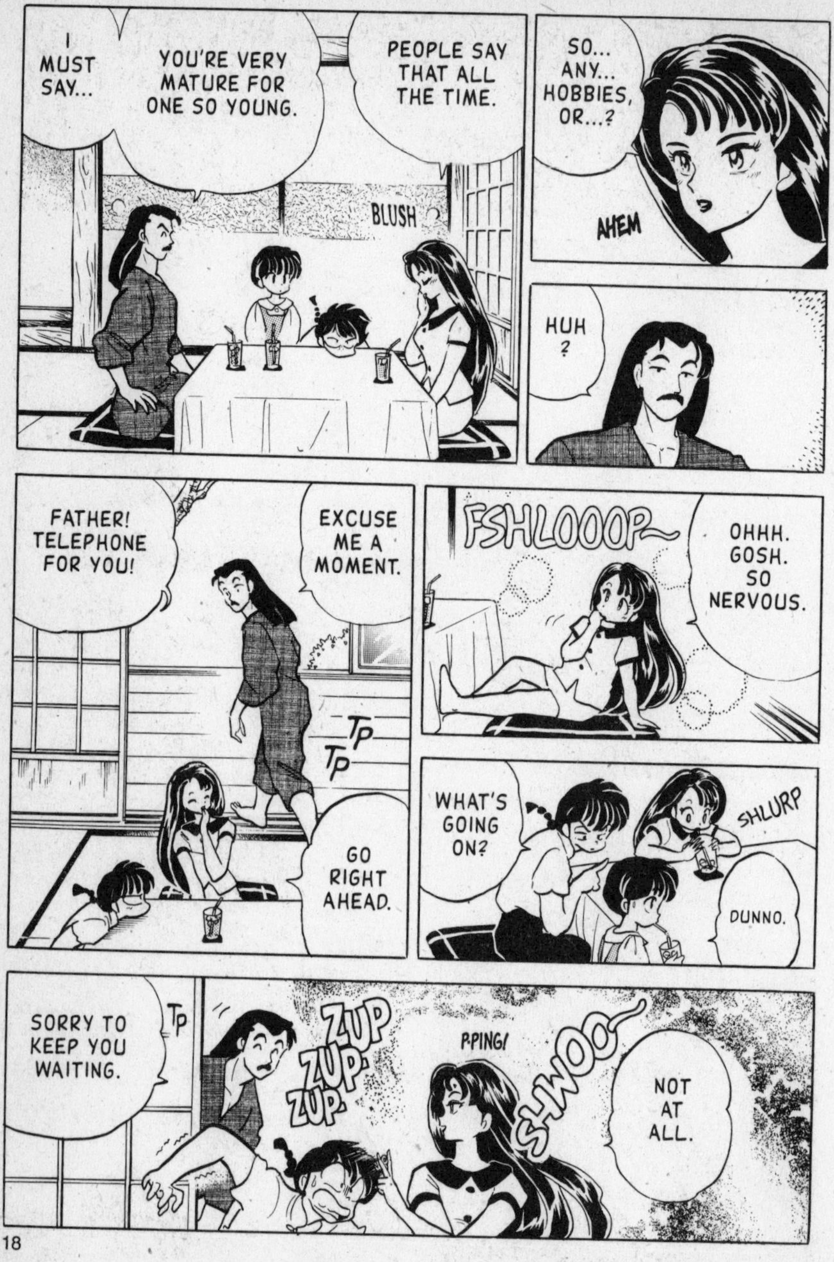
I MUST SAY...
YOU'RE VERY MATURE FOR ONE SO YOUNG.
PEOPLE SAY THAT ALL THE TIME.
BLUSH
SO... ANY... HOBBIES, OR...?
AHEM
HUH?
FATHER! TELEPHONE FOR YOU!
EXCUSE ME A MOMENT.
TP TP
GO RIGHT AHEAD.
FSHLOOOP~
OHHH. GOSH. SO NERVOUS.
WHAT'S GOING ON?
SHLURP
DUNNO.
SORRY TO KEEP YOU WAITING.
TP
ZUP ZUP ZUP
P-PING!
SHWOO~
NOT AT ALL.

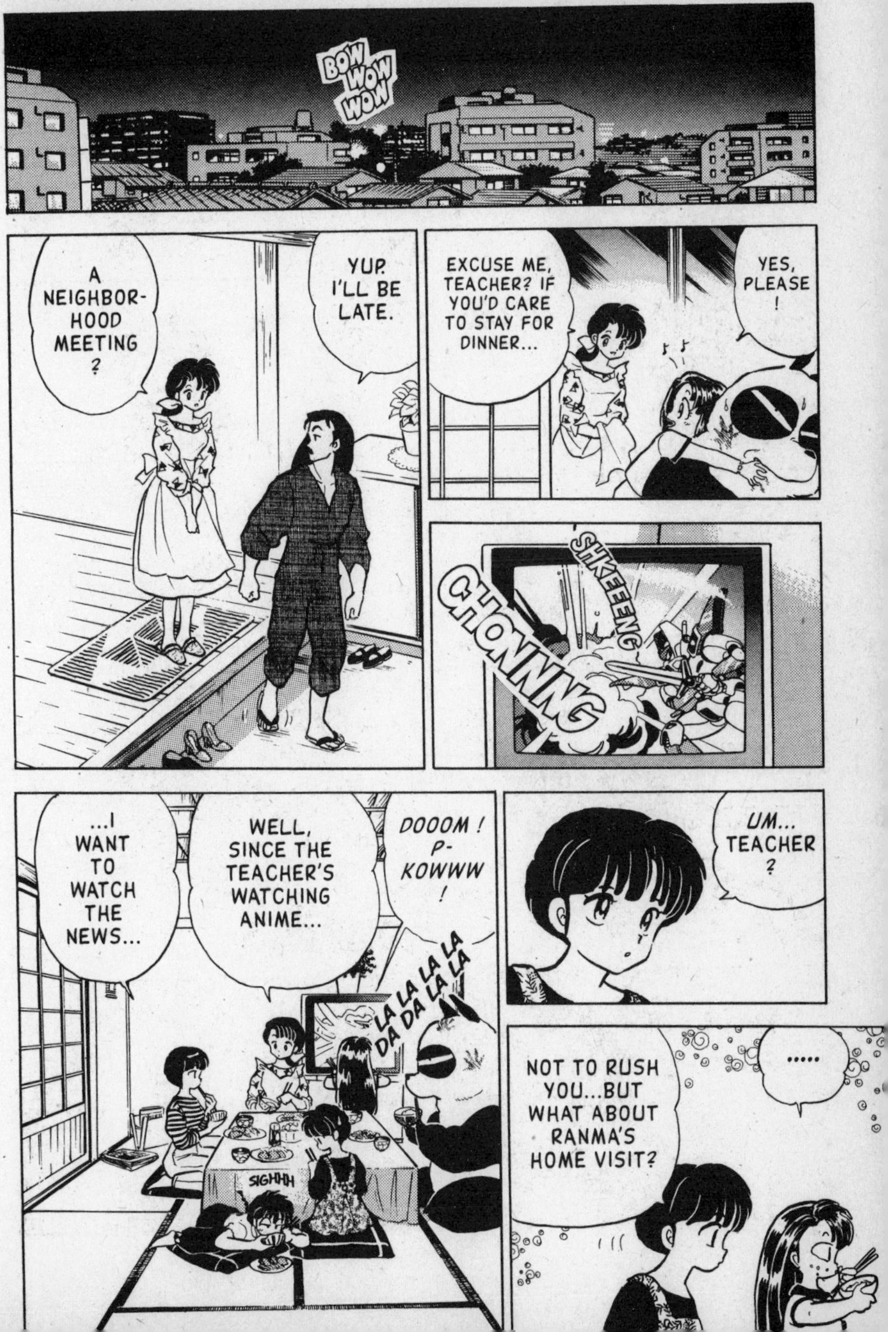
BOW WOW WOW
A NEIGHBOR-HOOD MEETING?
YUP. I'LL BE LATE.
EXCUSE ME, TEACHER? IF YOU'D CARE TO STAY FOR DINNER...
YES, PLEASE!
SHKEEENG
CHONNNG
...I WANT TO WATCH THE NEWS...
WELL, SINCE THE TEACHER'S WATCHING ANIME...
DOOOM! P-KOWWW!
LA LA LA LA DA DA LA LA
SIGHHH
UM... TEACHER?
NOT TO RUSH YOU...BUT WHAT ABOUT RANMA'S HOME VISIT?
.....

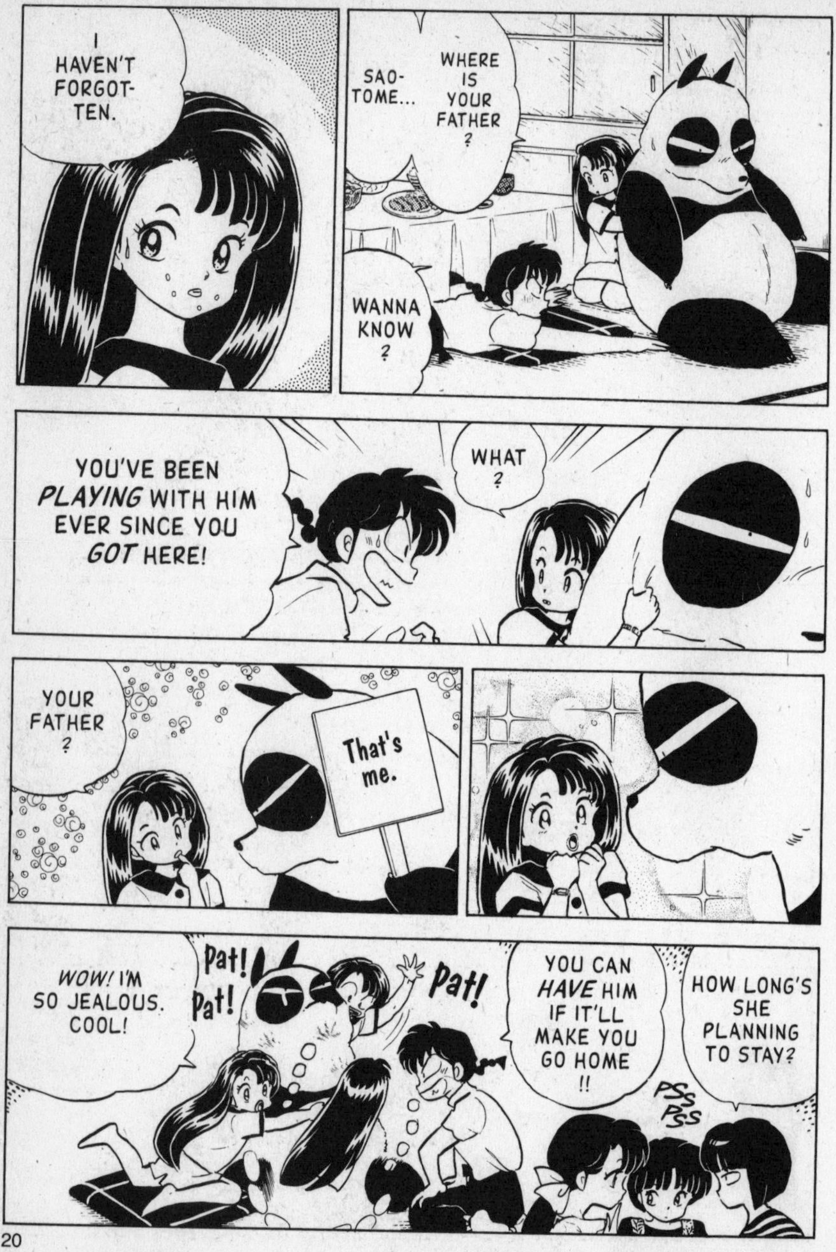

I HAVEN'T FORGOTTEN.
SAOTOME...
WHERE IS YOUR FATHER?
WANNA KNOW?
YOU'VE BEEN *PLAYING* WITH HIM EVER SINCE YOU *GOT* HERE!
WHAT?
YOUR FATHER?
That's me.
WOW! I'M SO JEALOUS. COOL!
Pat! Pat!
Pat!
YOU CAN *HAVE* HIM IF IT'LL MAKE YOU GO HOME!!
PSS PSS
HOW LONG'S SHE PLANNING TO STAY?

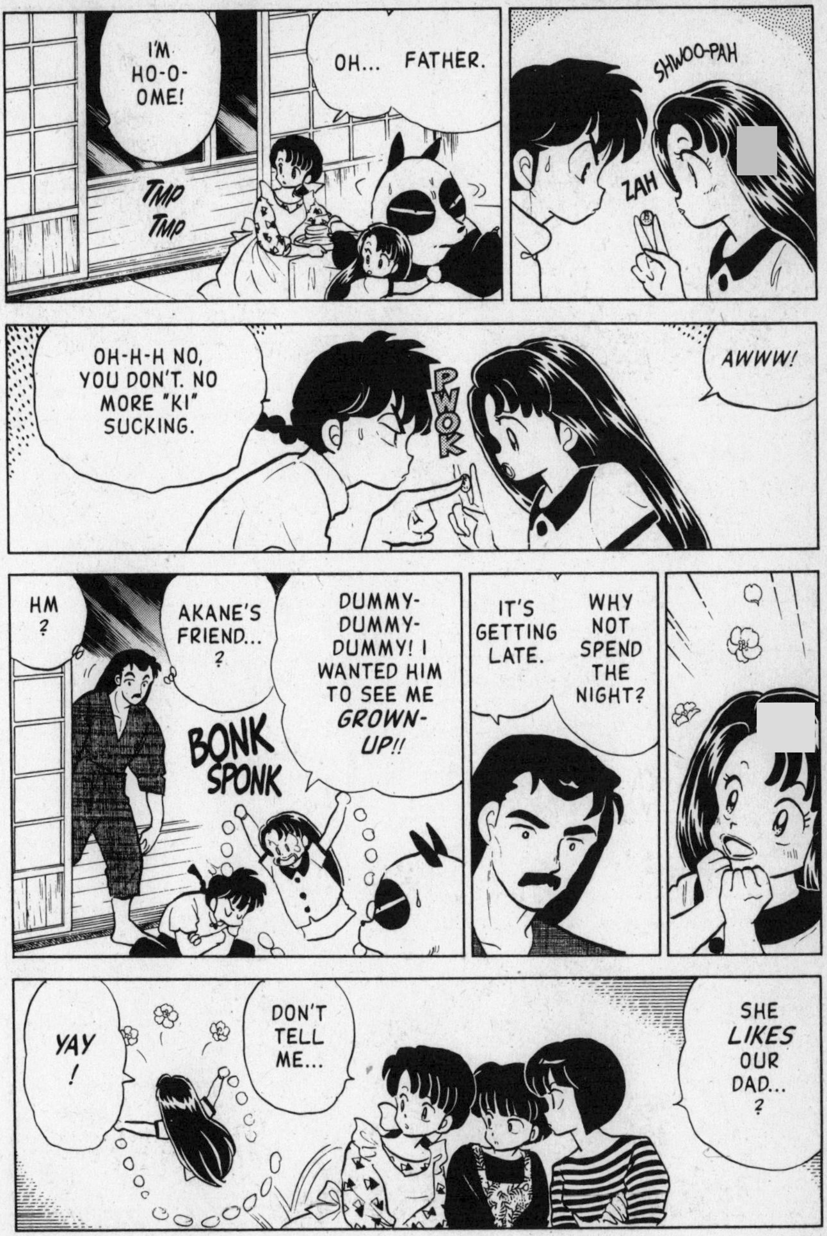
I'M HO-O-OME!
TMP TMP
OH... FATHER.
SHWOO-PAH
ZAH
OH-H-H NO, YOU DON'T. NO MORE "KI" SUCKING.
PWOK
AWWW!
HM?
AKANE'S FRIEND...?
DUMMY-DUMMY-DUMMY! I WANTED HIM TO SEE ME GROWN-UP!!
BONK SPONK
IT'S GETTING LATE.
WHY NOT SPEND THE NIGHT?
YAY!
DON'T TELL ME...
SHE LIKES OUR DAD...?

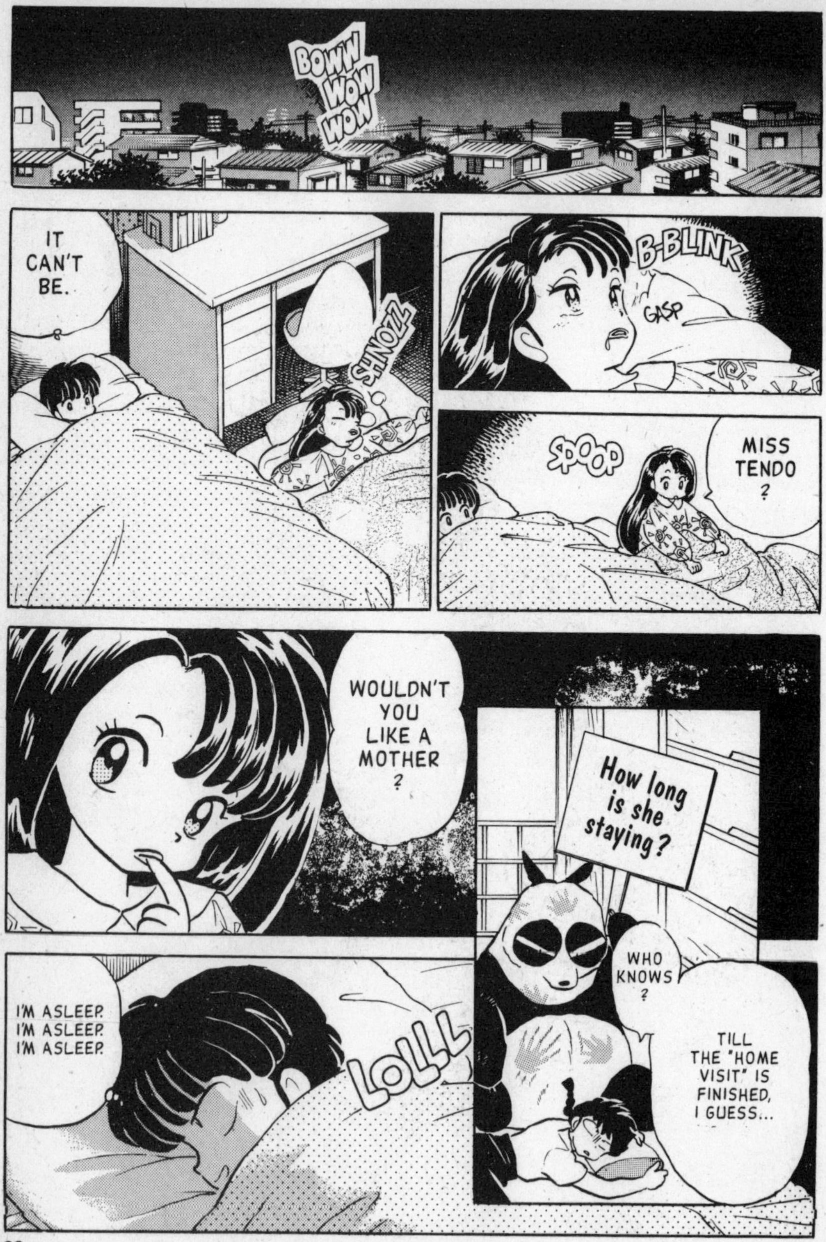
BOWW WOW WOW
IT CAN'T BE.
SHNOZZ
B-BLINK
GASP
SPOOP
MISS TENDO?
WOULDN'T YOU LIKE A MOTHER?
How long is she staying?
WHO KNOWS?
TILL THE "HOME VISIT" IS FINISHED, I GUESS...
I'M ASLEEP. I'M ASLEEP. I'M ASLEEP.
LOLLL

Part 2
TARGET: SOUN!

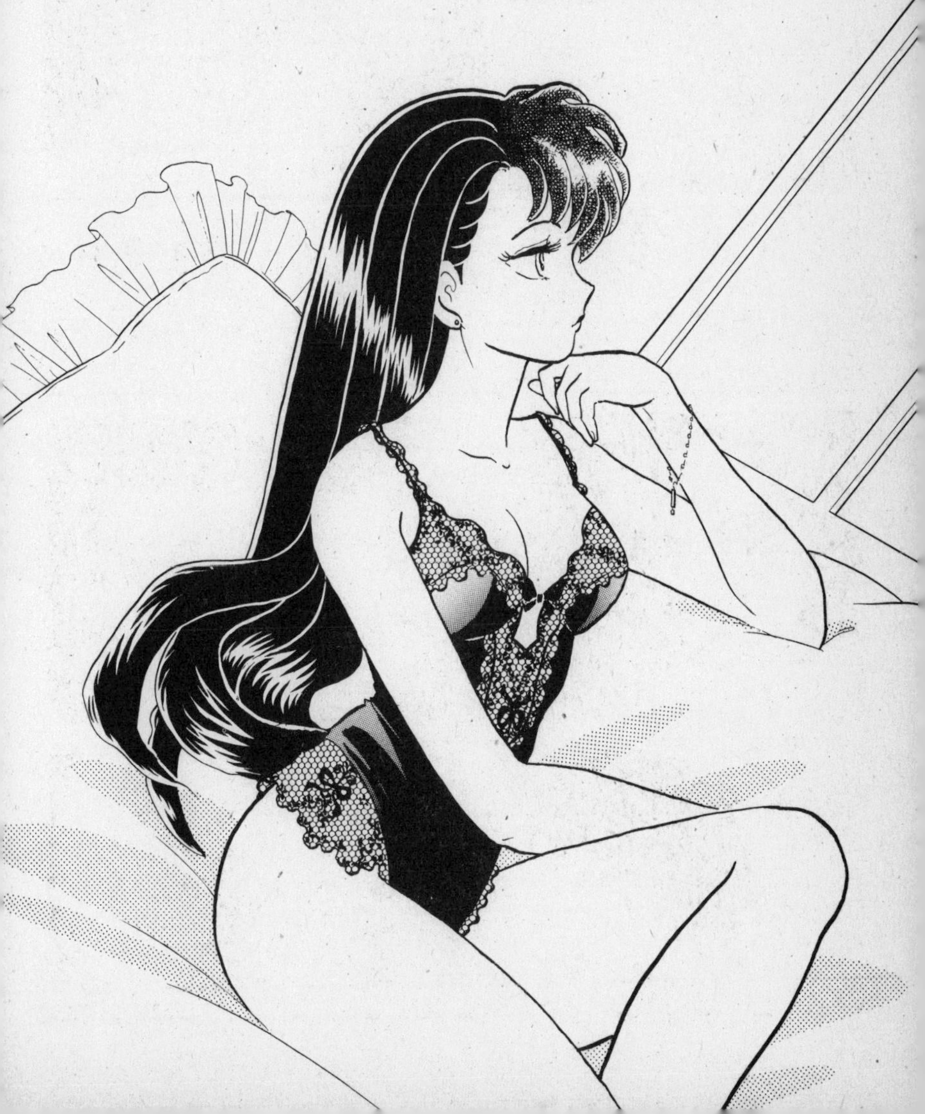

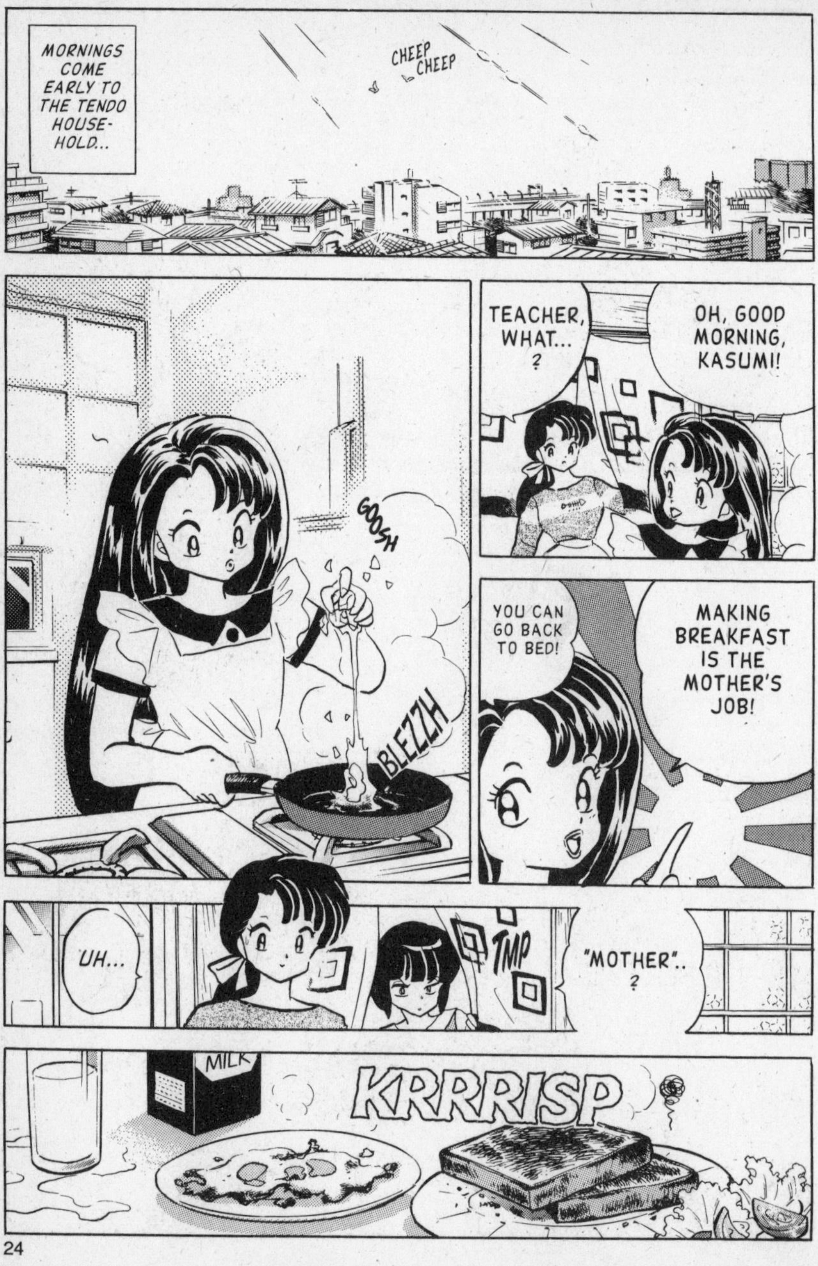
MORNINGS COME EARLY TO THE TENDO HOUSE-HOLD...
CHEEP CHEEP
GOOSH
BLEZZH
TEACHER, WHAT... ?
OH, GOOD MORNING, KASUMI!!
YOU CAN GO BACK TO BED!
MAKING BREAKFAST IS THE MOTHER'S JOB!
UH...
TMP
"MOTHER".. ?
MILK
KRRRISP

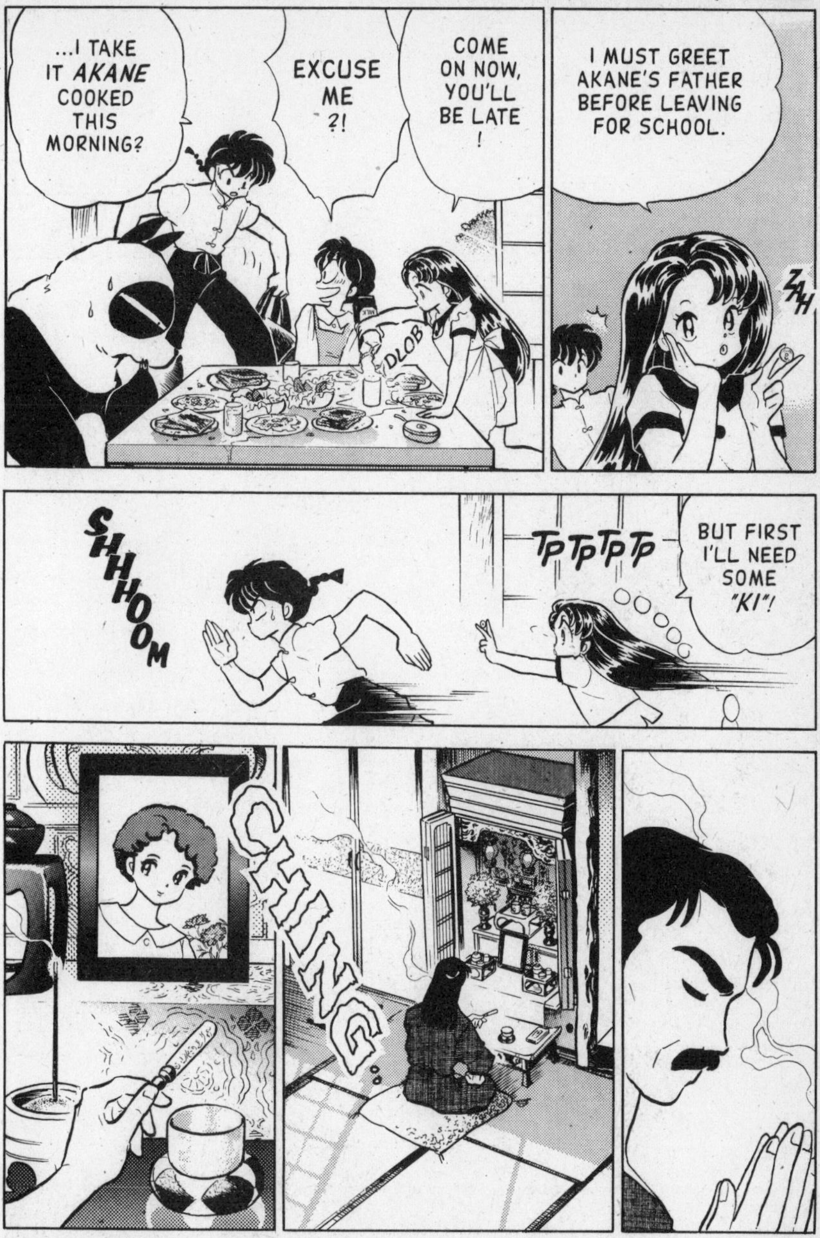
...I TAKE IT *AKANE* COOKED THIS MORNING?
EXCUSE ME ?!
COME ON NOW, YOU'LL BE LATE !
DLOB
I MUST GREET AKANE'S FATHER BEFORE LEAVING FOR SCHOOL.
ZAH
SHHHOOM
TPTPTPTP
BUT FIRST I'LL NEED SOME *"KI"*!
CHING

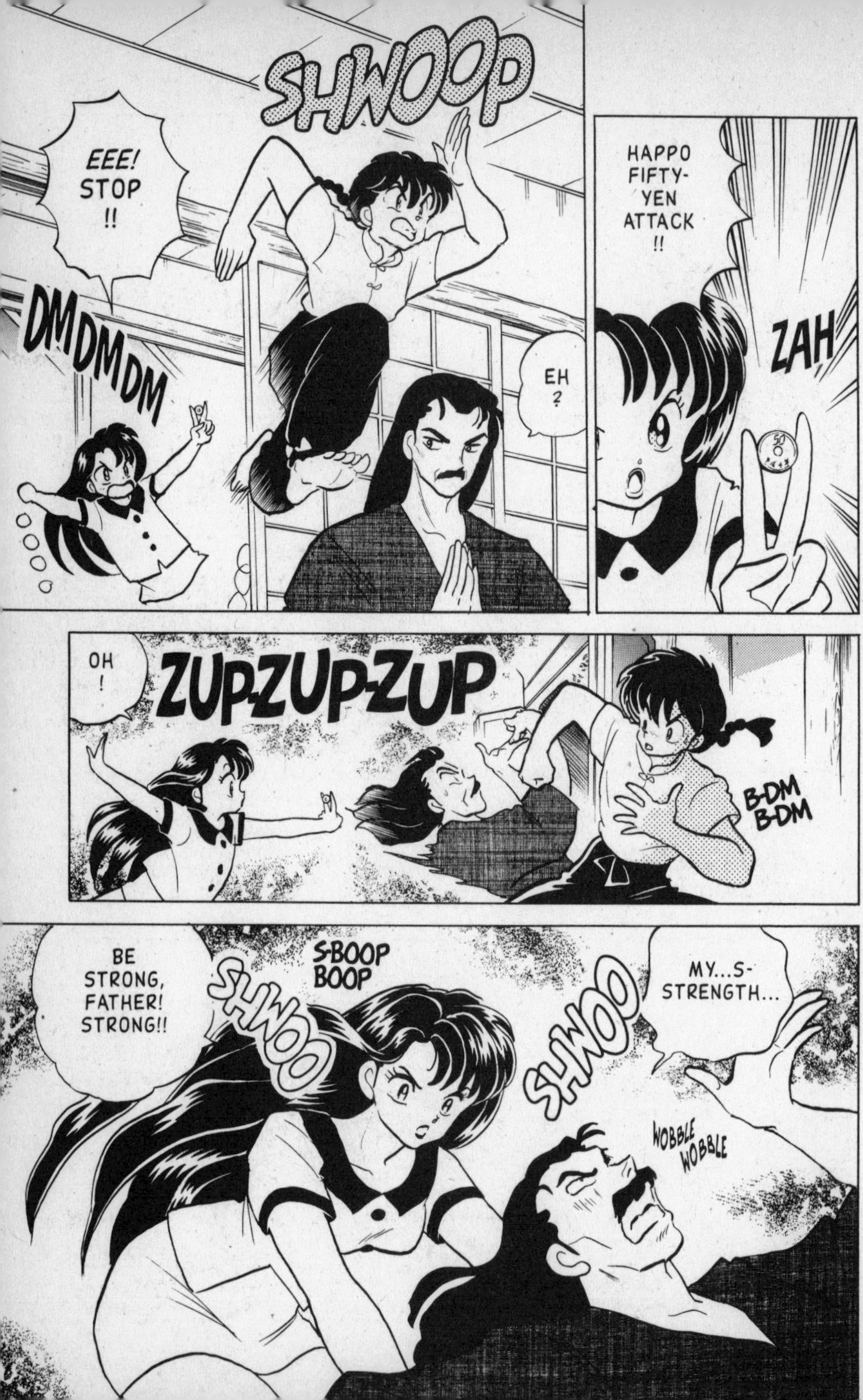
SHWOOP
EEE! STOP !!
DMDMDM
EH ?
HAPPO FIFTY-YEN ATTACK !!
ZAH
OH !
ZUP-ZUP-ZUP
B-DM B-DM
BE STRONG, FATHER! STRONG!!
S-BOOP BOOP
SHWOO
SHWOO
MY...S-STRENGTH...
WOBBLE WOBBLE

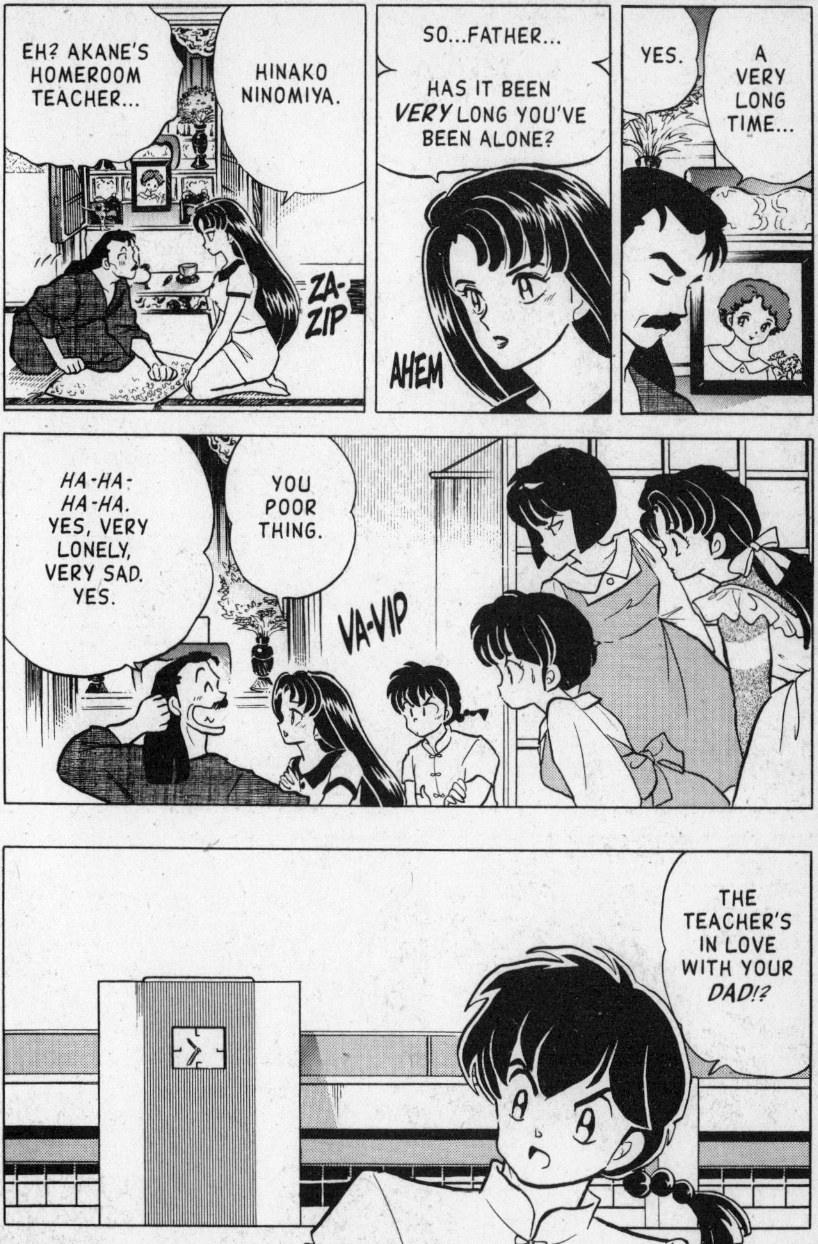
EH? AKANE'S HOMEROOM TEACHER...
HINAKO NINOMIYA.
ZA-ZIP
SO...FATHER...
HAS IT BEEN VERY LONG YOU'VE BEEN ALONE?
AHEM
YES.
A VERY LONG TIME...
HA-HA-HA-HA. YES, VERY LONELY, VERY SAD. YES.
YOU POOR THING.
VA-VIP
THE TEACHER'S IN LOVE WITH YOUR DAD!?

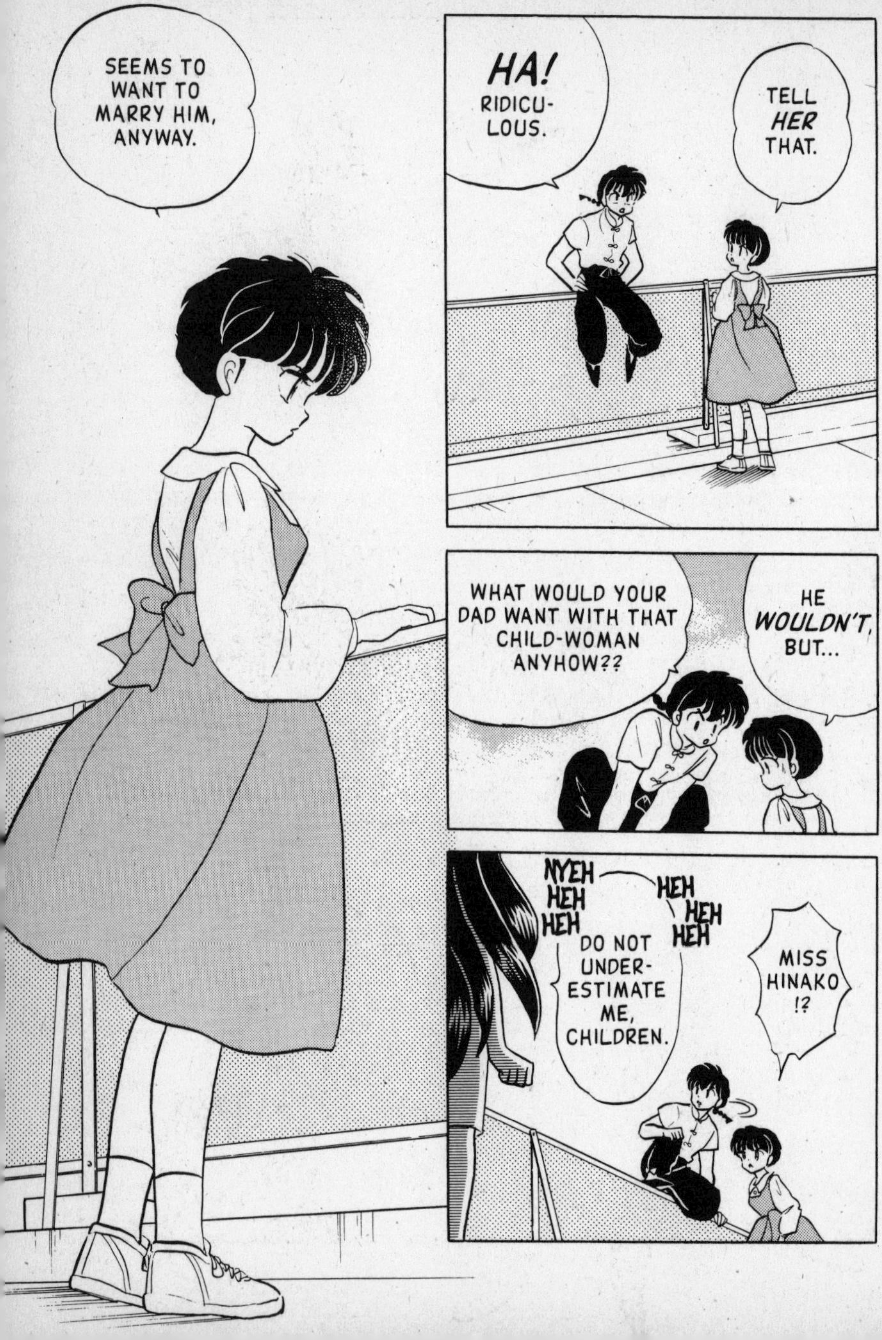
SEEMS TO WANT TO MARRY HIM, ANYWAY.
HA! RIDICU-LOUS.
TELL HER THAT.
WHAT WOULD YOUR DAD WANT WITH THAT CHILD-WOMAN ANYHOW??
HE WOULDN'T, BUT...
NYEH HEH HEH
HEH HEH HEH
DO NOT UNDER-ESTIMATE ME, CHILDREN.
MISS HINAKO !?

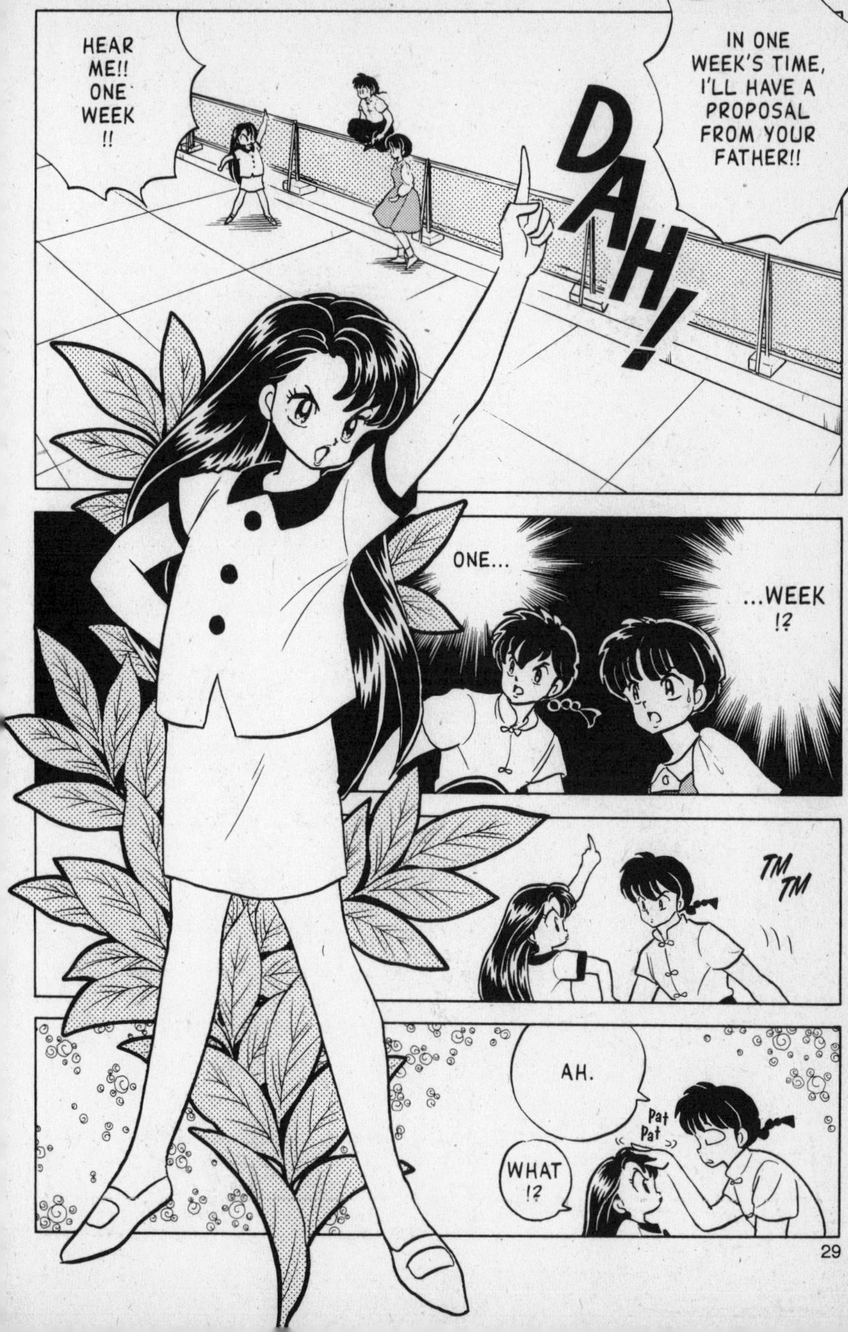
HEAR ME!! ONE WEEK !!
IN ONE WEEK'S TIME, I'LL HAVE A PROPOSAL FROM YOUR FATHER!!
DAH!
ONE...
...WEEK !?
TM TM
AH.
Pat Pat
WHAT !?

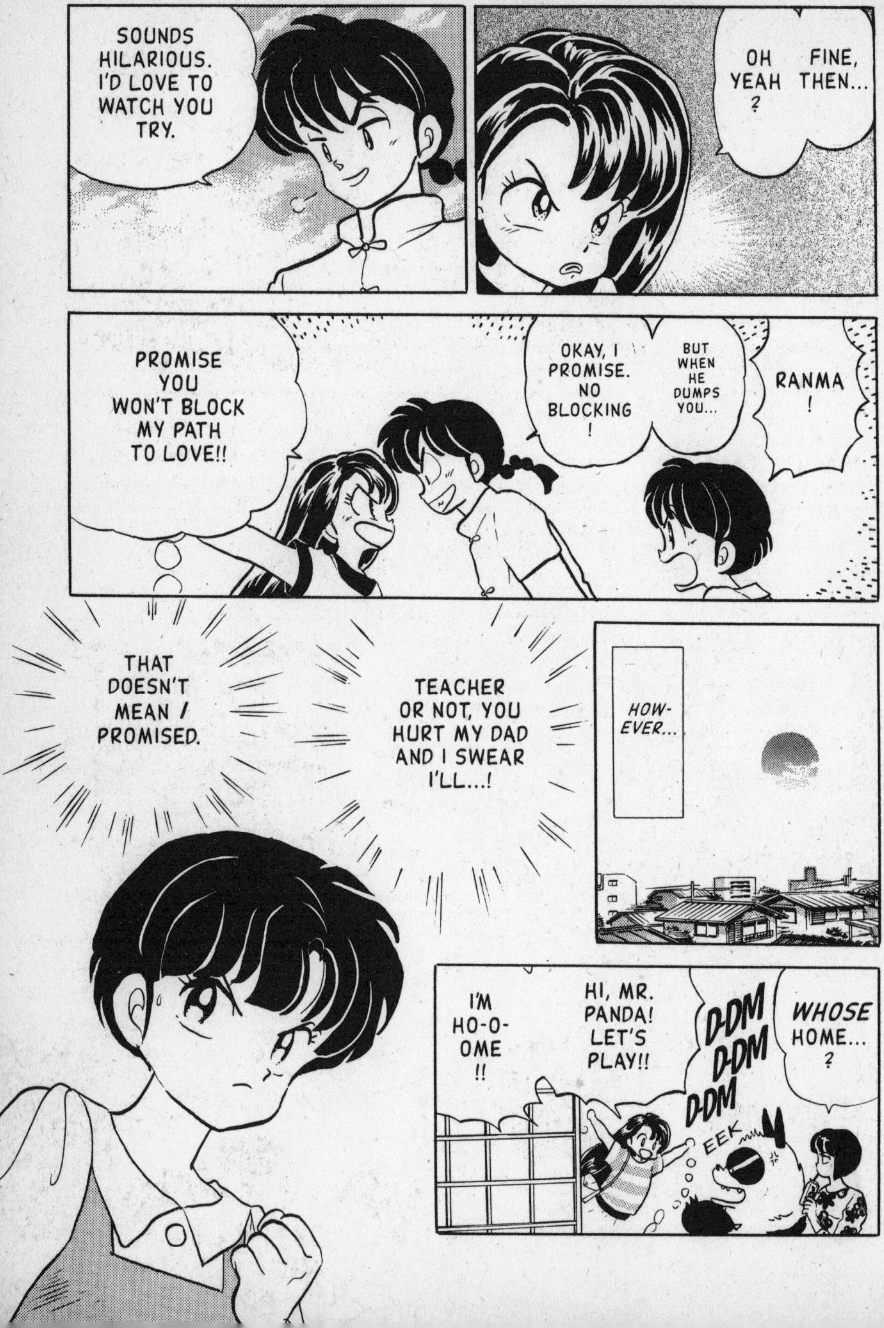
SOUNDS HILARIOUS. I'D LOVE TO WATCH YOU TRY.
OH YEAH?
FINE, THEN...
PROMISE YOU WON'T BLOCK MY PATH TO LOVE!!
OKAY, I PROMISE. NO BLOCKING!
BUT WHEN HE DUMPS YOU...
RANMA!
THAT DOESN'T MEAN *I* PROMISED.
TEACHER OR NOT, YOU HURT MY DAD AND I SWEAR I'LL...!
HOW-EVER...
I'M HO-O-OME!!
HI, MR. PANDA! LET'S PLAY!!
D-DM D-DM D-DM
EEK
WHOSE HOME...?

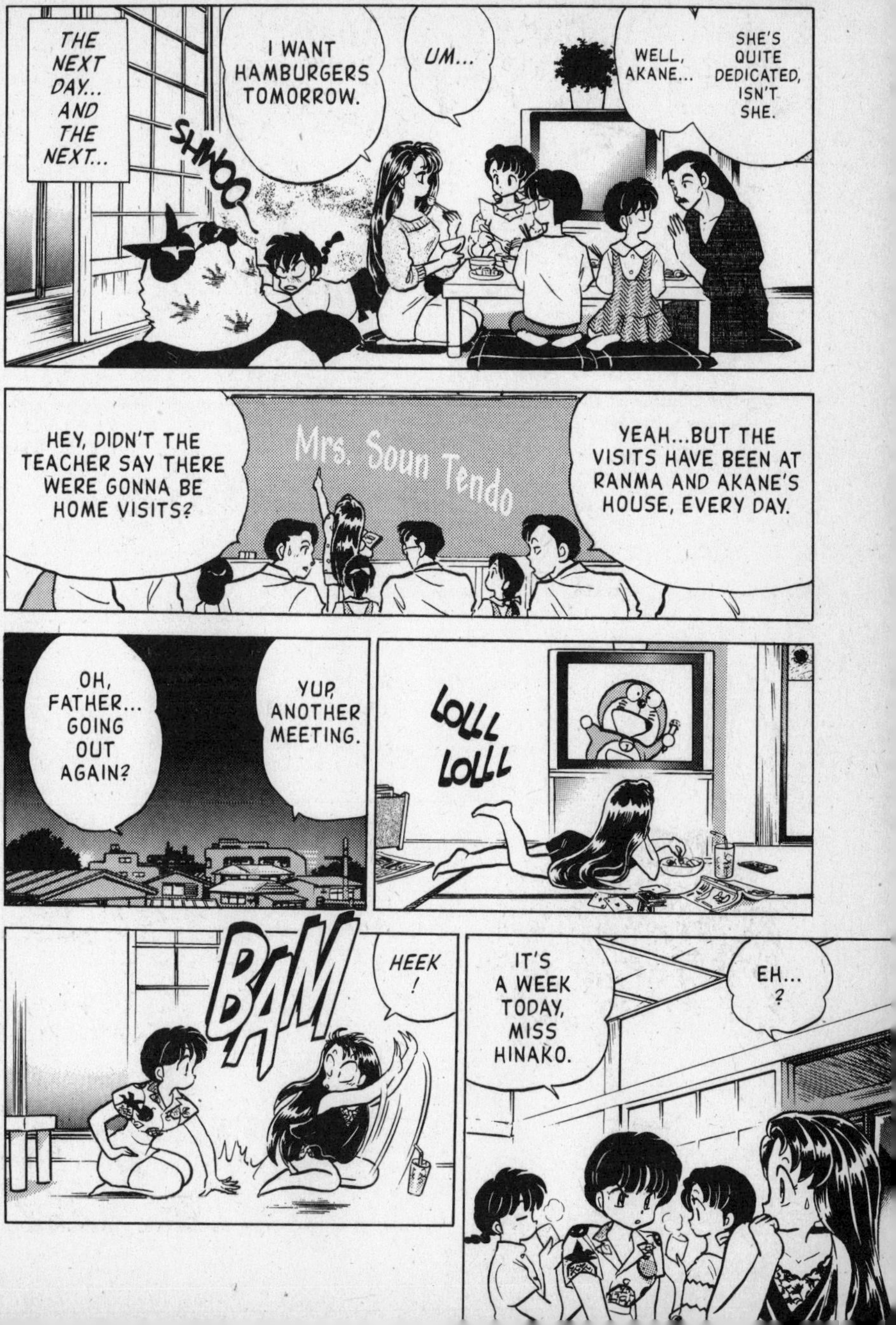
THE NEXT DAY... AND THE NEXT...
SHWOO
I WANT HAMBURGERS TOMORROW.
UM...
WELL, AKANE...
SHE'S QUITE DEDICATED, ISN'T SHE.
Mrs. Soun Tendo
HEY, DIDN'T THE TEACHER SAY THERE WERE GONNA BE HOME VISITS?
YEAH...BUT THE VISITS HAVE BEEN AT RANMA AND AKANE'S HOUSE, EVERY DAY.
OH, FATHER... GOING OUT AGAIN?
YUP, ANOTHER MEETING.
LOLLL LOLLL
BAM
HEEK!
IT'S A WEEK TODAY, MISS HINAKO.
EH...?

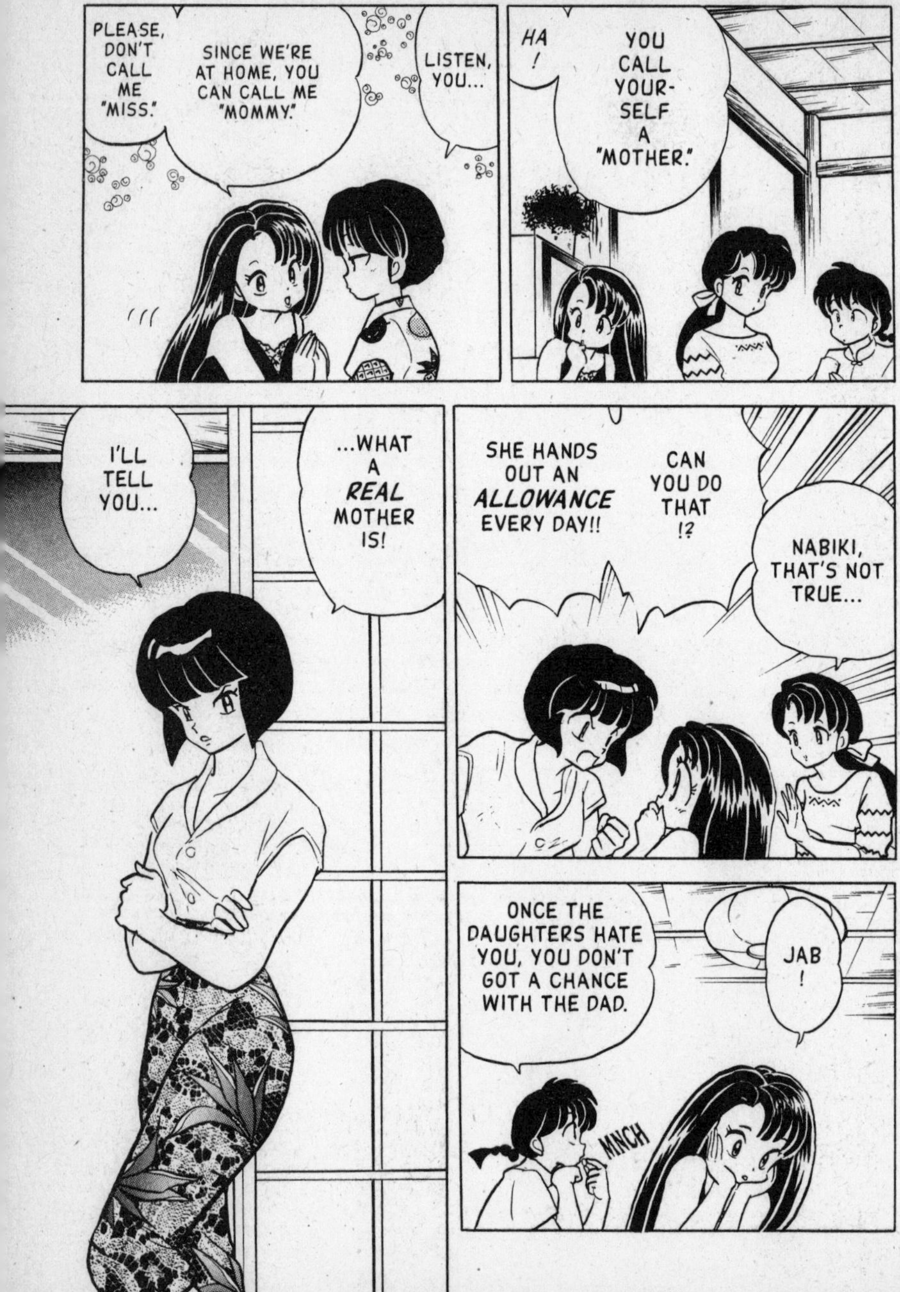
PLEASE, DON'T CALL ME "MISS."
SINCE WE'RE AT HOME, YOU CAN CALL ME "MOMMY."
LISTEN, YOU...
HA!
YOU CALL YOURSELF A "MOTHER."
I'LL TELL YOU...
...WHAT A REAL MOTHER IS!
SHE HANDS OUT AN ALLOWANCE EVERY DAY!!
CAN YOU DO THAT!?
NABIKI, THAT'S NOT TRUE...
ONCE THE DAUGHTERS HATE YOU, YOU DON'T GOT A CHANCE WITH THE DAD.
JAB!
MNCH

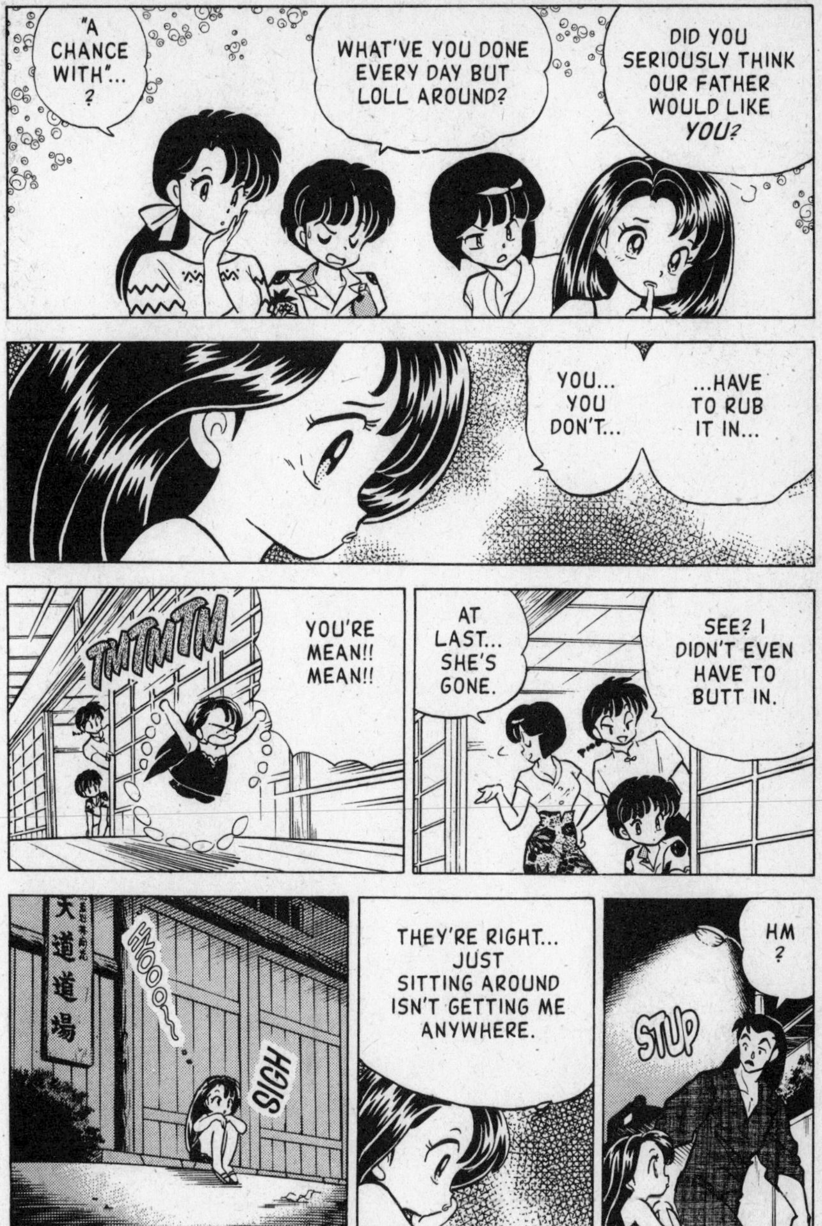
"A CHANCE WITH"... ?
WHAT'VE YOU DONE EVERY DAY BUT LOLL AROUND?
DID YOU SERIOUSLY THINK OUR FATHER WOULD LIKE *YOU*?
YOU... YOU DON'T...
...HAVE TO RUB IT IN...
TMTMTM
YOU'RE MEAN!! MEAN!!
AT LAST... SHE'S GONE.
SEE? I DIDN'T EVEN HAVE TO BUTT IN.
天道道場
HYOOO~
SIGH
THEY'RE RIGHT... JUST SITTING AROUND ISN'T GETTING ME ANYWHERE.
STUP
HM ?

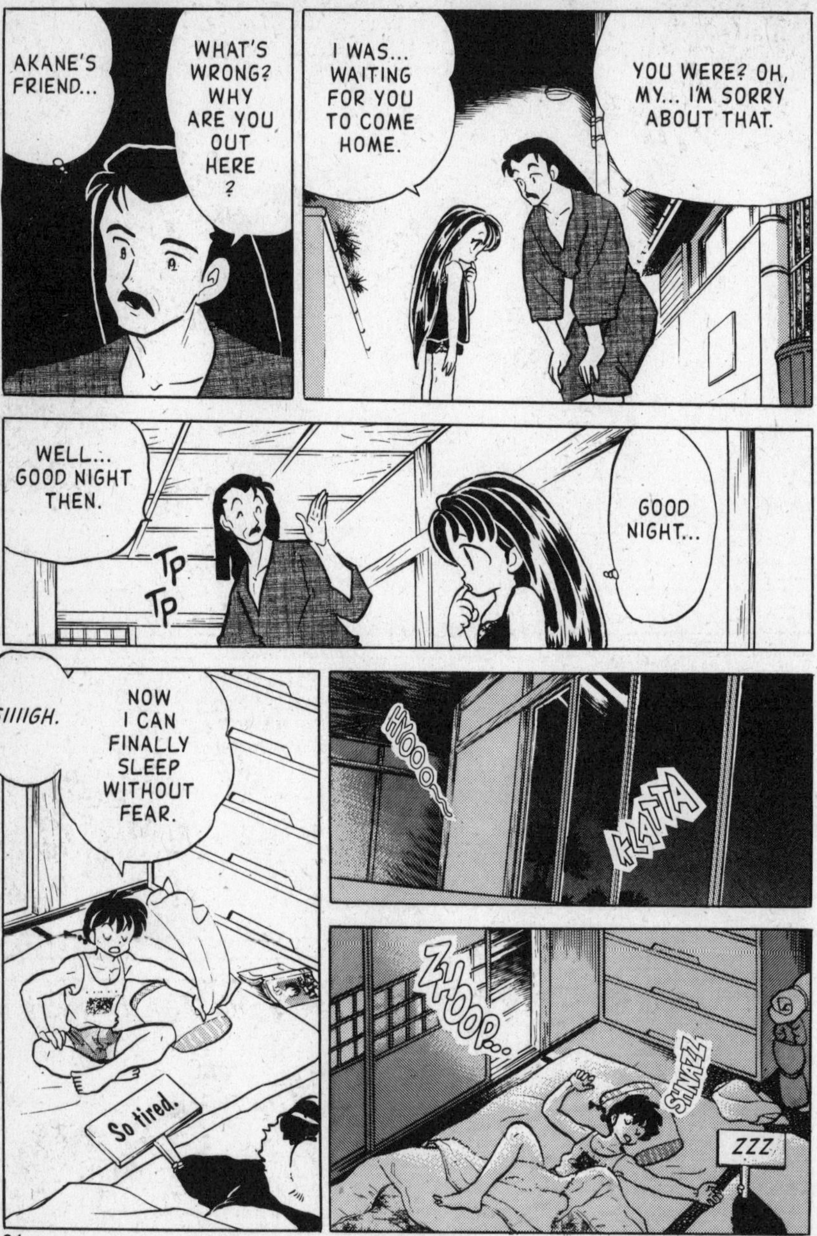
AKANE'S FRIEND...
WHAT'S WRONG? WHY ARE YOU OUT HERE?
I WAS... WAITING FOR YOU TO COME HOME.
YOU WERE? OH, MY... I'M SORRY ABOUT THAT.
WELL... GOOD NIGHT THEN.
TP TP
GOOD NIGHT...
SIIIGH.
NOW I CAN FINALLY SLEEP WITHOUT FEAR.
So tired.
HYOOO~~
KLATTA
ZHOOP...
SHNAZZ
ZZZ

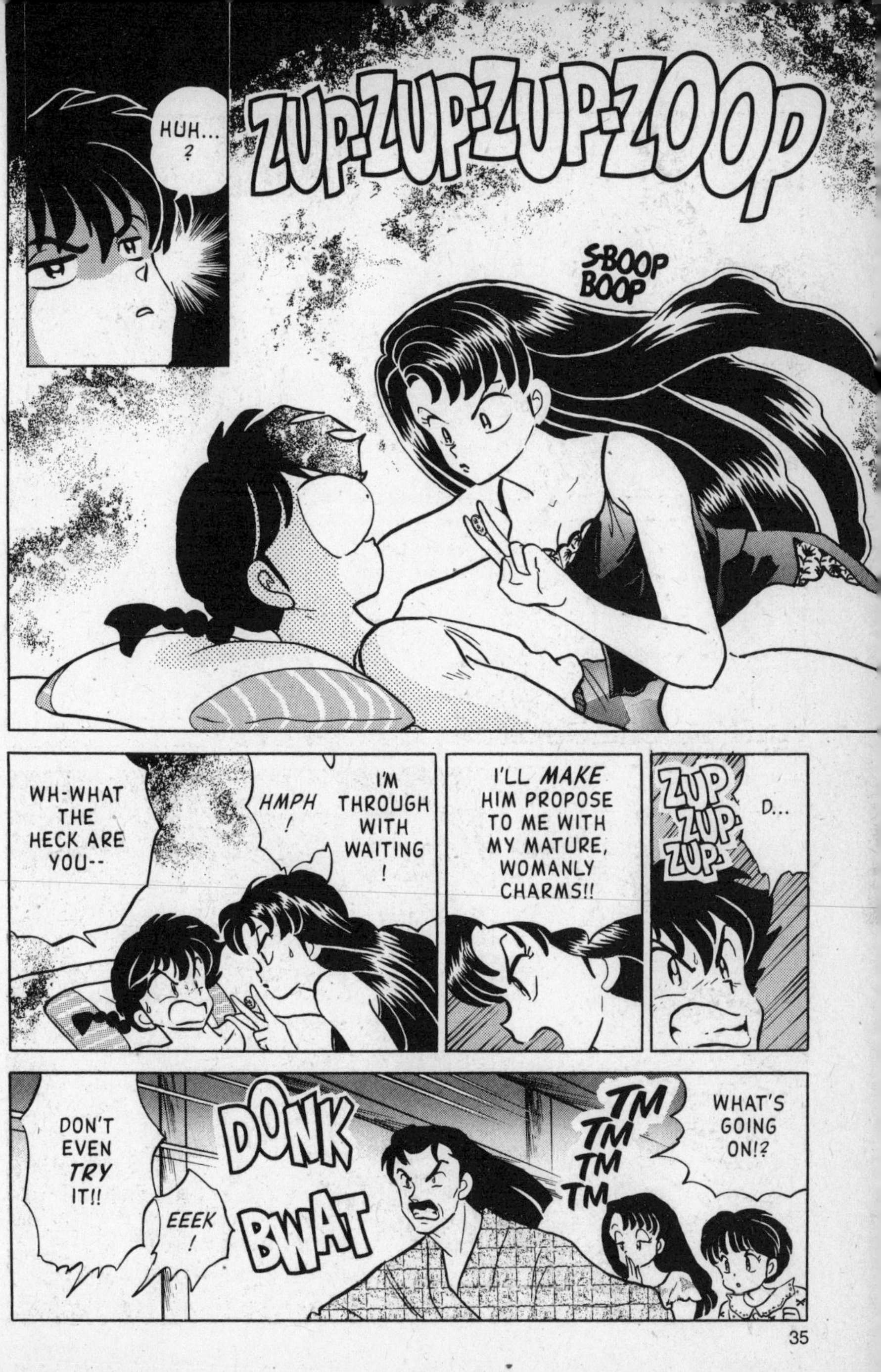
HUH... ?
ZUP-ZUP-ZUP-ZOOP
S-BOOP BOOP
WH-WHAT THE HECK ARE YOU--
HMPH !
I'M THROUGH WITH WAITING !
I'LL MAKE HIM PROPOSE TO ME WITH MY MATURE, WOMANLY CHARMS!!
ZUP ZUP ZUP
D...
DON'T EVEN TRY IT!!
DONK
EEEK !
BWAT
TM TM TM TM TM
WHAT'S GOING ON!?

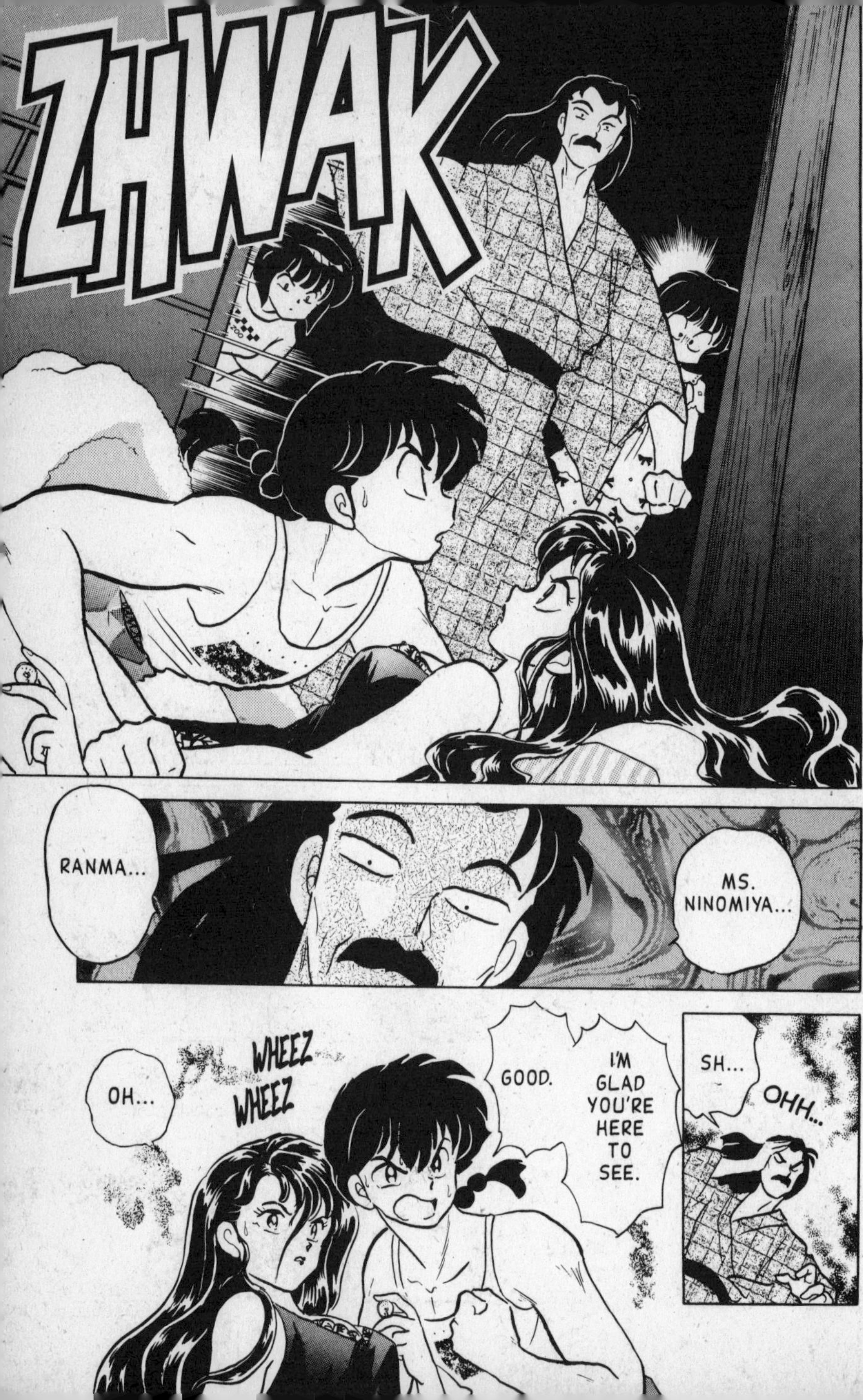
ZHWAK
RANMA...
MS. NINOMIYA...
OH...
WHEEZ WHEEZ
GOOD.
I'M GLAD YOU'RE HERE TO SEE.
SH...
OHH...

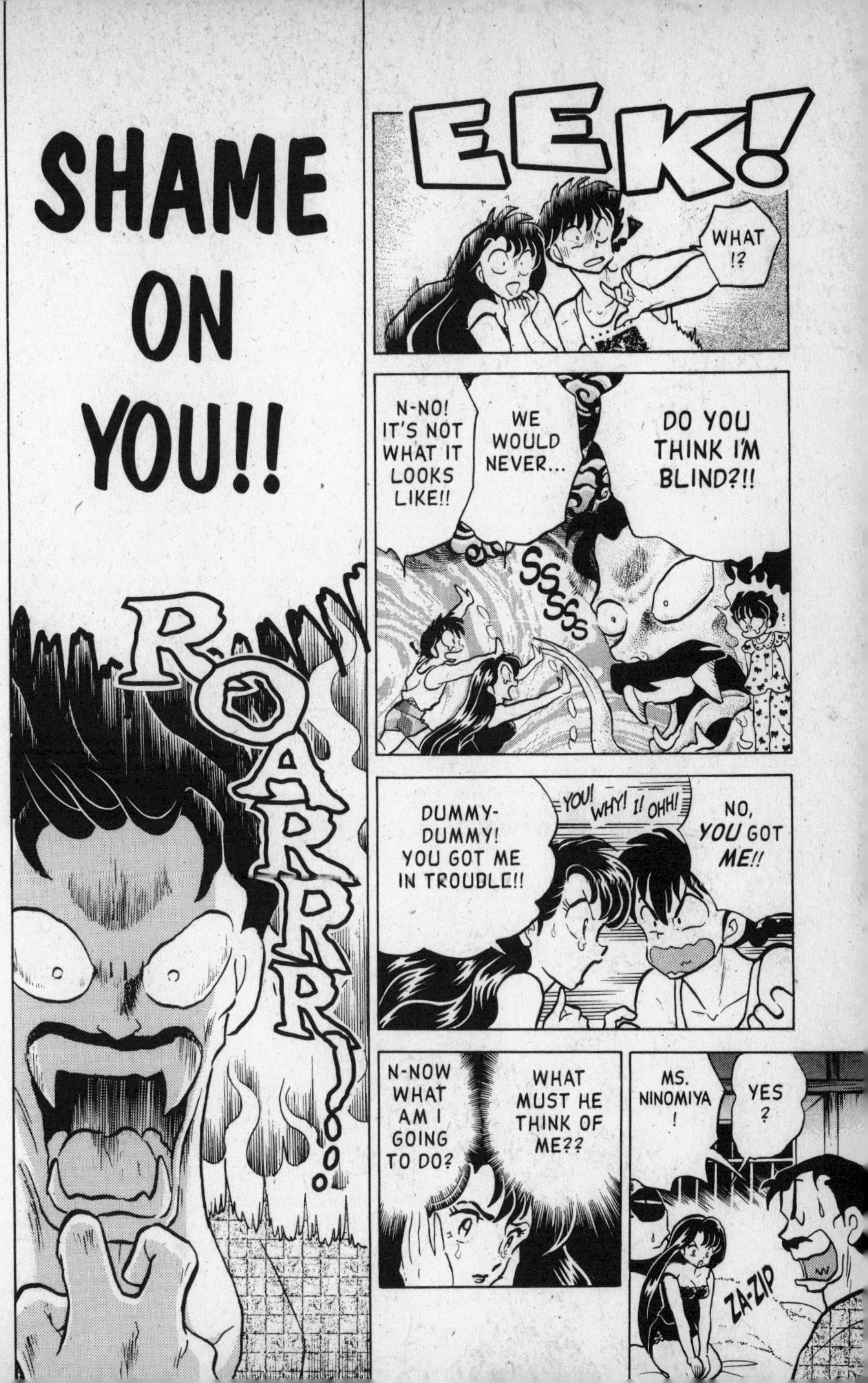
SHAME ON YOU!!
ROARRR!...
EEK!
WHAT !?
N-NO! IT'S NOT WHAT IT LOOKS LIKE!!
WE WOULD NEVER...
DO YOU THINK I'M BLIND?!!
SSSSSS
DUMMY-DUMMY! YOU GOT ME IN TROUBLE!!
YOU! WHY! I! OHH!
NO, YOU GOT ME!!
N-NOW WHAT AM I GOING TO DO?
WHAT MUST HE THINK OF ME??
MS. NINOMIYA!
YES?
ZA-ZIP

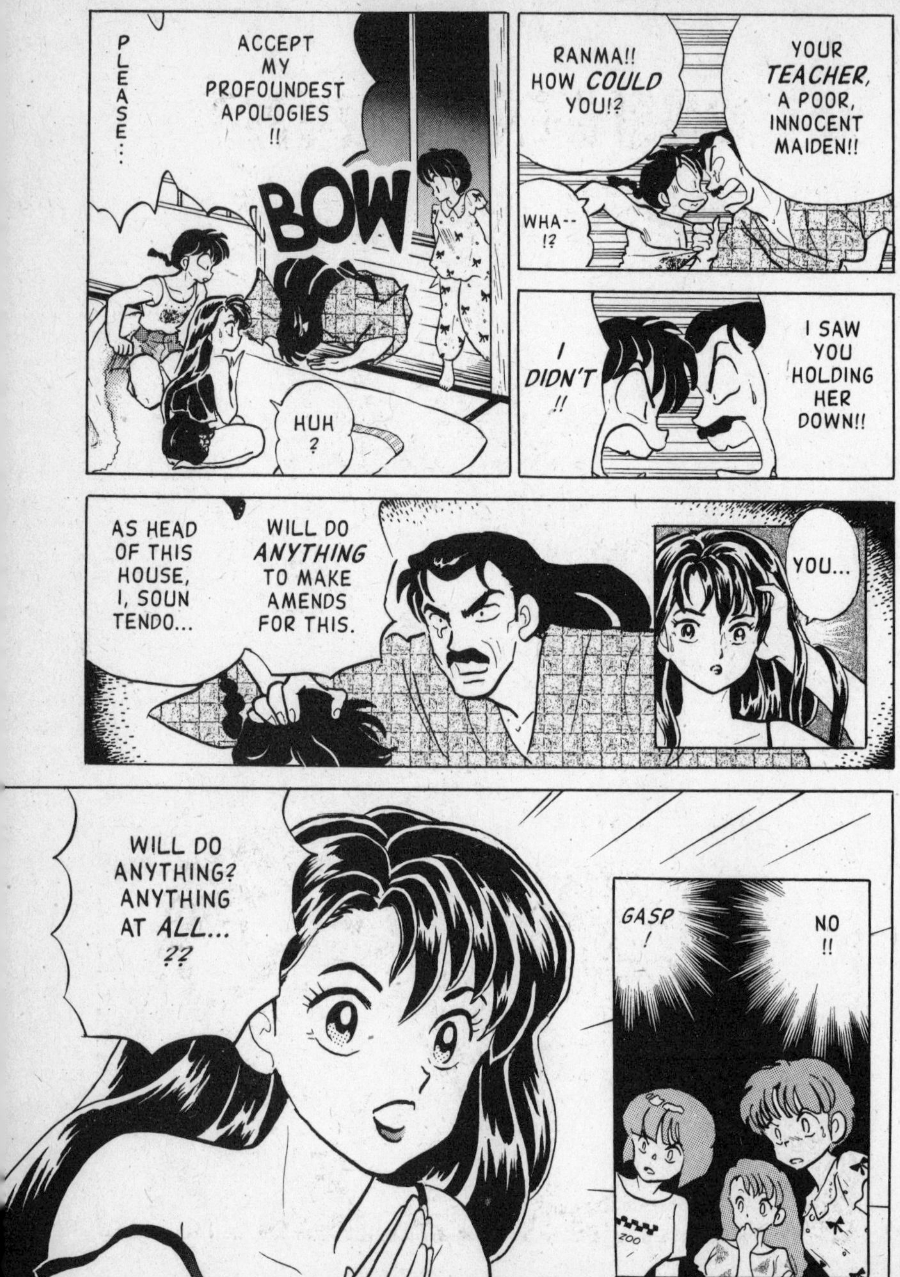
PLEASE...
ACCEPT MY PROFOUNDEST APOLOGIES !!
BOW
HUH ?
RANMA!! HOW COULD YOU!?
YOUR TEACHER, A POOR, INNOCENT MAIDEN!!
WHA-- !?
I DIDN'T !!
I SAW YOU HOLDING HER DOWN!!
AS HEAD OF THIS HOUSE, I, SOUN TENDO...
WILL DO ANYTHING TO MAKE AMENDS FOR THIS.
YOU...
WILL DO ANYTHING? ANYTHING AT ALL... ??
GASP !
NO !!

Part 3

DANGER: FLIGHT PATH OF LOVE!

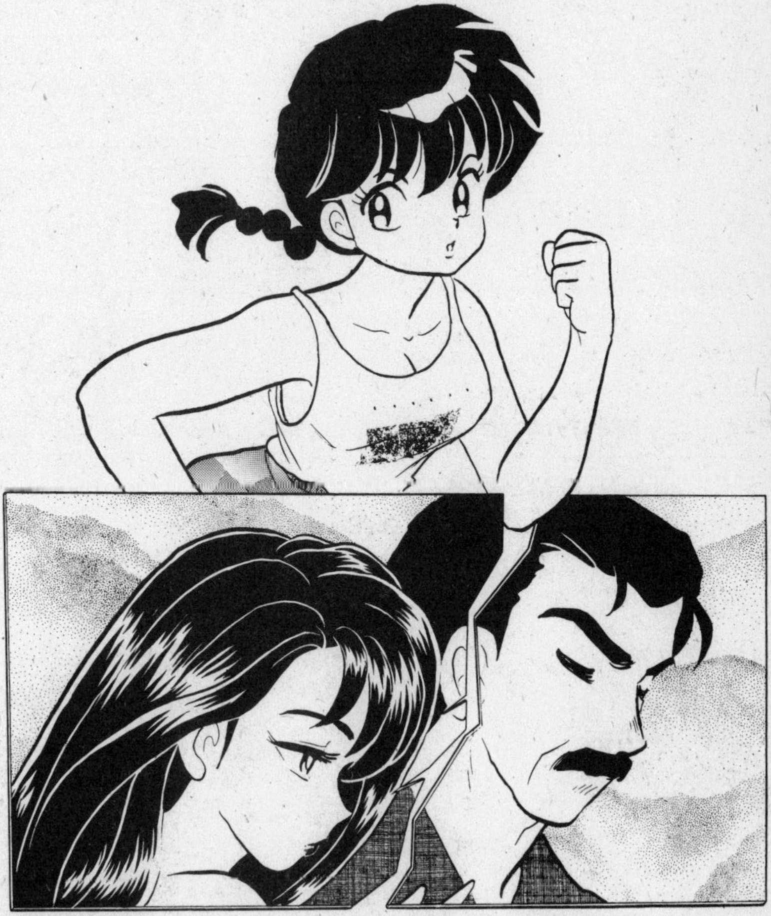

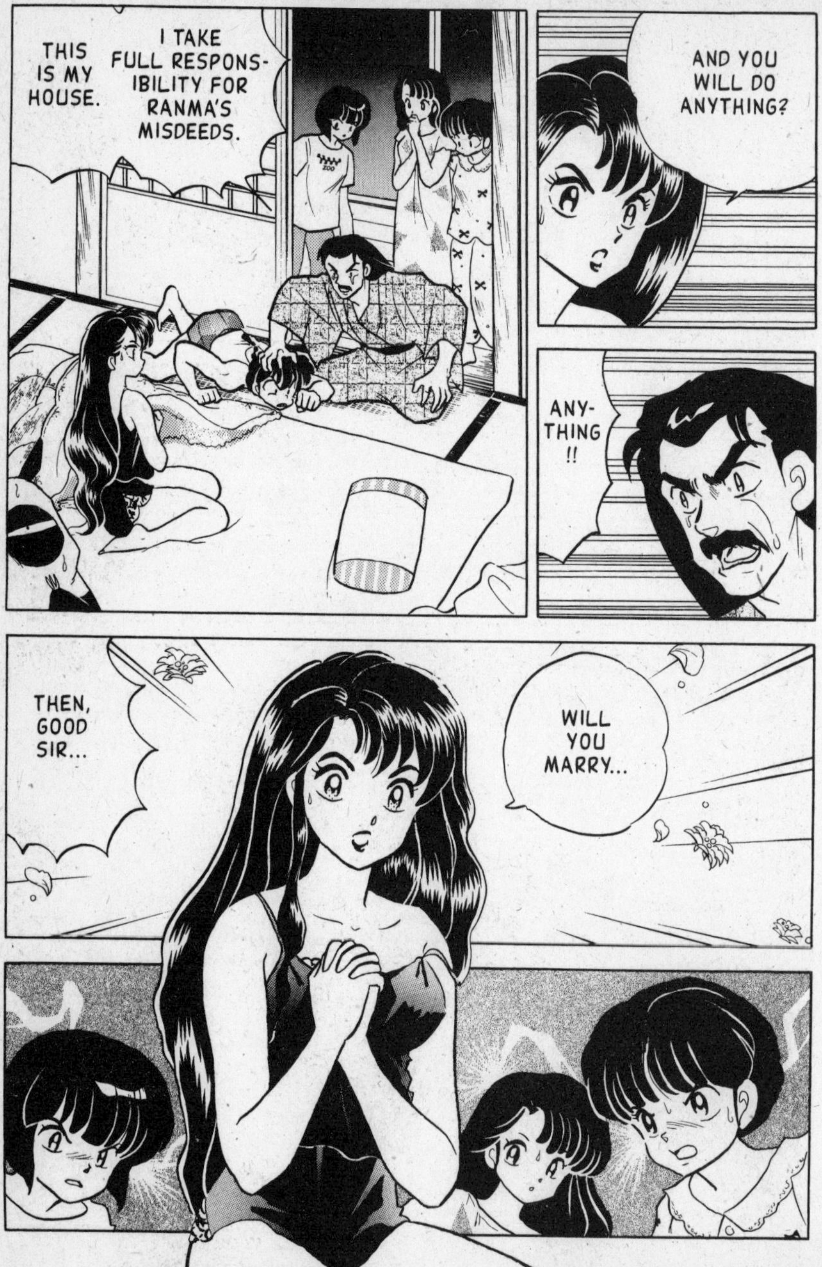
THIS IS MY HOUSE.
I TAKE FULL RESPONS-IBILITY FOR RANMA'S MISDEEDS.
AND YOU WILL DO ANYTHING?
ANY-THING !!
THEN, GOOD SIR...
WILL YOU MARRY...

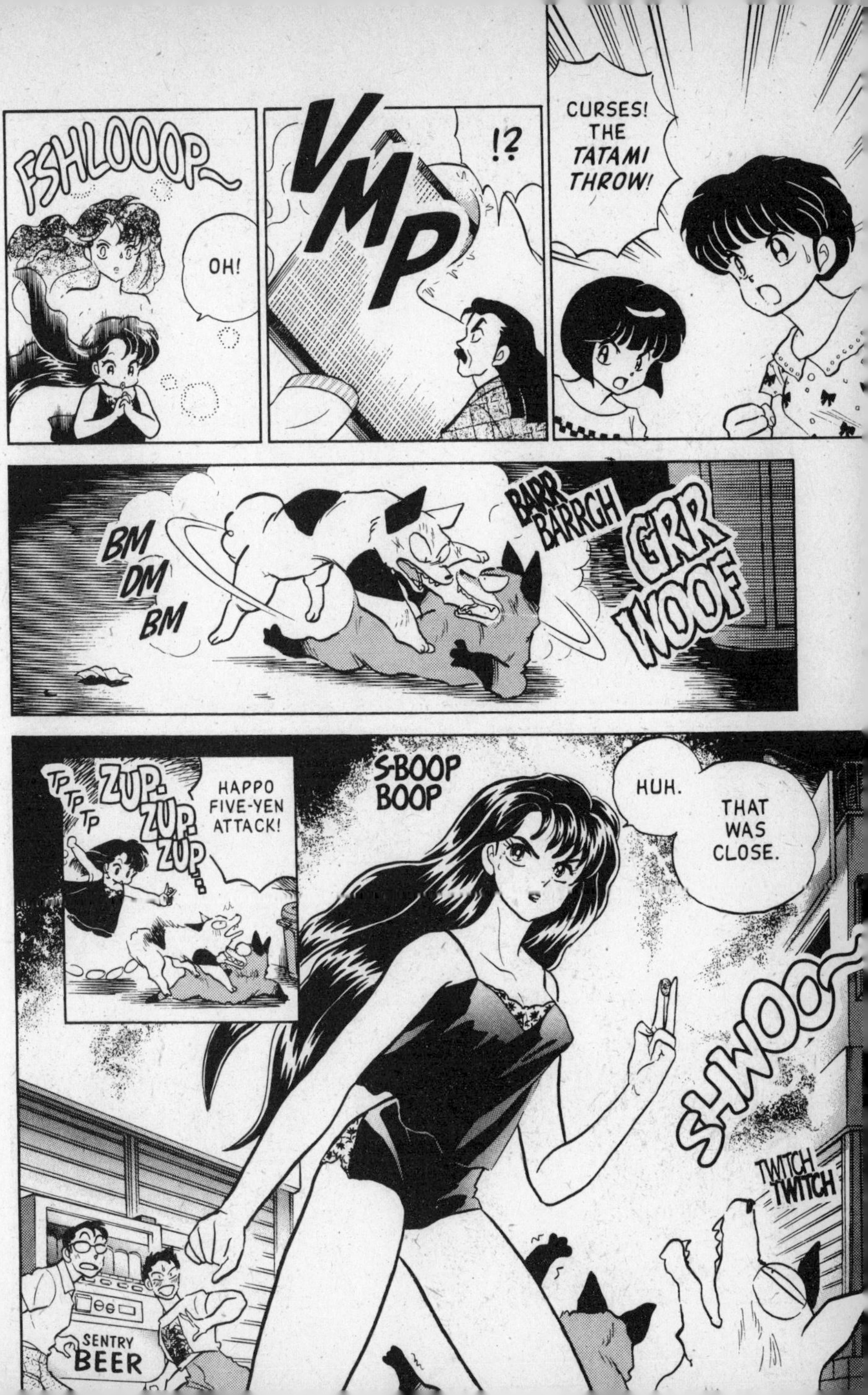
FSHLOOOP~
OH!
VMP
!?
CURSES! THE TATAMI THROW!
BM DM BM
BARR BARRGH
GRR WOOF
TP TP TP
ZUP-ZUP-ZUP
HAPPO FIVE-YEN ATTACK!
S-BOOP BOOP
HUH.
THAT WAS CLOSE.
SHWOO~
TWITCH TWITCH
SENTRY BEER

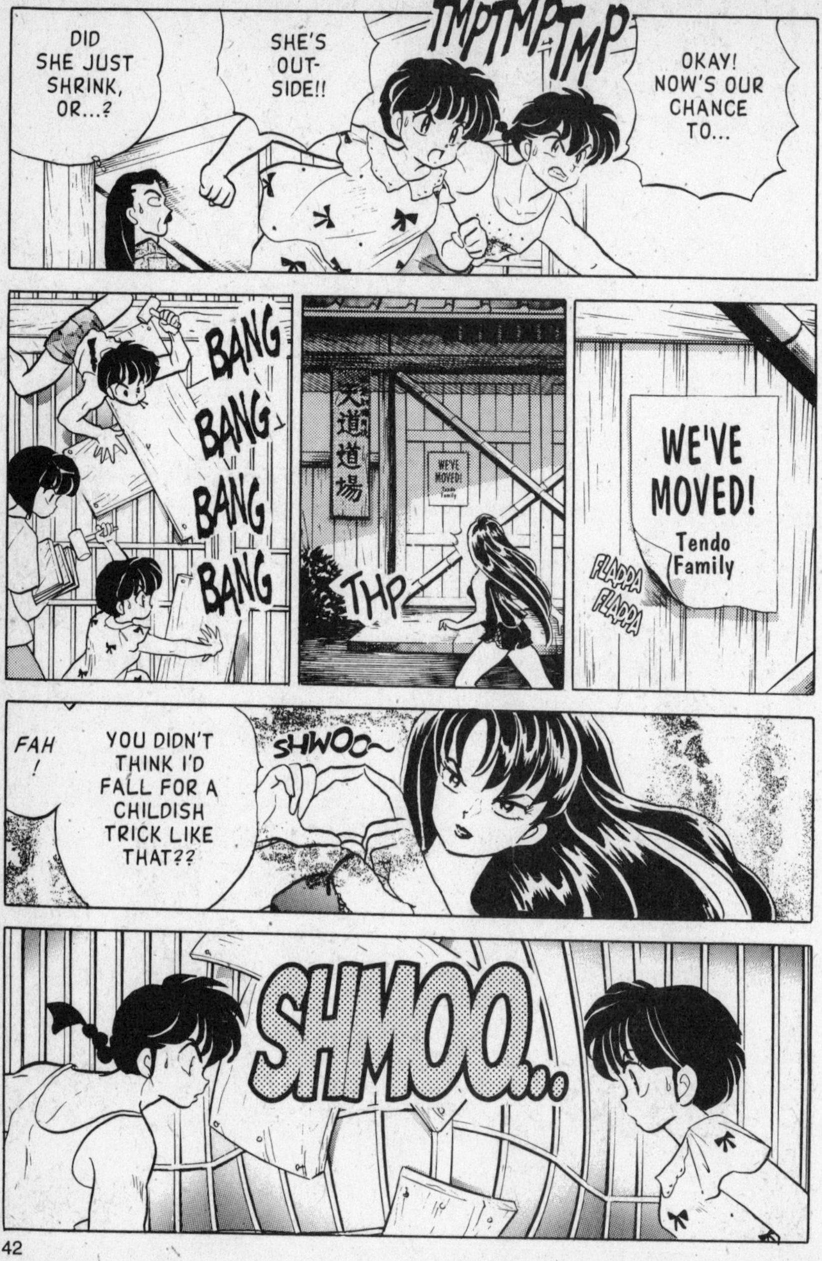
DID SHE JUST SHRINK, OR...?
SHE'S OUT-SIDE!!
TMPTMPTMP
OKAY! NOW'S OUR CHANCE TO...
BANG BANG BANG BANG
WE'VE MOVED! Tendo Family
THP
WE'VE MOVED! Tendo Family
FLAPPA FLAPPA
FAH!
YOU DIDN'T THINK I'D FALL FOR A CHILDISH TRICK LIKE THAT??
SHWOO~
SHMOO...

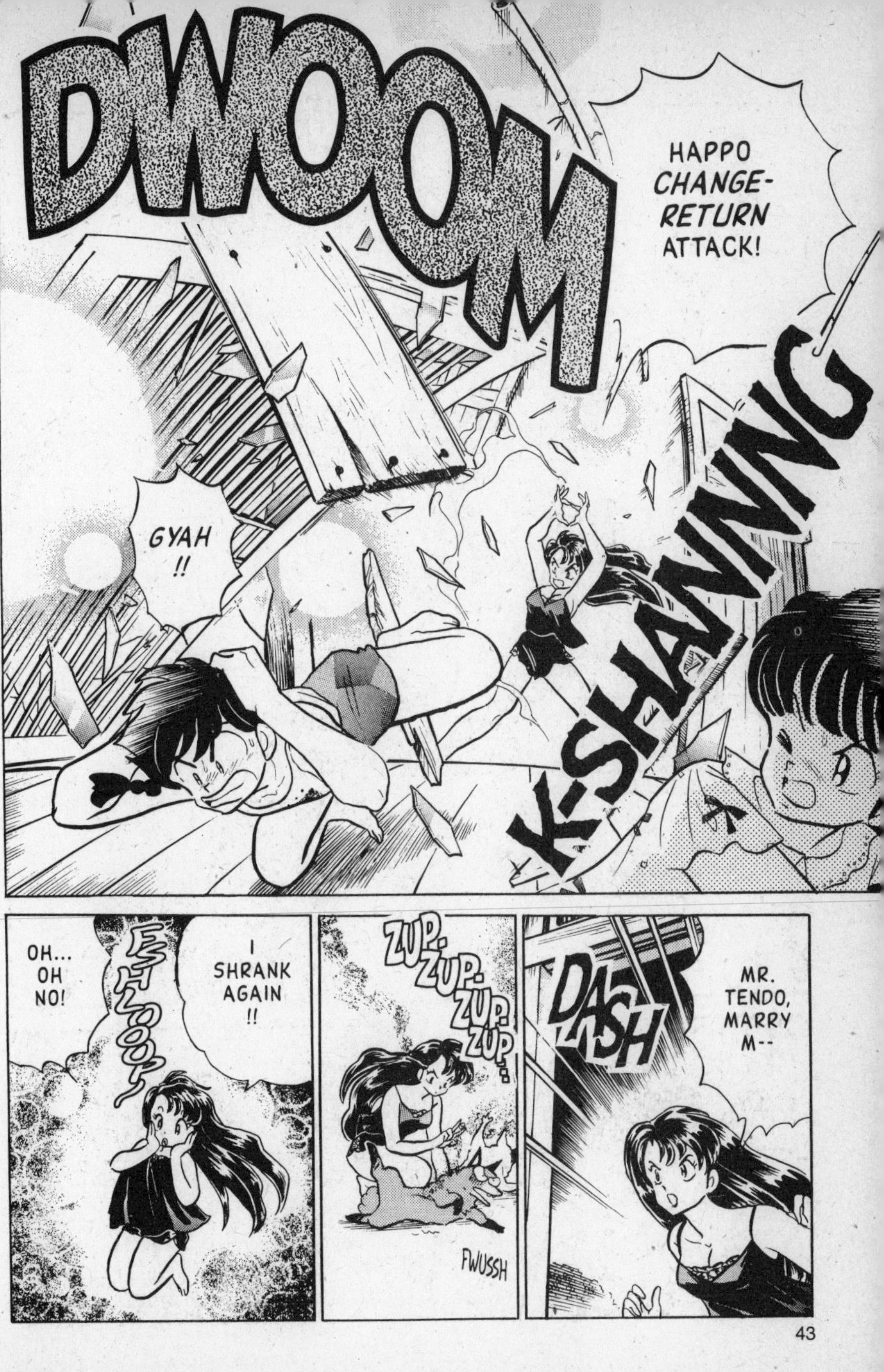
DWOOM
HAPPO CHANGE-RETURN ATTACK!
GYAH !!
K-SHANNNG
OH... OH NO!
FSHLOOP
I SHRANK AGAIN !!
ZUP-ZUP-ZUP-ZUP
FWUSSH
DASH
MR. TENDO, MARRY M--

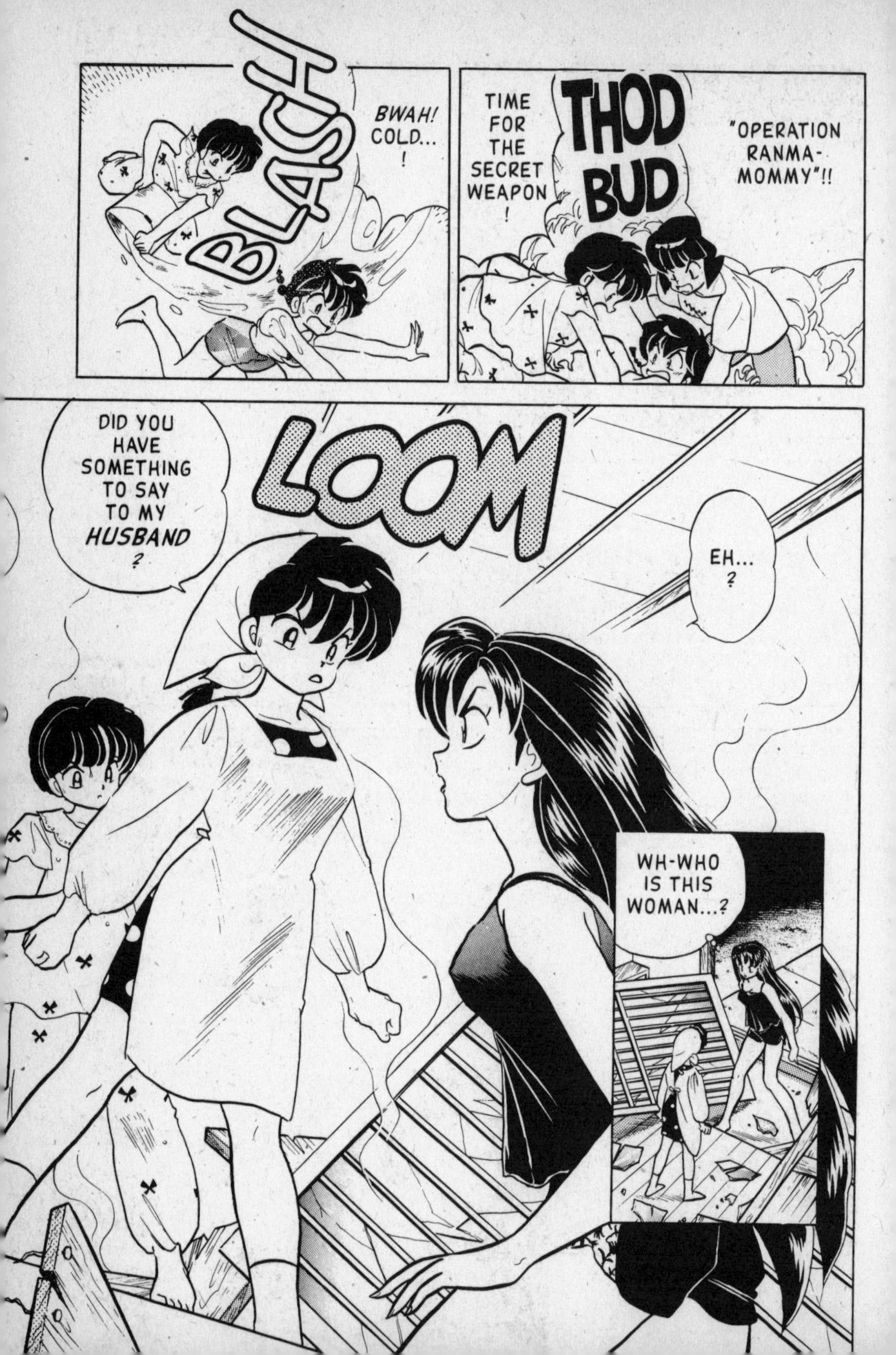
BLASCH
BWAH! COLD... !
TIME FOR THE SECRET WEAPON !
THOD BUD
"OPERATION RANMA-MOMMY"!!
DID YOU HAVE SOMETHING TO SAY TO MY *HUSBAND* ?
LOOM
EH... ?
WH-WHO IS THIS WOMAN...?

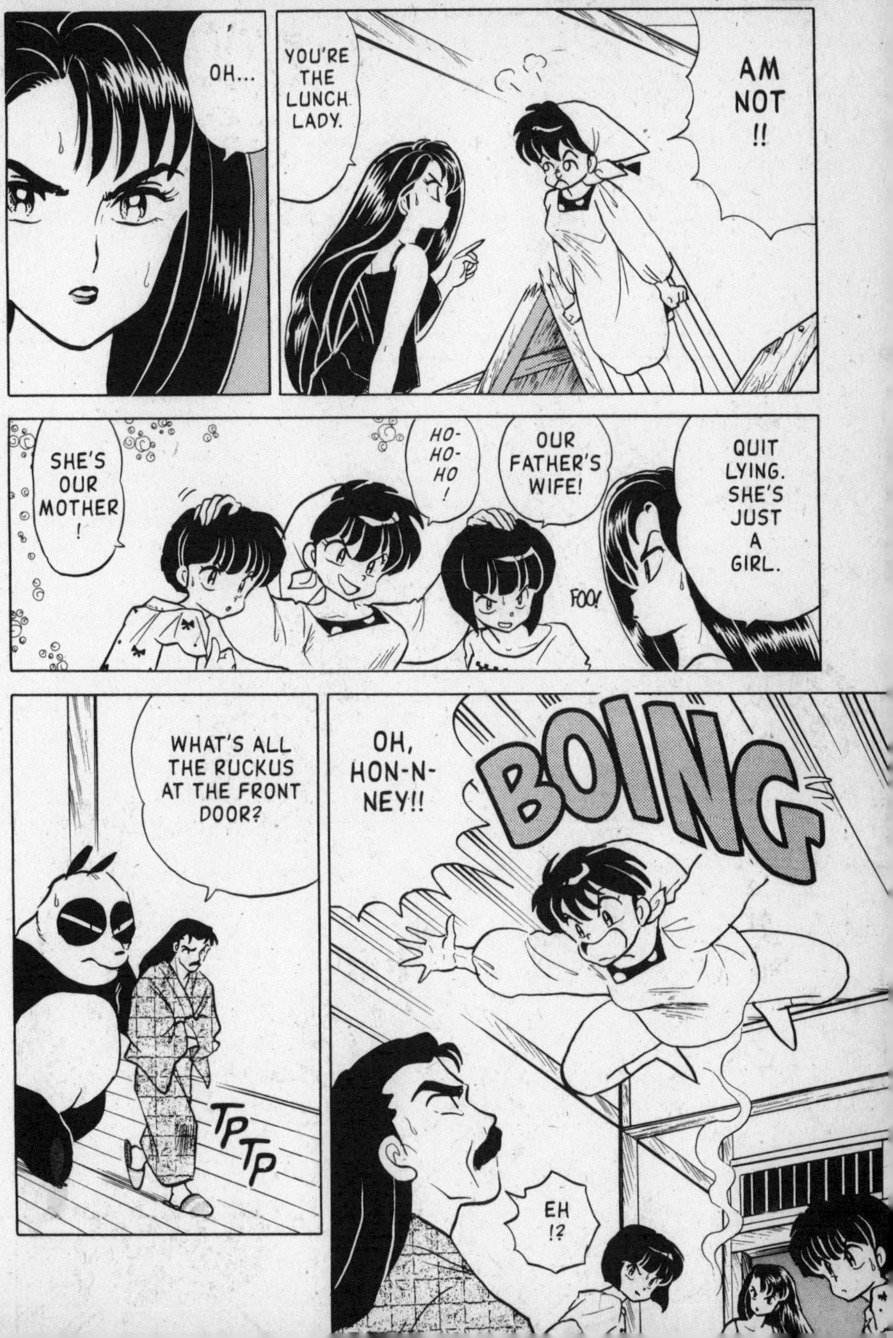
OH...
YOU'RE THE LUNCH LADY.
AM NOT !!
SHE'S OUR MOTHER !
HO-HO-HO !
OUR FATHER'S WIFE!
FOO!
QUIT LYING. SHE'S JUST A GIRL.
WHAT'S ALL THE RUCKUS AT THE FRONT DOOR?
TPTP
OH, HON-N-NEY!!
BOING
EH !?

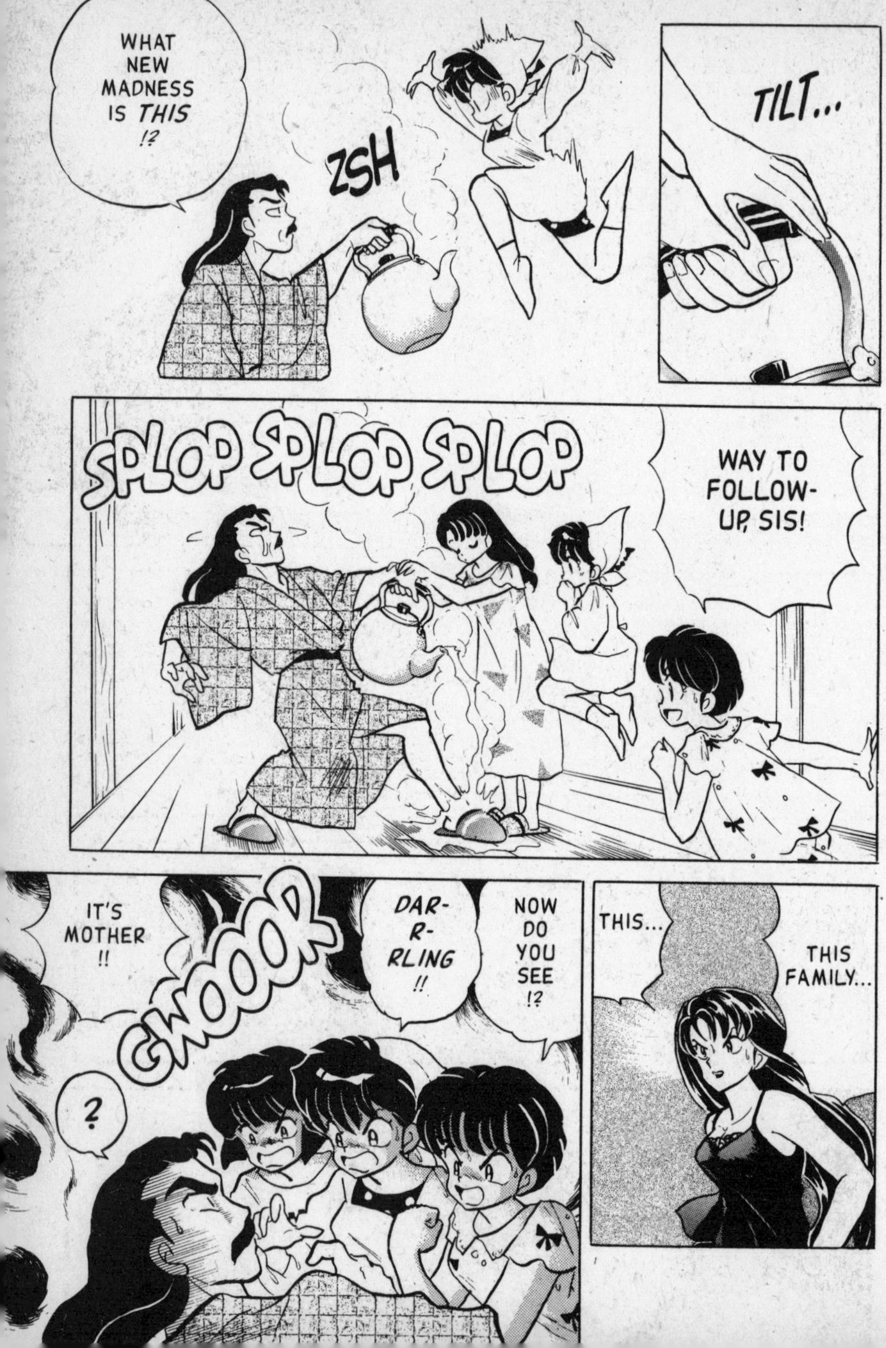
WHAT NEW MADNESS IS THIS !?
ZSH
TILT...
SPLOP SPLOP SPLOP
WAY TO FOLLOW-UP, SIS!
IT'S MOTHER !!
GWOOOR
DAR-R-RLING !!
NOW DO YOU SEE !?
?
THIS...
THIS FAMILY...

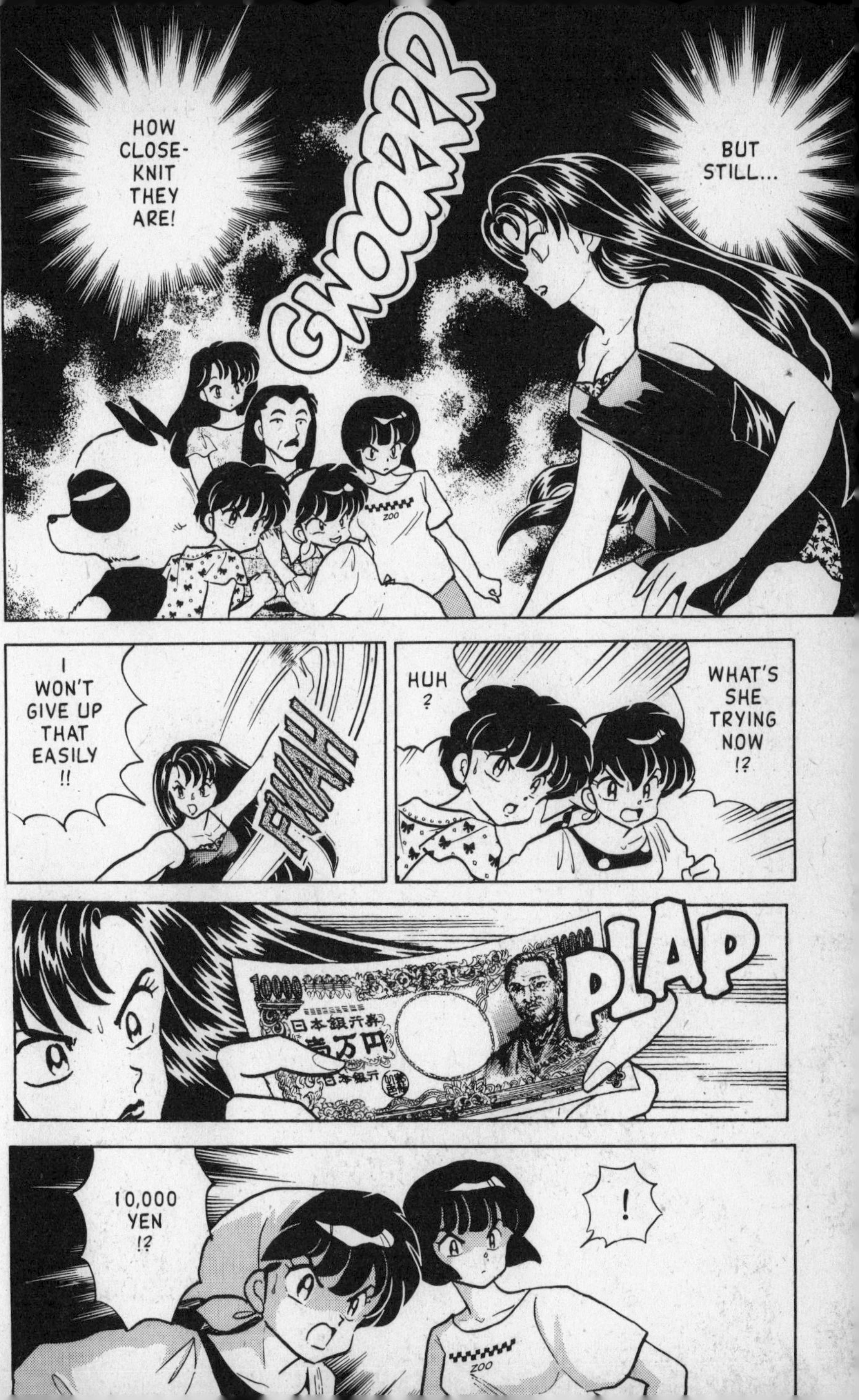
HOW CLOSE-KNIT THEY ARE!
GWOOARP
BUT STILL...
I WON'T GIVE UP THAT EASILY !!
FWAH
HUH ?
WHAT'S SHE TRYING NOW !?
PLAP
10,000 YEN !?
!

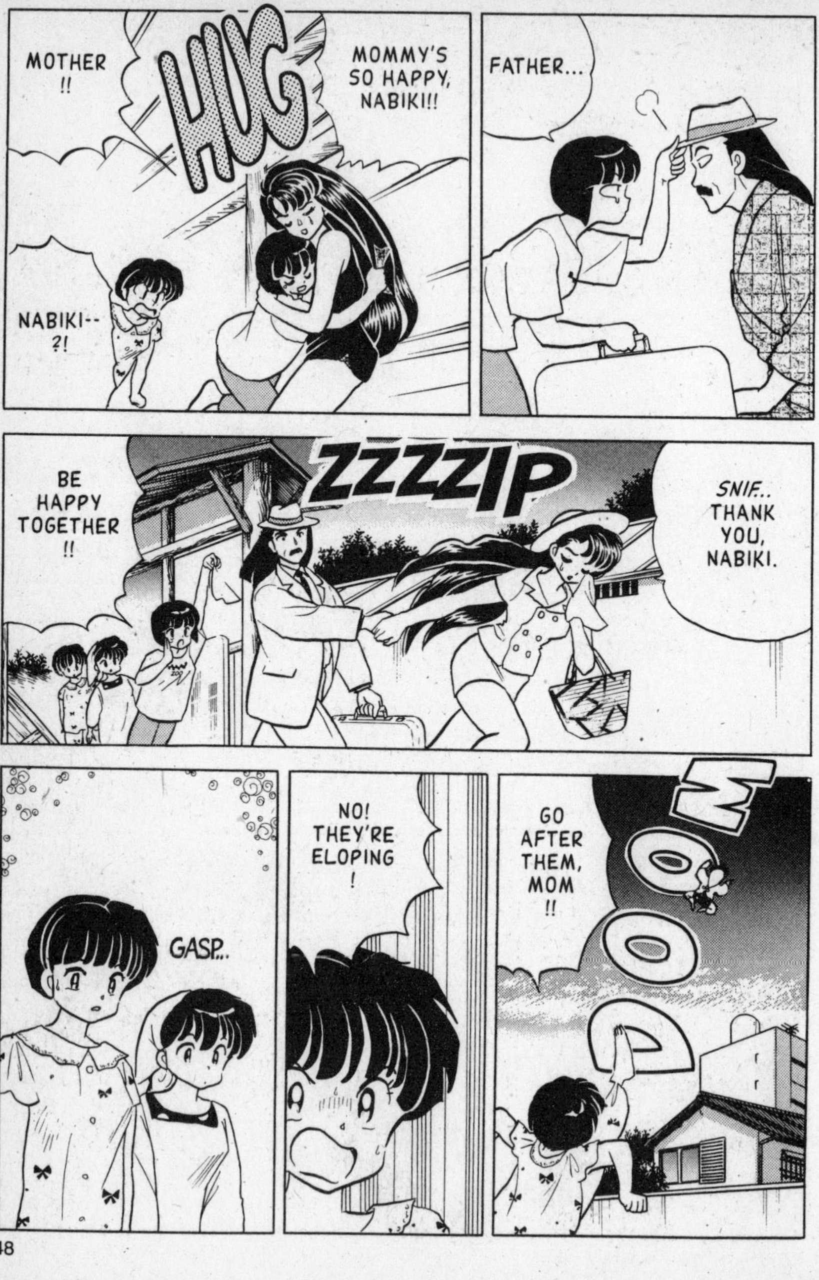
FATHER...
MOMMY'S SO HAPPY, NABIKI!!!
HUG
MOTHER !!
NABIKI-- ?!
SNIF.. THANK YOU, NABIKI.
ZZZZIP
BE HAPPY TOGETHER !!
GO AFTER THEM, MOM !!
NO! THEY'RE ELOPING !
GASP...

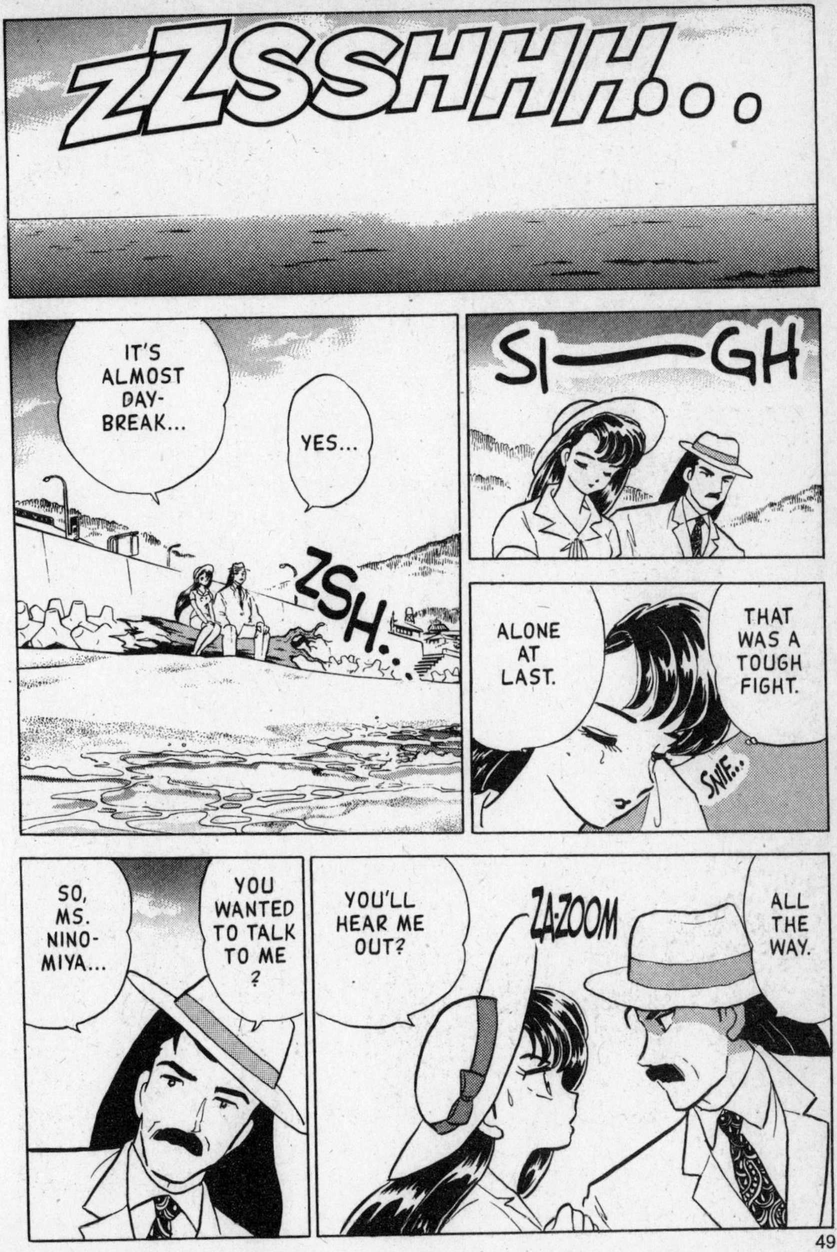
zZSSHHH...
IT'S ALMOST DAY-BREAK...
YES...
ZSSH...
SI——GH
ALONE AT LAST.
THAT WAS A TOUGH FIGHT.
SNIF...
SO, MS. NINO-MIYA...
YOU WANTED TO TALK TO ME?
YOU'LL HEAR ME OUT?
ZA-ZOOM
ALL THE WAY.

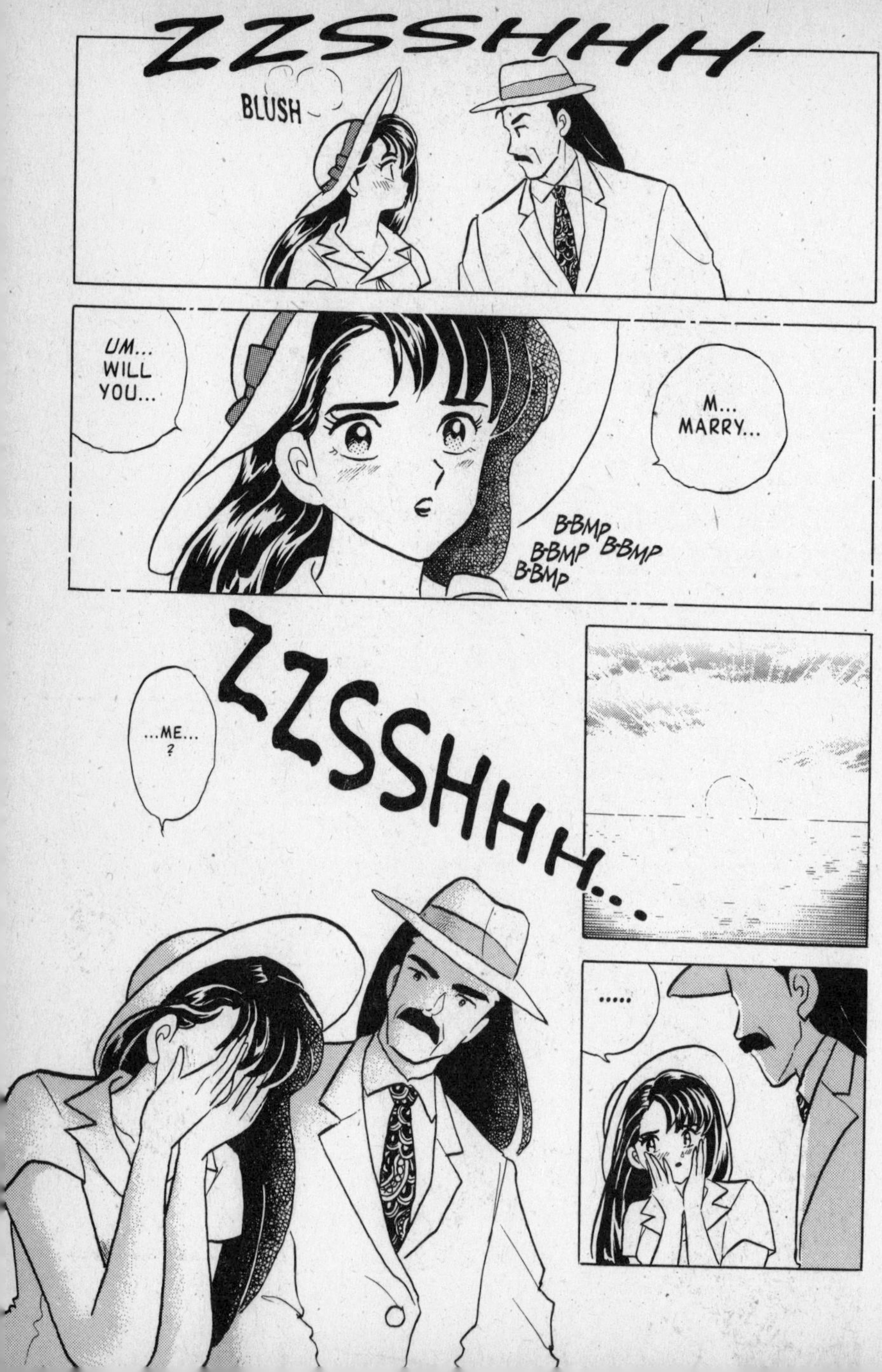
ZZSSHHHH
BLUSH
UM... WILL YOU...
M... MARRY...
B-BMP B-BMP B-BMP B-BMP
...ME... ?
ZZSSHHHH...
.....

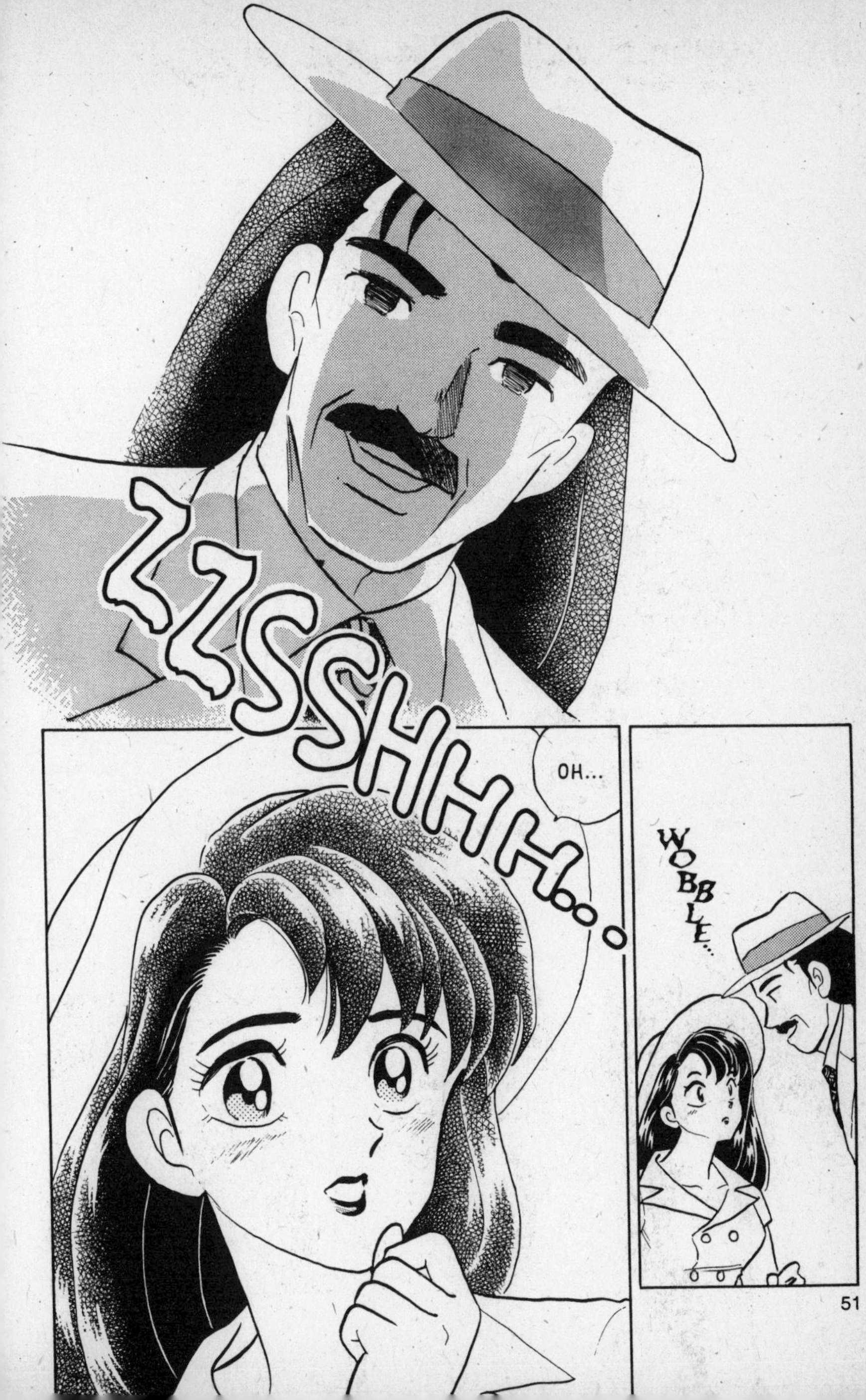
ZZSSHHH...
OH...
WOBBLE...

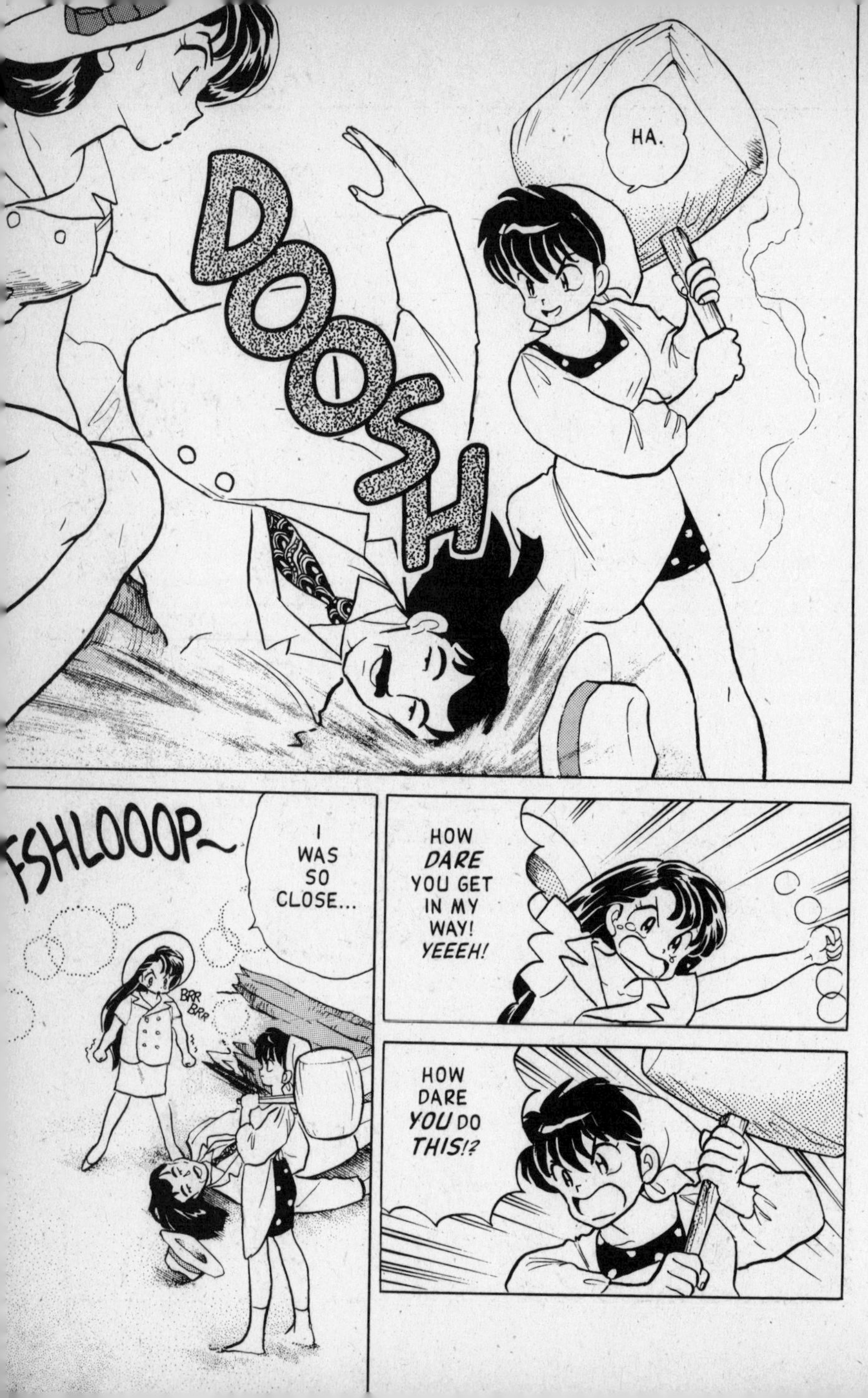

HA.
DOOOSH
FSHLOOOP~
I WAS SO CLOSE...
BRR BRR
HOW DARE YOU GET IN MY WAY! YEEEH!
HOW DARE YOU DO THIS!?

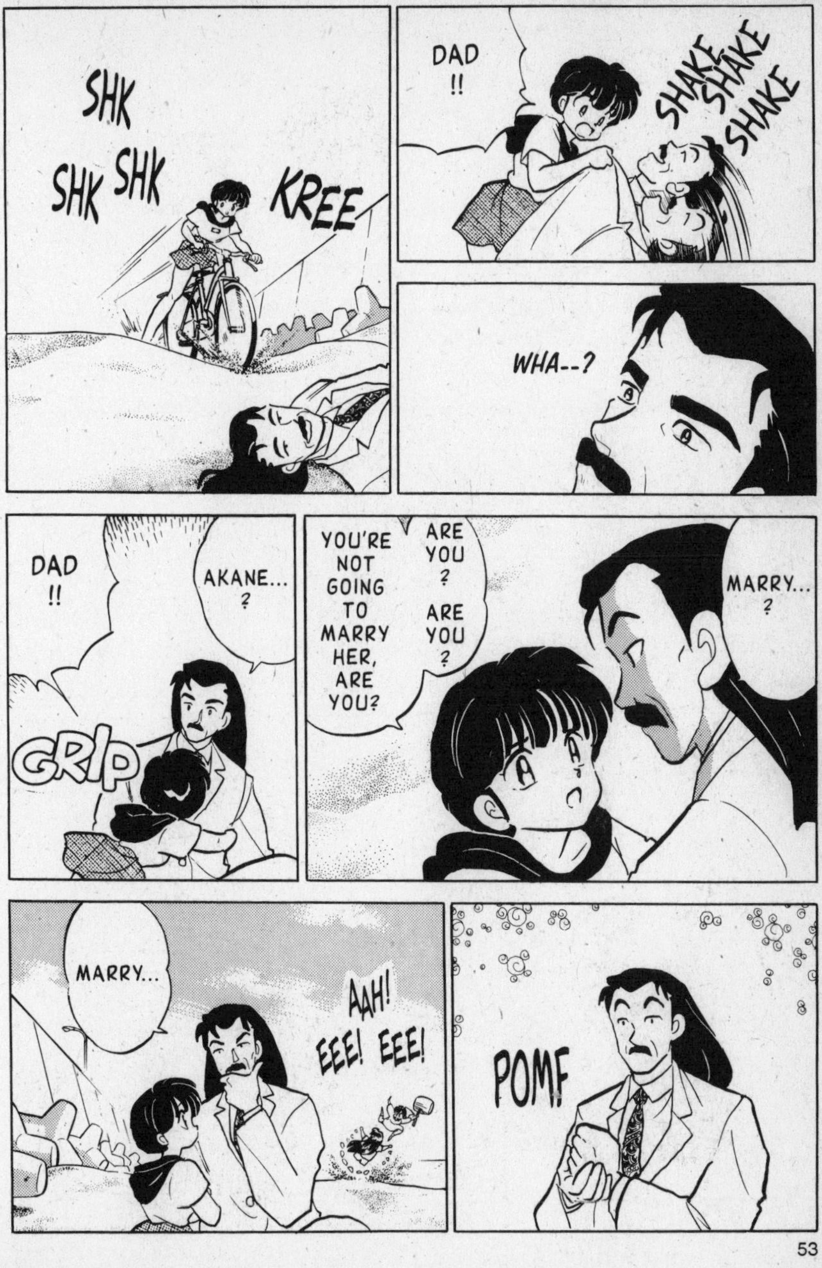
SHK
SHK SHK
KREE
DAD !!
SHAKE SHAKE SHAKE
WHA--?
DAD !!
AKANE... ?
YOU'RE NOT GOING TO MARRY HER, ARE YOU?
ARE YOU ? ARE YOU ?
MARRY... ?
GRIP
MARRY...
AAH! EEE! EEE!
POMF

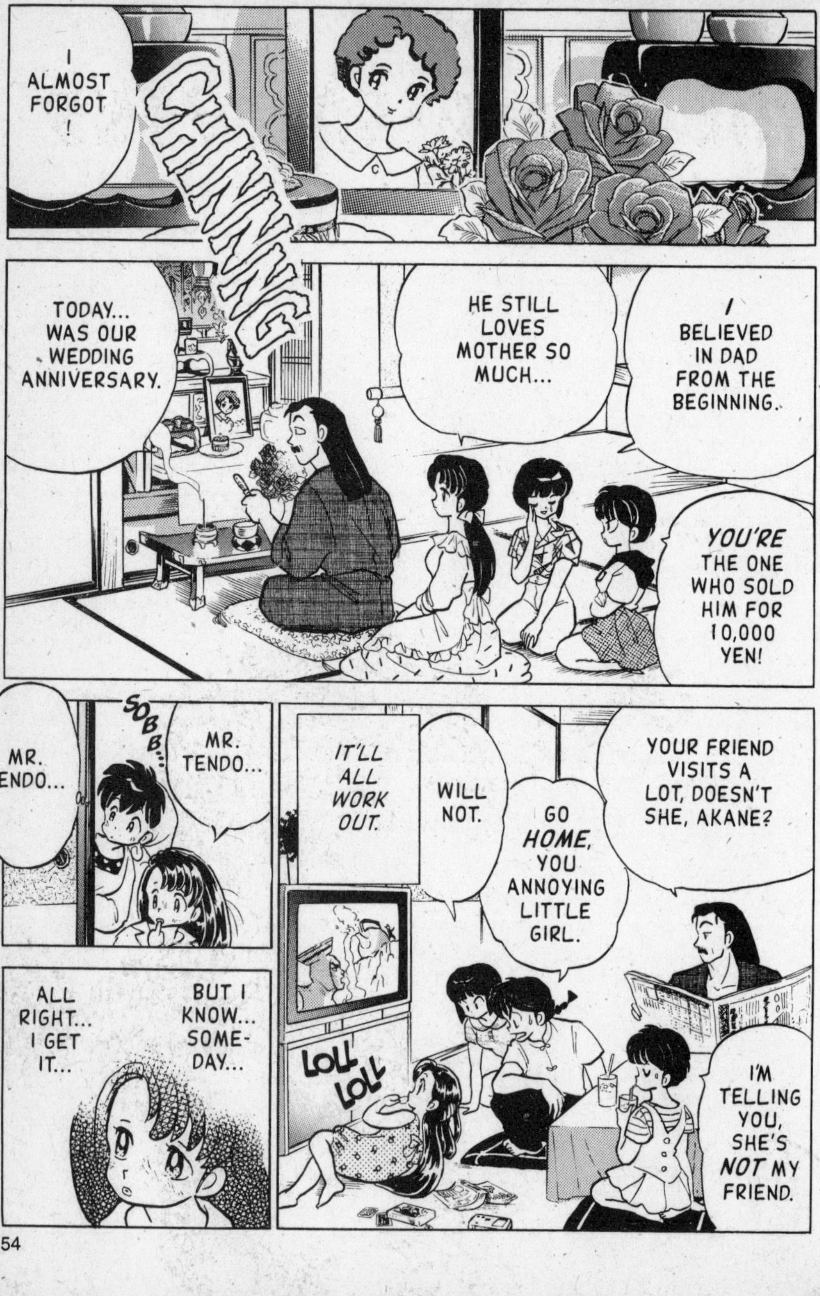
I ALMOST FORGOT!
CHINNNG
TODAY... WAS OUR WEDDING ANNIVERSARY.
HE STILL LOVES MOTHER SO MUCH...
I BELIEVED IN DAD FROM THE BEGINNING.
YOU'RE THE ONE WHO SOLD HIM FOR 10,000 YEN!
MR. TENDO...
SOBB...
MR. TENDO...
ALL RIGHT... I GET IT...
BUT I KNOW... SOME-DAY...
IT'LL ALL WORK OUT.
WILL NOT.
GO *HOME*, YOU ANNOYING LITTLE GIRL.
YOUR FRIEND VISITS A LOT, DOESN'T SHE, AKANE?
LOLL LOLL
I'M TELLING YOU, SHE'S *NOT* MY FRIEND.

Part 4

THE UNBEATABLE LENS

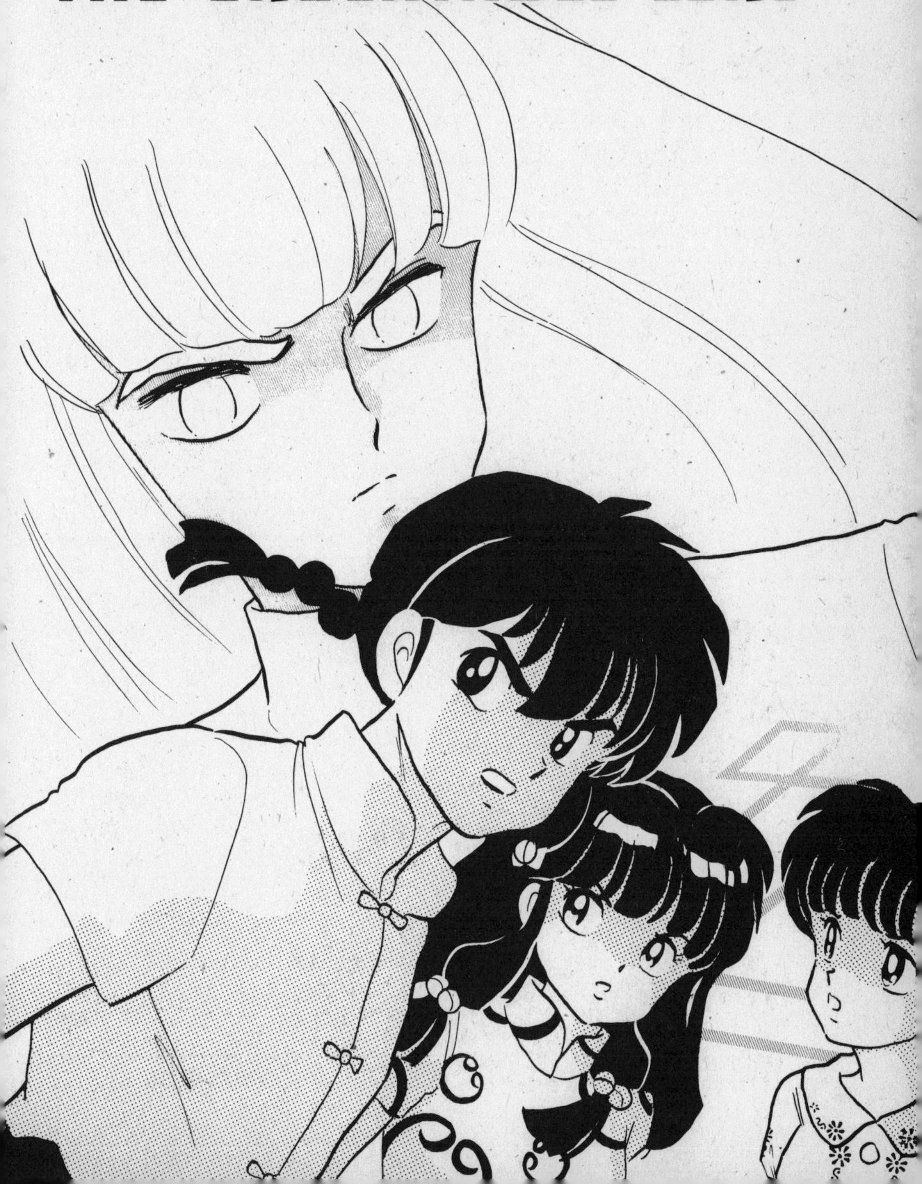

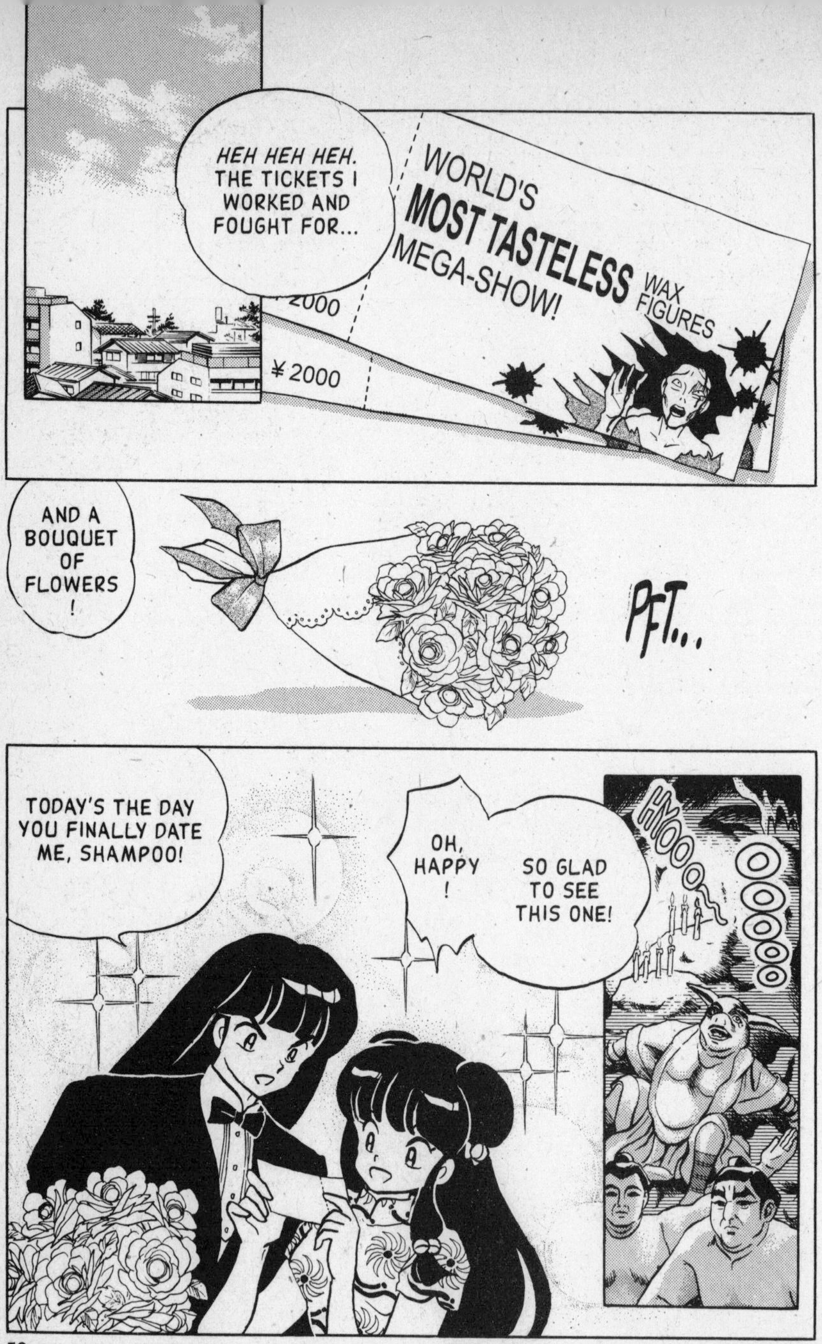
HEH HEH HEH. THE TICKETS I WORKED AND FOUGHT FOR...
WORLD'S MOST TASTELESS WAX FIGURES MEGA-SHOW!
¥2000
¥2000
AND A BOUQUET OF FLOWERS!
PFT...
TODAY'S THE DAY YOU FINALLY DATE ME, SHAMPOO!
OH, HAPPY!
SO GLAD TO SEE THIS ONE!
HYOOOOOOOOO

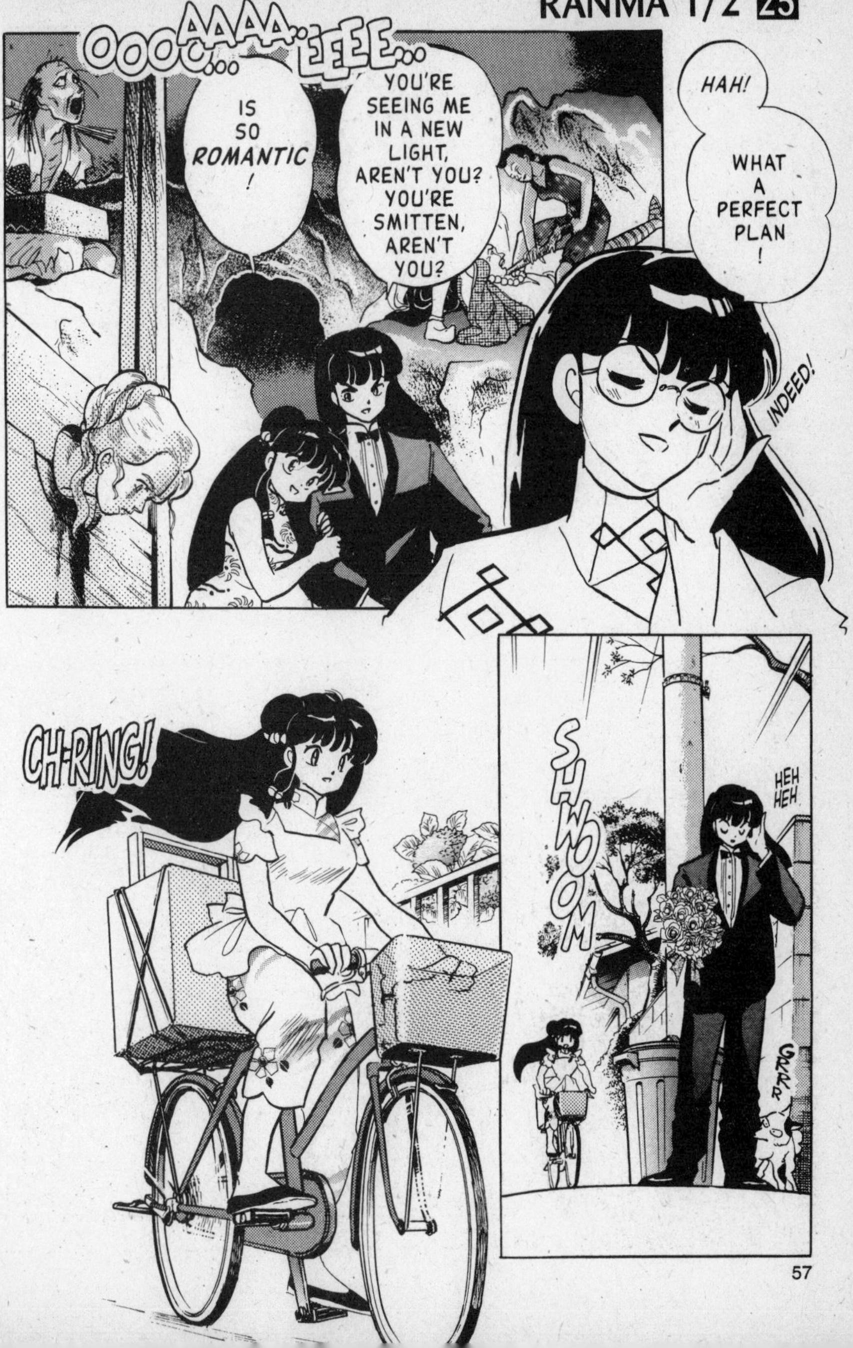
OOOO...AAAA...EEEE...
IS SO ROMANTIC!
YOU'RE SEEING ME IN A NEW LIGHT, AREN'T YOU? YOU'RE SMITTEN, AREN'T YOU?
HAH!
WHAT A PERFECT PLAN!
INDEED!
CH-RING!
SHWOOM
HEH HEH
GRRR

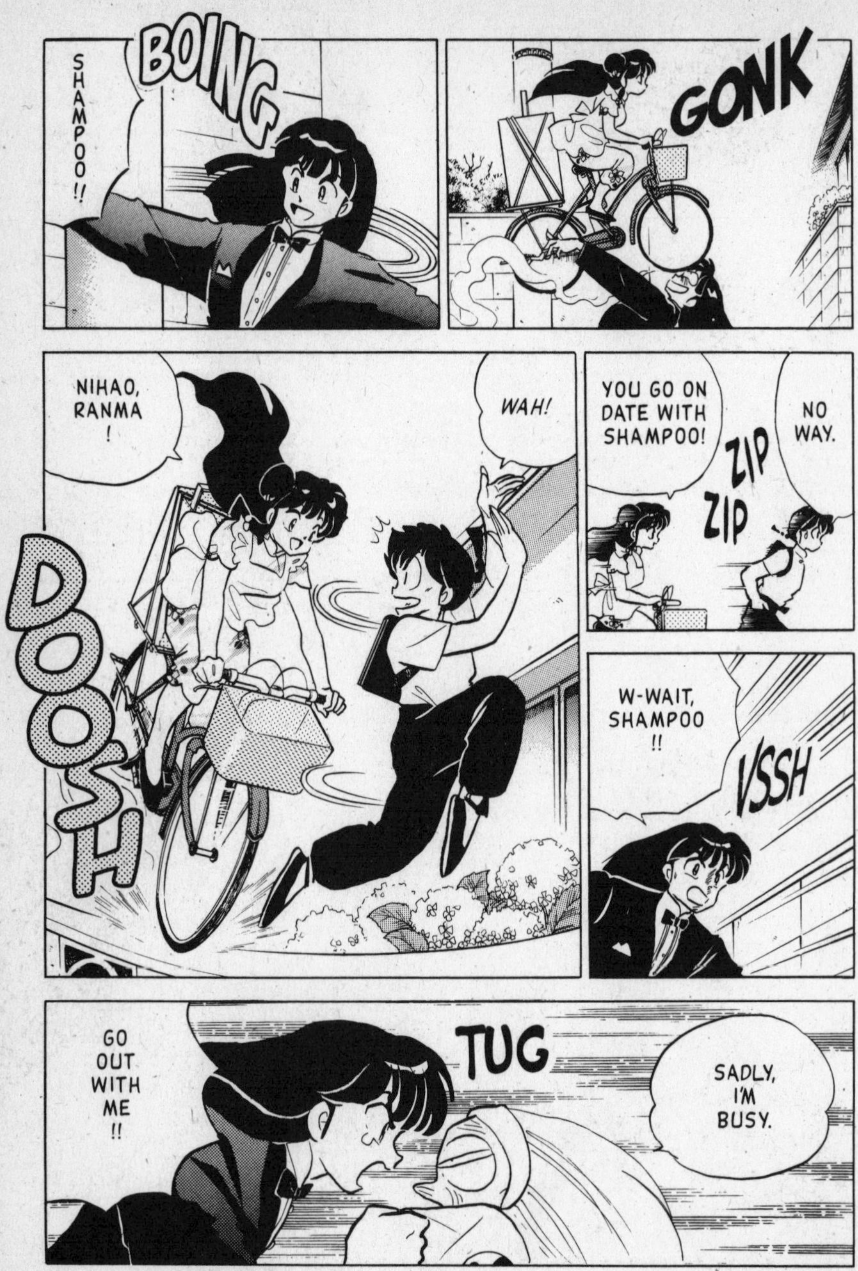
SHAMPOO!!
BOING
GONK
NIHAO, RANMA!
WAH!
DOOSH
YOU GO ON DATE WITH SHAMPOO!
NO WAY.
ZIP ZIP
W-WAIT, SHAMPOO!!
VSSH
GO OUT WITH ME!!
TUG
SADLY, I'M BUSY.

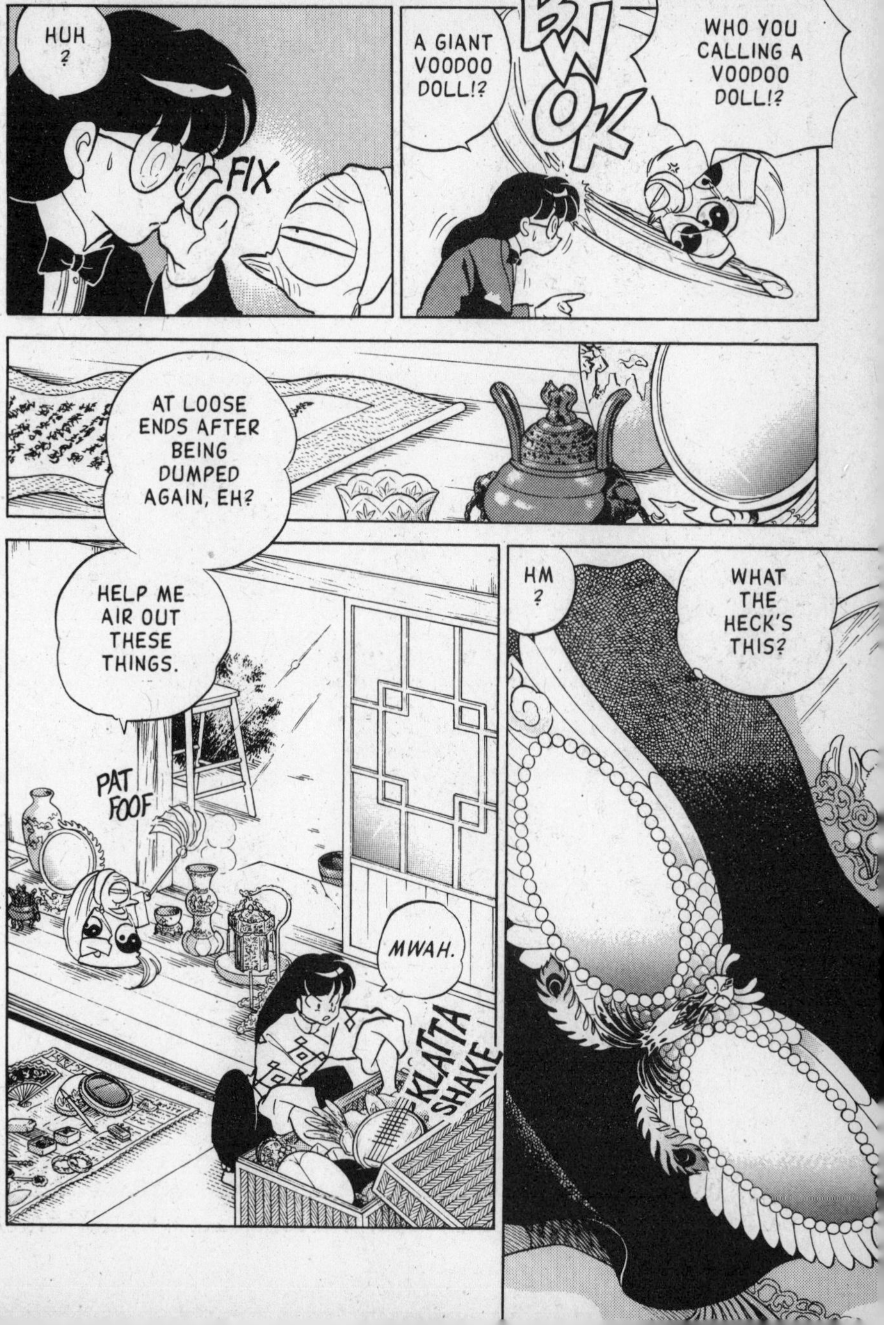
HUH ?
FIX
A GIANT VOODOO DOLL!?
BWOK
WHO YOU CALLING A VOODOO DOLL!?
AT LOOSE ENDS AFTER BEING DUMPED AGAIN, EH?
HELP ME AIR OUT THESE THINGS.
PAT FOOF
MWAH.
KLATTA SHAKE
HM ?
WHAT THE HECK'S THIS?

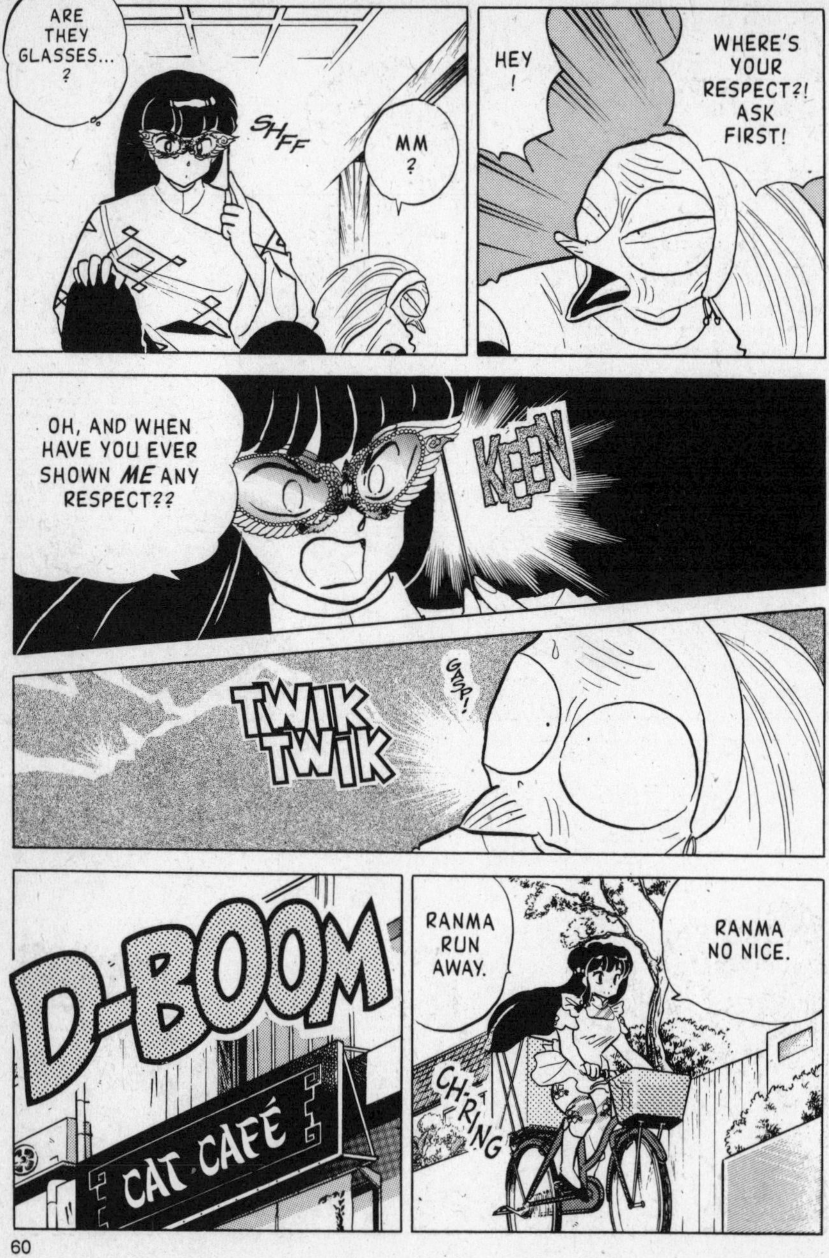
ARE THEY GLASSES...?
SHFF
MM?
HEY!
WHERE'S YOUR RESPECT?! ASK FIRST!
OH, AND WHEN HAVE YOU EVER SHOWN ME ANY RESPECT??
KEEN
TWIK TWIK
GASP!
D-BOOM
CAT CAFÉ
RANMA RUN AWAY.
RANMA NO NICE.
CH-RING

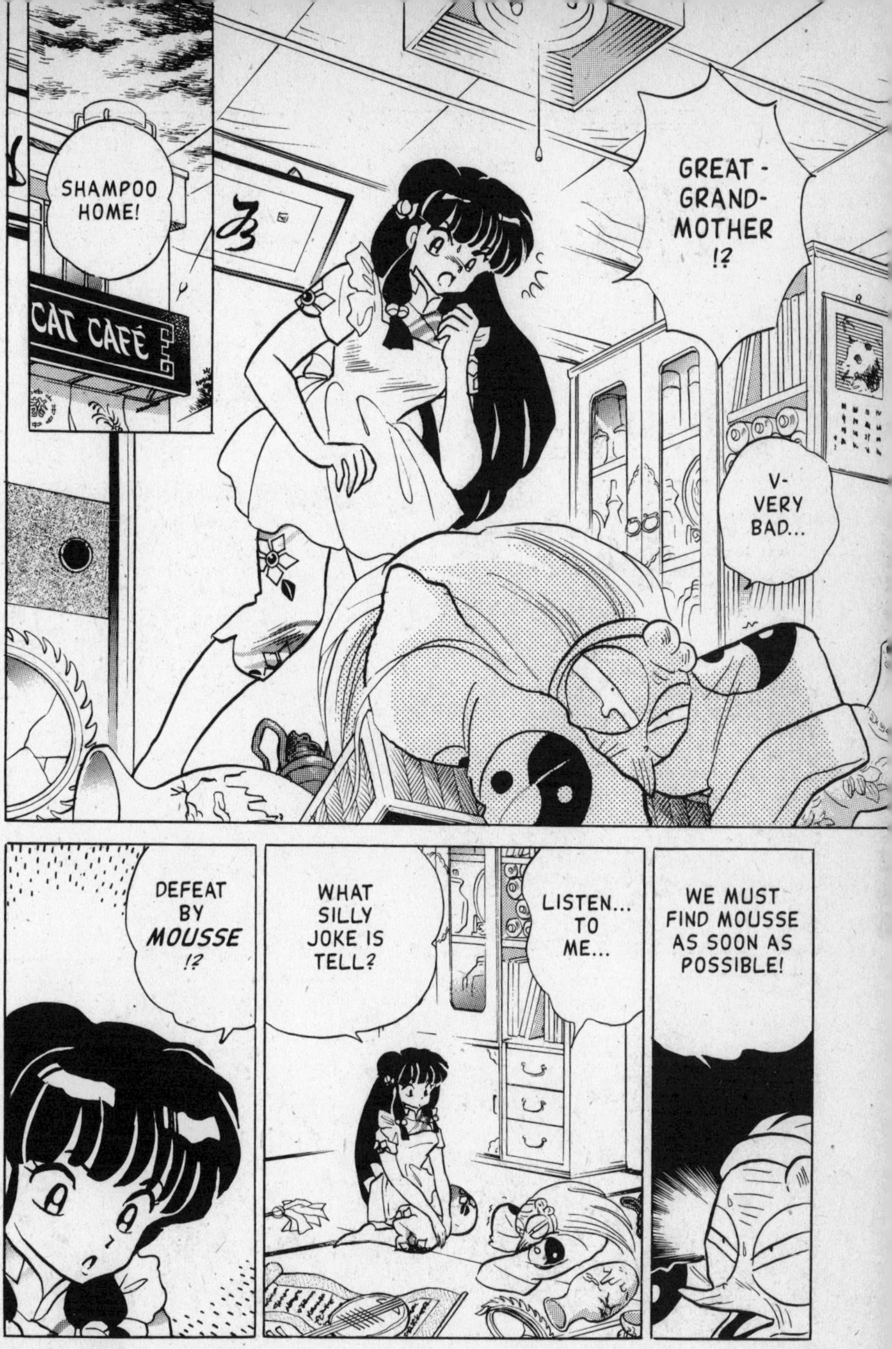
CAT CAFÉ
SHAMPOO HOME!
GREAT-GRANDMOTHER !?
V-VERY BAD...
DEFEAT BY *MOUSSE* !?
WHAT SILLY JOKE IS TELL?
LISTEN... TO ME...
WE MUST FIND MOUSSE AS SOON AS POSSIBLE!

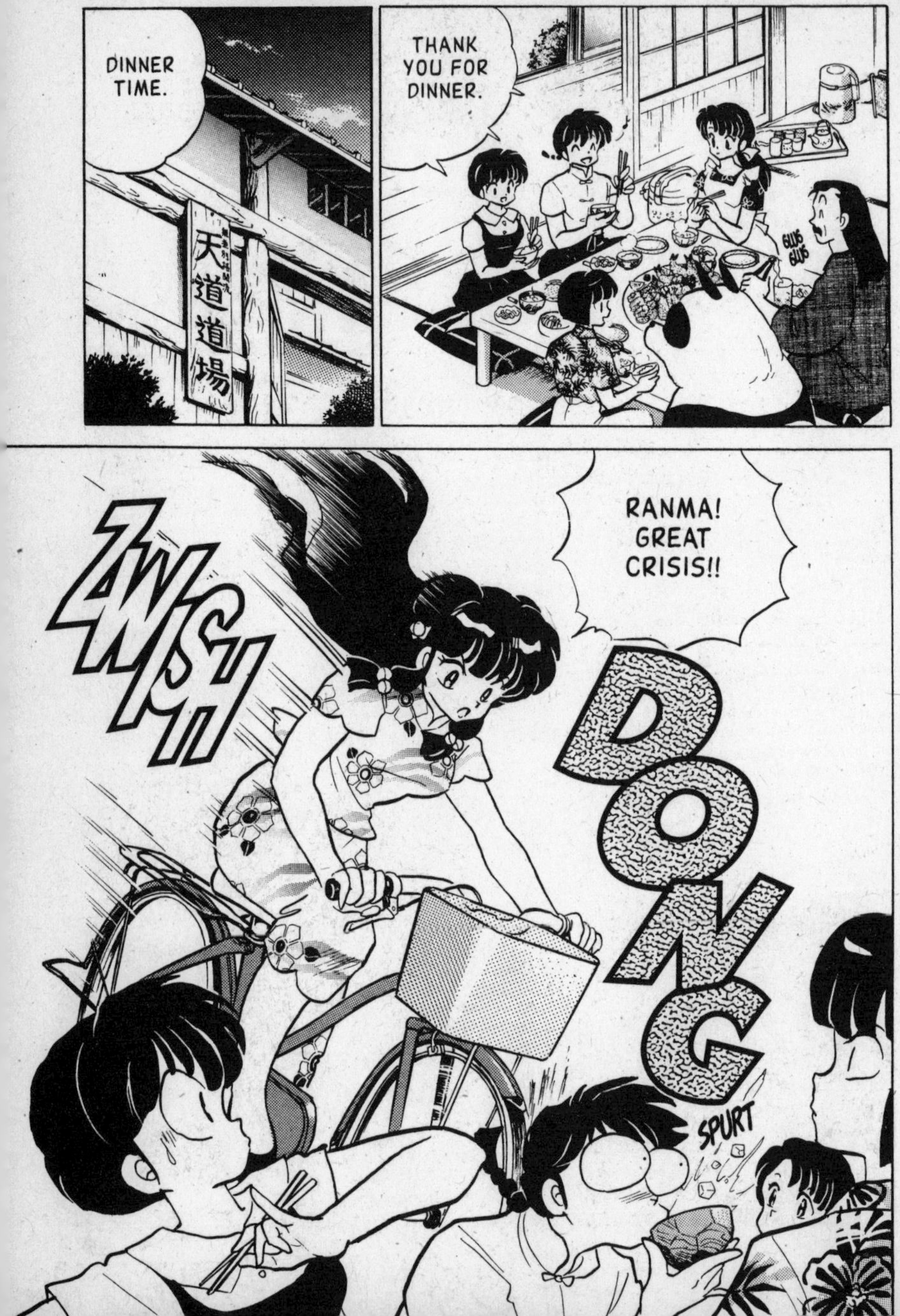
DINNER TIME.
天道道場
THANK YOU FOR DINNER.
GLUG GLUG
ZWISH
RANMA! GREAT CRISIS!!
DONG
SPURT

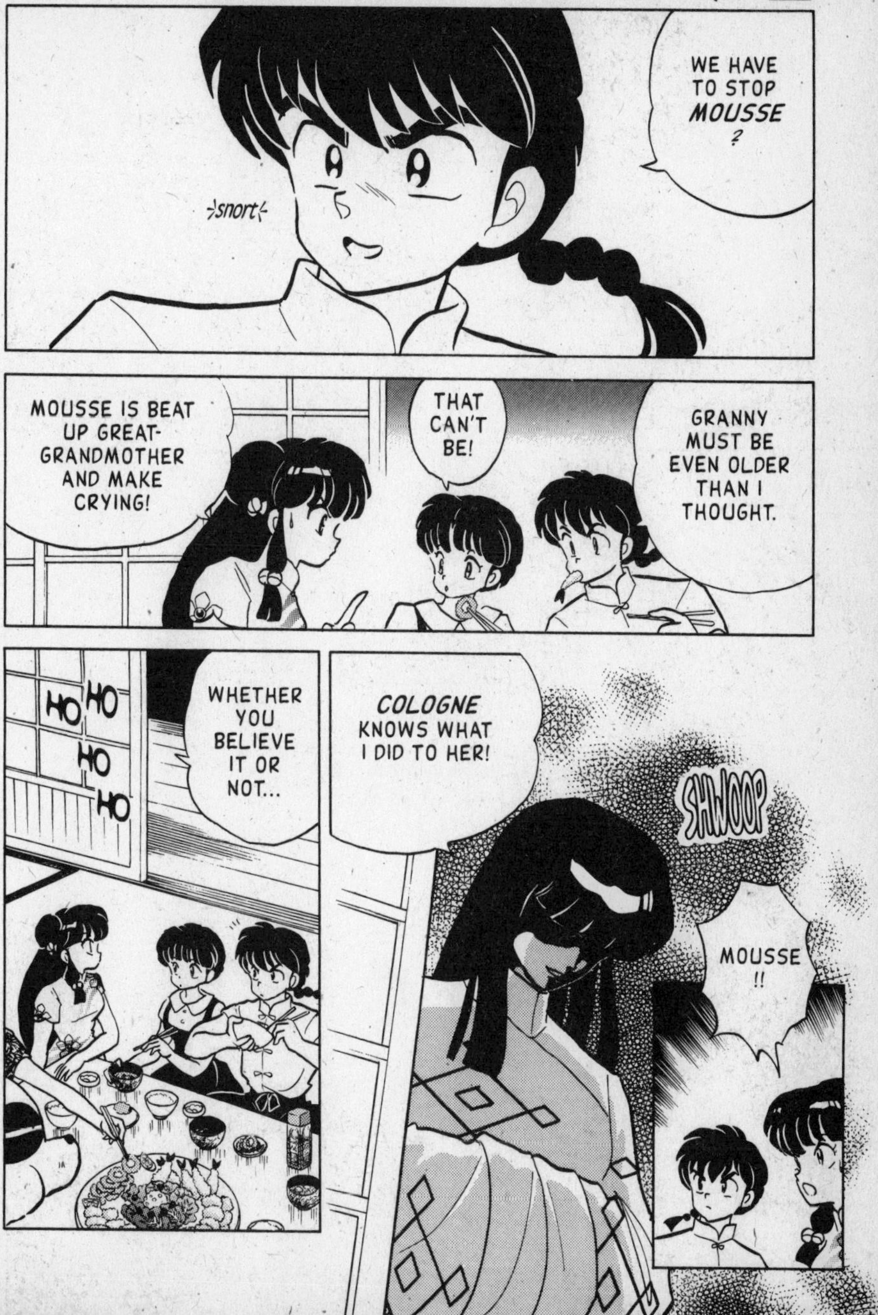

WE HAVE TO STOP MOUSSE ?
-snort-
MOUSSE IS BEAT UP GREAT-GRANDMOTHER AND MAKE CRYING!
THAT CAN'T BE!
GRANNY MUST BE EVEN OLDER THAN I THOUGHT.
HO HO HO HO
WHETHER YOU BELIEVE IT OR NOT...
COLOGNE KNOWS WHAT I DID TO HER!
SHWOOP
MOUSSE !!

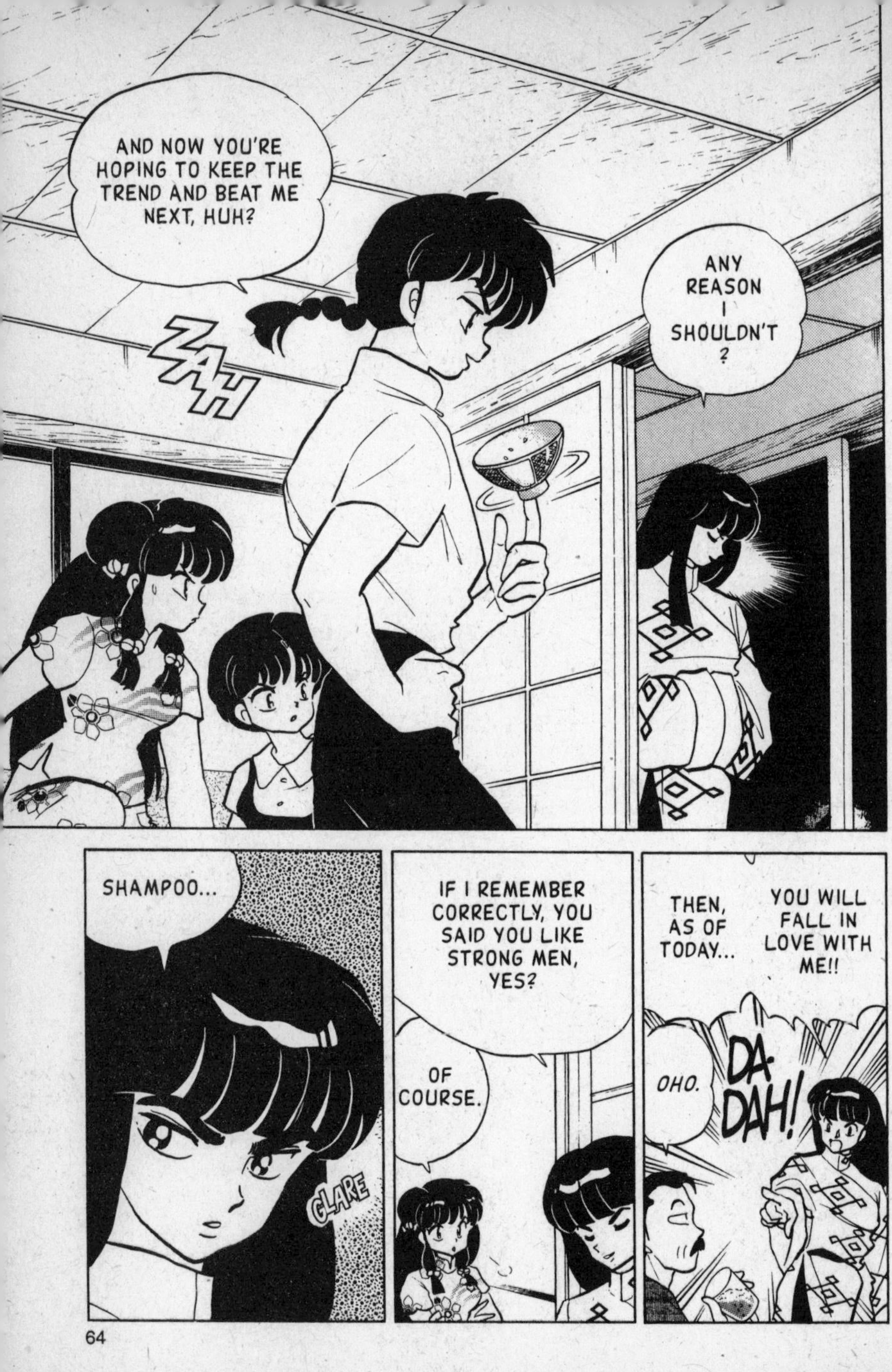
AND NOW YOU'RE HOPING TO KEEP THE TREND AND BEAT ME NEXT, HUH?
ZAH
ANY REASON I SHOULDN'T ?
SHAMPOO...
GLARE
IF I REMEMBER CORRECTLY, YOU SAID YOU LIKE STRONG MEN, YES?
OF COURSE.
THEN, AS OF TODAY...
YOU WILL FALL IN LOVE WITH ME!!
OHO.
DA-DAH!

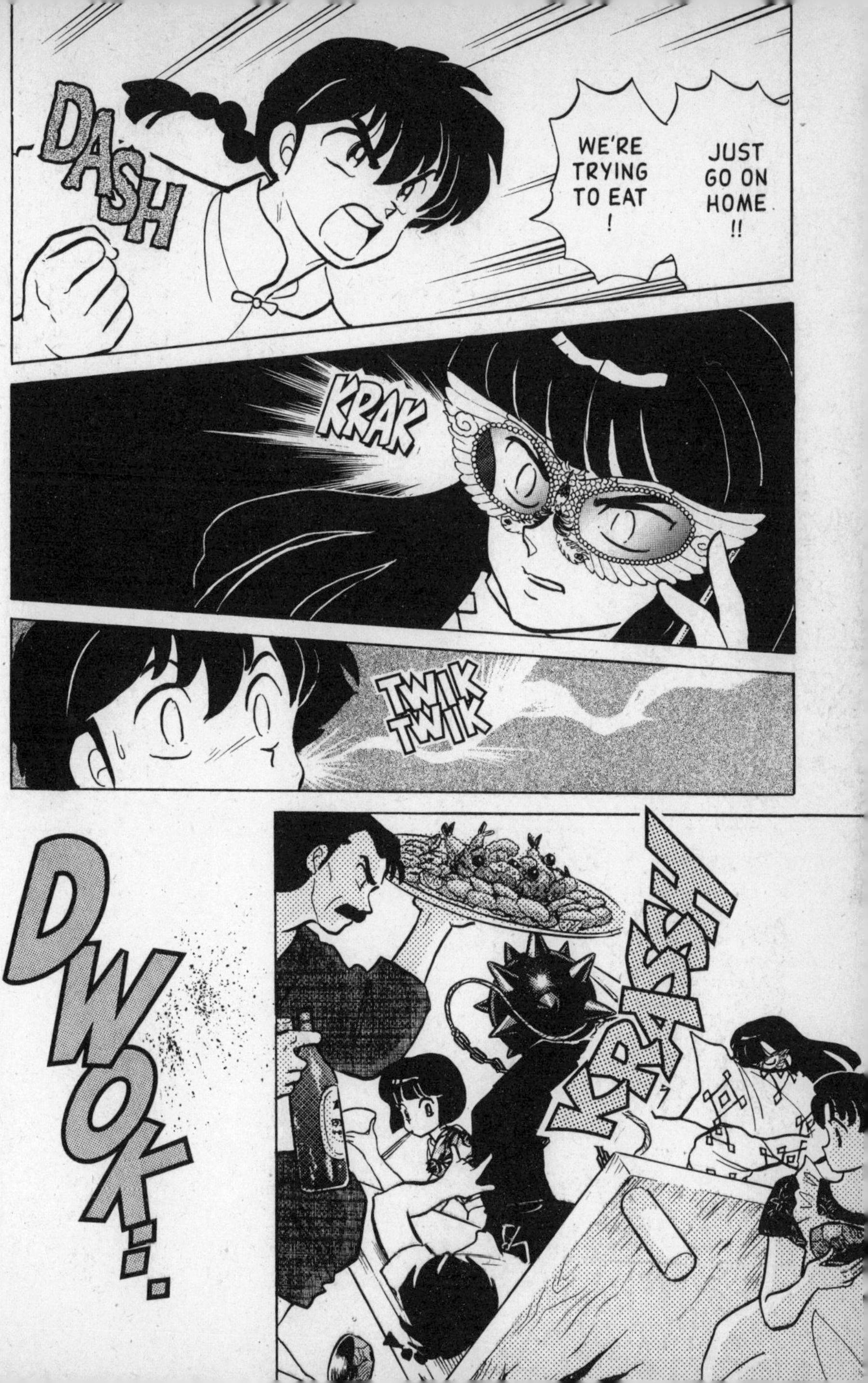
DASH
WE'RE TRYING TO EAT !
JUST GO ON HOME !!
KRAK
TWIK TWIK
DWOK..
KRASH

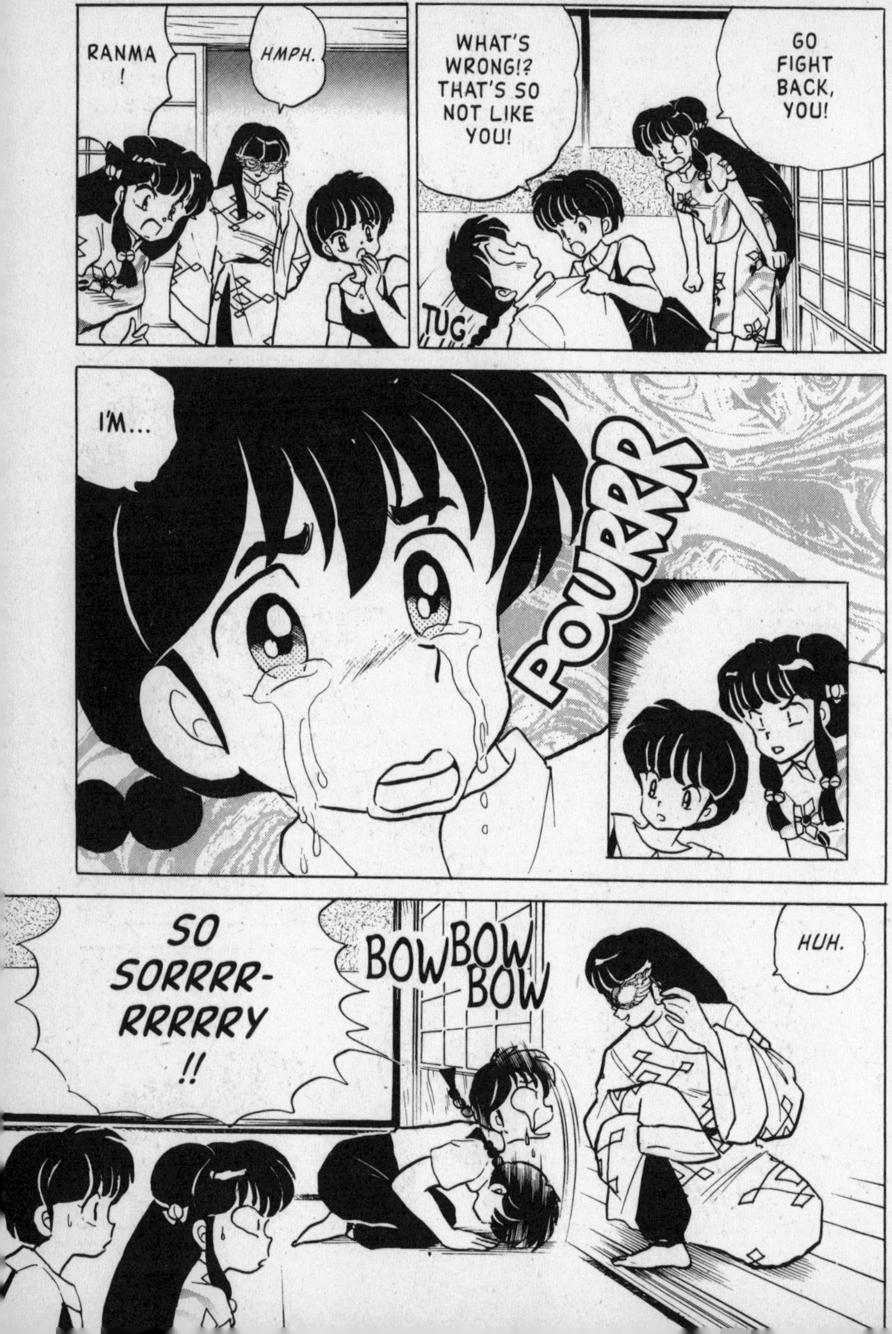
RANMA!
HMPH.
WHAT'S WRONG!? THAT'S SO NOT LIKE YOU!
GO FIGHT BACK, YOU!
TUG
I'M...
POURRR
SO SORRRRR-RRRRRY !!
BOW BOW BOW BOW
HUH.

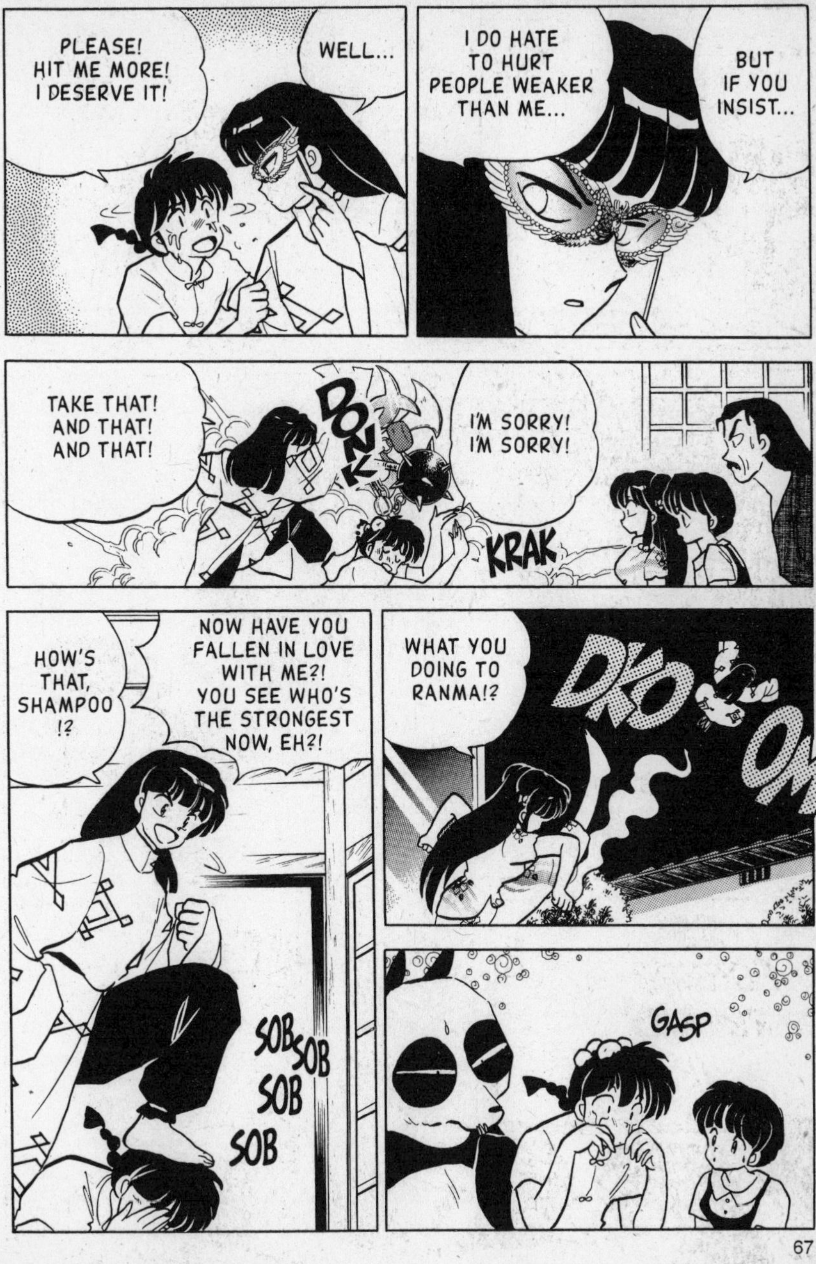
PLEASE! HIT ME MORE! I DESERVE IT!
WELL...
I DO HATE TO HURT PEOPLE WEAKER THAN ME...
BUT IF YOU INSIST...
TAKE THAT! AND THAT! AND THAT!
DONK
I'M SORRY! I'M SORRY!
KRAK
HOW'S THAT, SHAMPOO !?
NOW HAVE YOU FALLEN IN LOVE WITH ME?! YOU SEE WHO'S THE STRONGEST NOW, EH?!
SOB SOB SOB SOB
WHAT YOU DOING TO RANMA!?
DKOOM
GASP

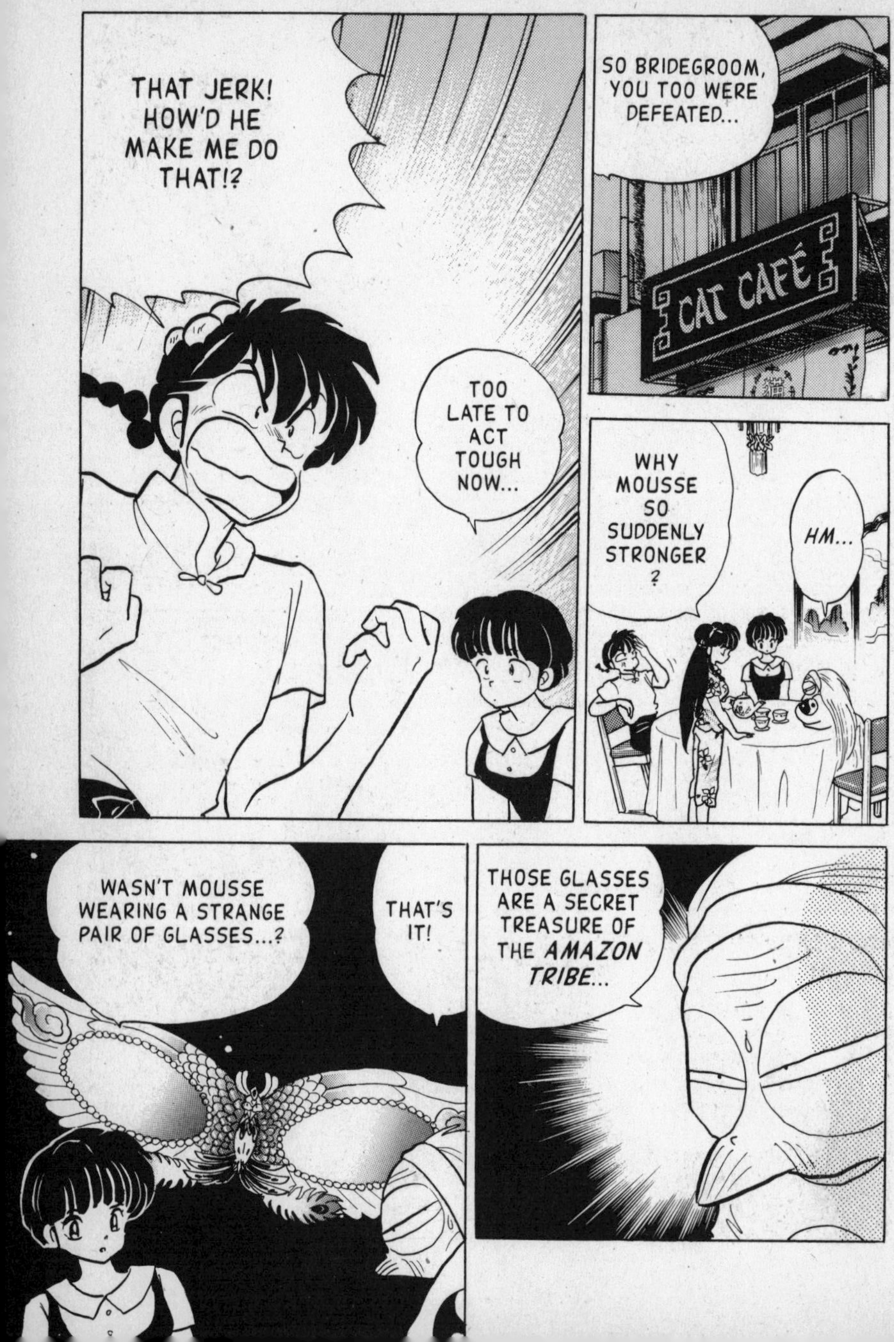
THAT JERK! HOW'D HE MAKE ME DO THAT!?
TOO LATE TO ACT TOUGH NOW...
SO BRIDEGROOM, YOU TOO WERE DEFEATED...
CAT CAFÉ
WHY MOUSSE SO SUDDENLY STRONGER ?
HM...
WASN'T MOUSSE WEARING A STRANGE PAIR OF GLASSES...?
THAT'S IT!
THOSE GLASSES ARE A SECRET TREASURE OF THE *AMAZON* TRIBE...

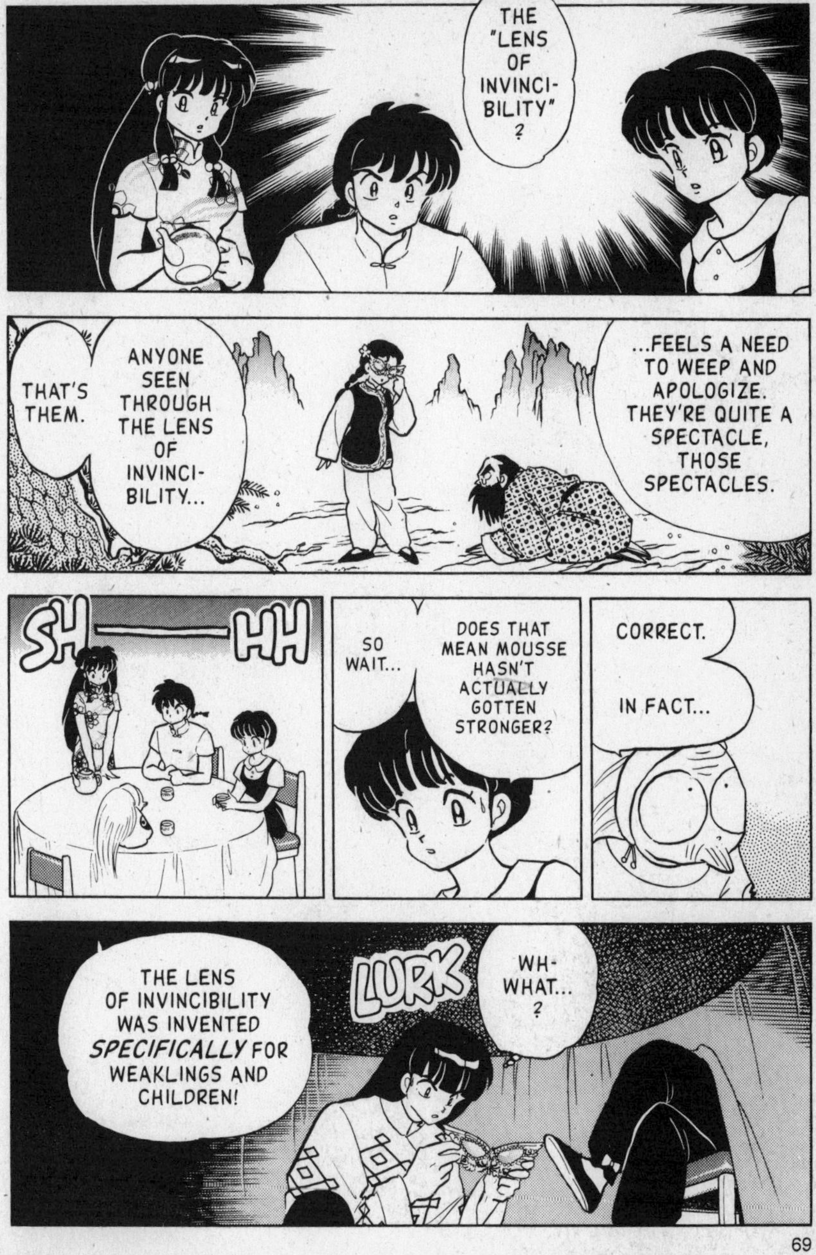

THE "LENS OF INVINCIBILITY"?
THAT'S THEM.
ANYONE SEEN THROUGH THE LENS OF INVINCIBILITY...
...FEELS A NEED TO WEEP AND APOLOGIZE. THEY'RE QUITE A SPECTACLE, THOSE SPECTACLES.
SH—HH
SO WAIT...
DOES THAT MEAN MOUSSE HASN'T ACTUALLY GOTTEN STRONGER?
CORRECT.
IN FACT...
THE LENS OF INVINCIBILITY WAS INVENTED SPECIFICALLY FOR WEAKLINGS AND CHILDREN!
LURK
WH-WHAT...?

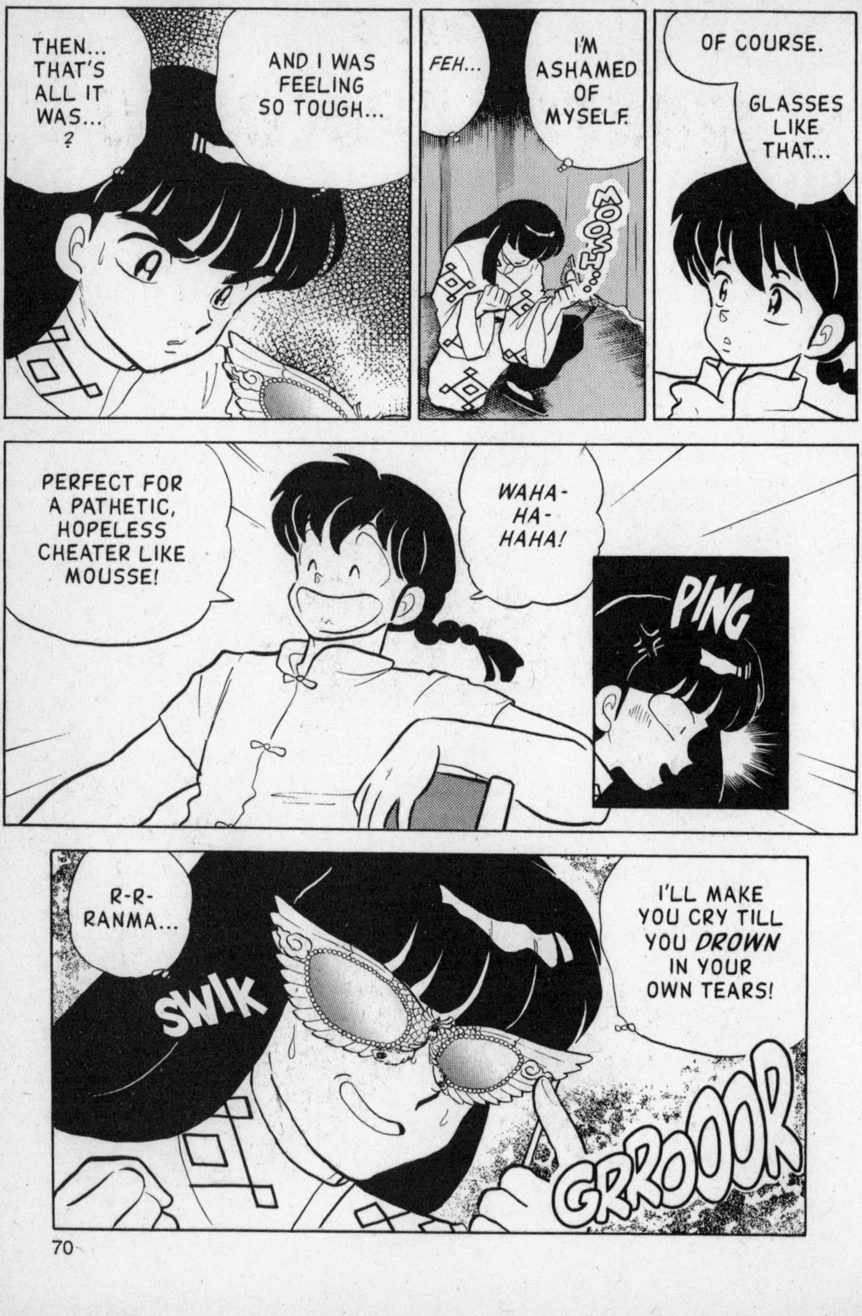
THEN... THAT'S ALL IT WAS...?
AND I WAS FEELING SO TOUGH...
FEH...
I'M ASHAMED OF MYSELF.
MOOSH...
OF COURSE.
GLASSES LIKE THAT...
PERFECT FOR A PATHETIC, HOPELESS CHEATER LIKE MOUSSE!
WAHA-HA-HAHA!
PING
R-R-RANMA...
SWIK
I'LL MAKE YOU CRY TILL YOU *DROWN* IN YOUR OWN TEARS!
GRROOOR

Part 5
TEARFUL APOLOGY!!

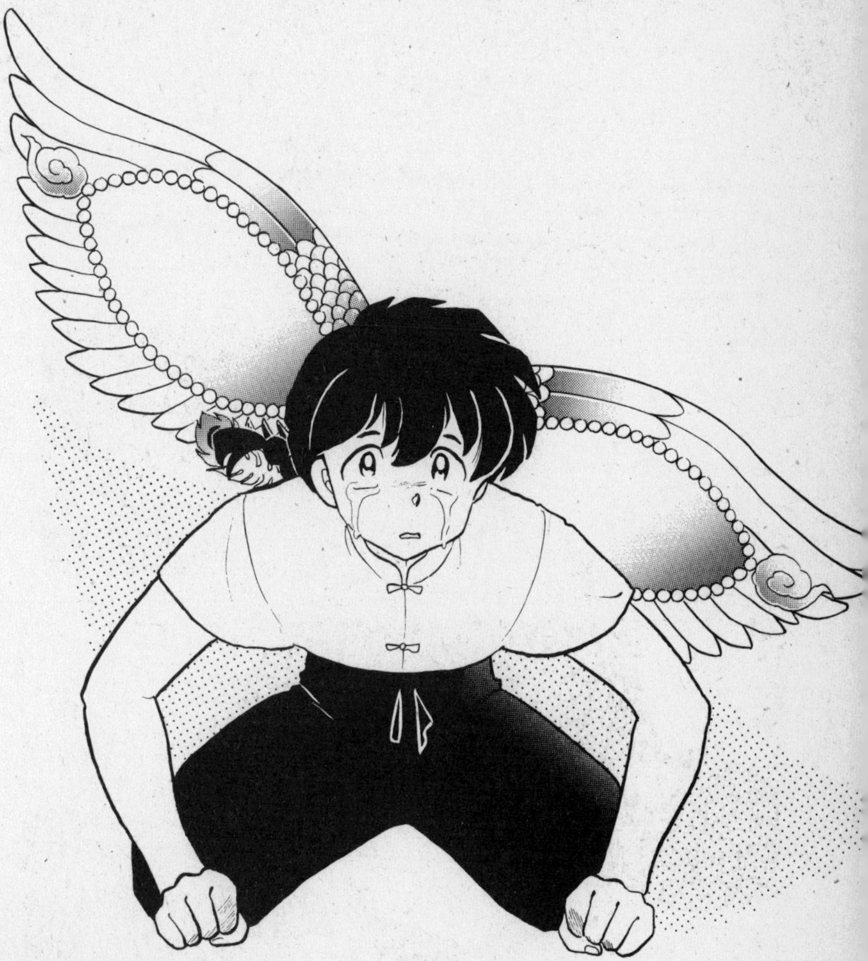

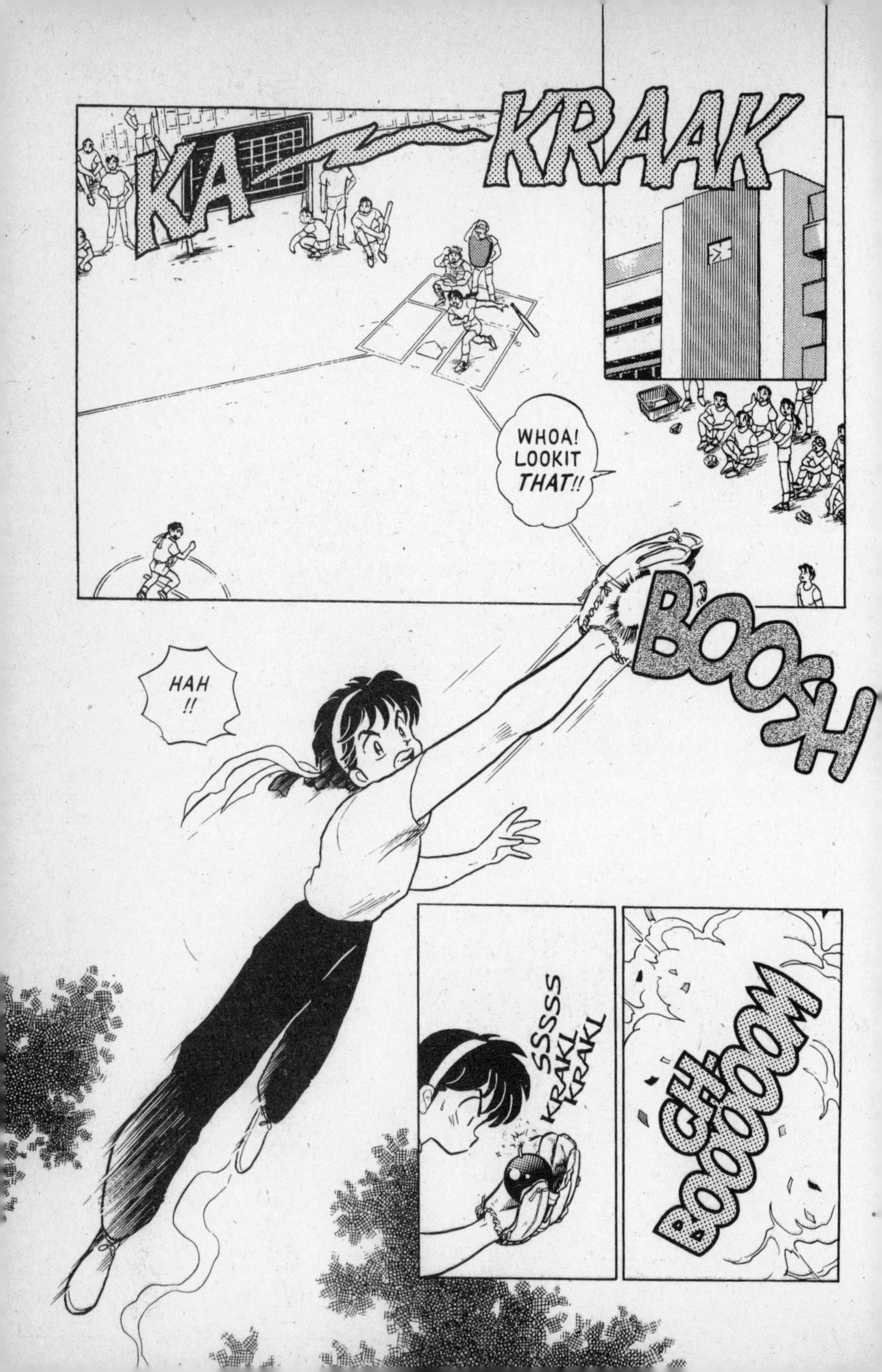
KA-KRAAK
WHOA! LOOKIT THAT!!
HAH !!
BOOSH
SSSSS KRAKL KRAKL
BCHOOOOOOM

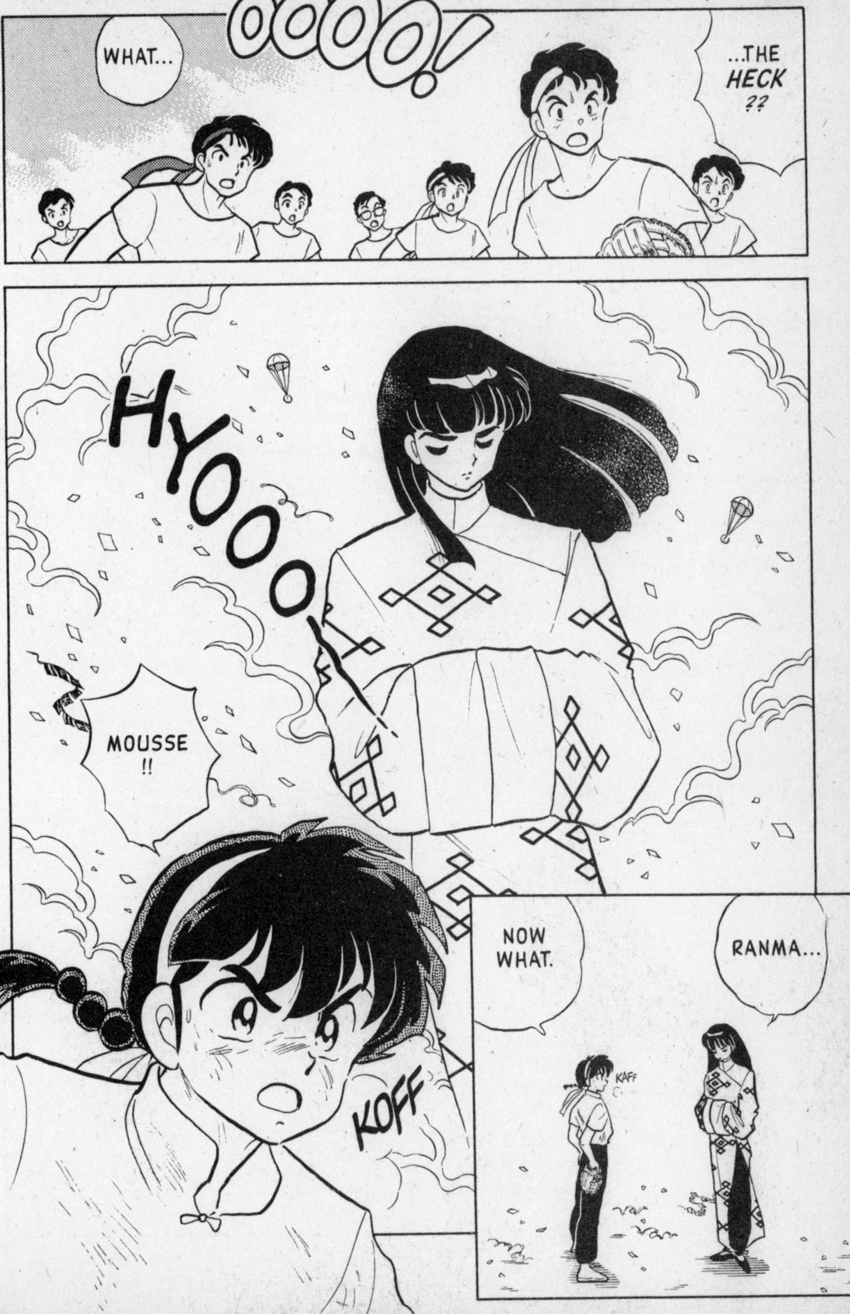
WHAT...
OOOO!
...THE HECK ??
HYOOOO
MOUSSE !!
KOFF
NOW WHAT.
RANMA...
KAFF

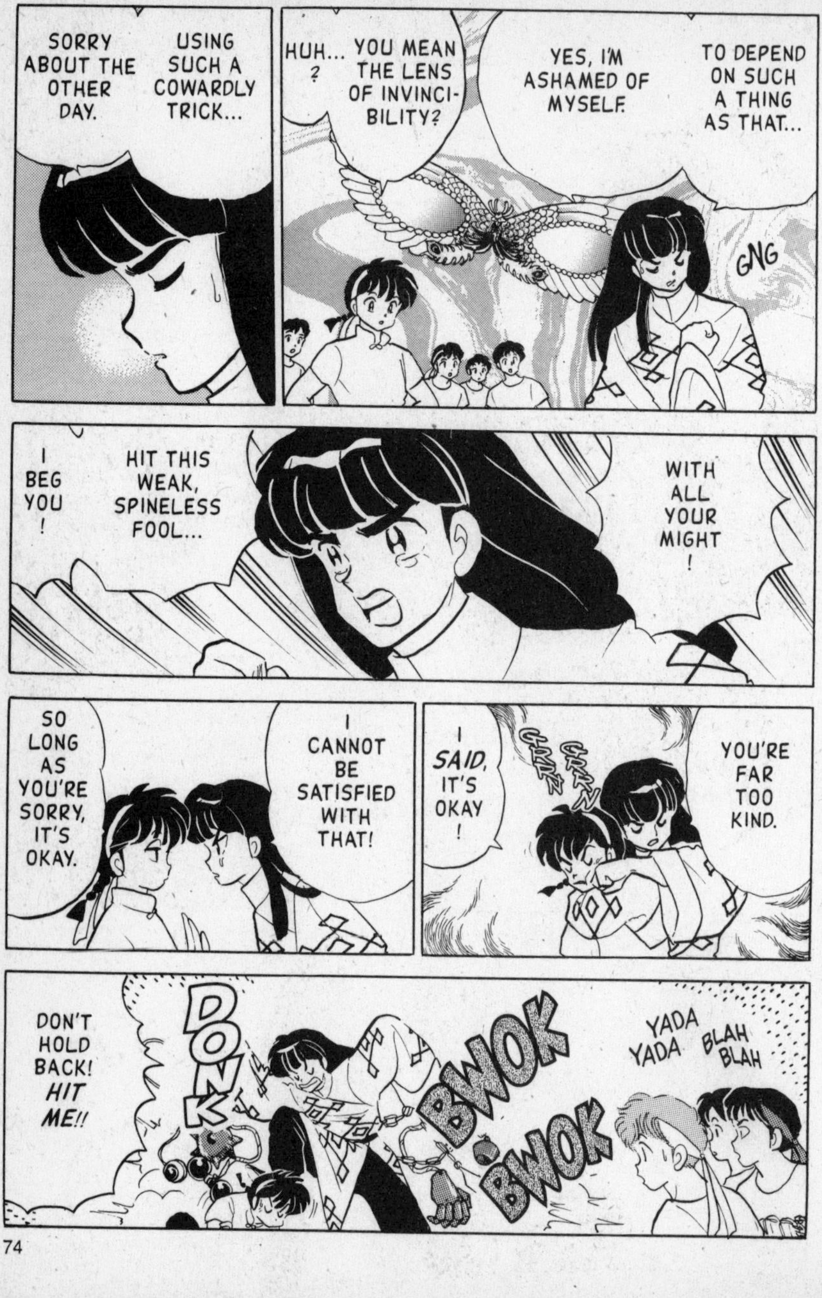
SORRY ABOUT THE OTHER DAY.
USING SUCH A COWARDLY TRICK...
HUH...?
YOU MEAN THE LENS OF INVINCIBILITY?
YES, I'M ASHAMED OF MYSELF.
TO DEPEND ON SUCH A THING AS THAT...
GNG
I BEG YOU!
HIT THIS WEAK, SPINELESS FOOL...
WITH ALL YOUR MIGHT!
SO LONG AS YOU'RE SORRY, IT'S OKAY.
I CANNOT BE SATISFIED WITH THAT!
I SAID, IT'S OKAY!
GRRN GRRN
YOU'RE FAR TOO KIND.
DON'T HOLD BACK! HIT ME!!
DONK
BWOK
BWOK
YADA YADA
BLAH BLAH

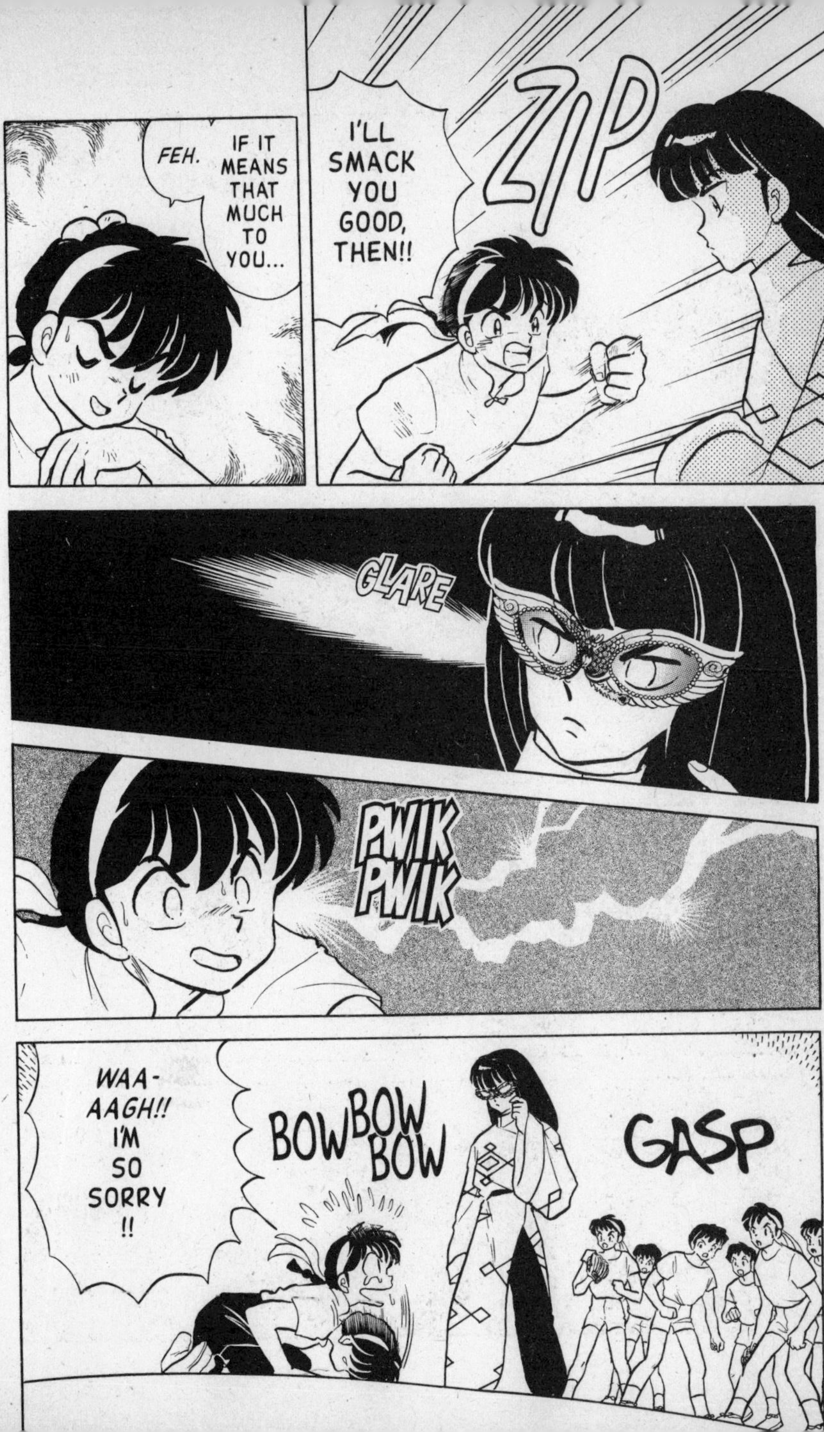
FEH.
IF IT MEANS THAT MUCH TO YOU...
I'LL SMACK YOU GOOD, THEN!!
ZIP
GLARE
PWIK PWIK
WAA-AAGH!! I'M SO SORRY !!
BOW BOW BOW
GASP

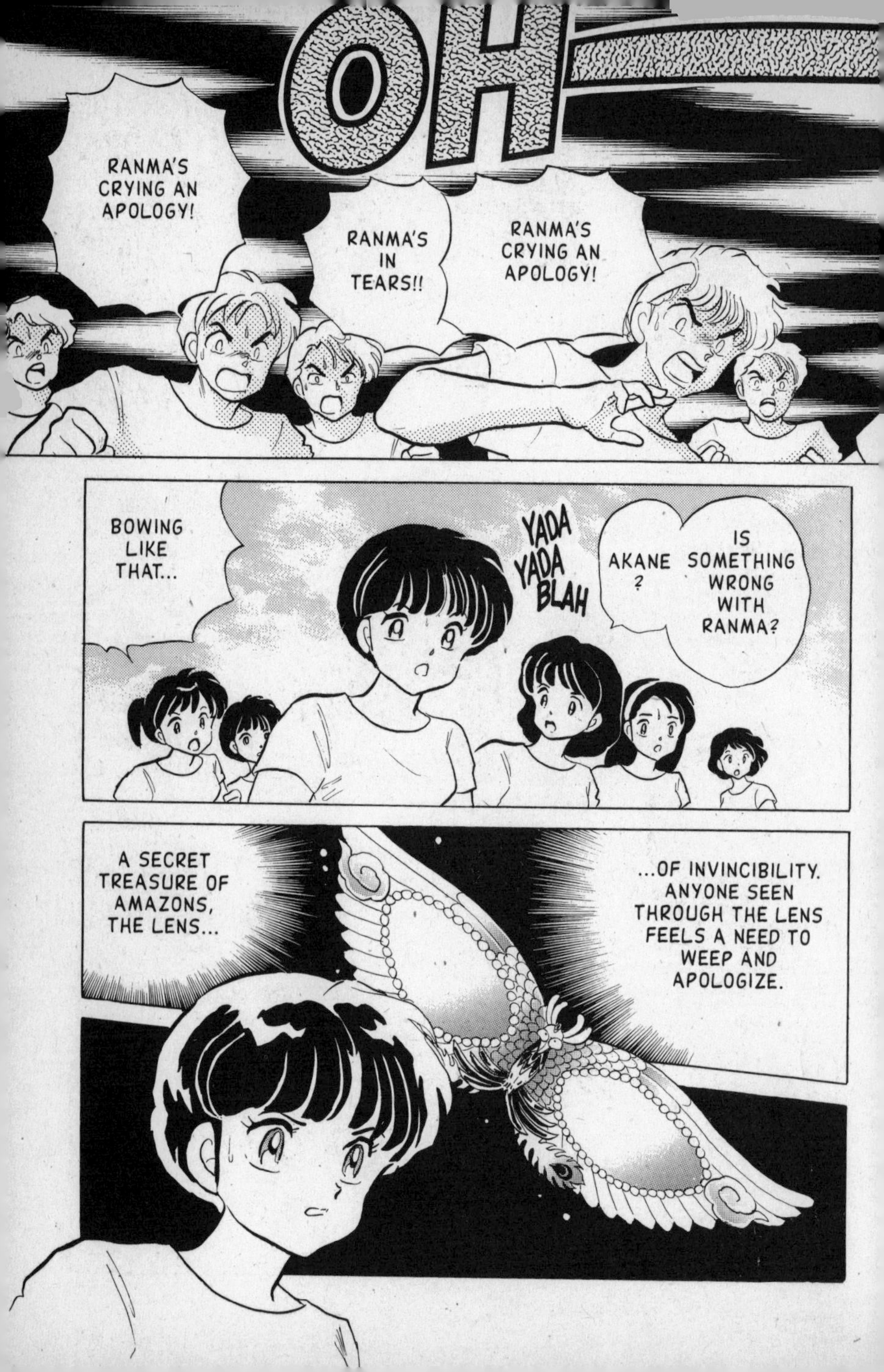
OH
RANMA'S CRYING AN APOLOGY!
RANMA'S IN TEARS!!
RANMA'S CRYING AN APOLOGY!
BOWING LIKE THAT...
YADA YADA BLAH
AKANE ?
IS SOMETHING WRONG WITH RANMA?
A SECRET TREASURE OF AMAZONS, THE LENS...
...OF INVINCIBILITY. ANYONE SEEN THROUGH THE LENS FEELS A NEED TO WEEP AND APOLOGIZE.

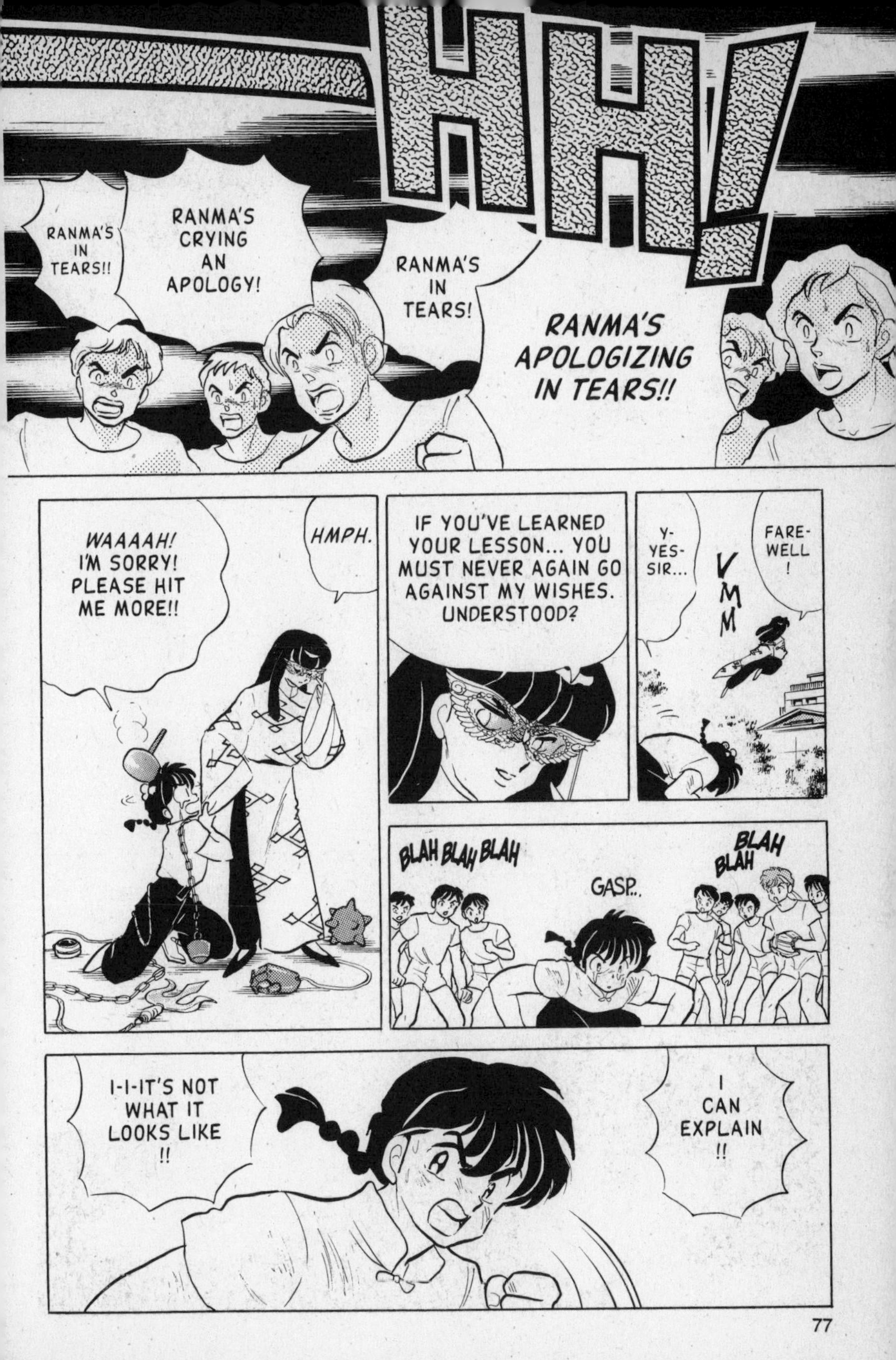
HH!
RANMA'S IN TEARS!!
RANMA'S CRYING AN APOLOGY!
RANMA'S IN TEARS!
RANMA'S APOLOGIZING IN TEARS!!
WAAAAH! I'M SORRY! PLEASE HIT ME MORE!!
HMPH.
IF YOU'VE LEARNED YOUR LESSON... YOU MUST NEVER AGAIN GO AGAINST MY WISHES. UNDERSTOOD?
Y-YES-SIR...
VMM
FARE-WELL!
BLAH BLAH BLAH
GASP...
BLAH BLAH
I-I-IT'S NOT WHAT IT LOOKS LIKE !!
I CAN EXPLAIN !!

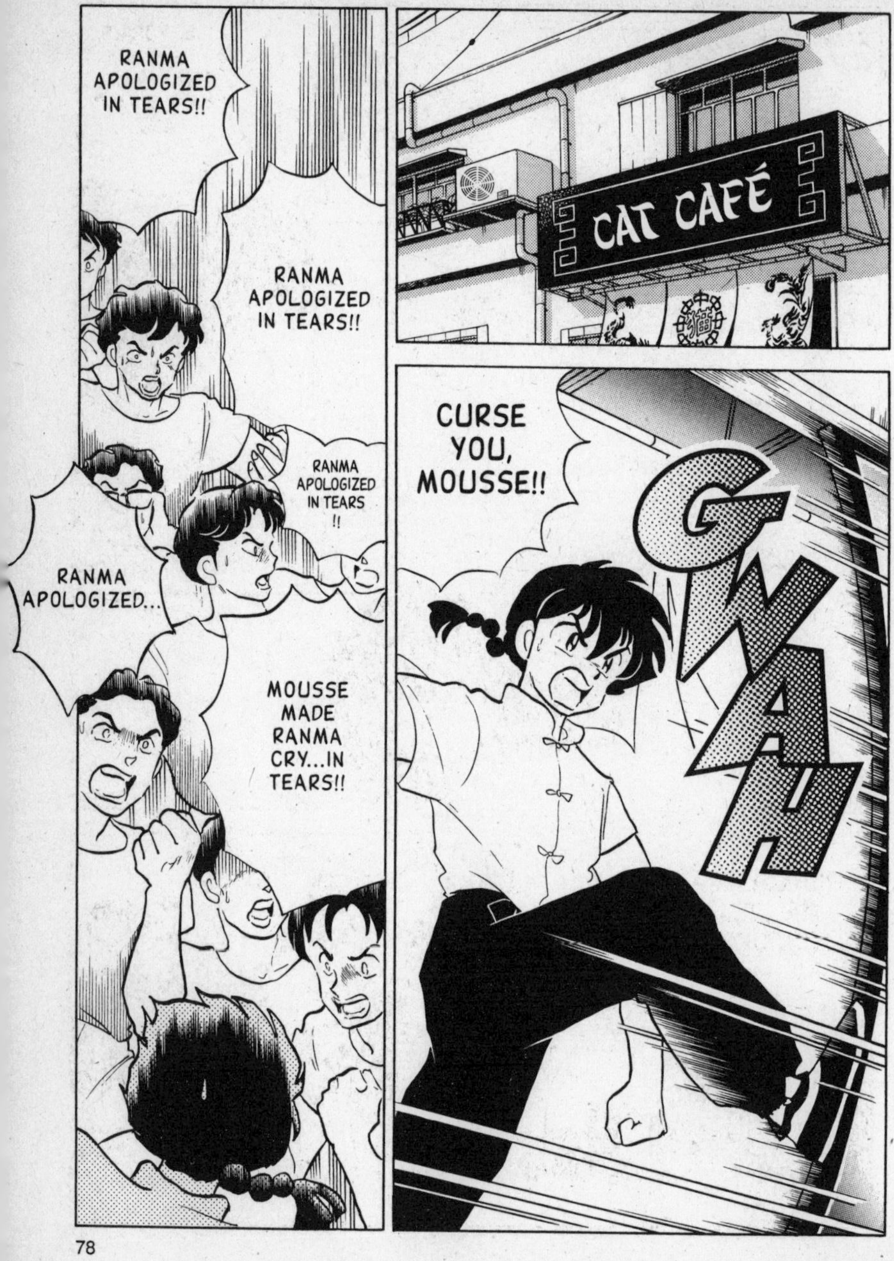
RANMA APOLOGIZED IN TEARS!!
RANMA APOLOGIZED IN TEARS!!
RANMA APOLOGIZED IN TEARS !!
RANMA APOLOGIZED...
MOUSSE MADE RANMA CRY...IN TEARS!!
CAT CAFÉ
CURSE YOU, MOUSSE!!
GWAAH

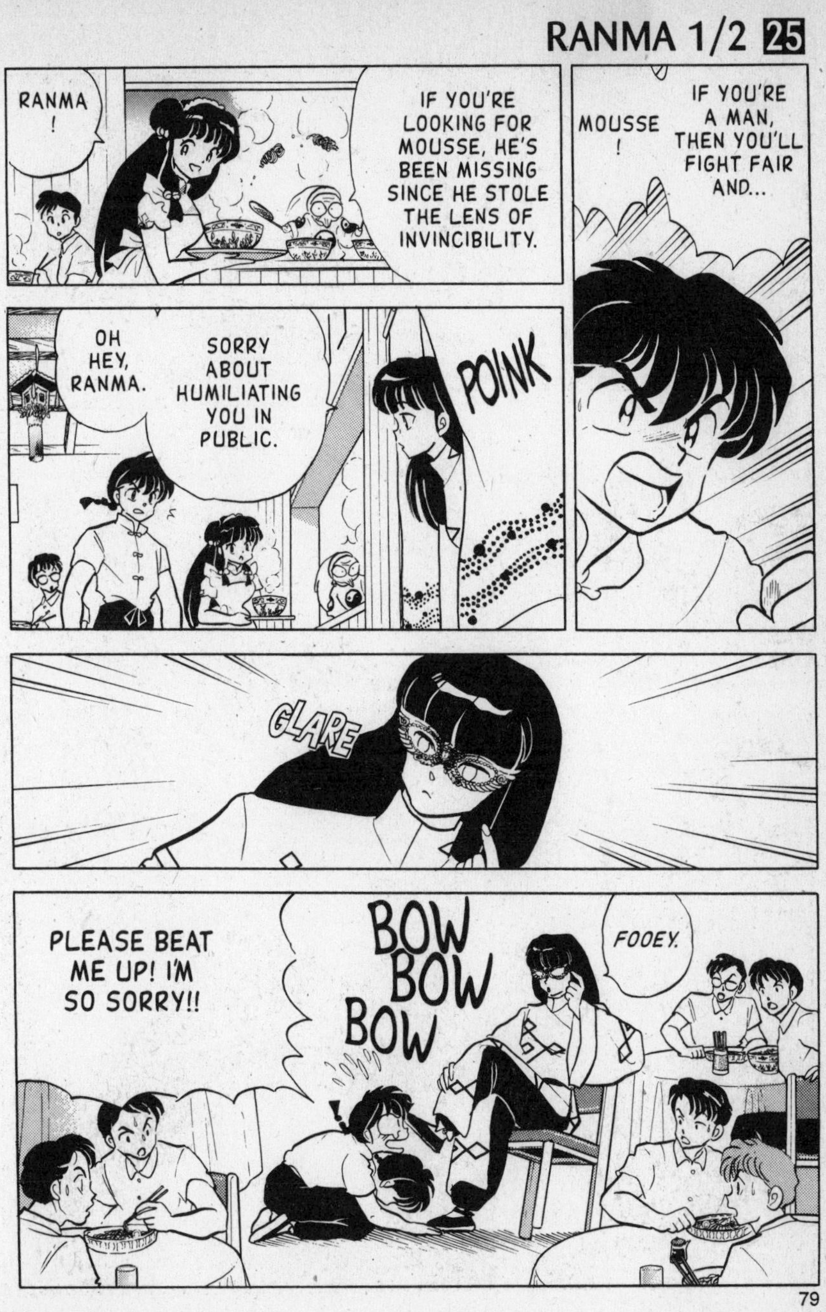
RANMA !
IF YOU'RE LOOKING FOR MOUSSE, HE'S BEEN MISSING SINCE HE STOLE THE LENS OF INVINCIBILITY.
OH HEY, RANMA.
SORRY ABOUT HUMILIATING YOU IN PUBLIC.
POINK
MOUSSE !
IF YOU'RE A MAN, THEN YOU'LL FIGHT FAIR AND...
GLARE
PLEASE BEAT ME UP! I'M SO SORRY!!
BOW BOW BOW
FOOEY.

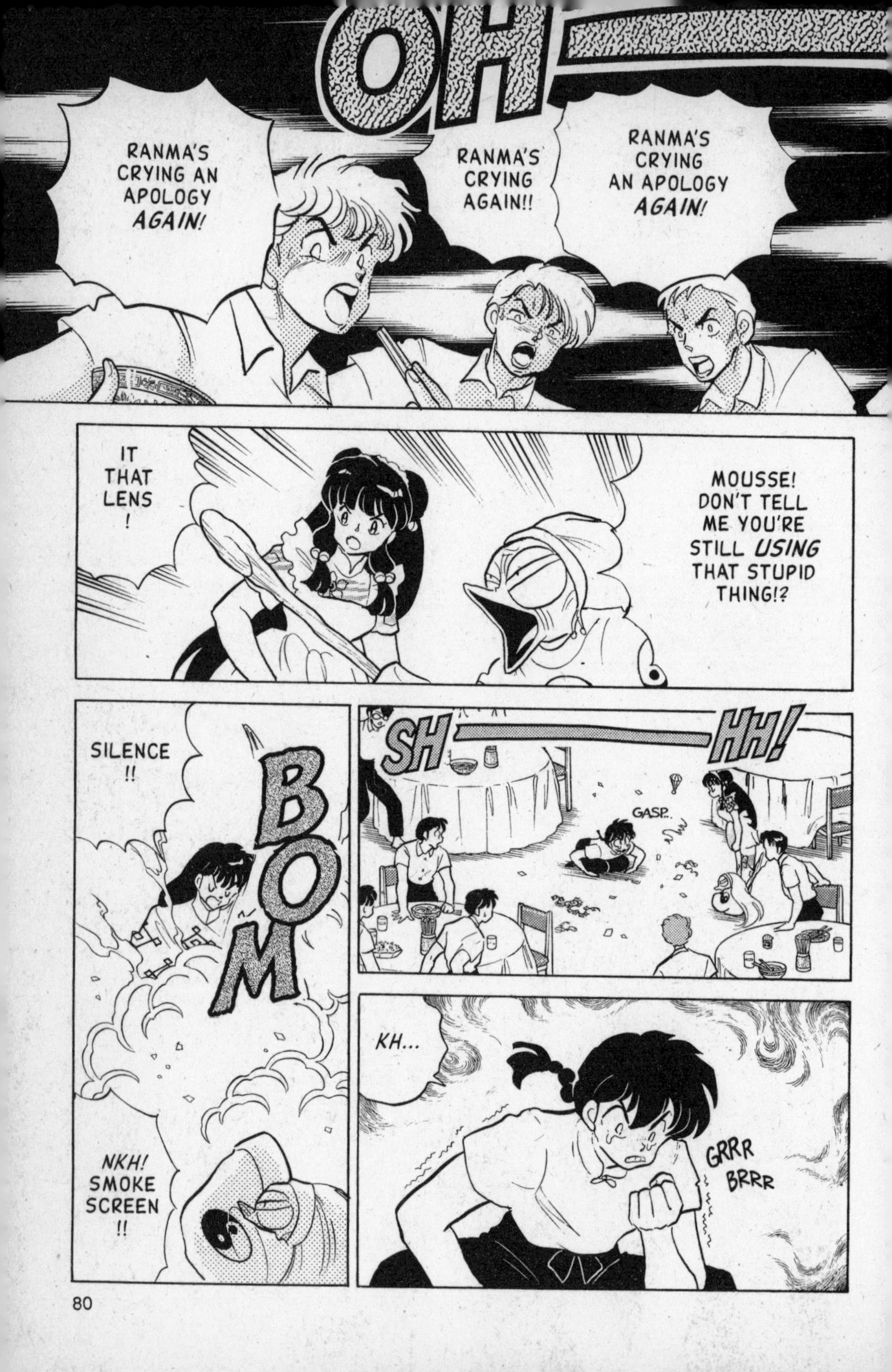
OH—
RANMA'S CRYING AN APOLOGY AGAIN!
RANMA'S CRYING AGAIN!!
RANMA'S CRYING AN APOLOGY AGAIN!
IT THAT LENS!
MOUSSE! DON'T TELL ME YOU'RE STILL USING THAT STUPID THING!?
SILENCE!!
BOM
NKH! SMOKE SCREEN!!
SH—HH!
GASP..
KH...
GRRR BRRR

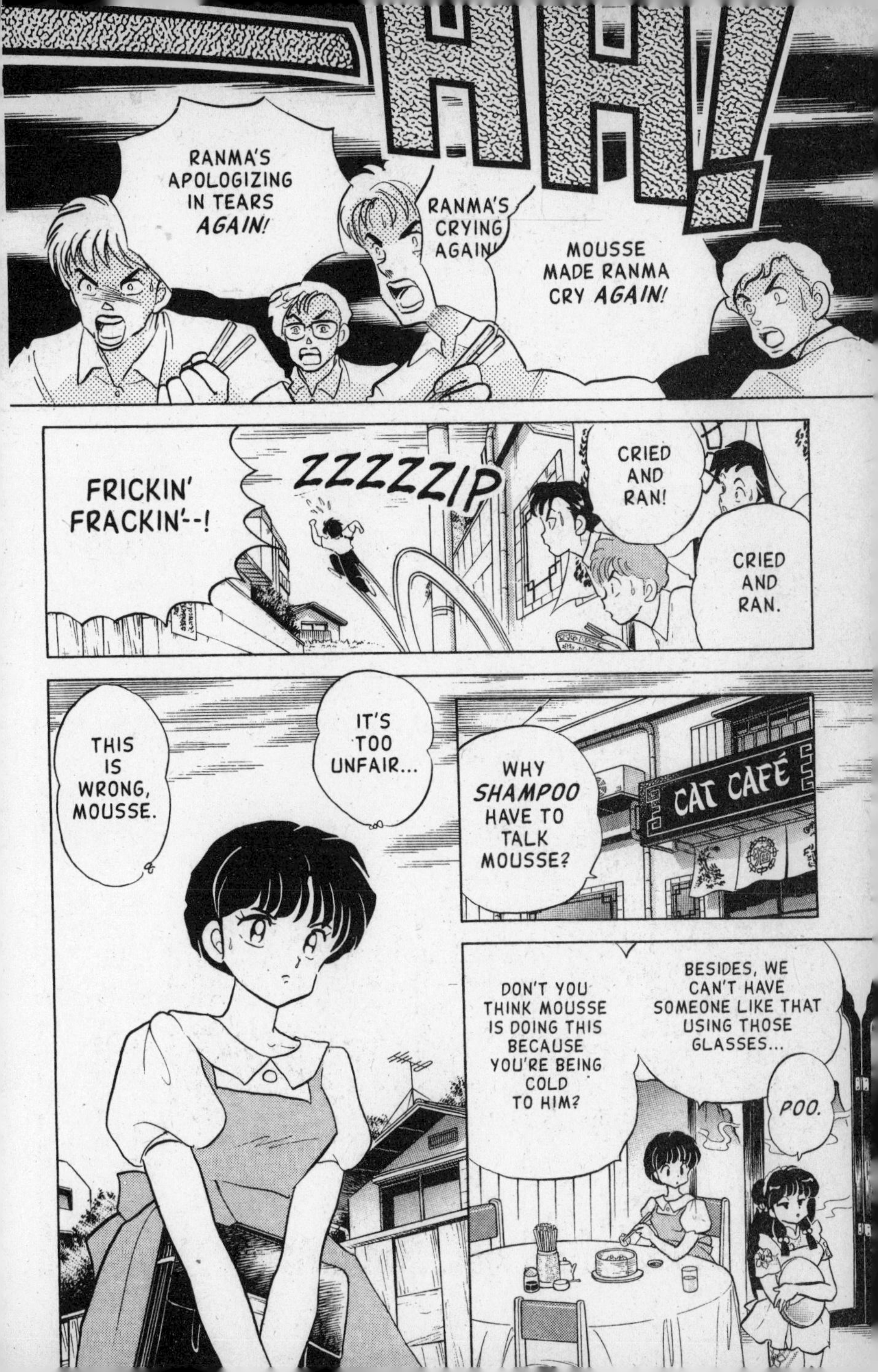

HH!
RANMA'S APOLOGIZING IN TEARS AGAIN!
RANMA'S CRYING AGAIN!
MOUSSE MADE RANMA CRY AGAIN!
FRICKIN' FRACKIN'--!
ZZZZZZIP
CRIED AND RAN!
CRIED AND RAN.
THIS IS WRONG, MOUSSE.
IT'S TOO UNFAIR...
WHY SHAMPOO HAVE TO TALK MOUSSE?
CAT CAFÉ
DON'T YOU THINK MOUSSE IS DOING THIS BECAUSE YOU'RE BEING COLD TO HIM?
BESIDES, WE CAN'T HAVE SOMEONE LIKE THAT USING THOSE GLASSES...
POO.

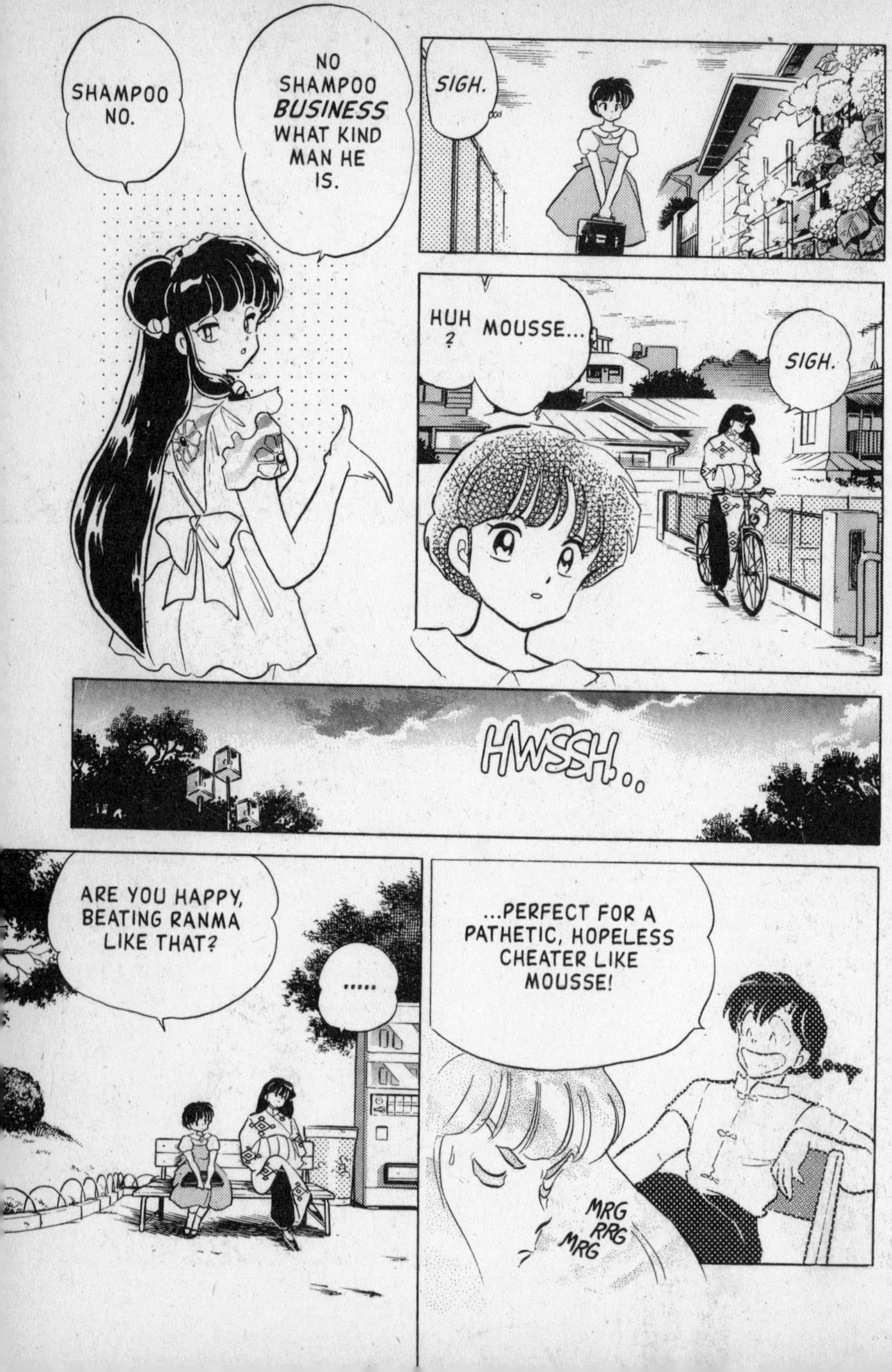
SHAMPOO NO.
NO SHAMPOO BUSINESS WHAT KIND MAN HE IS.
SIGH.
HUH ? MOUSSE...
SIGH.
HWSSH..
ARE YOU HAPPY, BEATING RANMA LIKE THAT?
.....
...PERFECT FOR A PATHETIC, HOPELESS CHEATER LIKE MOUSSE!
MRG RRG MRG

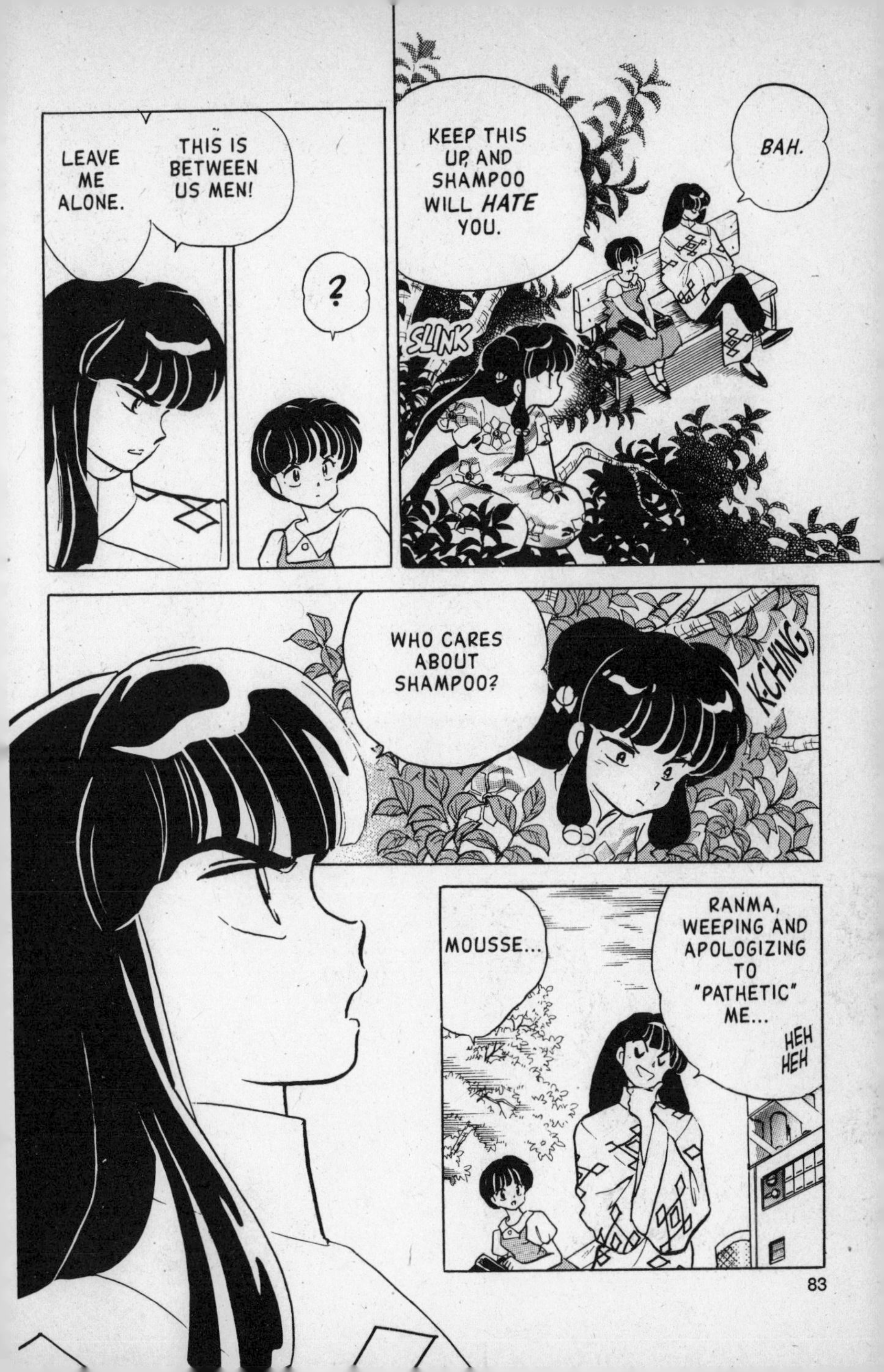
LEAVE ME ALONE.
THIS IS BETWEEN US MEN!
?
KEEP THIS UP, AND SHAMPOO WILL HATE YOU.
BAH.
SLINK
WHO CARES ABOUT SHAMPOO?
K-CHING
MOUSSE...
RANMA, WEEPING AND APOLOGIZING TO "PATHETIC" ME...
HEH HEH

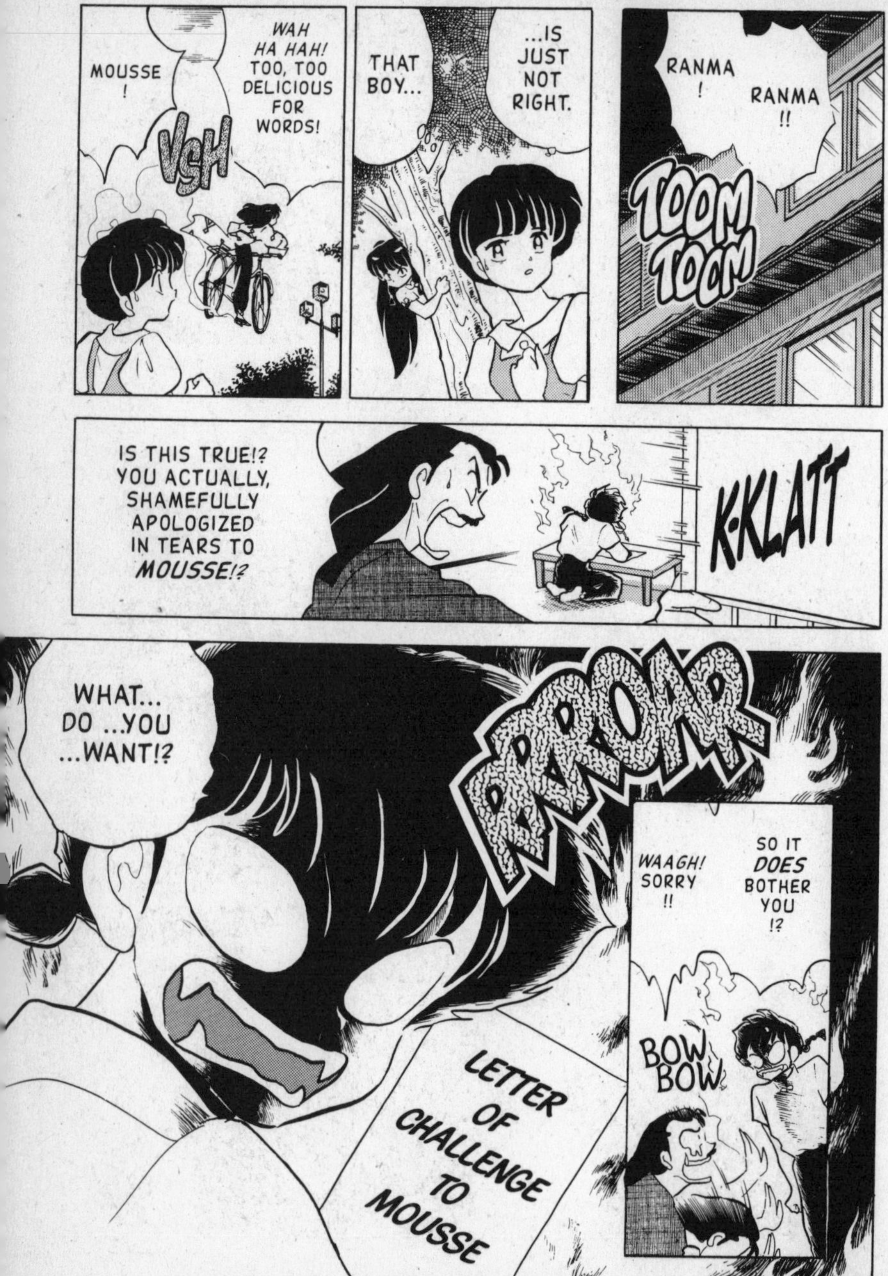
MOUSSE !
WAH HA HAH! TOO, TOO DELICIOUS FOR WORDS!
VSH
THAT BOY...
...IS JUST NOT RIGHT.
RANMA !
RANMA !!
TOOM TOOM
IS THIS TRUE!? YOU ACTUALLY, SHAMEFULLY APOLOGIZED IN TEARS TO MOUSSE!?
K-KLATT
WHAT... DO ...YOU ...WANT!?
RRROAR
LETTER OF CHALLENGE TO MOUSSE
WAAGH! SORRY !!
SO IT DOES BOTHER YOU !?
BOW BOW

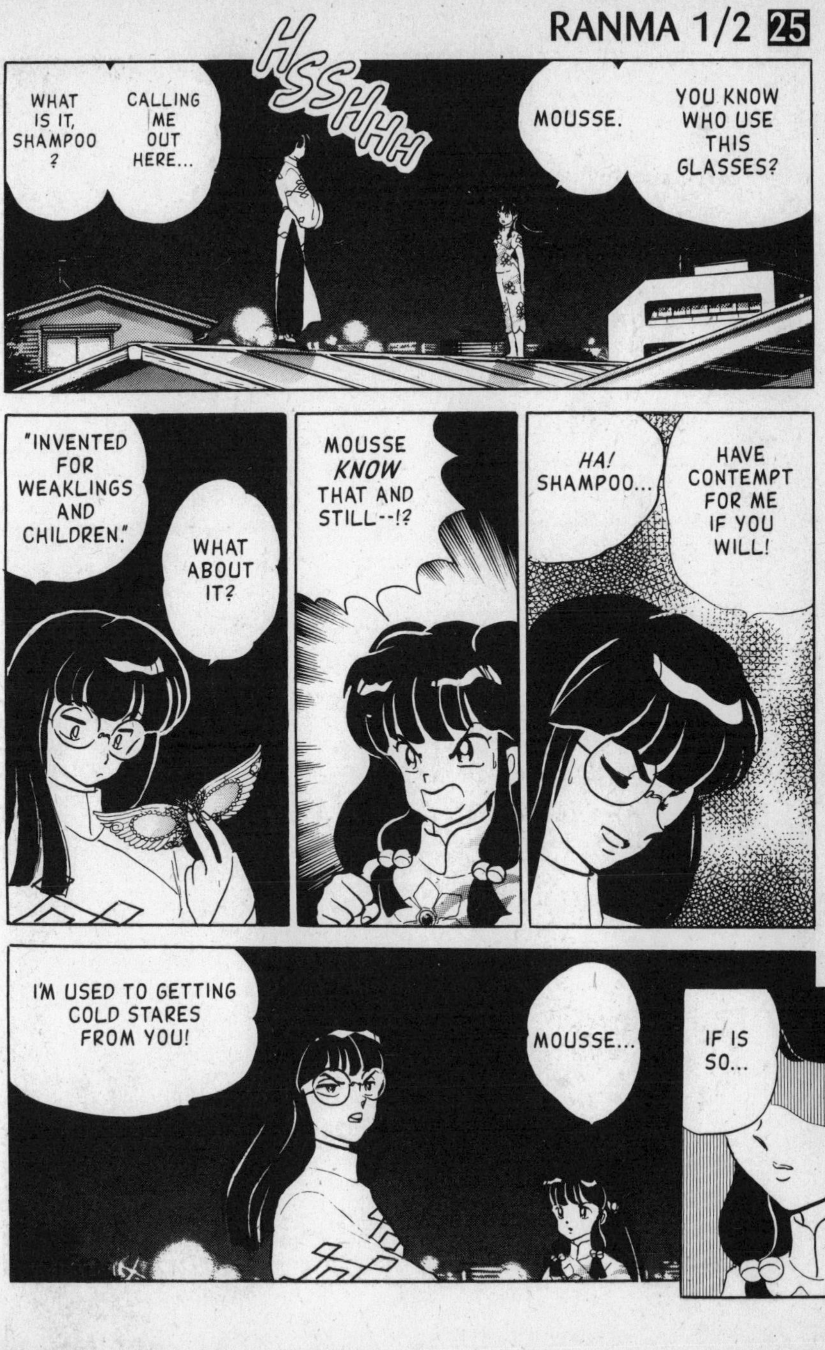
HSSHHH
WHAT IS IT, SHAMPOO ?
CALLING ME OUT HERE...
MOUSSE.
YOU KNOW WHO USE THIS GLASSES?
"INVENTED FOR WEAKLINGS AND CHILDREN."
WHAT ABOUT IT?
MOUSSE *KNOW* THAT AND STILL--!?
HA! SHAMPOO...
HAVE CONTEMPT FOR ME IF YOU WILL!
I'M USED TO GETTING COLD STARES FROM YOU!
MOUSSE...
IF IS SO...

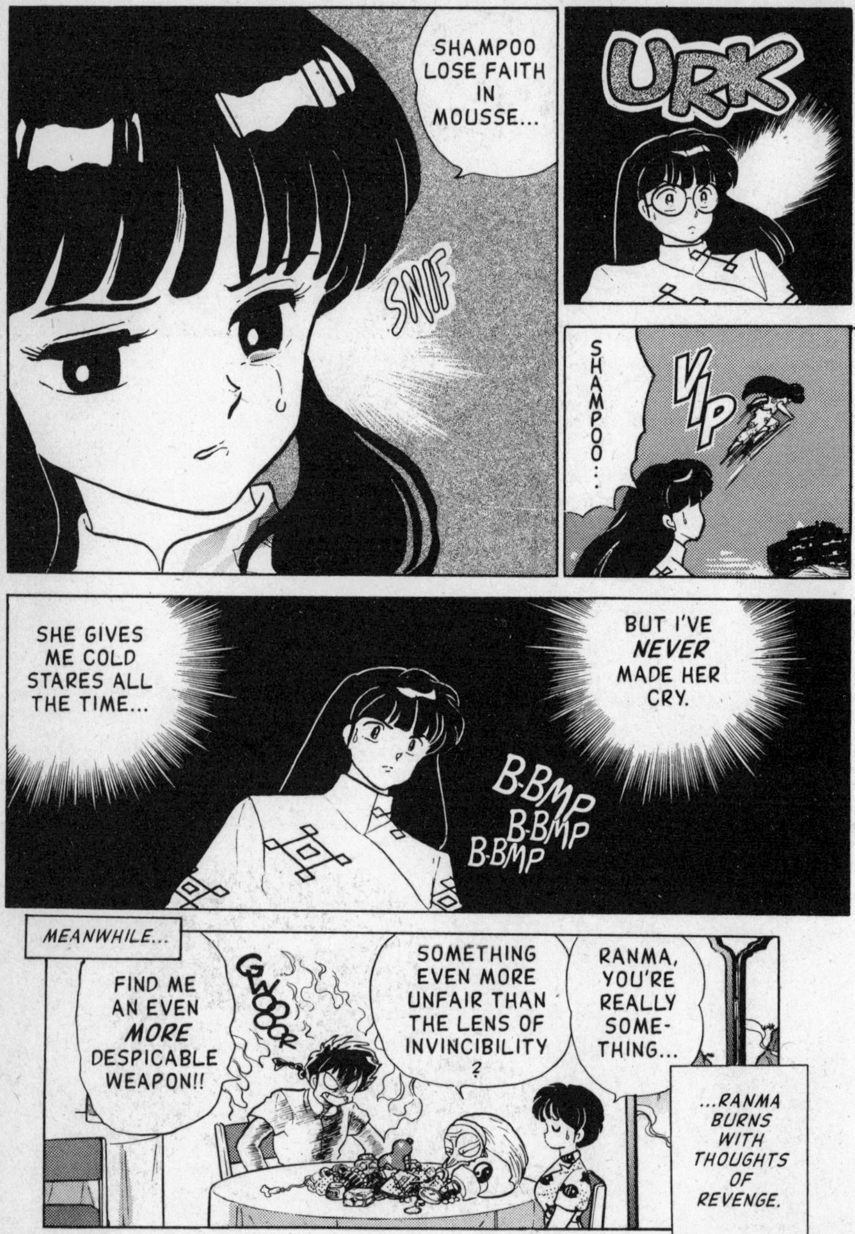
SHAMPOO LOSE FAITH IN MOUSSE...
SNIF
URK
SHAMPOO...
VIP
SHE GIVES ME COLD STARES ALL THE TIME...
BUT I'VE *NEVER* MADE HER CRY.
B-BMP
B-BMP
B-BMP
MEANWHILE...
FIND ME AN EVEN *MORE* DESPICABLE WEAPON!!
GWOOOOR
SOMETHING EVEN MORE UNFAIR THAN THE LENS OF INVINCIBILITY?
RANMA, YOU'RE REALLY SOME-THING...
...RANMA BURNS WITH THOUGHTS OF REVENGE.

Part 6

THE LOWLIEST JERK

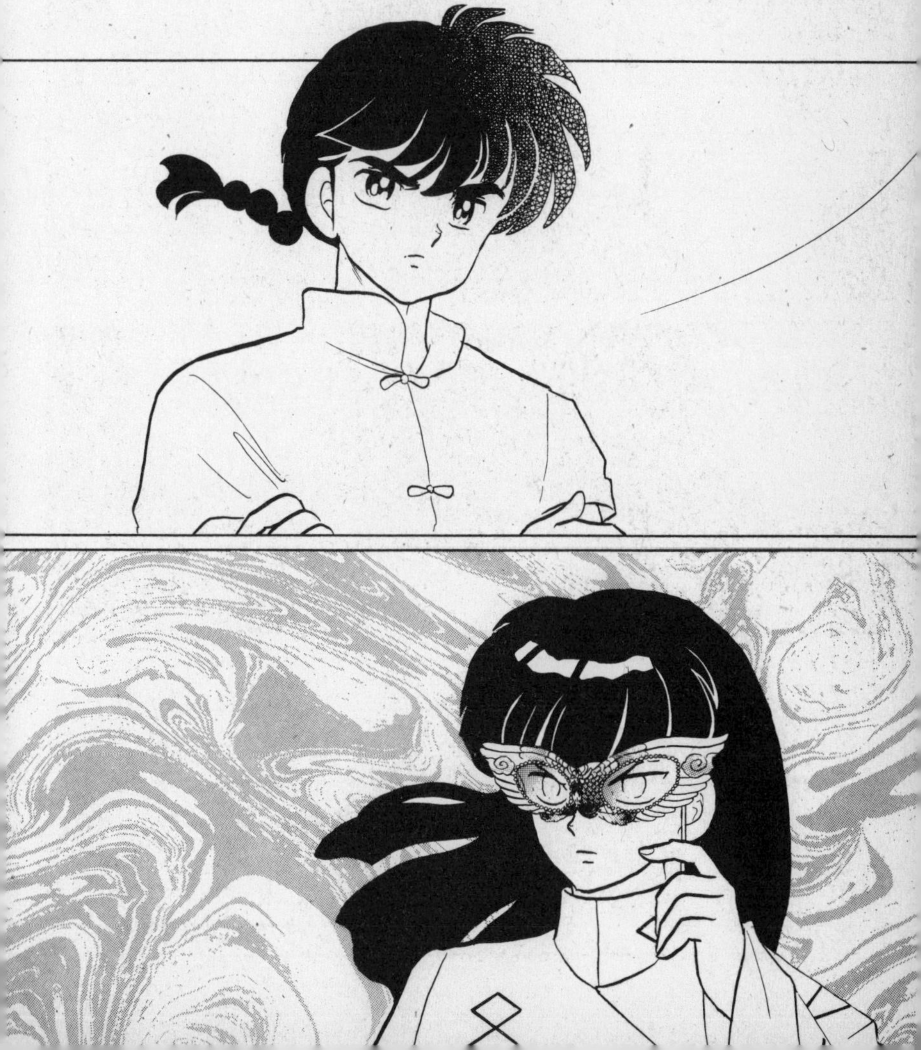

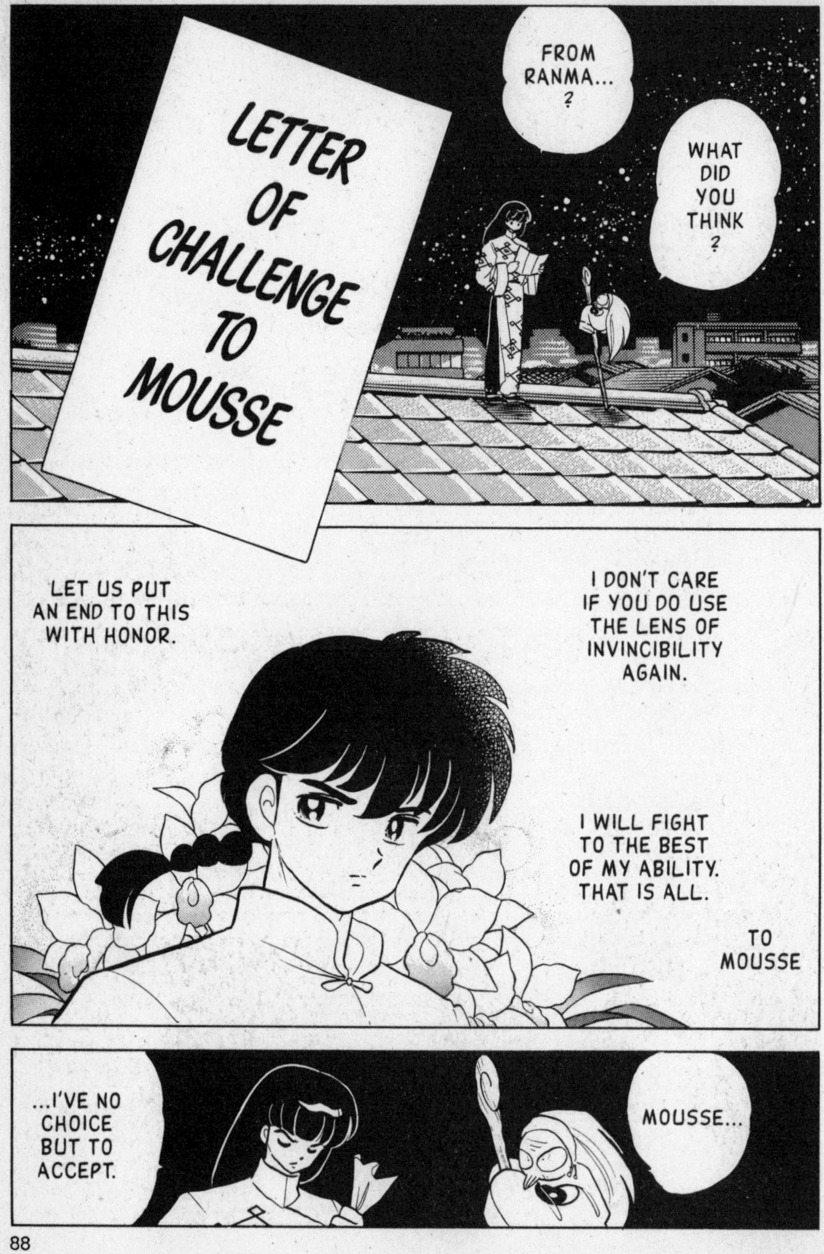
LETTER OF CHALLENGE TO MOUSSE
FROM RANMA...?
WHAT DID YOU THINK?
LET US PUT AN END TO THIS WITH HONOR.
I DON'T CARE IF YOU DO USE THE LENS OF INVINCIBILITY AGAIN.
I WILL FIGHT TO THE BEST OF MY ABILITY. THAT IS ALL.
TO MOUSSE
...I'VE NO CHOICE BUT TO ACCEPT.
MOUSSE...

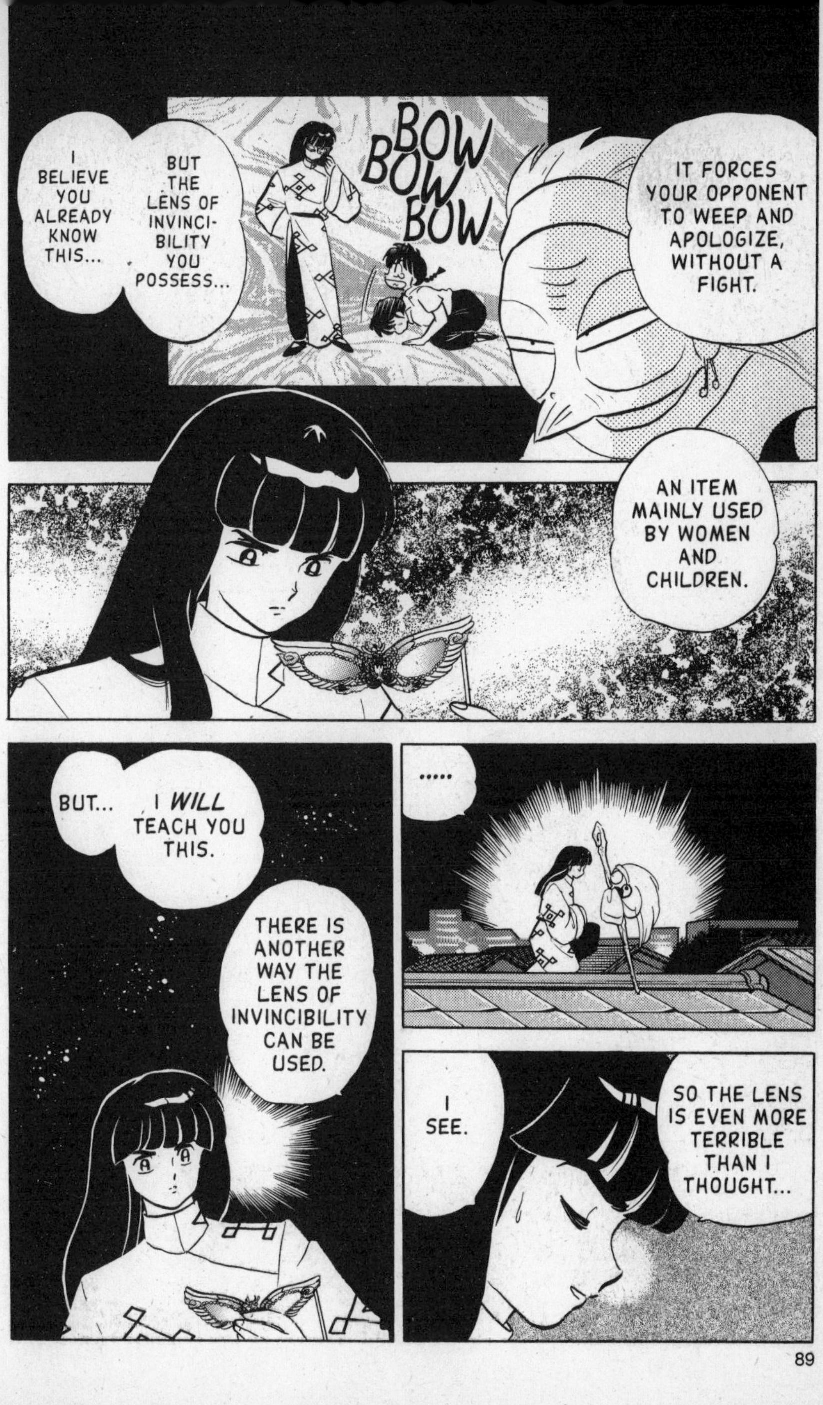
I BELIEVE YOU ALREADY KNOW THIS...
BUT THE LENS OF INVINCI-BILITY YOU POSSESS...
BOW BOW BOW
IT FORCES YOUR OPPONENT TO WEEP AND APOLOGIZE, WITHOUT A FIGHT.
AN ITEM MAINLY USED BY WOMEN AND CHILDREN.
BUT...
I *WILL* TEACH YOU THIS.
THERE IS ANOTHER WAY THE LENS OF INVINCIBILITY CAN BE USED.
.....
I SEE.
SO THE LENS IS EVEN MORE TERRIBLE THAN I THOUGHT...

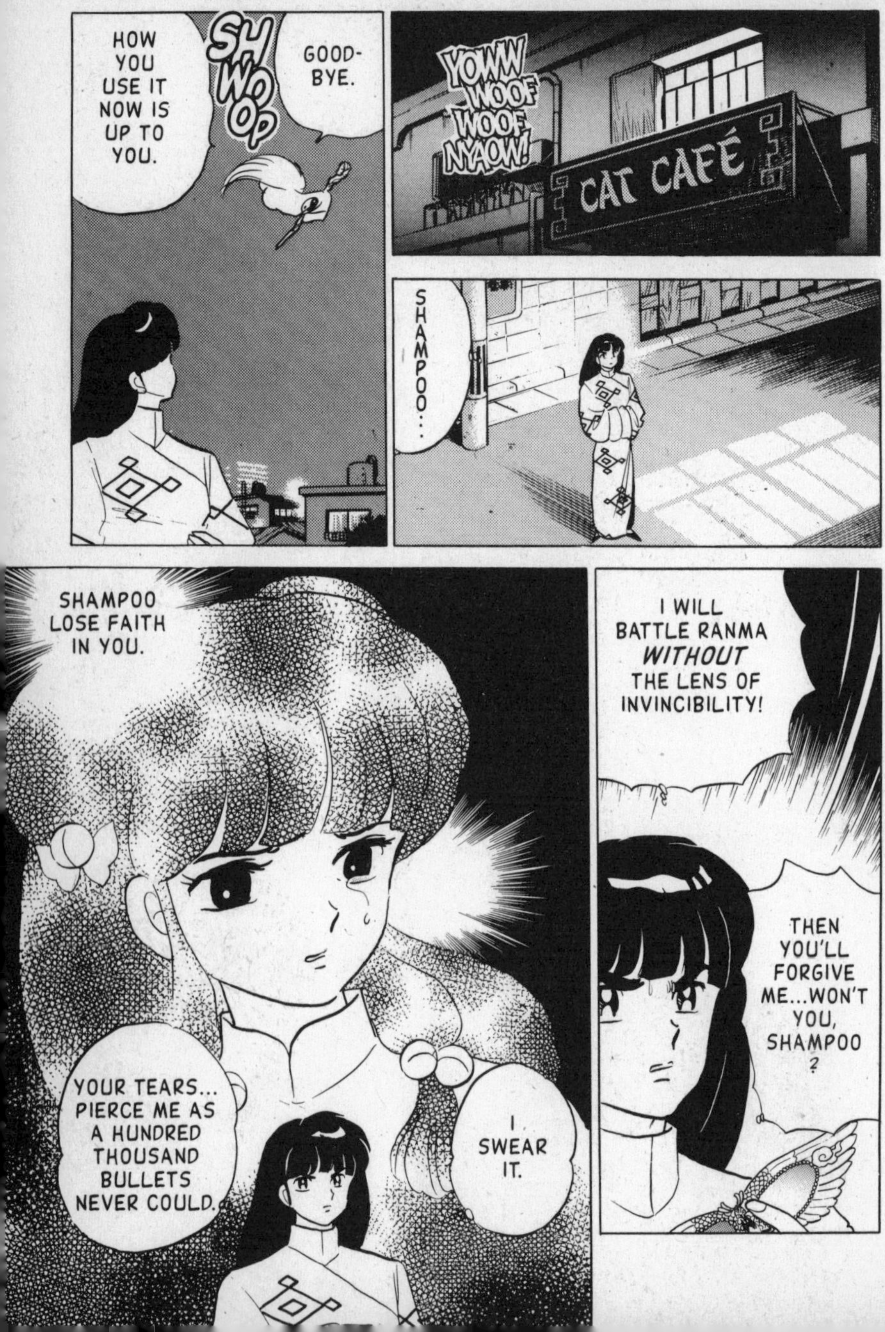
HOW YOU USE IT NOW IS UP TO YOU.
SHWOOP
GOOD-BYE.
YOWW WOOF WOOF NYAOW!
CAT CAFÉ
SHAMPOO...
SHAMPOO LOSE FAITH IN YOU.
YOUR TEARS... PIERCE ME AS A HUNDRED THOUSAND BULLETS NEVER COULD.
I SWEAR IT.
I WILL BATTLE RANMA *WITHOUT* THE LENS OF INVINCIBILITY!
THEN YOU'LL FORGIVE ME...WON'T YOU, SHAMPOO?

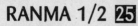

TIME CHANGE WATER IN FLOWER VASE.

KKAT

PSH

HWOOO

KWAK

HYOOOOO

BLAH BLAH

YADA

RANMA AND MOUSSE ARE GONNA FIGHT!!

YADA YADA BLAH

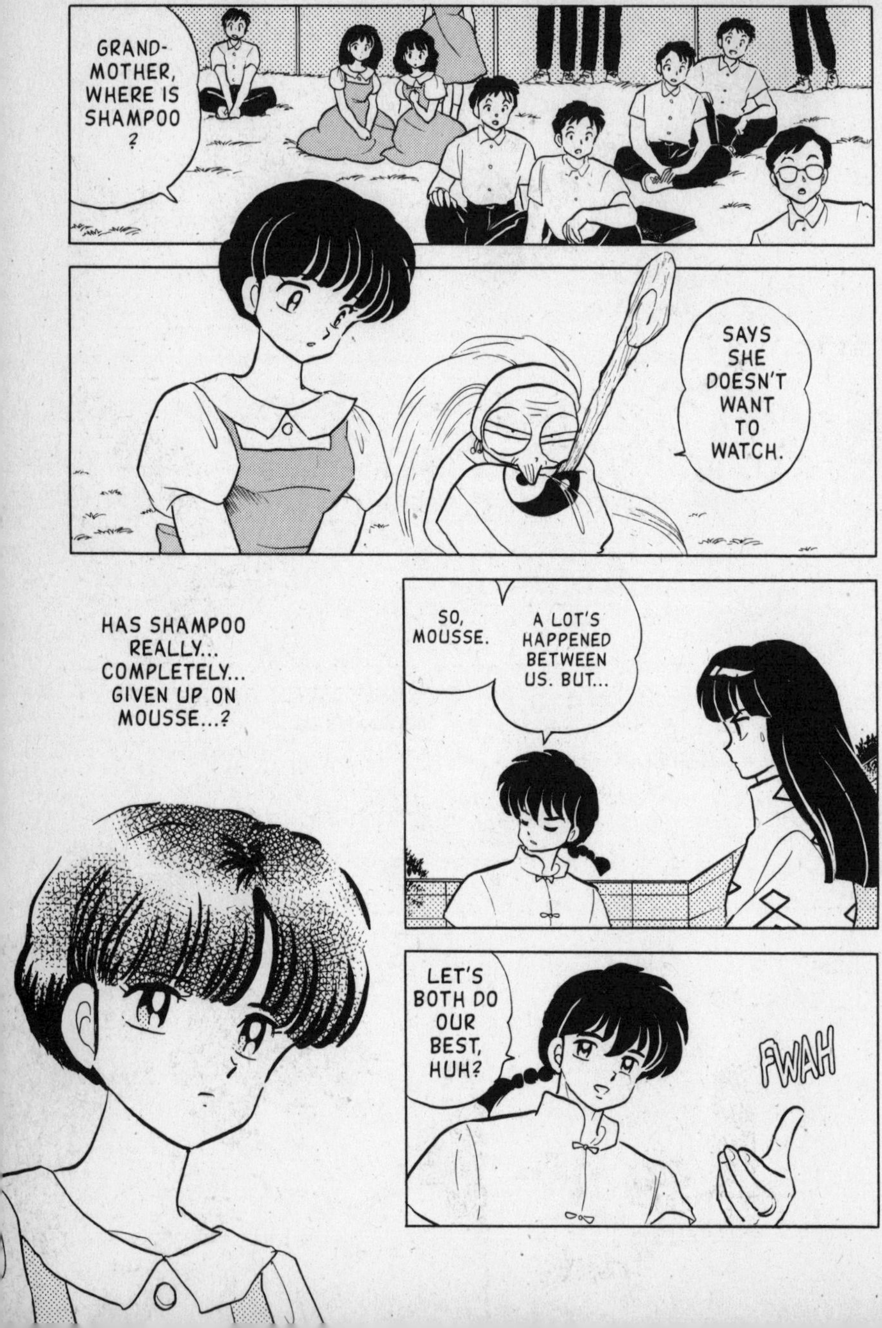
GRAND-MOTHER, WHERE IS SHAMPOO?
SAYS SHE DOESN'T WANT TO WATCH.
HAS SHAMPOO REALLY... COMPLETELY... GIVEN UP ON MOUSSE...?
SO, MOUSSE.
A LOT'S HAPPENED BETWEEN US. BUT...
LET'S BOTH DO OUR BEST, HUH?
FWAH

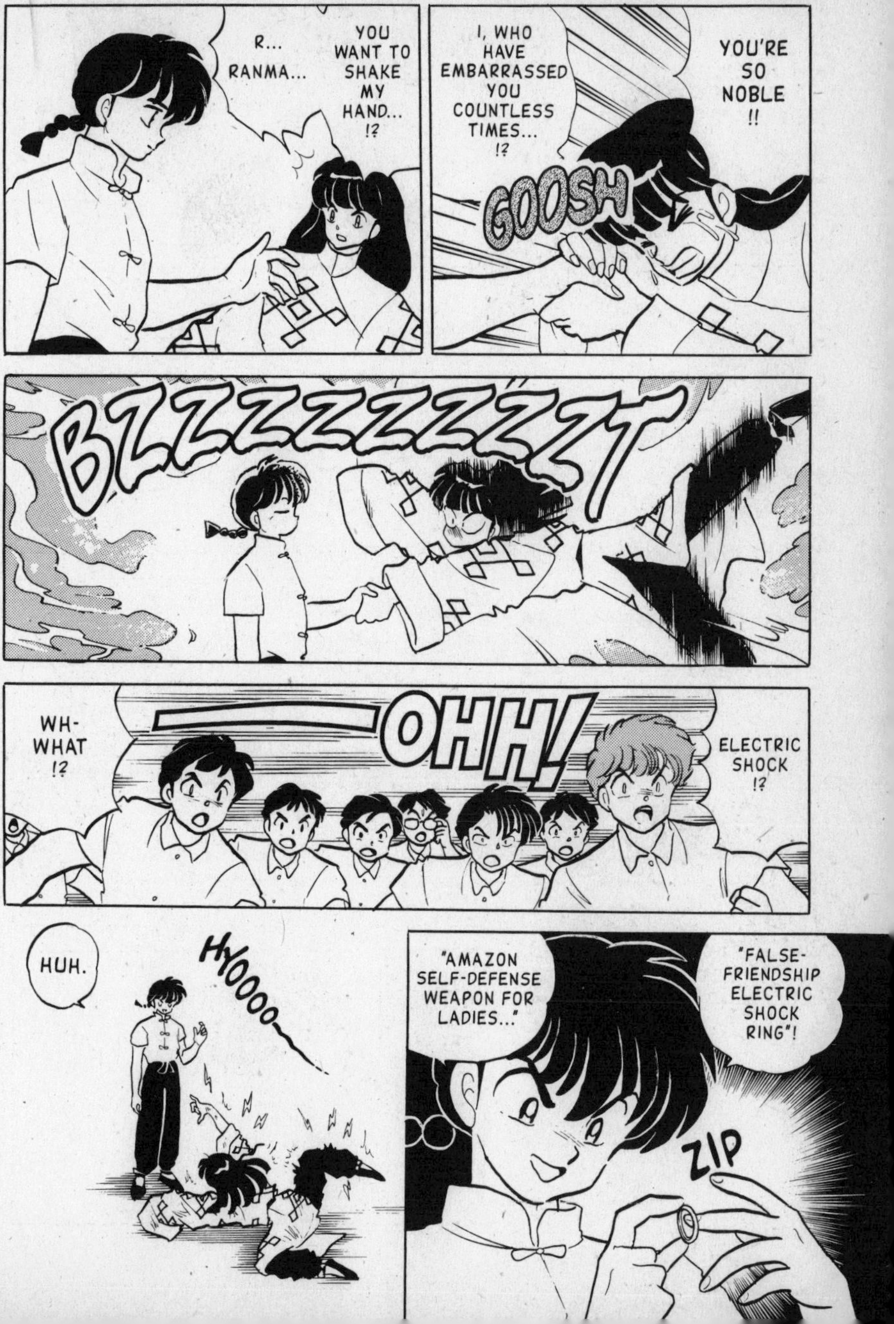
R... RANMA...
YOU WANT TO SHAKE MY HAND... !?
I, WHO HAVE EMBARRASSED YOU COUNTLESS TIMES... !?
YOU'RE SO NOBLE !!
GOOSH
BZZZZZZZZZT
WH-WHAT !?
———OHH!
ELECTRIC SHOCK !?
HUH.
HYOOOO—
"AMAZON SELF-DEFENSE WEAPON FOR LADIES..."
"FALSE-FRIENDSHIP ELECTRIC SHOCK RING"!
ZIP

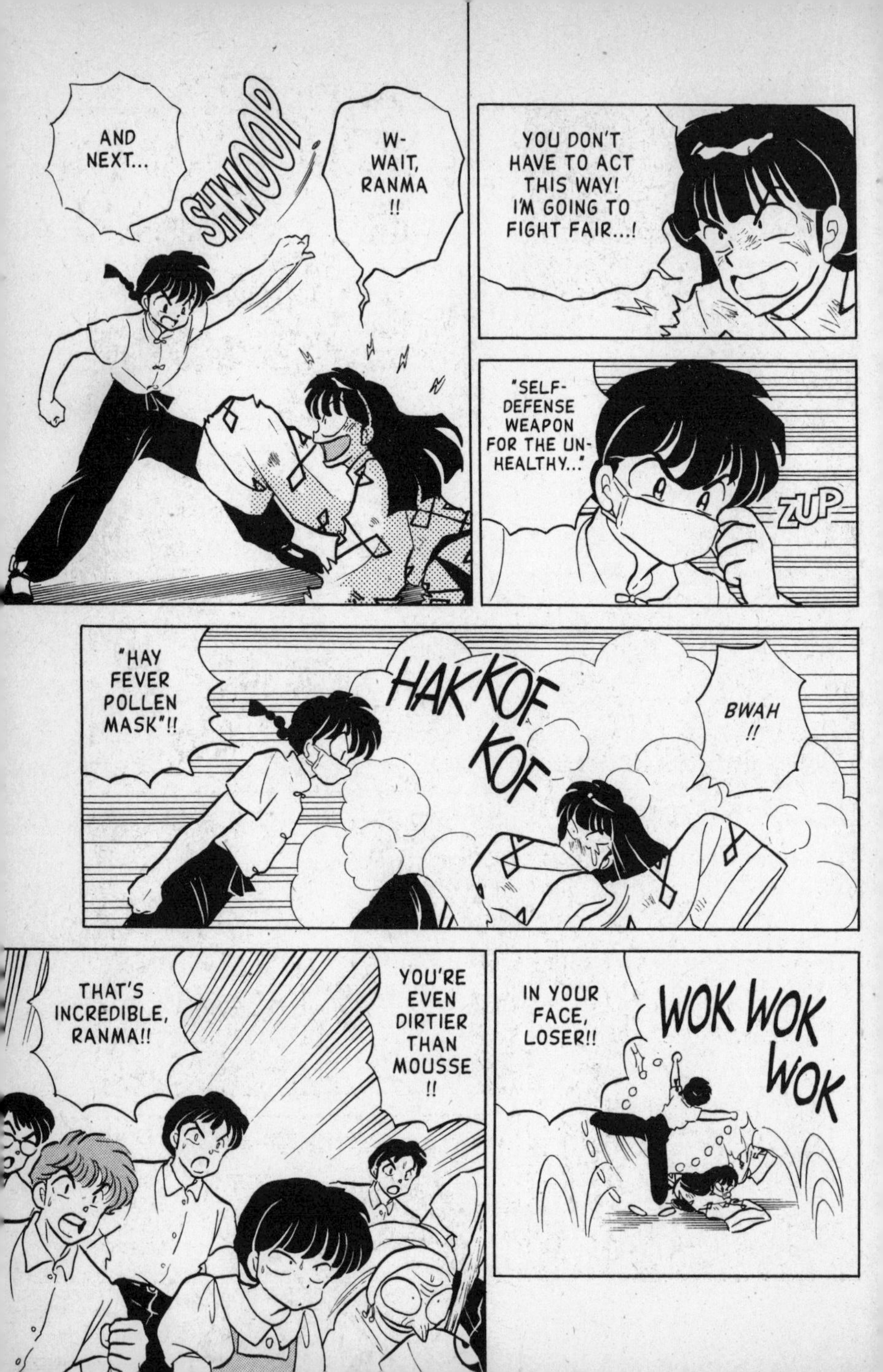
AND NEXT...
SHWOOP
W-WAIT, RANMA!!
YOU DON'T HAVE TO ACT THIS WAY! I'M GOING TO FIGHT FAIR...!
"SELF-DEFENSE WEAPON FOR THE UN-HEALTHY..."
ZUP
"HAY FEVER POLLEN MASK"!!
HAK KOF KOF
BWAH!!
THAT'S INCREDIBLE, RANMA!!
YOU'RE EVEN DIRTIER THAN MOUSSE!!
IN YOUR FACE, LOSER!!
WOK WOK WOK

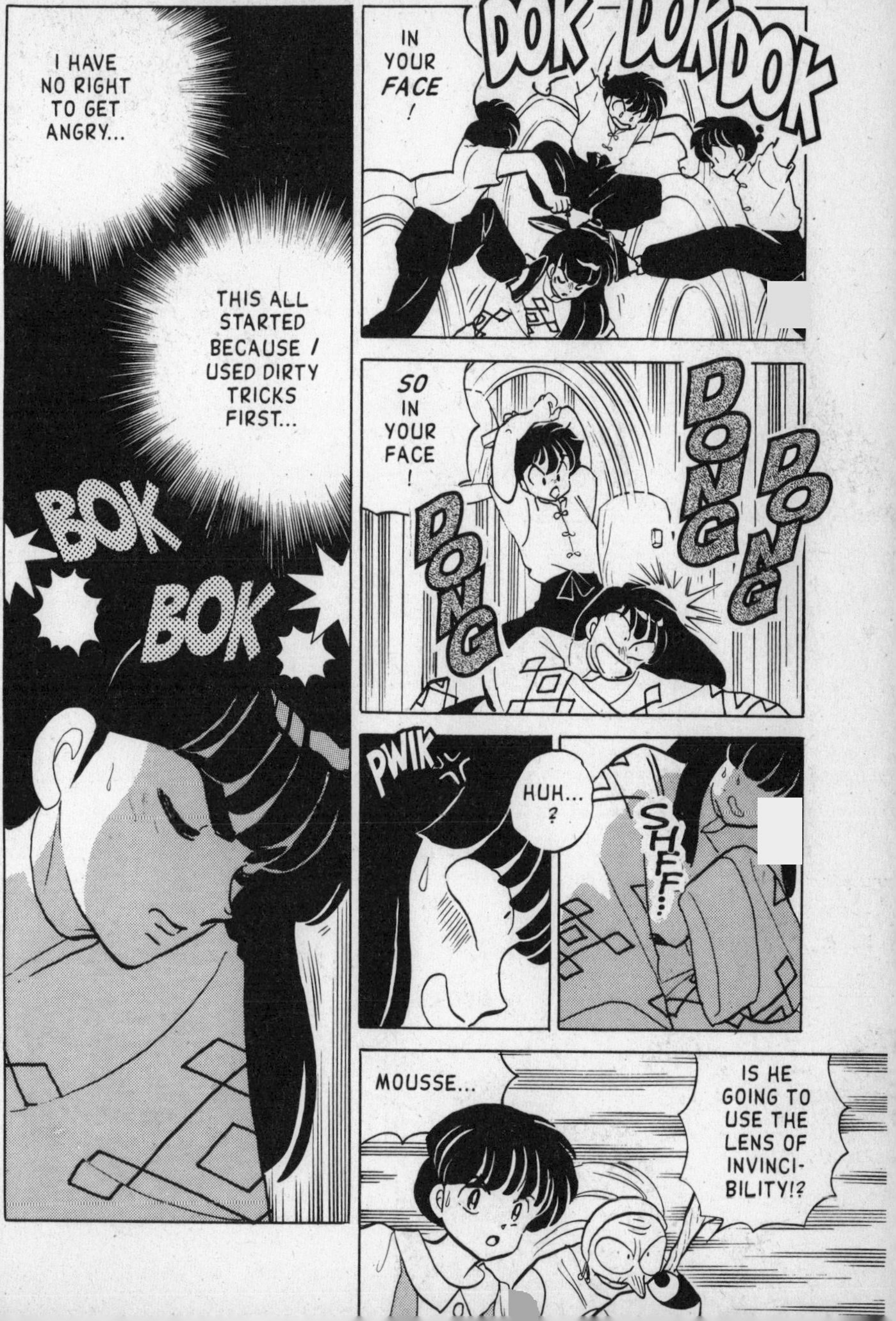
I HAVE NO RIGHT TO GET ANGRY...
THIS ALL STARTED BECAUSE I USED DIRTY TRICKS FIRST...
BOK
BOK
IN YOUR FACE!
DOK DOK DOK
SO IN YOUR FACE!
DONG
DONG
DONG
PWIK
HUH...?
SHFF...
MOUSSE...
IS HE GOING TO USE THE LENS OF INVINCI-BILITY!?

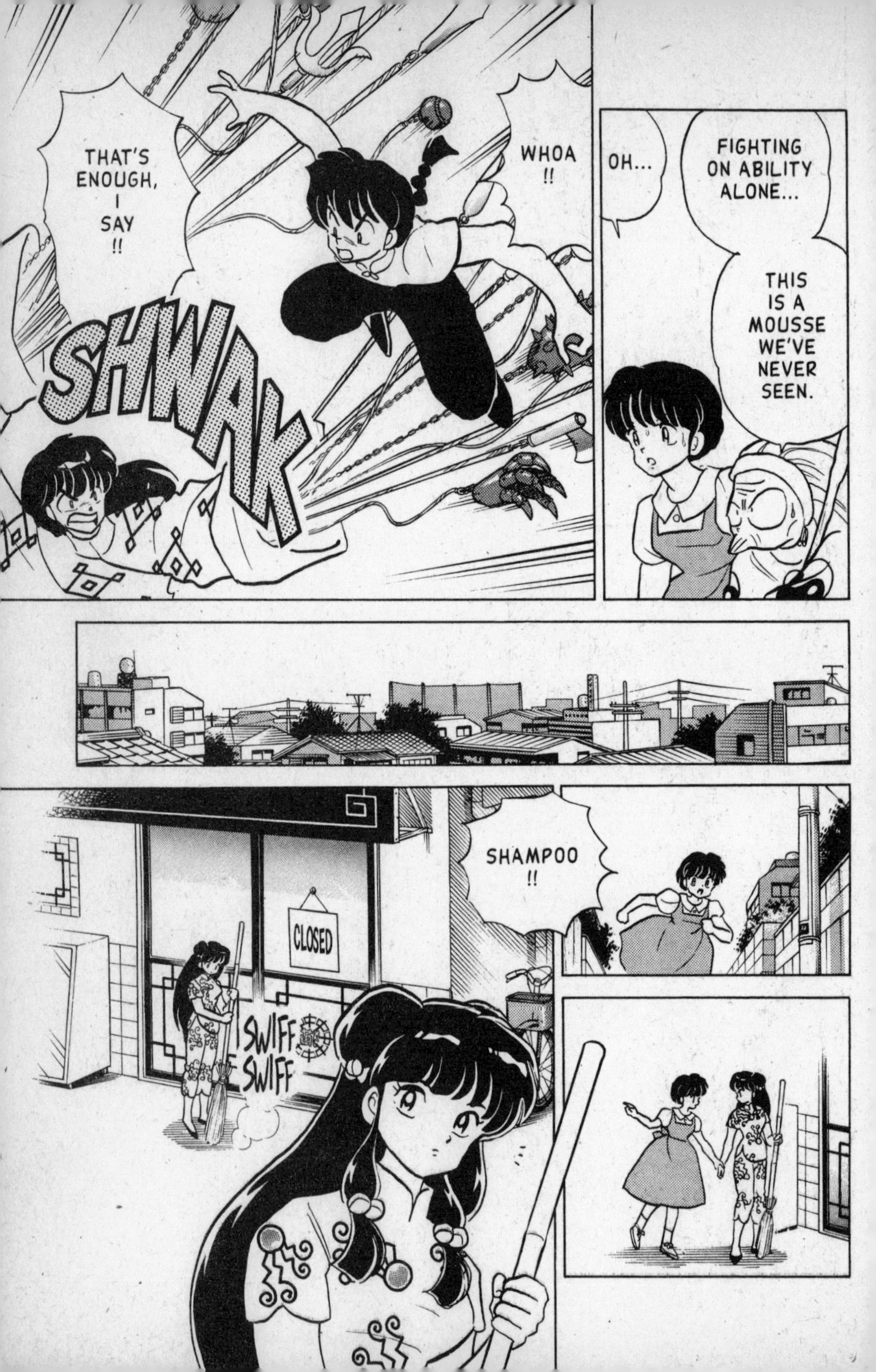
THAT'S ENOUGH, I SAY !!
WHOA !!
SHWAK
OH...
FIGHTING ON ABILITY ALONE...
THIS IS A MOUSSE WE'VE NEVER SEEN.
CLOSED
SWIFF SWIFF
SHAMPOO !!

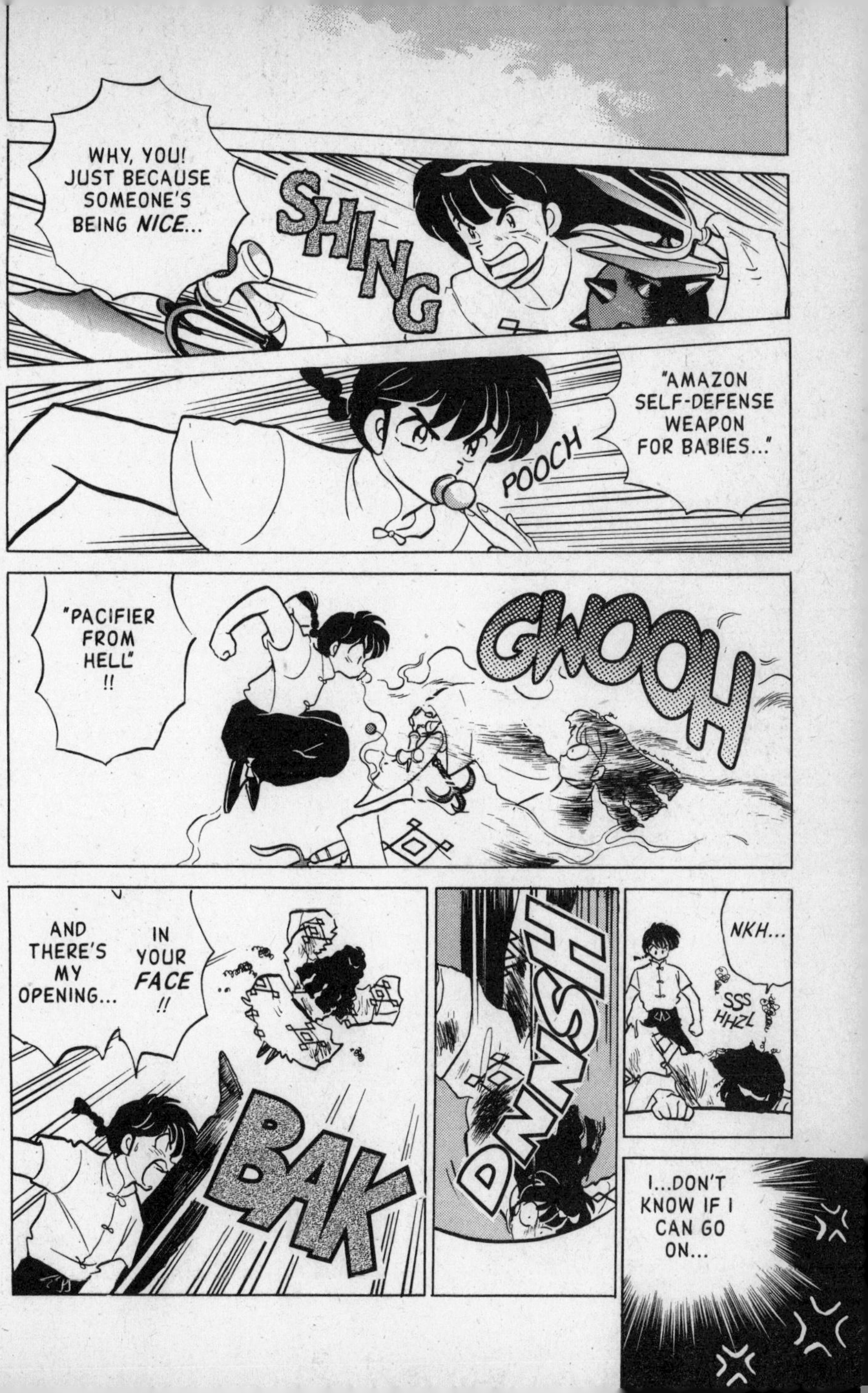
WHY, YOU! JUST BECAUSE SOMEONE'S BEING *NICE*...
SHING
"AMAZON SELF-DEFENSE WEAPON FOR BABIES..."
POOCH
"PACIFIER FROM HELL" !!
GWOOOH
AND THERE'S MY OPENING...
IN YOUR *FACE* !!
BAK
DNNSH
NKH...
SSS HHZL
I...DON'T KNOW IF I CAN GO ON...

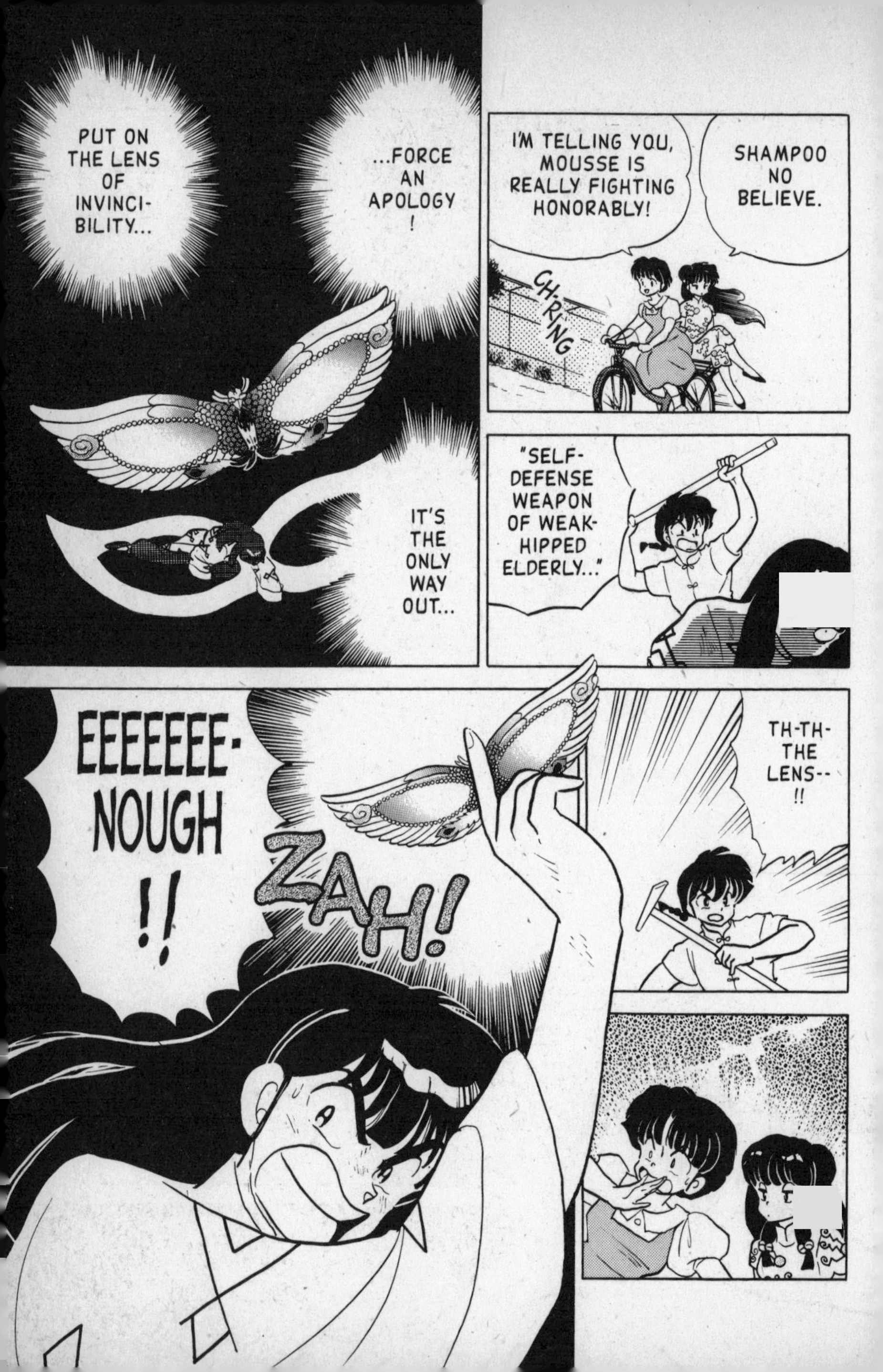
PUT ON THE LENS OF INVINCI-BILITY...
...FORCE AN APOLOGY!
IT'S THE ONLY WAY OUT...
I'M TELLING YOU, MOUSSE IS REALLY FIGHTING HONORABLY!
SHAMPOO NO BELIEVE.
CH-RING
"SELF-DEFENSE WEAPON OF WEAK-HIPPED ELDERLY..."
EEEEEEE-NOUGH !!
ZAH!
TH-TH-THE LENS--!!

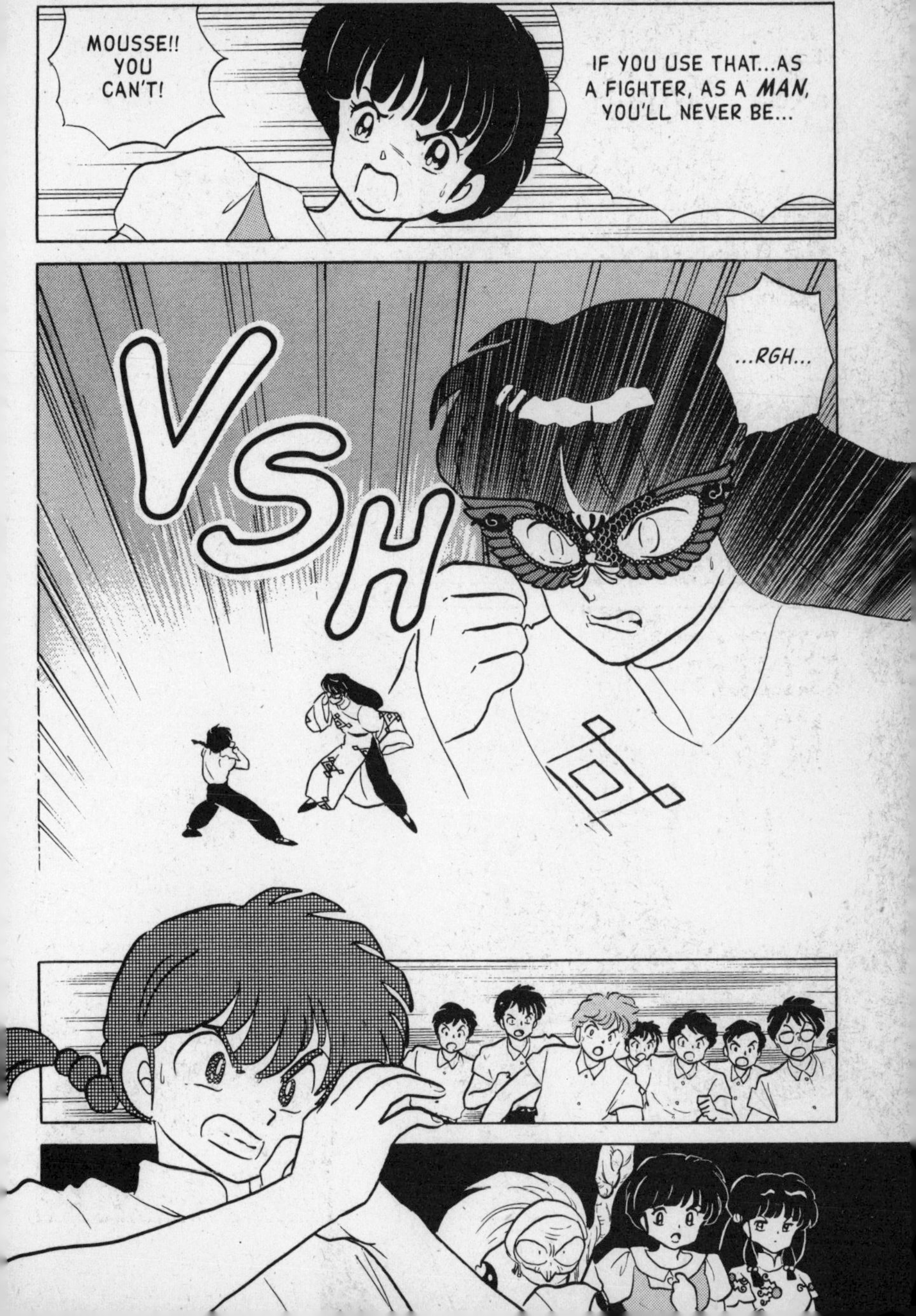
MOUSSE!! YOU CAN'T!
IF YOU USE THAT...AS A FIGHTER, AS A *MAN*, YOU'LL NEVER BE...
VSH
...RGH...

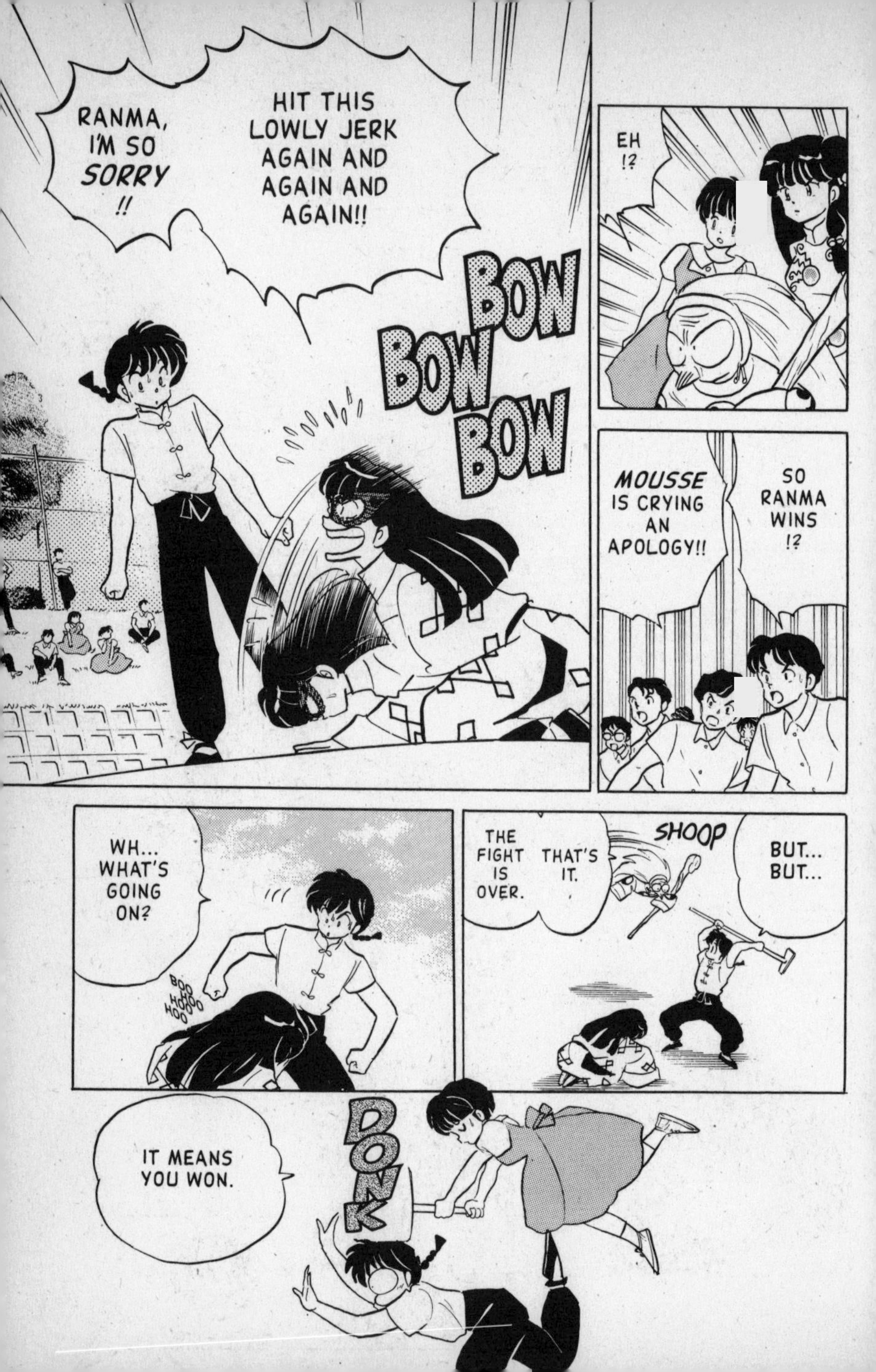
RANMA, I'M SO SORRY !!
HIT THIS LOWLY JERK AGAIN AND AGAIN AND AGAIN!!
BOW BOW BOW BOW
EH !?
MOUSSE IS CRYING AN APOLOGY!!
SO RANMA WINS !?
WH... WHAT'S GOING ON?
BOO HOO HOO HOO
THE FIGHT IS OVER.
THAT'S IT.
SHOOP
BUT... BUT...
IT MEANS YOU WON.
DONK

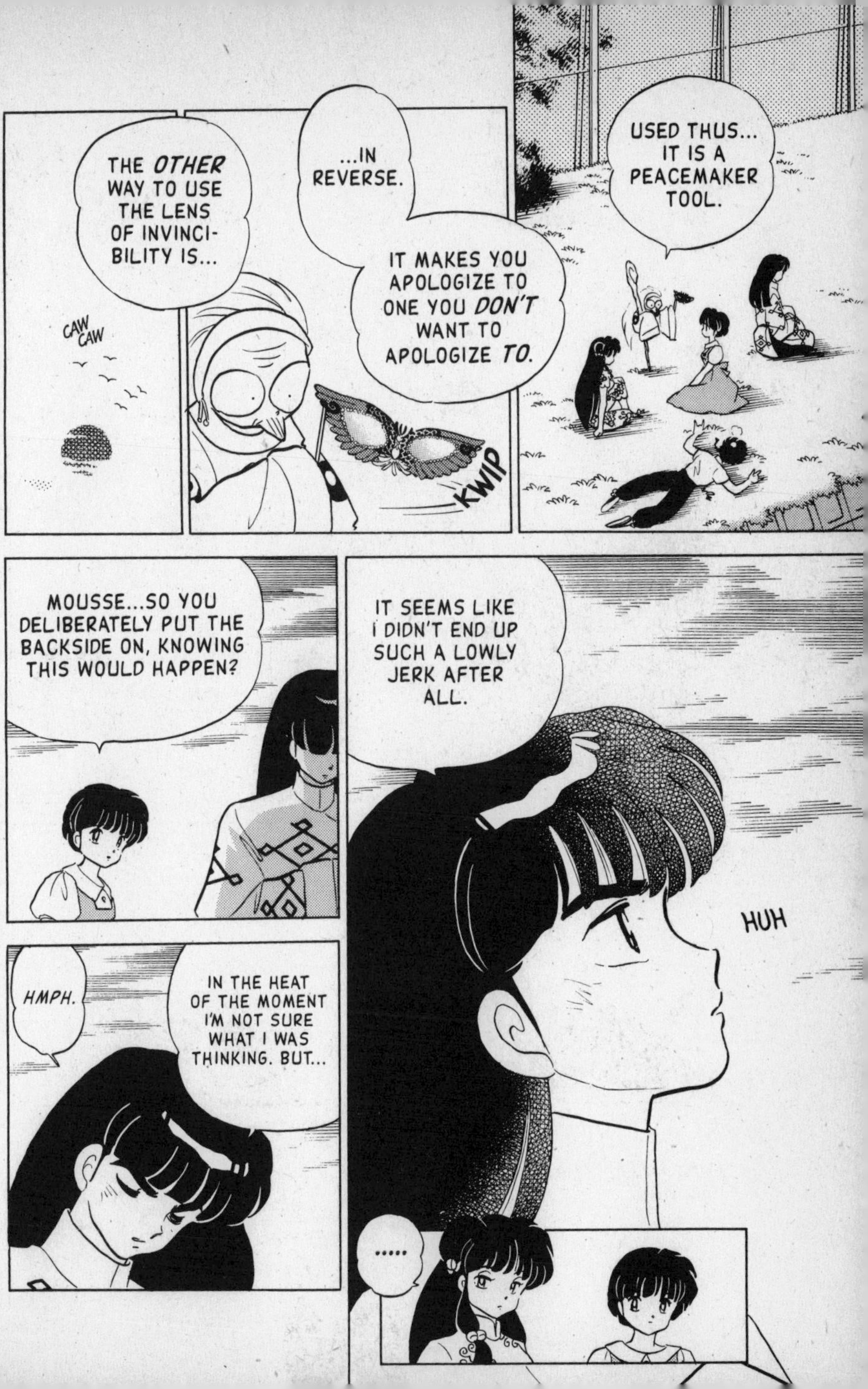
THE *OTHER* WAY TO USE THE LENS OF INVINCI-BILITY IS...
CAW CAW
...IN REVERSE.
IT MAKES YOU APOLOGIZE TO ONE YOU *DON'T* WANT TO APOLOGIZE *TO.*
KWIP
USED THUS... IT IS A PEACEMAKER TOOL.
MOUSSE...SO YOU DELIBERATELY PUT THE BACKSIDE ON, KNOWING THIS WOULD HAPPEN?
HMPH.
IN THE HEAT OF THE MOMENT I'M NOT SURE WHAT I WAS THINKING. BUT...
IT SEEMS LIKE I DIDN'T END UP SUCH A LOWLY JERK AFTER ALL.
HUH
.....

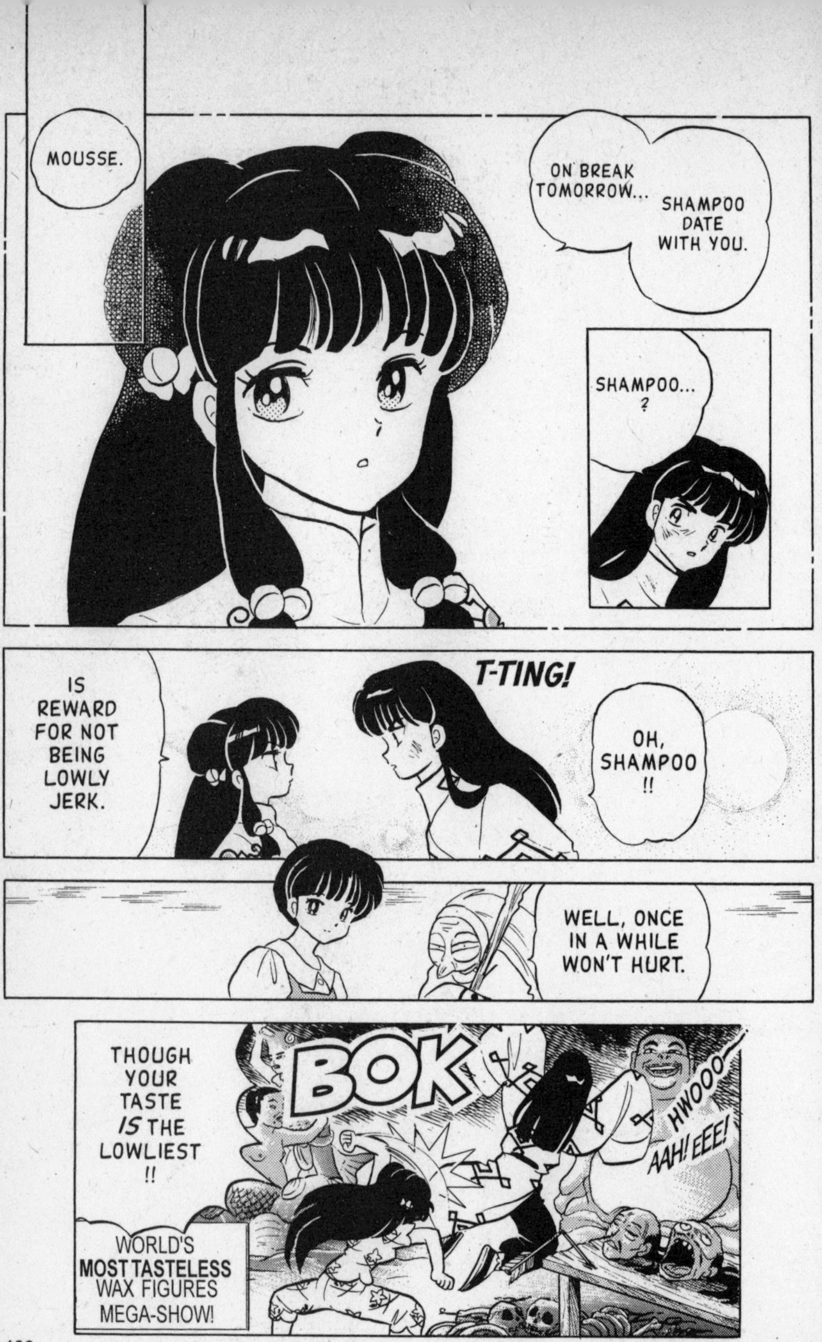

MOUSSE.
ON BREAK TOMORROW... SHAMPOO DATE WITH YOU.
SHAMPOO...?
IS REWARD FOR NOT BEING LOWLY JERK.
T-TING!
OH, SHAMPOO!!
WELL, ONCE IN A WHILE WON'T HURT.
THOUGH YOUR TASTE IS THE LOWLIEST!!
BOK
HWOOO—
AAH! EEE!
WORLD'S MOST TASTELESS WAX FIGURES MEGA-SHOW!

Part 7

DEMON DOG OF THE SEA

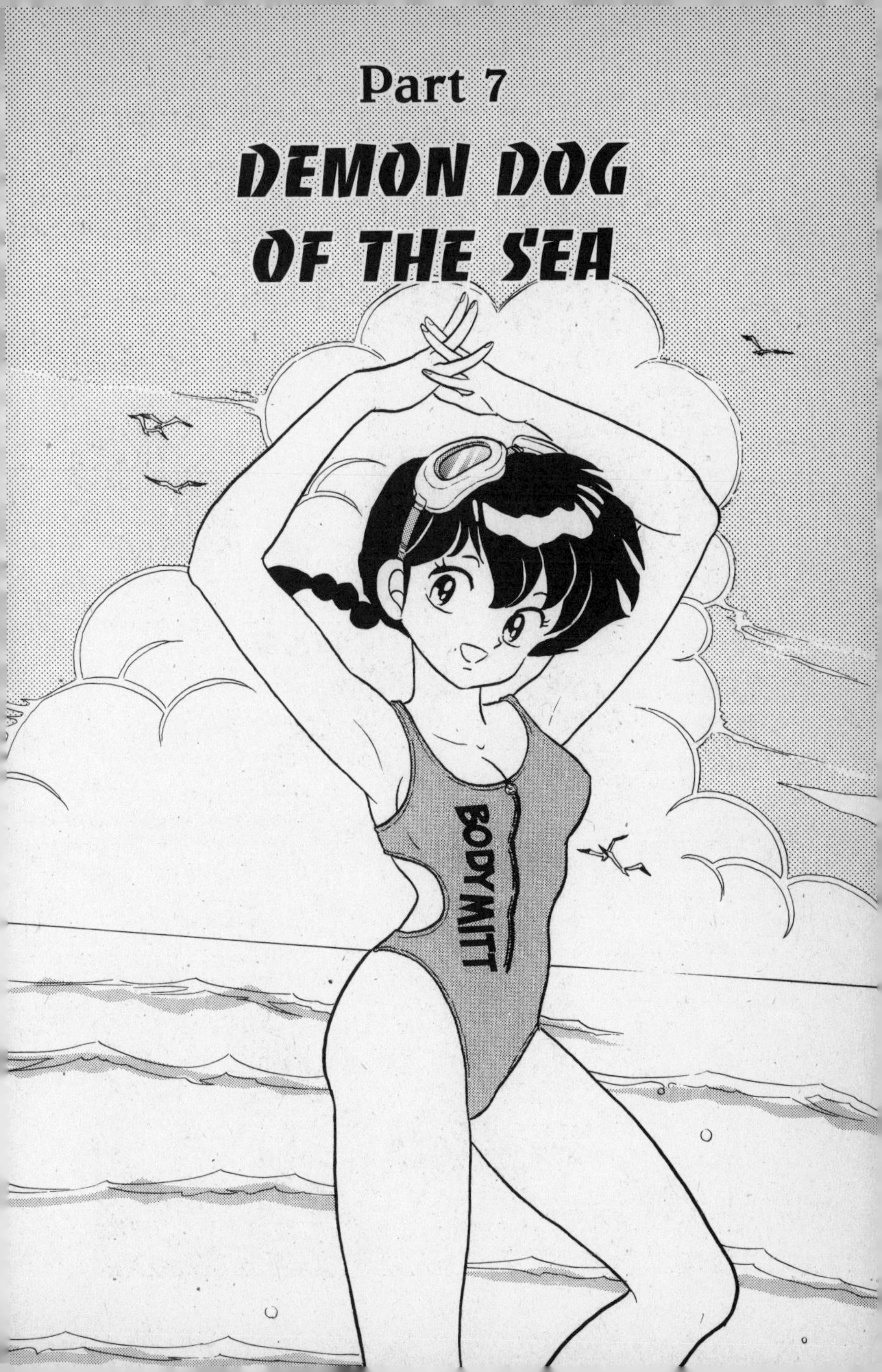
BODYMITT

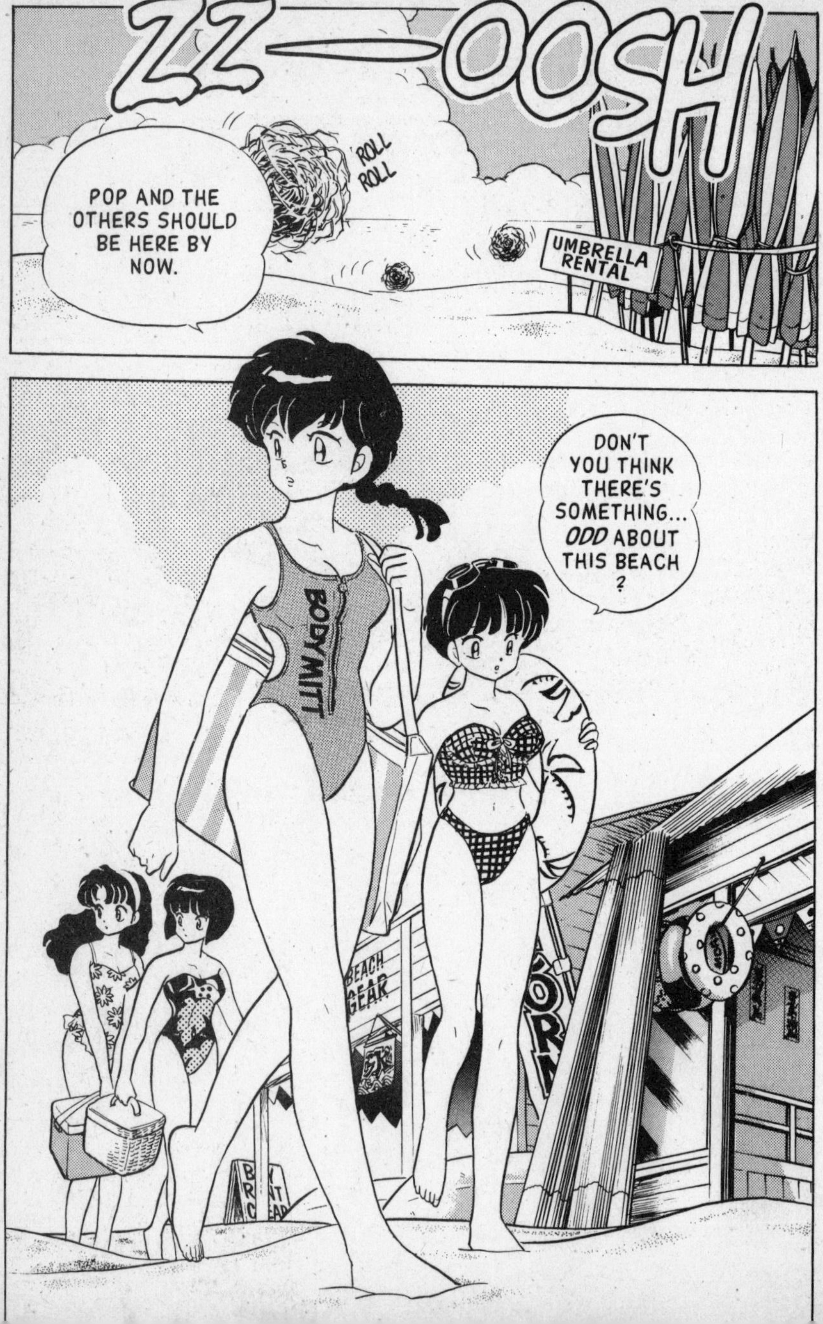
ZZ—OOSH
ROLL ROLL
POP AND THE OTHERS SHOULD BE HERE BY NOW.
UMBRELLA RENTAL
DON'T YOU THINK THERE'S SOMETHING... *ODD* ABOUT THIS BEACH ?
BODY MITT
BEACH GEAR

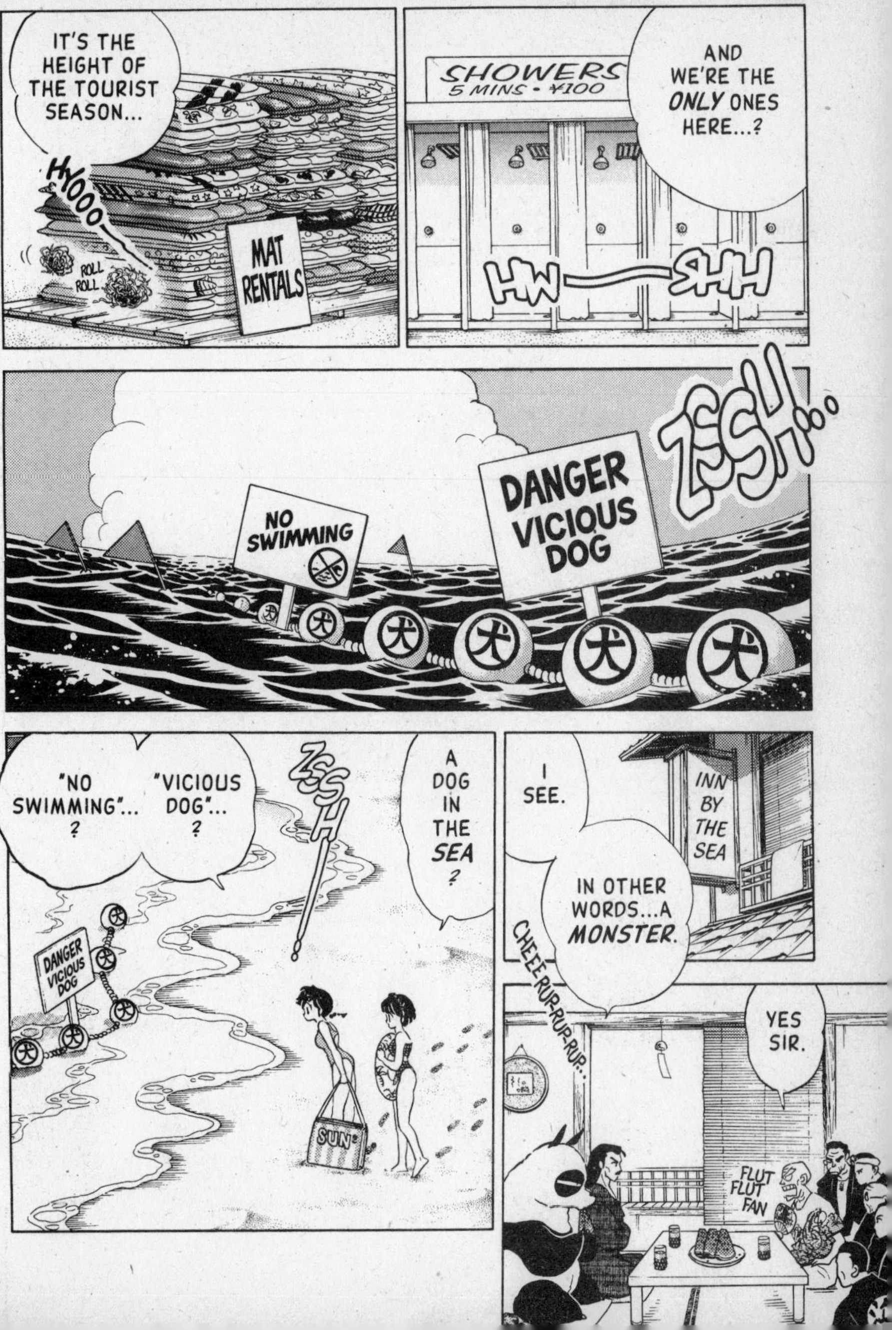
IT'S THE HEIGHT OF THE TOURIST SEASON...
HYOOO
ROLL ROLL
MAT RENTALS
SHOWERS 5 MINS - ¥100
AND WE'RE THE *ONLY* ONES HERE...?
HW—SHH
NO SWIMMING
DANGER VICIOUS DOG
ZESH...
"NO SWIMMING"...?
"VICIOUS DOG"...?
ZESH
A DOG IN THE *SEA*?
DANGER VICIOUS DOG
SUN
I SEE.
INN BY THE SEA
IN OTHER WORDS...A *MONSTER*.
CHEEE RUP-RUP-RUP...
YES SIR.
FLUT FLUT FAN

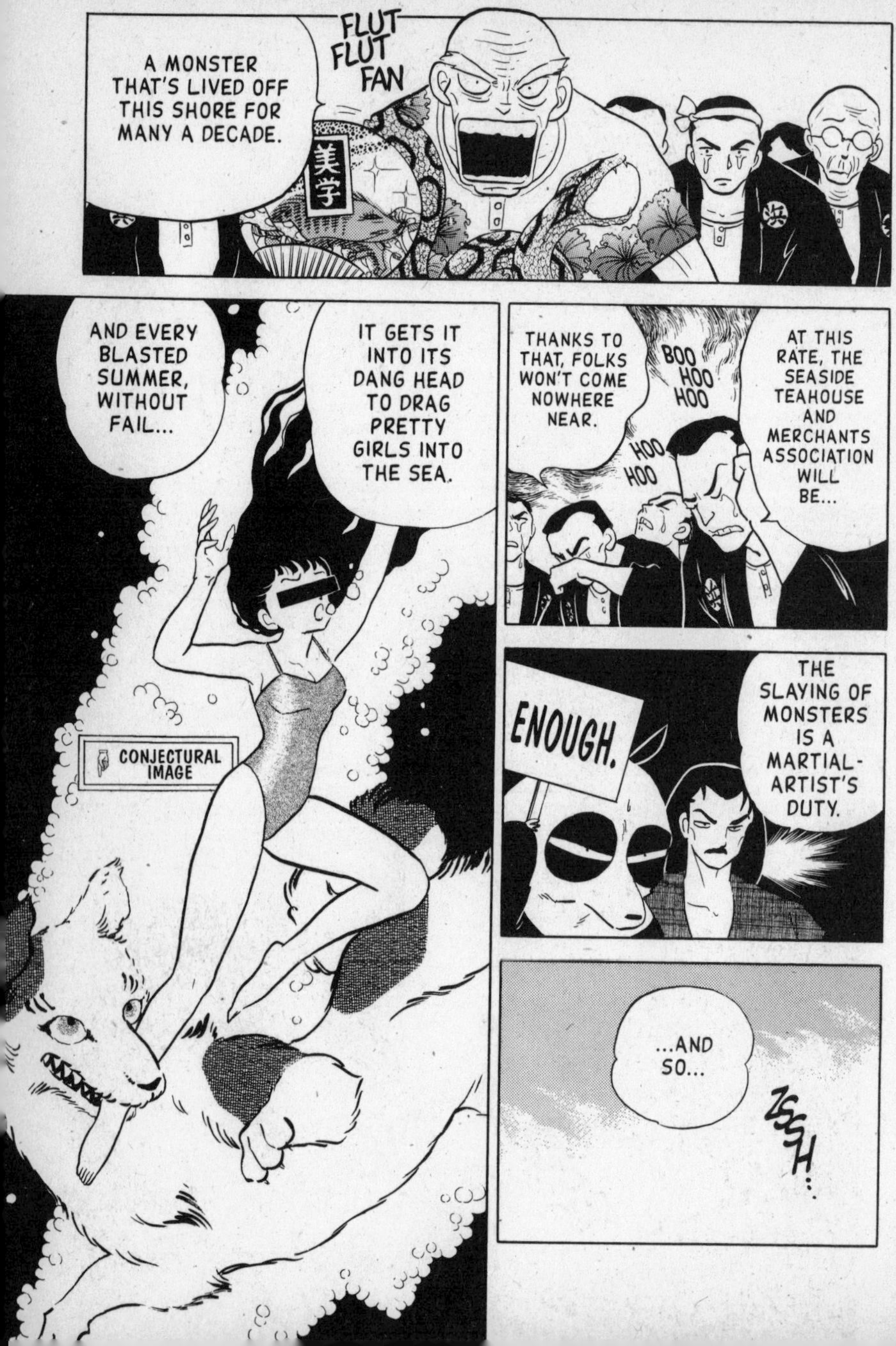
A MONSTER THAT'S LIVED OFF THIS SHORE FOR MANY A DECADE.
FLUT FLUT FAN
美学
AND EVERY BLASTED SUMMER, WITHOUT FAIL...
IT GETS IT INTO ITS DANG HEAD TO DRAG PRETTY GIRLS INTO THE SEA.
CONJECTURAL IMAGE
THANKS TO THAT, FOLKS WON'T COME NOWHERE NEAR.
BOO HOO HOO
HOO HOO
AT THIS RATE, THE SEASIDE TEAHOUSE AND MERCHANTS ASSOCIATION WILL BE...
ENOUGH.
THE SLAYING OF MONSTERS IS A MARTIAL-ARTIST'S DUTY.
...AND SO...
ZSSH...

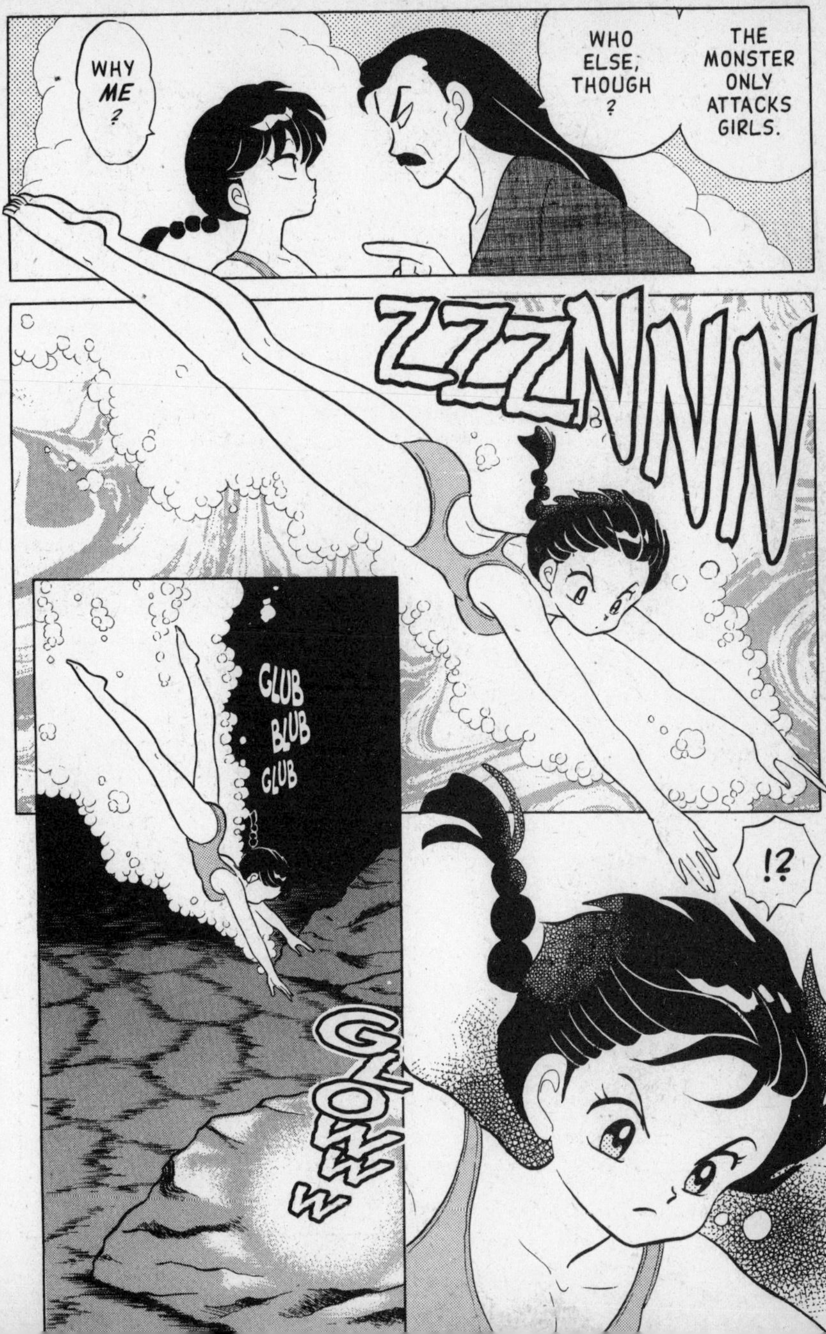
WHY ME?
WHO ELSE, THOUGH?
THE MONSTER ONLY ATTACKS GIRLS.
ZZZNNN
GLUB
BLUB
GLUB
GYOWWw
!?

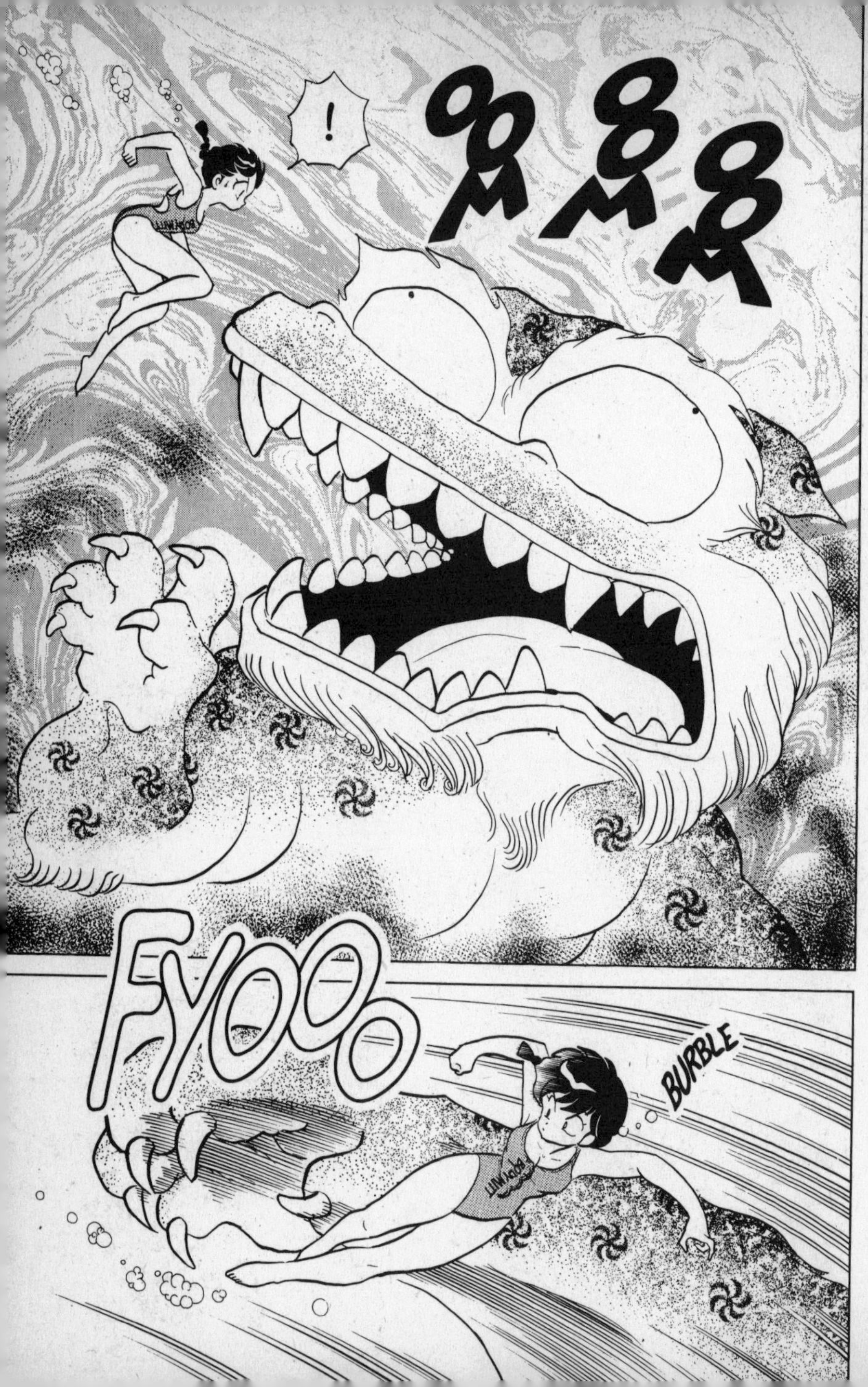
!
OOM OOM OOM
FYOOO
BURBLE

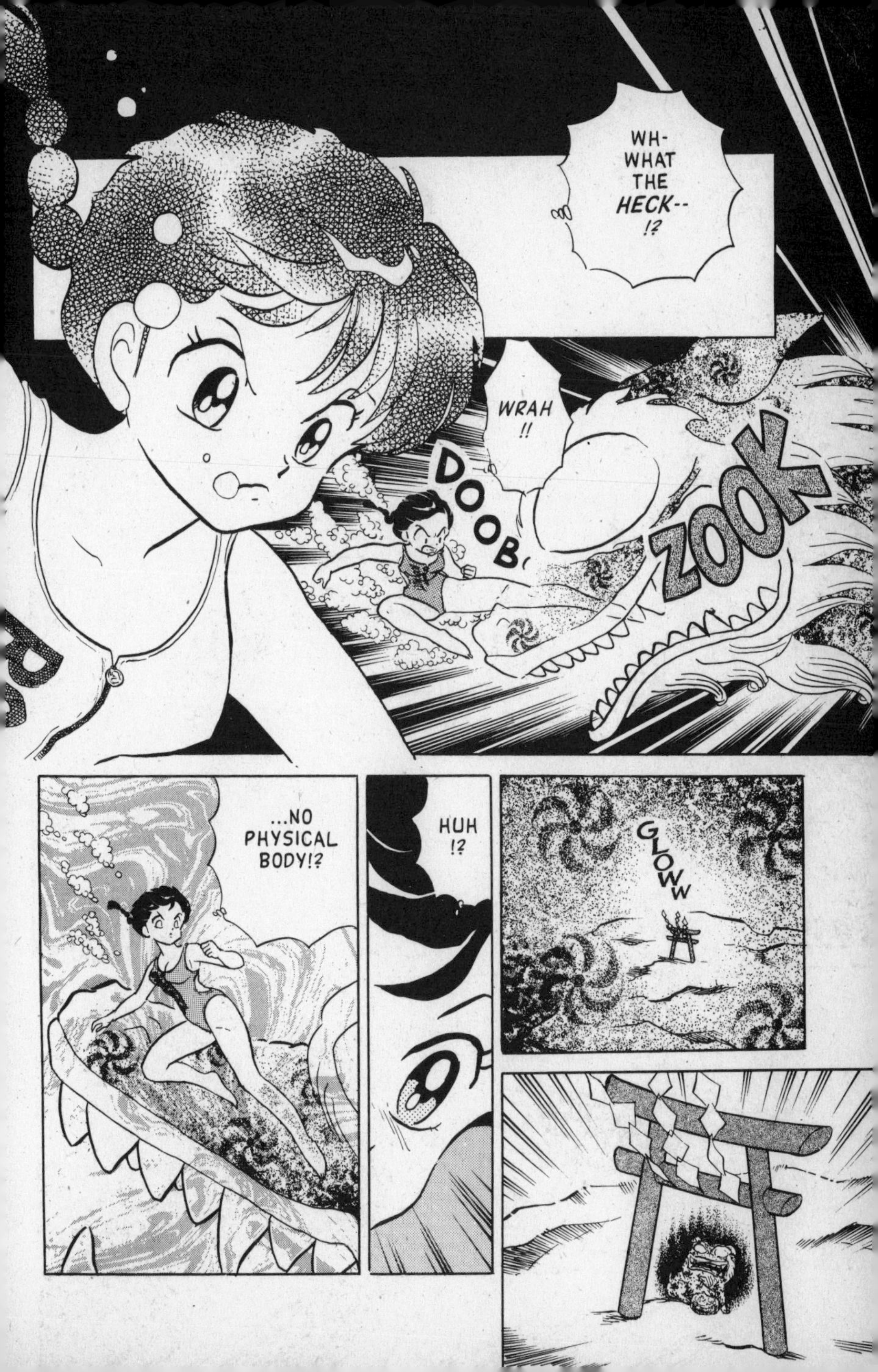
WH- WHAT THE HECK-- !?
WRAH !!
DOOB
ZOOK
...NO PHYSICAL BODY!?
HUH !?
GLOWW

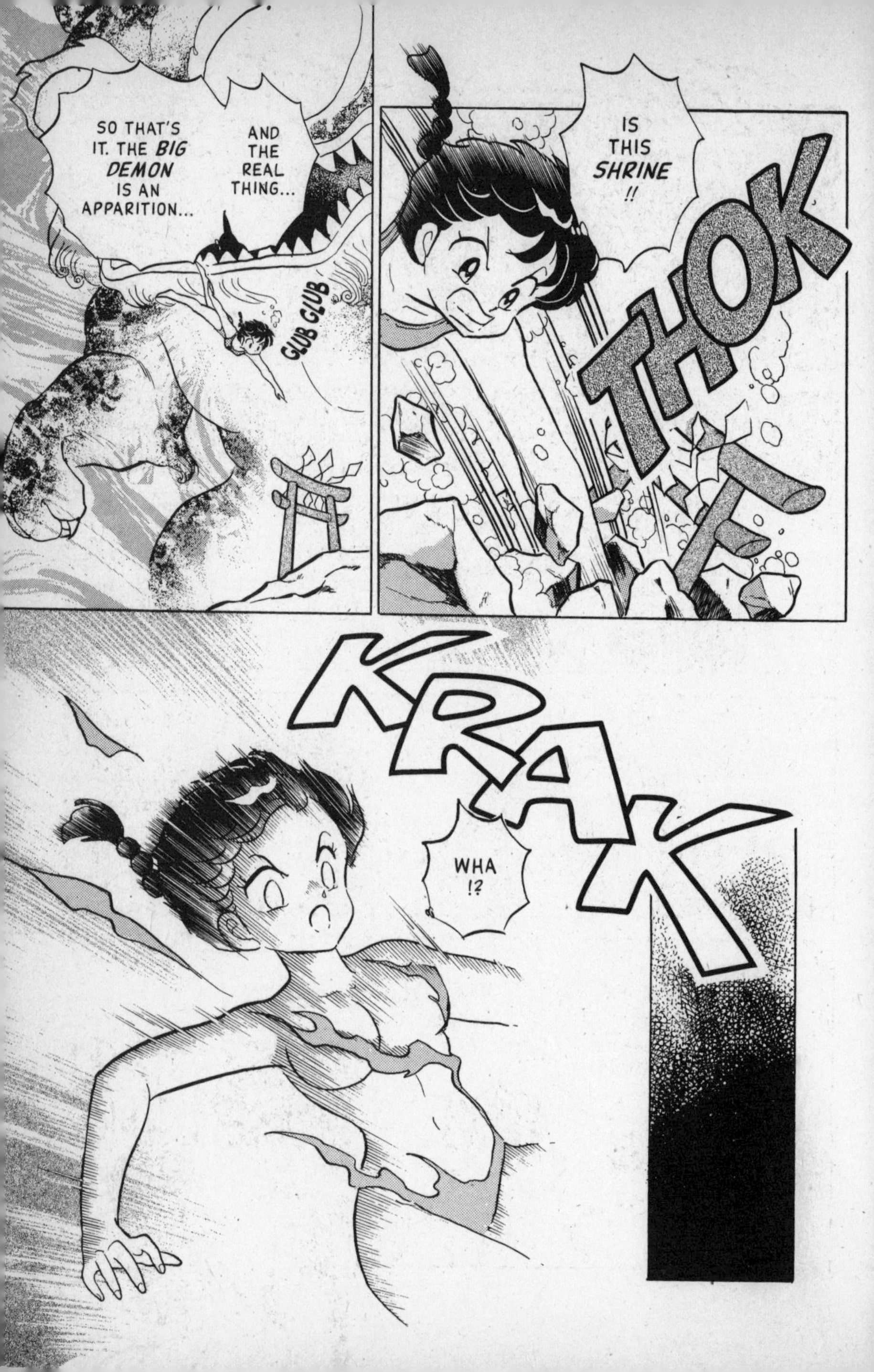
SO THAT'S IT. THE *BIG DEMON* IS AN APPARITION...
AND THE REAL THING...
GLUB GLUB
IS THIS *SHRINE* !!
THOK
KRAK
WHA !?

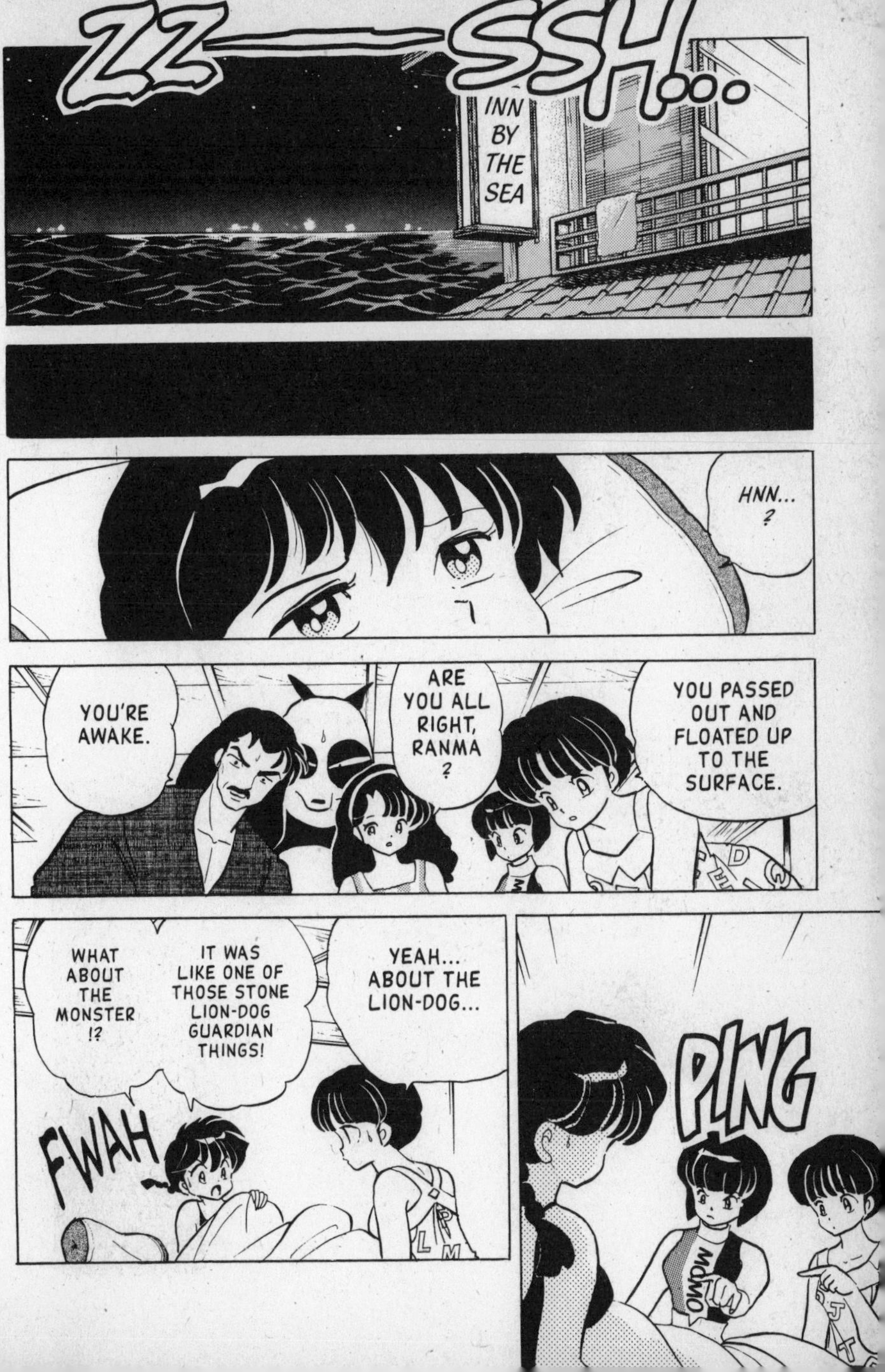
ZZ——SSH...
INN BY THE SEA
HNN...?
YOU'RE AWAKE.
ARE YOU ALL RIGHT, RANMA?
YOU PASSED OUT AND FLOATED UP TO THE SURFACE.
WHAT ABOUT THE MONSTER!?
IT WAS LIKE ONE OF THOSE STONE LION-DOG GUARDIAN THINGS!
YEAH... ABOUT THE LION-DOG...
FWAH
PING

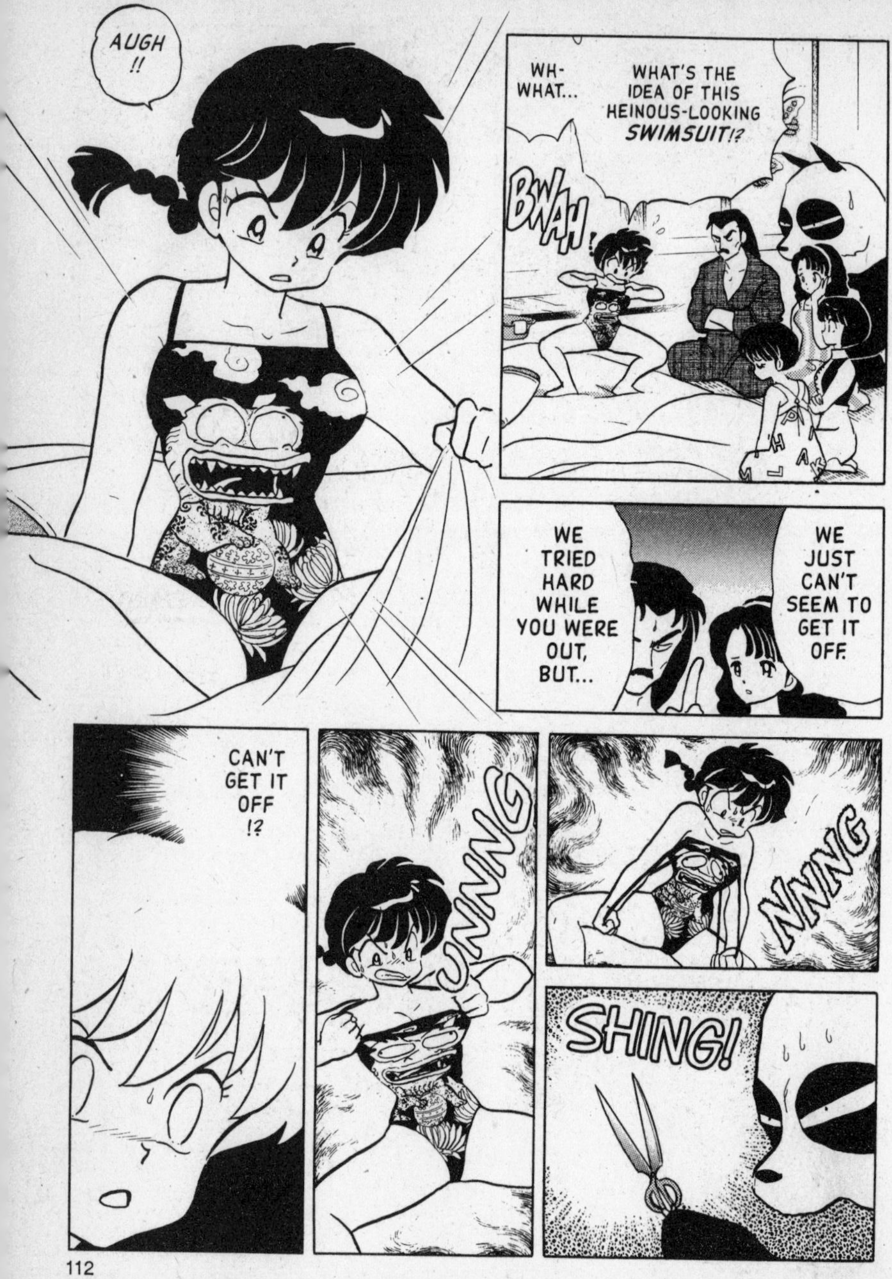
AUGH !!
WH- WHAT...
WHAT'S THE IDEA OF THIS HEINOUS-LOOKING SWIMSUIT!?
BWAH
WE TRIED HARD WHILE YOU WERE OUT, BUT...
WE JUST CAN'T SEEM TO GET IT OFF.
CAN'T GET IT OFF !?
UNNNG
NNNG
SHING!

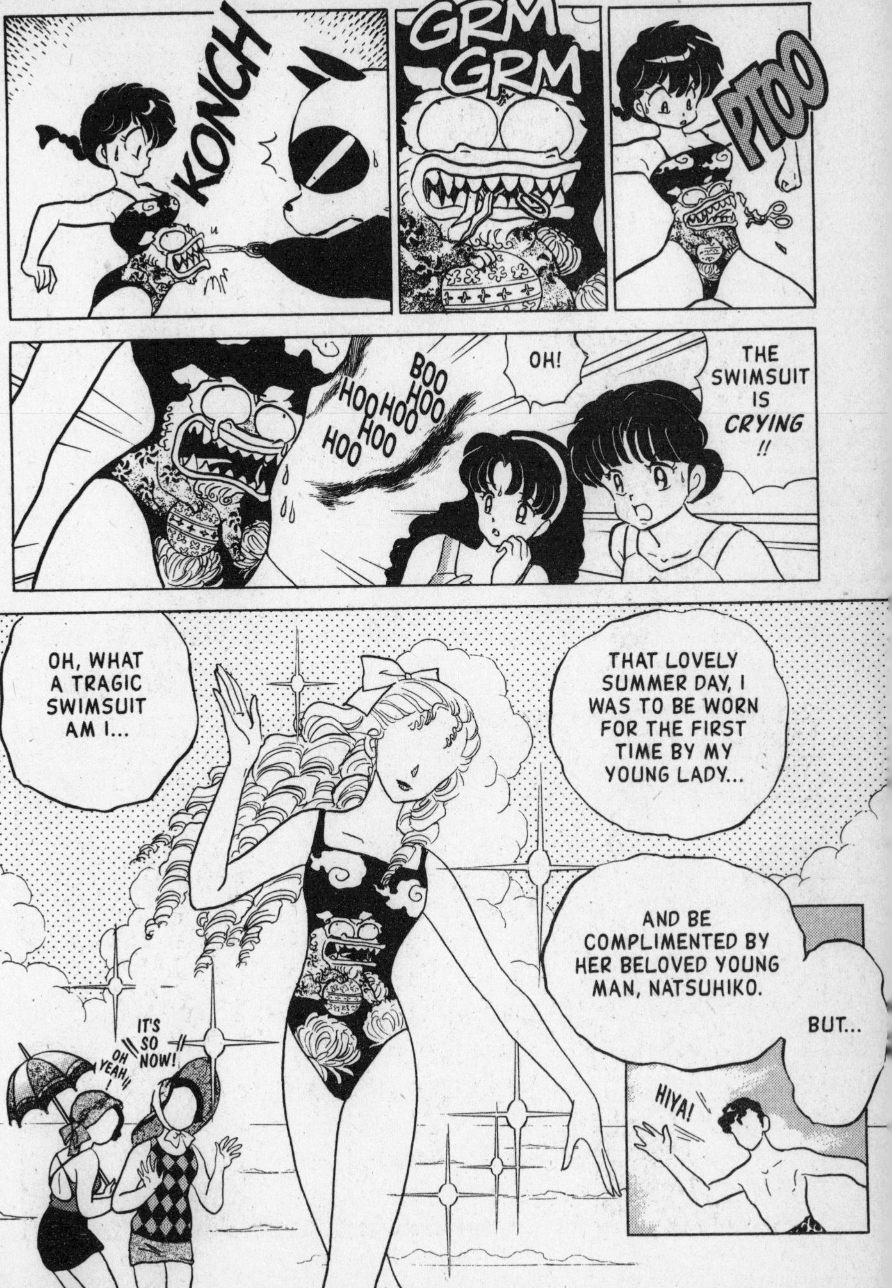
KONCH
GRM GRM
PTOO
BOO HOO HOO HOO HOO HOO
OH!
THE SWIMSUIT IS *CRYING* !!
OH, WHAT A TRAGIC SWIMSUIT AM I...
THAT LOVELY SUMMER DAY, I WAS TO BE WORN FOR THE FIRST TIME BY MY YOUNG LADY...
AND BE COMPLIMENTED BY HER BELOVED YOUNG MAN, NATSUHIKO.
BUT...
IT'S SO NOW!
OH YEAH!!
HIYA!

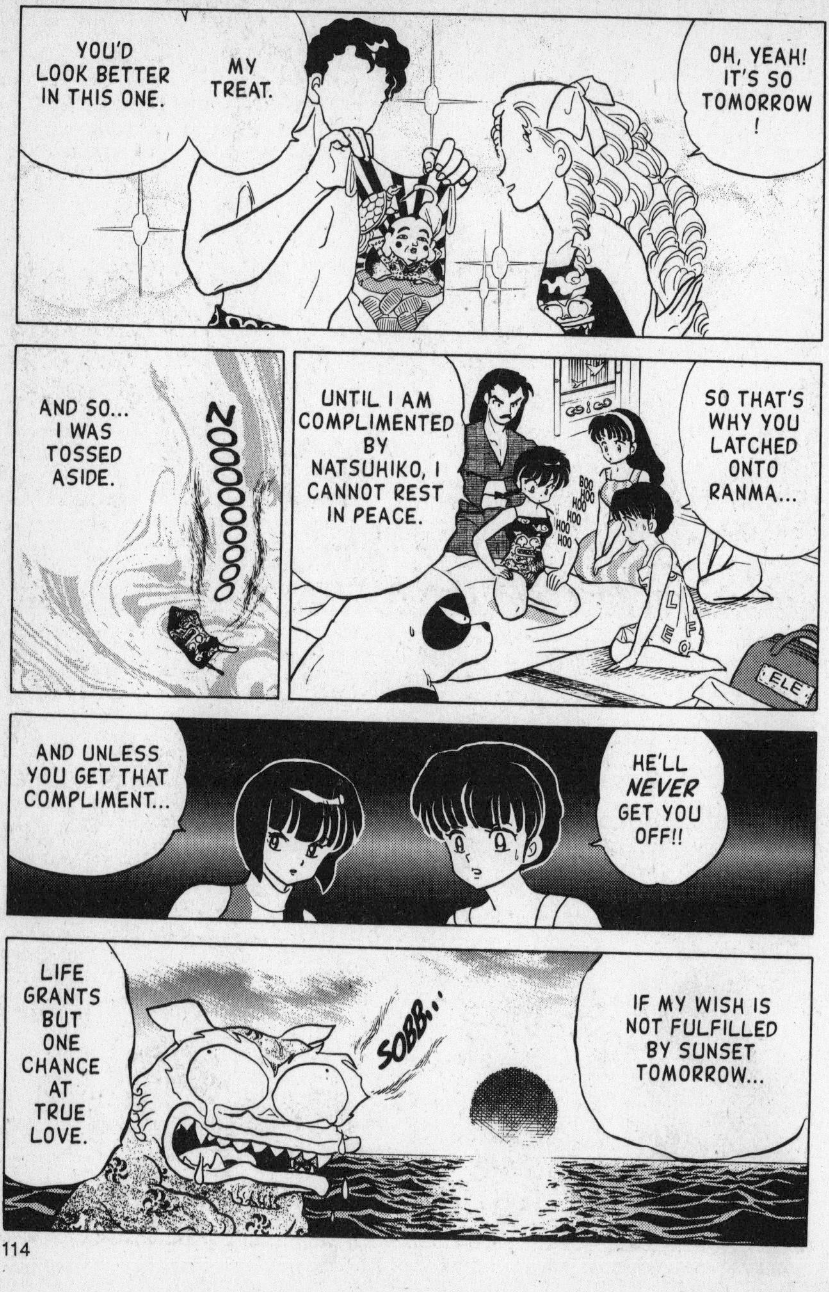
YOU'D LOOK BETTER IN THIS ONE.
MY TREAT.
OH, YEAH! IT'S SO TOMORROW!
AND SO... I WAS TOSSED ASIDE.
NOOOOOOOOOOO
UNTIL I AM COMPLIMENTED BY NATSUHIKO, I CANNOT REST IN PEACE.
BOO HOO HOO HOO HOO HOO
SO THAT'S WHY YOU LATCHED ONTO RANMA...
ELE
AND UNLESS YOU GET THAT COMPLIMENT...
HE'LL *NEVER* GET YOU OFF!!
LIFE GRANTS BUT ONE CHANCE AT TRUE LOVE.
SOBB...
IF MY WISH IS NOT FULFILLED BY SUNSET TOMORROW...

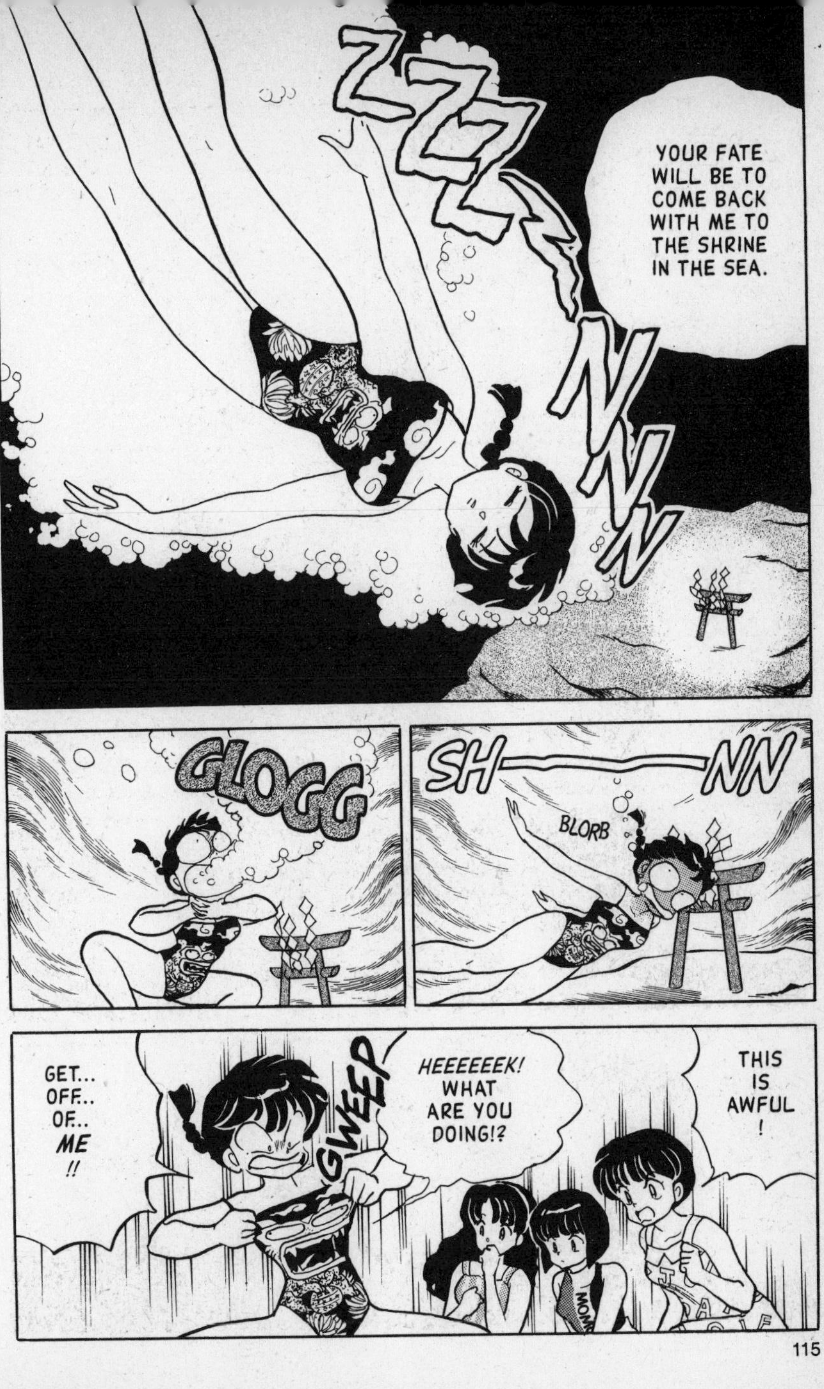
ZZZZZNNNN
YOUR FATE WILL BE TO COME BACK WITH ME TO THE SHRINE IN THE SEA.
GLOGG
SH——NN
BLORB
GET... OFF... OF... ME !!
GWEEP
HEEEEEEK! WHAT ARE YOU DOING!?
THIS IS AWFUL !

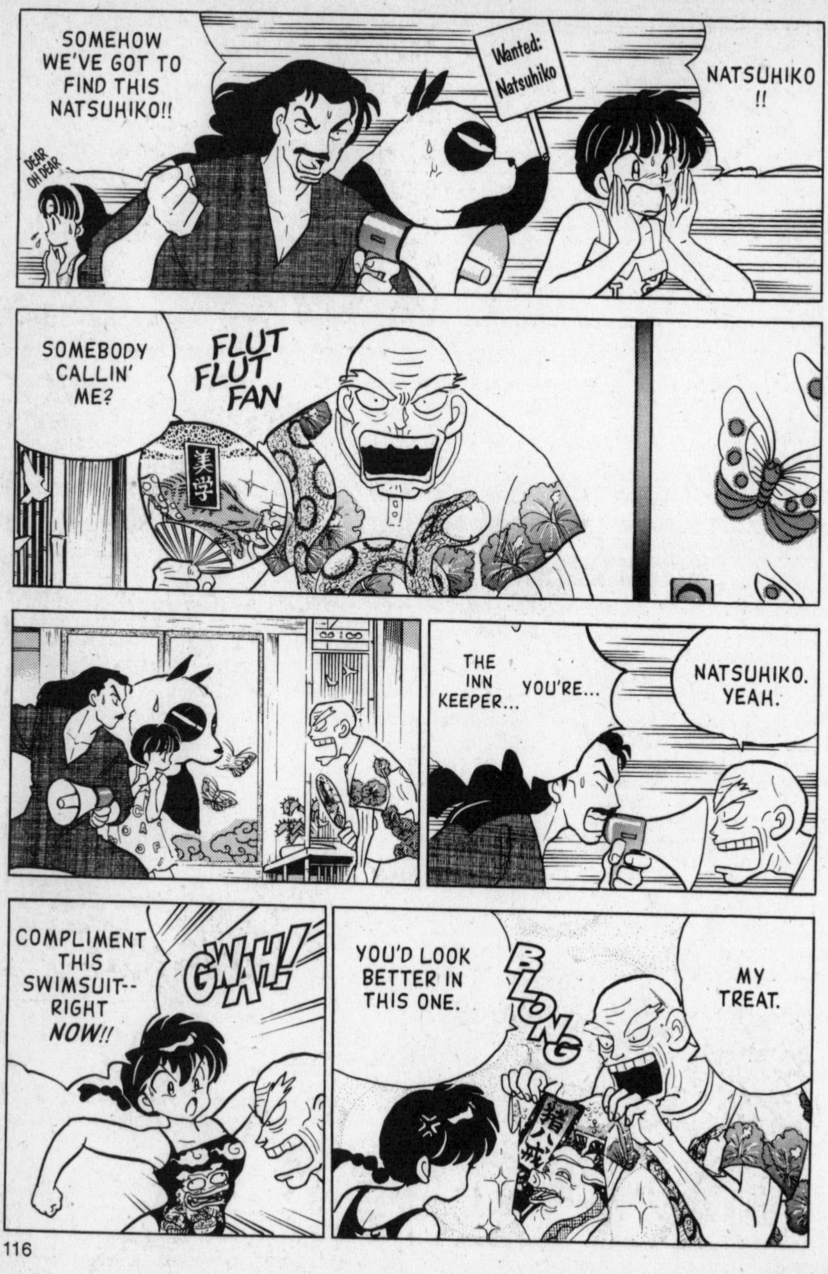
SOMEHOW WE'VE GOT TO FIND THIS NATSUHIKO!!
DEAR OH DEAR
Wanted: Natsuhiko
NATSUHIKO !!
SOMEBODY CALLIN' ME?
FLUT FLUT FAN
美学
THE INN KEEPER...
YOU'RE...
NATSUHIKO. YEAH.
COMPLIMENT THIS SWIMSUIT-- RIGHT NOW!!
GWAH!
YOU'D LOOK BETTER IN THIS ONE.
BLONG
MY TREAT.

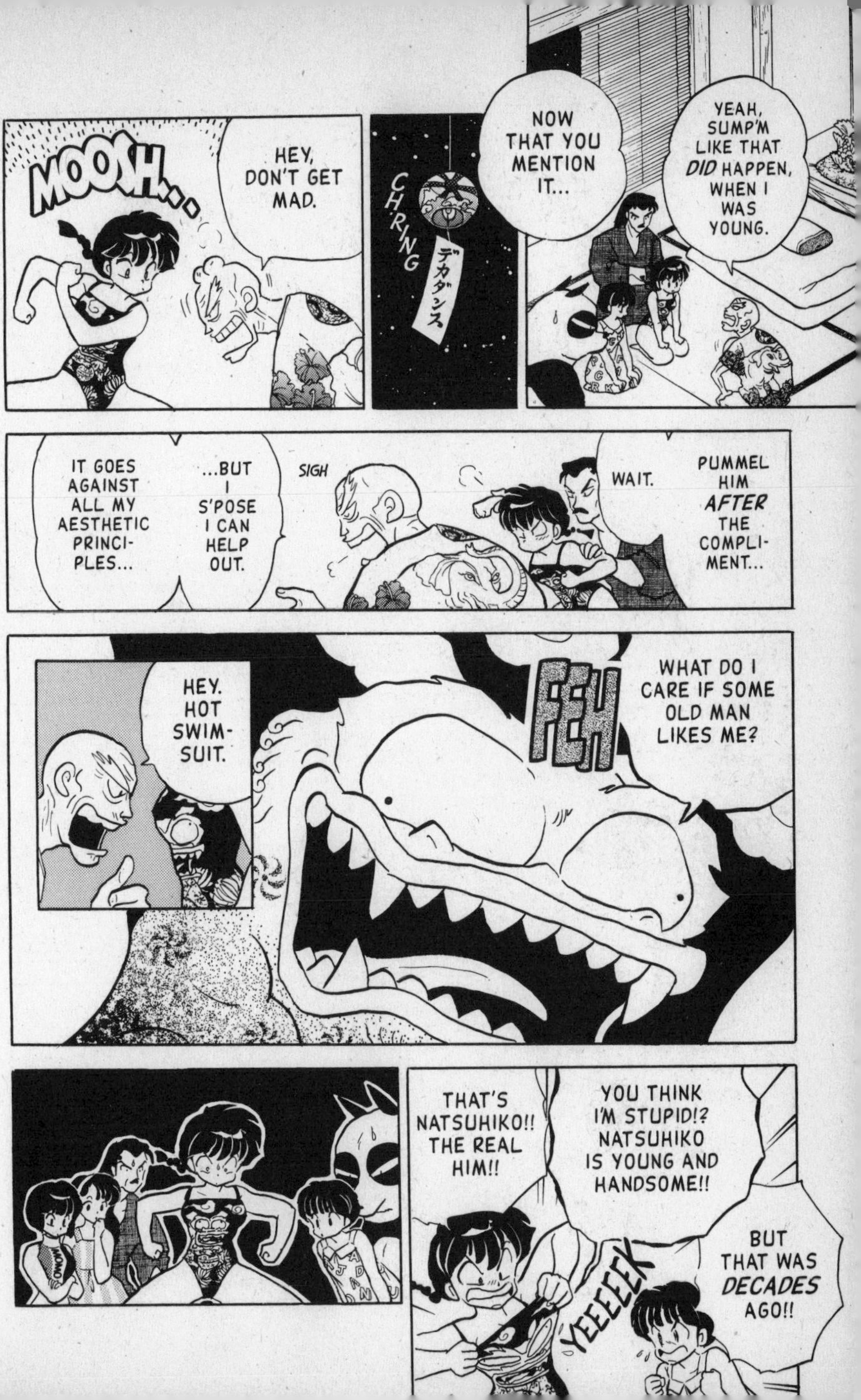
MOOSH...
HEY, DON'T GET MAD.
CHRING
デカダンス
NOW THAT YOU MENTION IT...
YEAH, SUMP'M LIKE THAT *DID* HAPPEN, WHEN I WAS YOUNG.
IT GOES AGAINST ALL MY AESTHETIC PRINCIPLES...
...BUT I S'POSE I CAN HELP OUT.
SIGH
WAIT.
PUMMEL HIM *AFTER* THE COMPLIMENT...
HEY. HOT SWIMSUIT.
FEH
WHAT DO I CARE IF SOME OLD MAN LIKES ME?
THAT'S NATSUHIKO!! THE REAL HIM!!
YOU THINK I'M STUPID!? NATSUHIKO IS YOUNG AND HANDSOME!!
YEEEEEK
BUT THAT WAS *DECADES* AGO!!

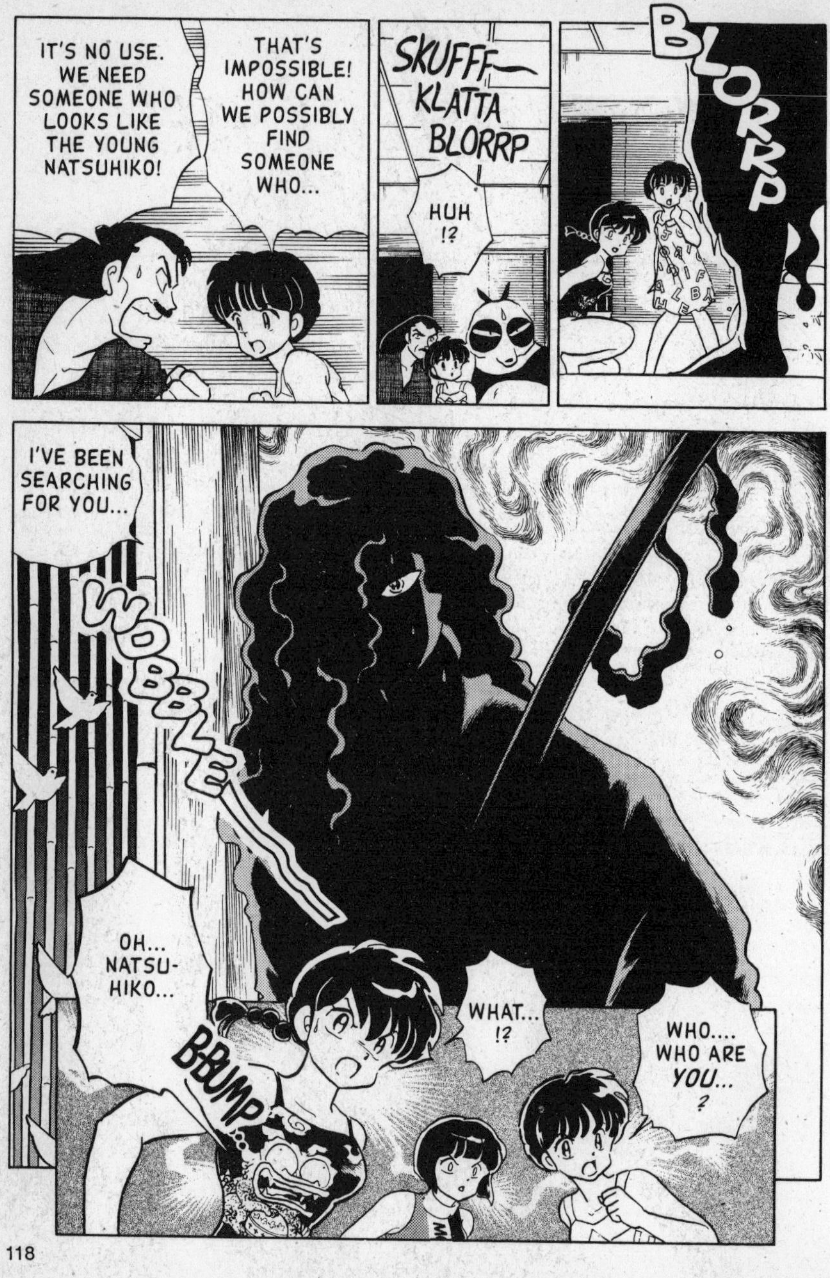
IT'S NO USE. WE NEED SOMEONE WHO LOOKS LIKE THE YOUNG NATSUHIKO!
THAT'S IMPOSSIBLE! HOW CAN WE POSSIBLY FIND SOMEONE WHO...
SKUFFF—KLATTA BLORRP
HUH !?
BLORRP
I'VE BEEN SEARCHING FOR YOU...
WOBBLE
OH... NATSU-HIKO...
B-BUMP...
WHAT... !?
WHO.... WHO ARE YOU... ?

Part 8

COMPLIMENT ME!

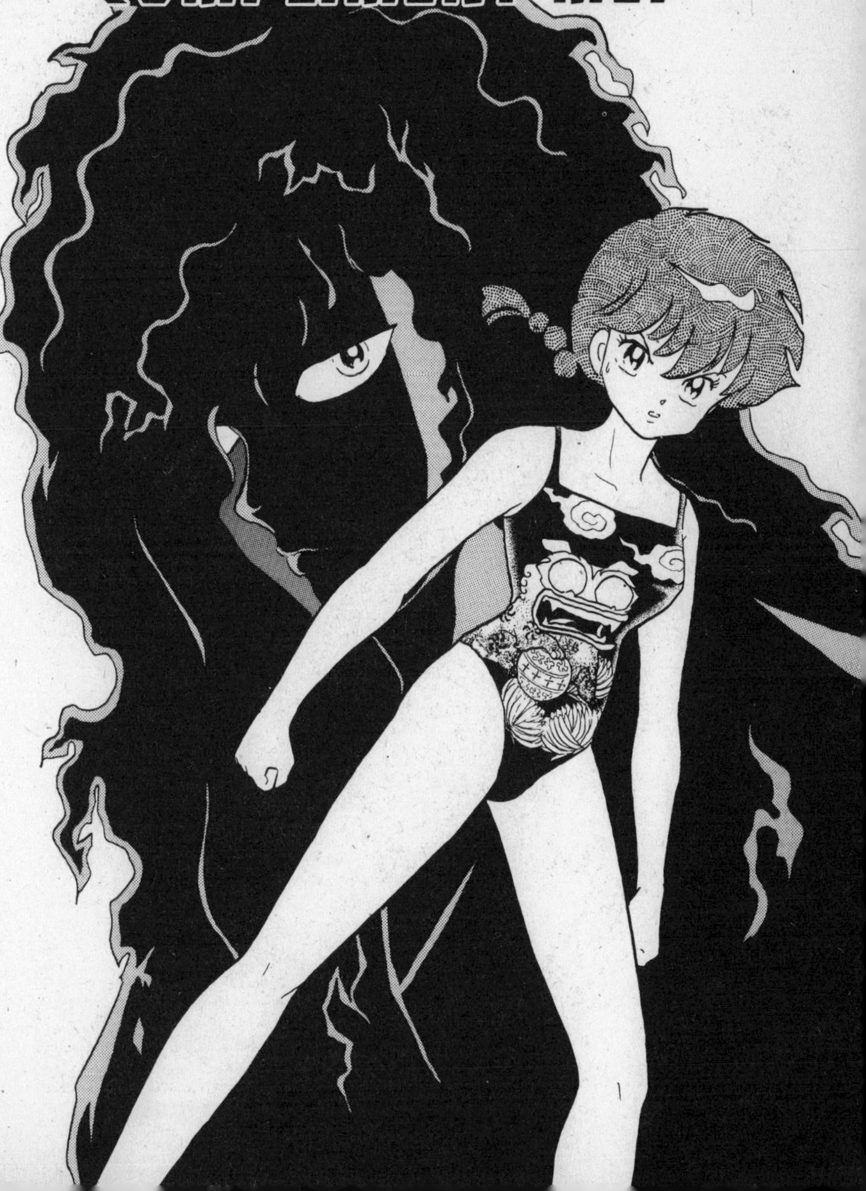

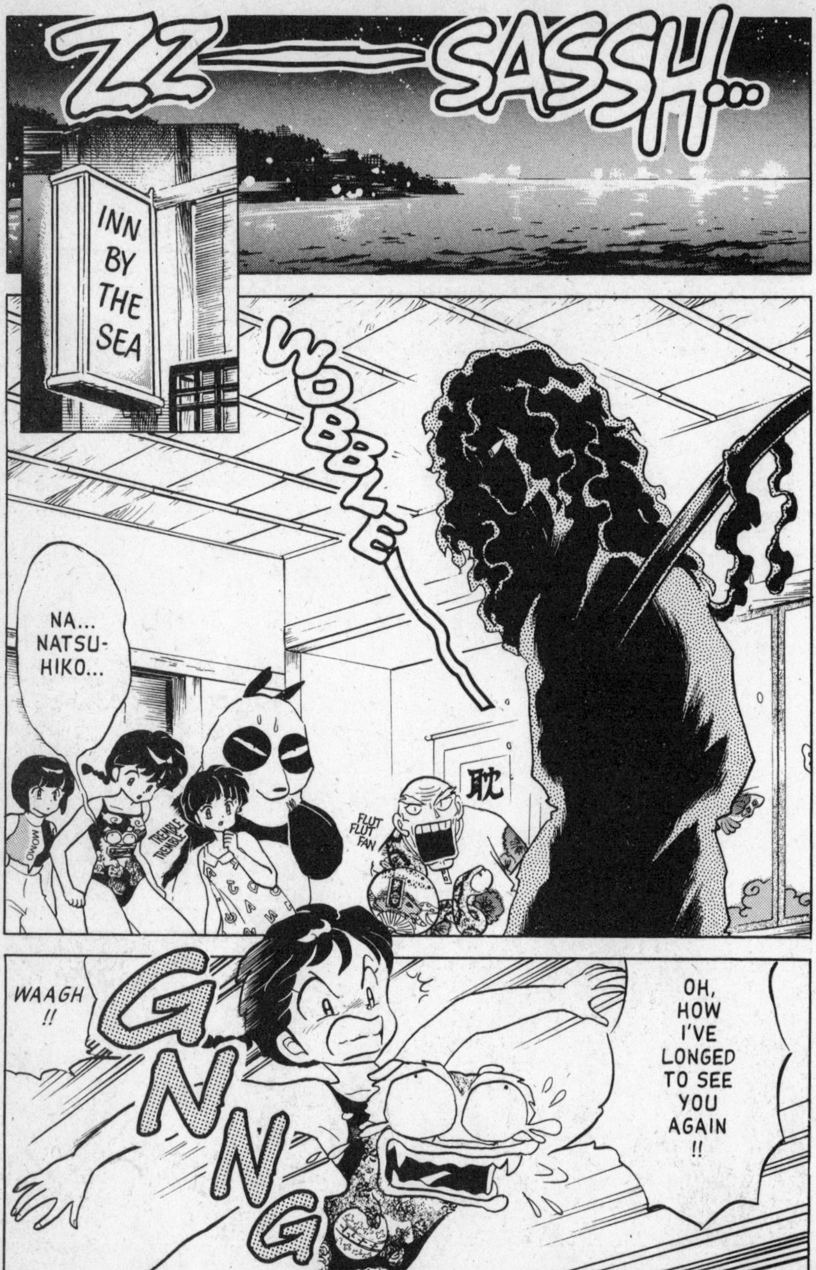
ZZ—SASSH...
INN BY THE SEA
WOBBLE
NA... NATSU-HIKO...
TREMBLE TREMBLE
FLUT FLUT FAN
耽
WAAGH !!
GNNNG
OH, HOW I'VE LONGED TO SEE YOU AGAIN !!

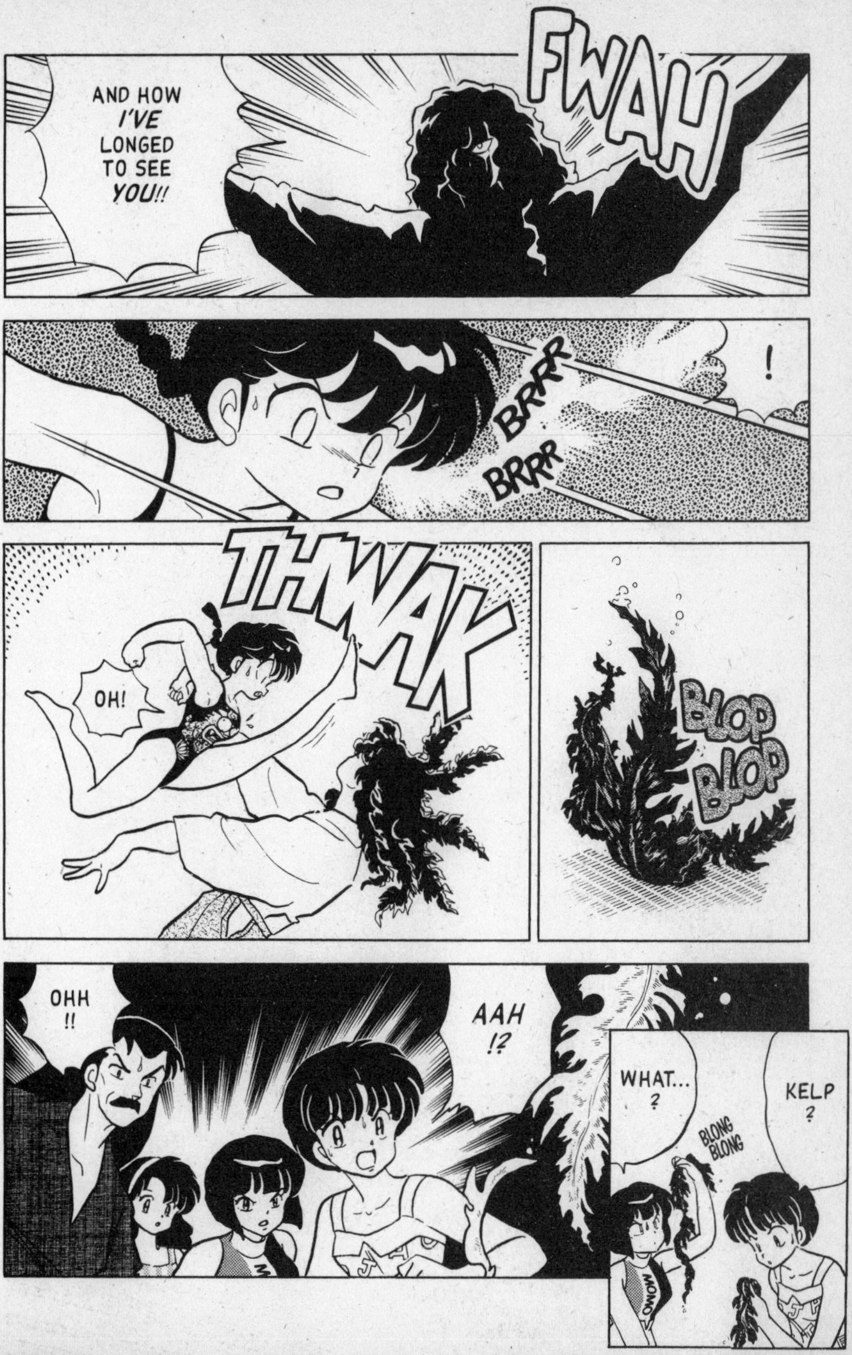
AND HOW I'VE LONGED TO SEE YOU!!
FWAH
!
BRRR BRRR
THWAK
OH!
BLOP BLOP
OHH !!
AAH !?
WHAT... ?
KELP ?
BLONG BLONG

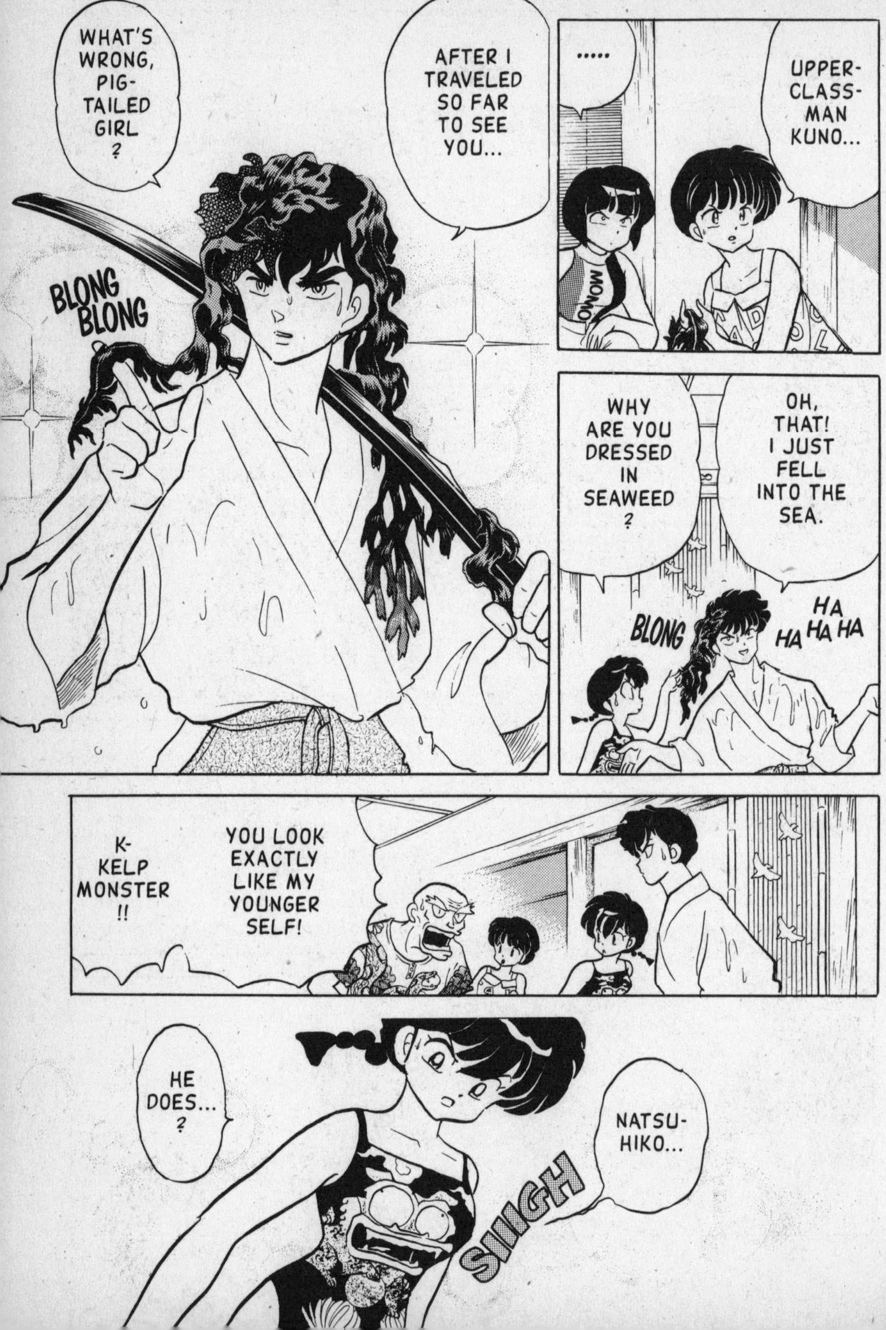
WHAT'S WRONG, PIG-TAILED GIRL?
AFTER I TRAVELED SO FAR TO SEE YOU...
BLONG BLONG
.....
UPPER-CLASSMAN KUNO...
WHY ARE YOU DRESSED IN SEAWEED?
OH, THAT! I JUST FELL INTO THE SEA.
BLONG
HA HA HA HA HA
K-KELP MONSTER!!
YOU LOOK EXACTLY LIKE MY YOUNGER SELF!
HE DOES...?
NATSU-HIKO...
SIIIGH

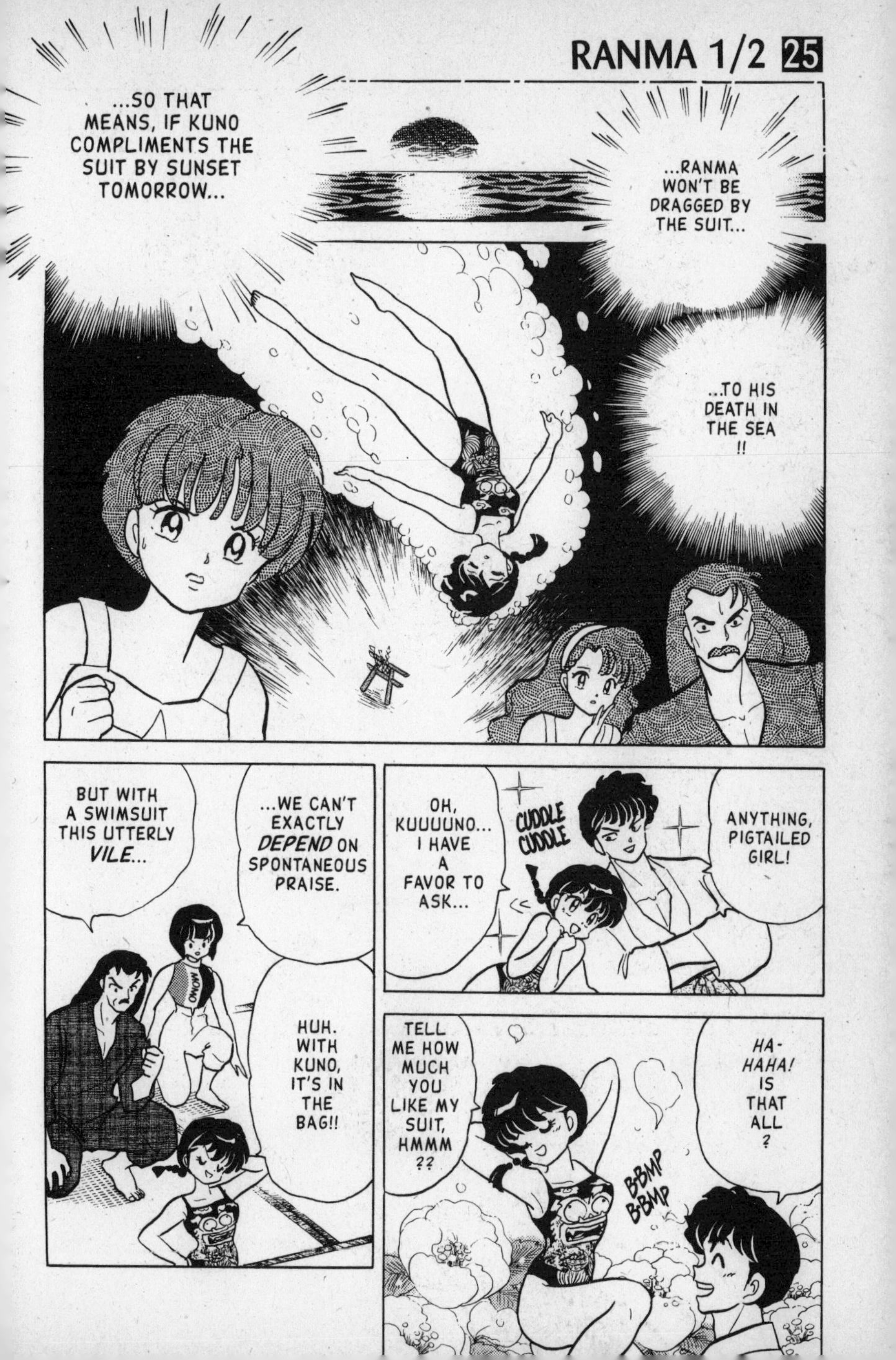
...SO THAT MEANS, IF KUNO COMPLIMENTS THE SUIT BY SUNSET TOMORROW...
...RANMA WON'T BE DRAGGED BY THE SUIT...
...TO HIS DEATH IN THE SEA !!
BUT WITH A SWIMSUIT THIS UTTERLY VILE...
...WE CAN'T EXACTLY DEPEND ON SPONTANEOUS PRAISE.
HUH. WITH KUNO, IT'S IN THE BAG!!
MOMO
OH, KUUUUNO... I HAVE A FAVOR TO ASK...
CUDDLE CUDDLE
ANYTHING, PIGTAILED GIRL!
TELL ME HOW MUCH YOU LIKE MY SUIT, HMMM ??
B-BMP B-BMP
HA-HAHA! IS THAT ALL ?

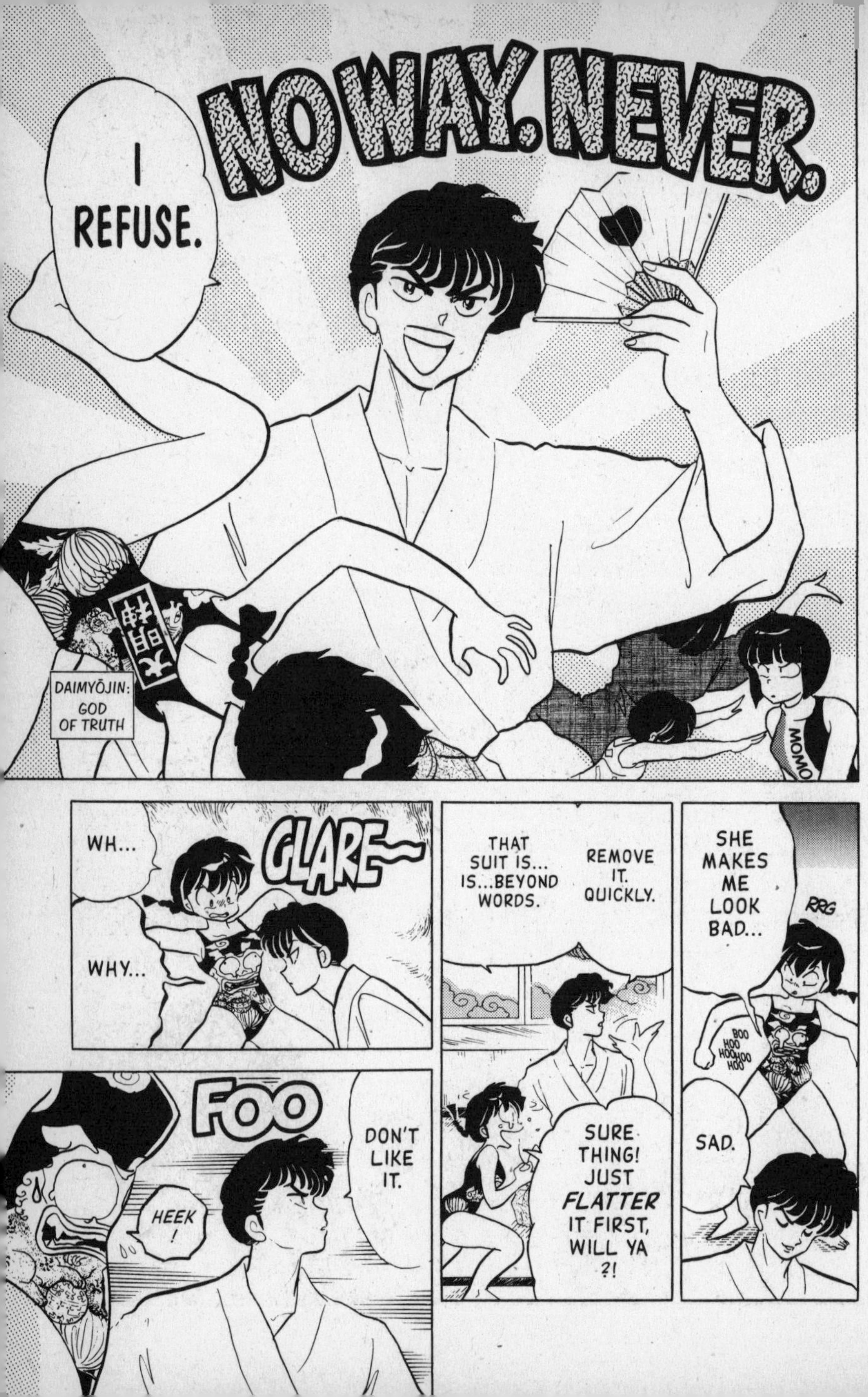
I REFUSE.
NO WAY. NEVER.
DAIMYŌJIN: GOD OF TRUTH
MOMO
WH...
GLARE~
WHY...
FOO
DON'T LIKE IT.
HEEK!
THAT SUIT IS... IS...BEYOND WORDS.
REMOVE IT. QUICKLY.
SURE THING! JUST *FLATTER* IT FIRST, WILL YA ?!
SHE MAKES ME LOOK BAD...
RRG
BOO HOO HOO HOO HOO
SAD.

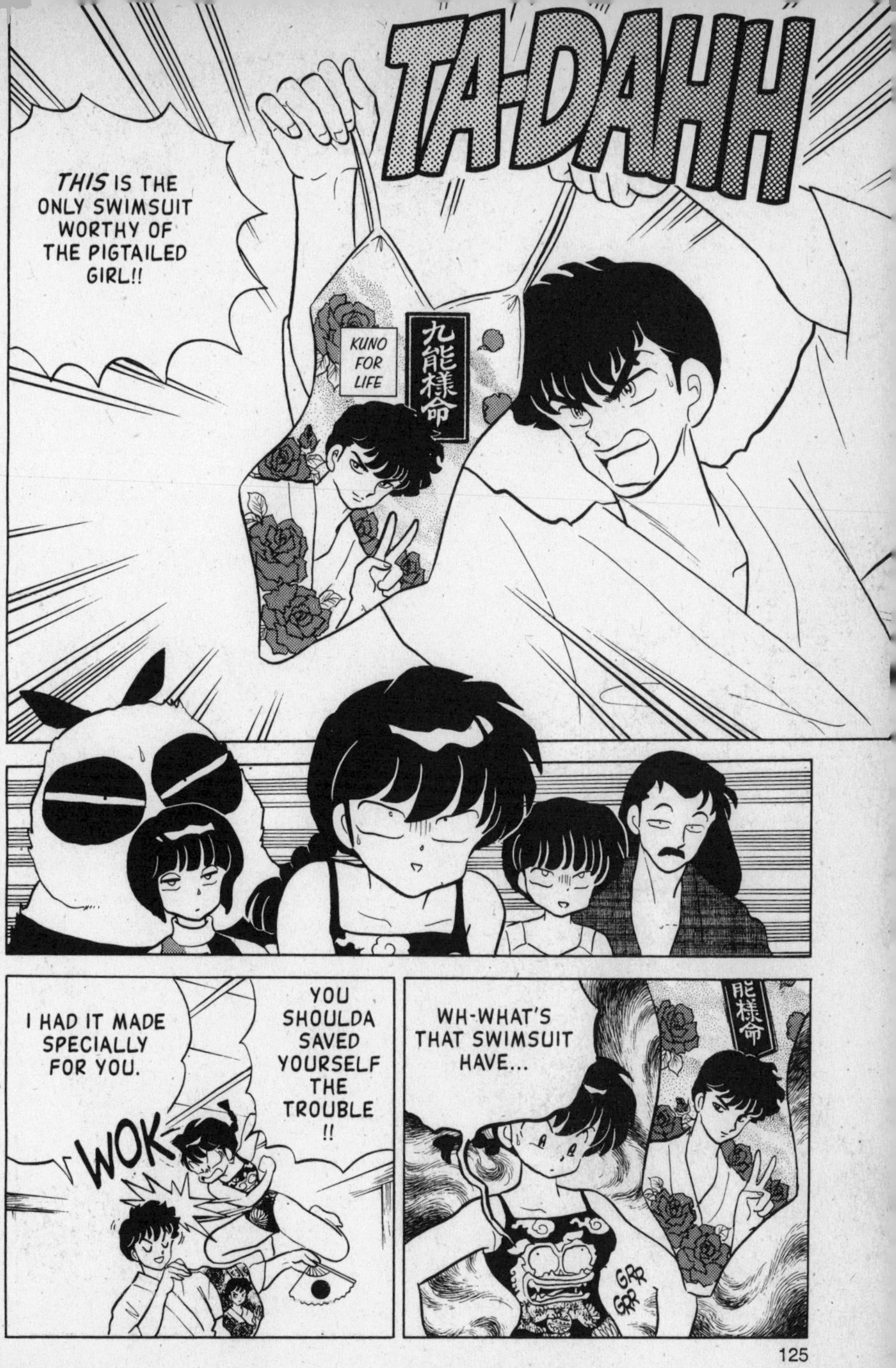
THIS IS THE ONLY SWIMSUIT WORTHY OF THE PIGTAILED GIRL!!
TA-DAHH
KUNO FOR LIFE
九能様命
I HAD IT MADE SPECIALLY FOR YOU.
YOU SHOULDA SAVED YOURSELF THE TROUBLE !!
WOK
WH-WHAT'S THAT SWIMSUIT HAVE...
能様命
GRR GRR

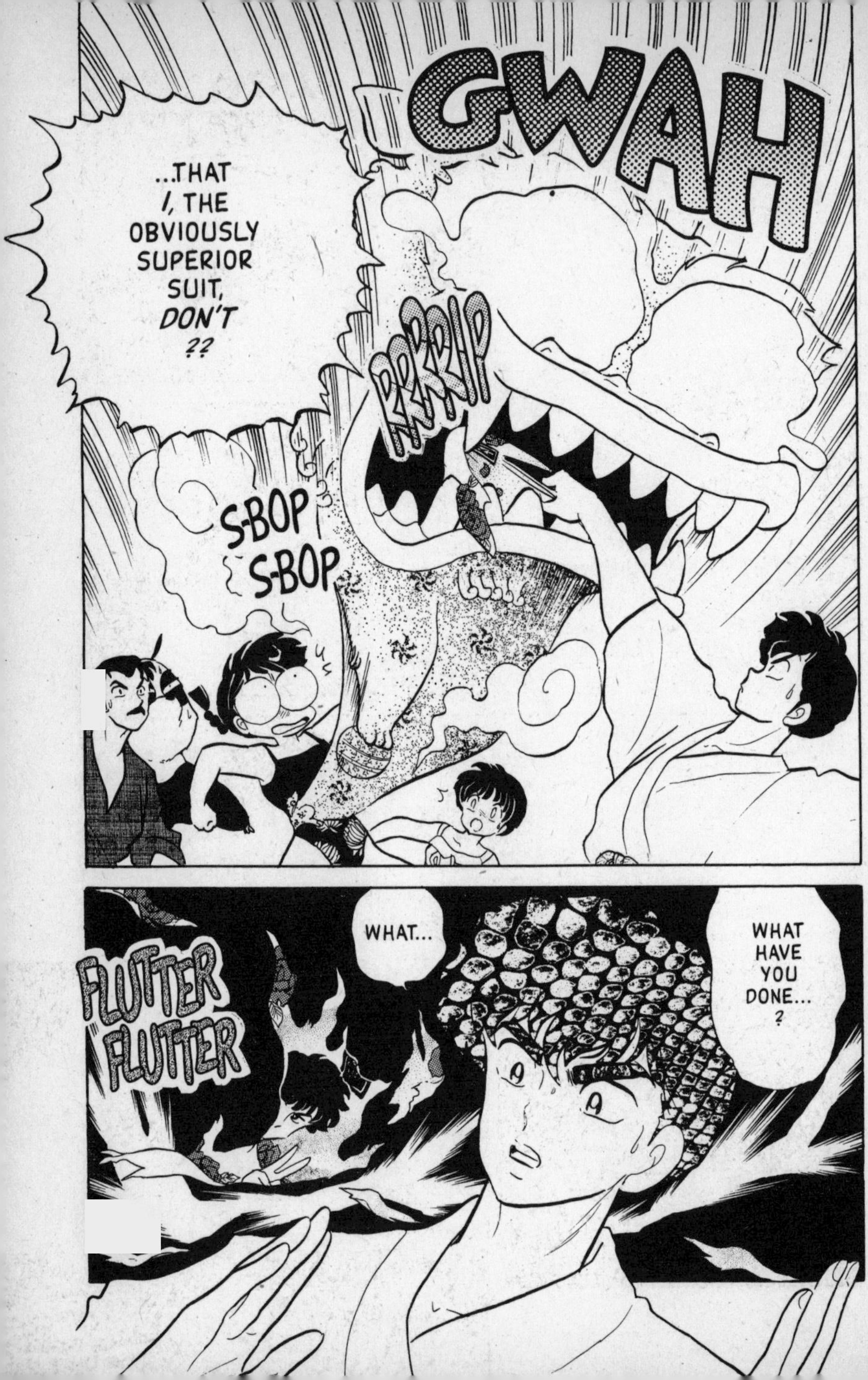
...THAT I, THE OBVIOUSLY SUPERIOR SUIT, DON'T ??
GWAH
RRRRIP
S-BOP S-BOP
FLUTTER FLUTTER
WHAT...
WHAT HAVE YOU DONE... ?

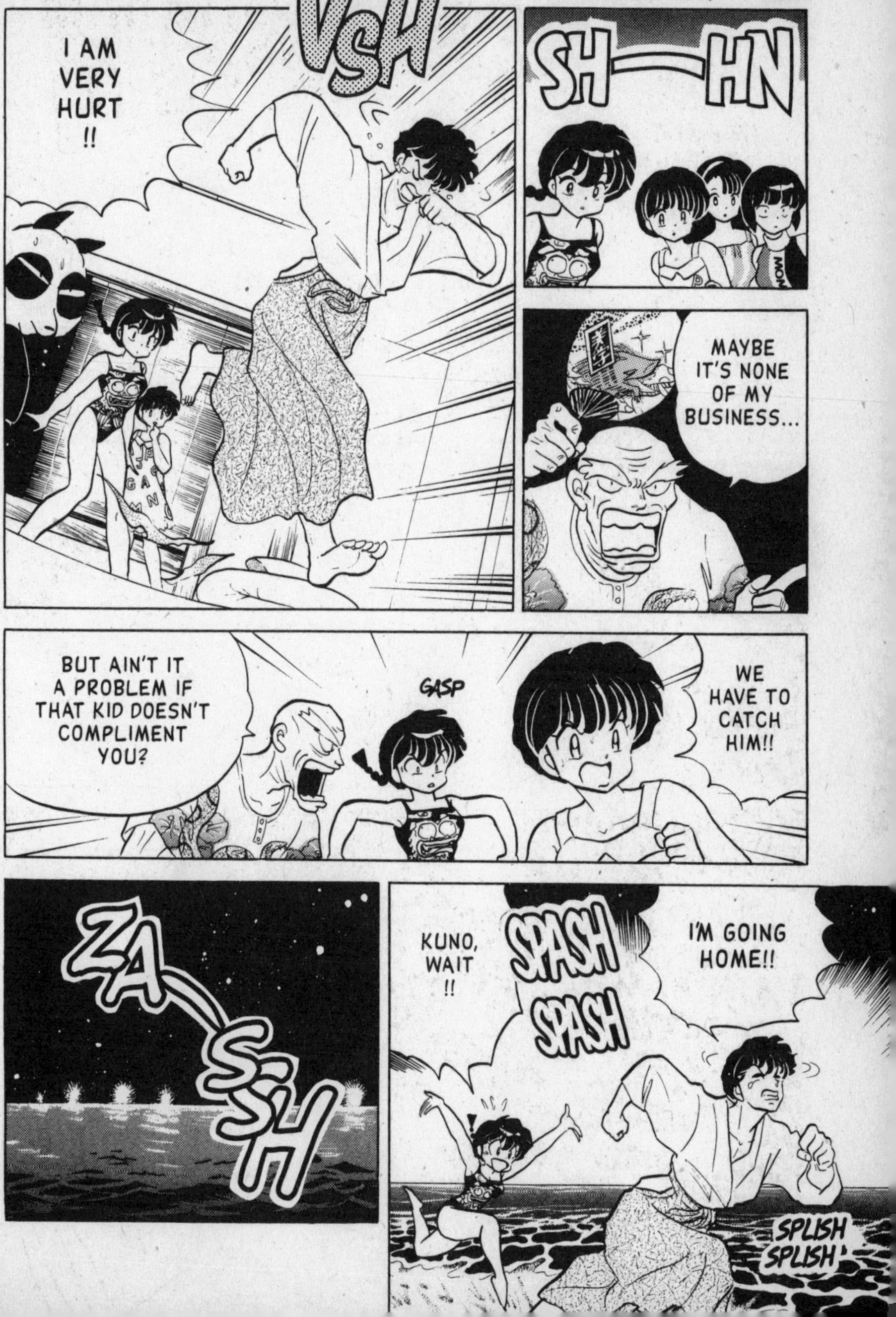
VSH
I AM VERY HURT !!
SH—HN
MAYBE IT'S NONE OF MY BUSINESS...
BUT AIN'T IT A PROBLEM IF THAT KID DOESN'T COMPLIMENT YOU?
GASP
WE HAVE TO CATCH HIM!!
ZA-S-S-H
KUNO, WAIT !!
SPASH SPASH
I'M GOING HOME!!
SPLISH SPLISH

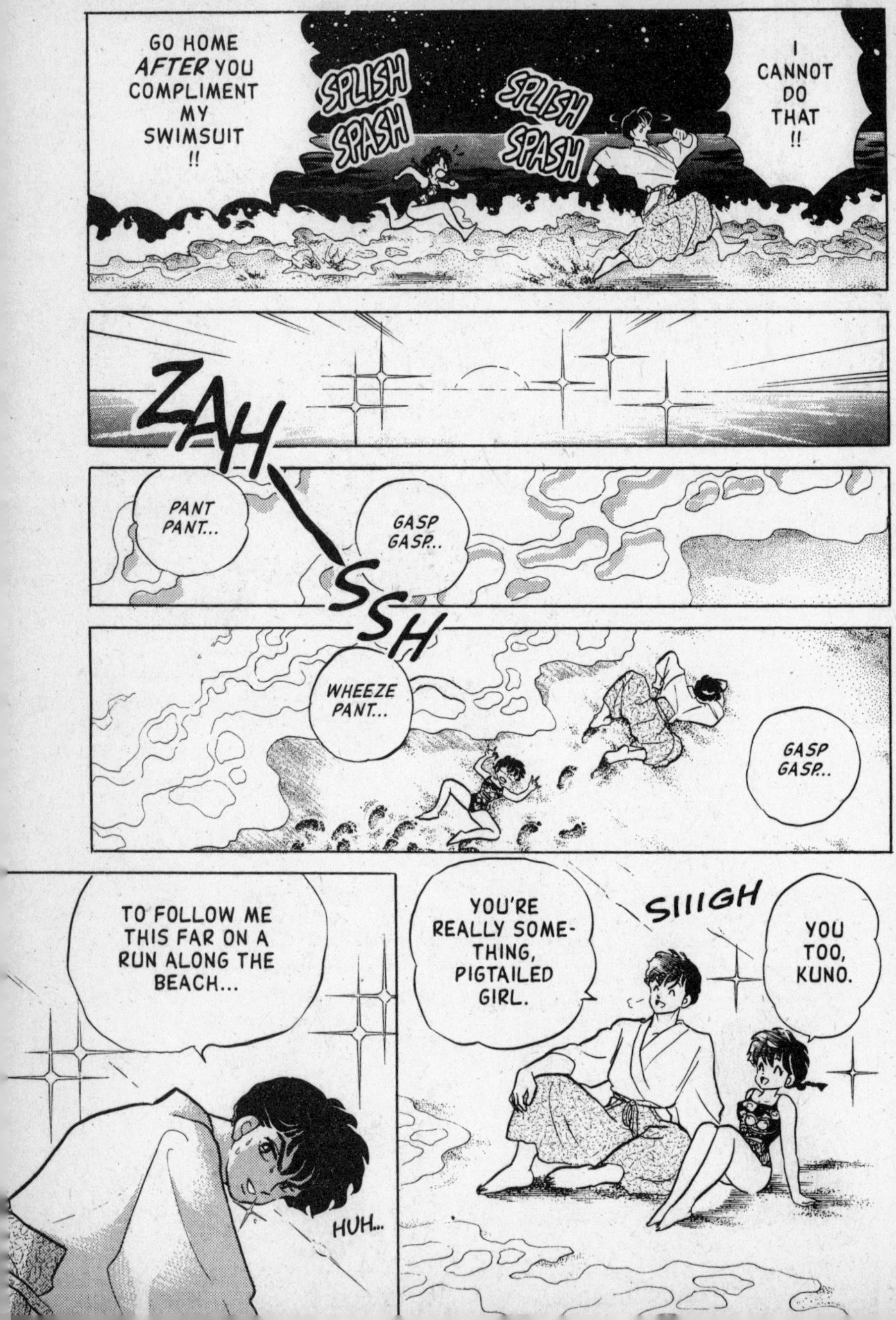
GO HOME *AFTER* YOU COMPLIMENT MY SWIMSUIT !!
SPLISH SPASH
SPLISH SPASH
I CANNOT DO THAT !!
ZAH
PANT PANT...
GASP GASP...
SSH
WHEEZE PANT...
GASP GASP...
TO FOLLOW ME THIS FAR ON A RUN ALONG THE BEACH...
HUH...
YOU'RE REALLY SOME-THING, PIGTAILED GIRL.
SIIIGH
YOU TOO, KUNO.

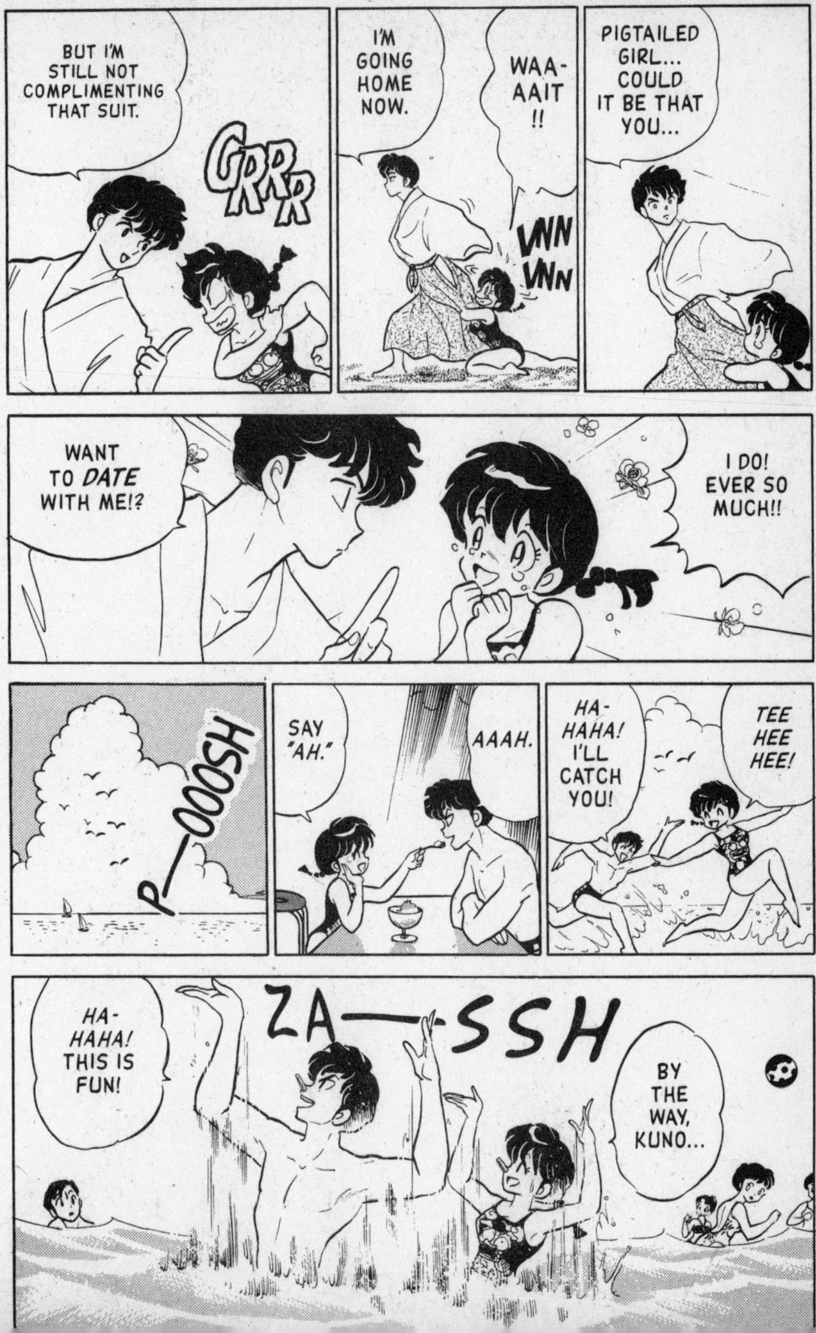

BUT I'M STILL NOT COMPLIMENTING THAT SUIT.
GRRR
I'M GOING HOME NOW.
WAA-AAIT !!
VNN VNN
PIGTAILED GIRL... COULD IT BE THAT YOU...
WANT TO DATE WITH ME!?
I DO! EVER SO MUCH!!
P—OOOSH
SAY "AH."
AAAH.
HA-HAHA! I'LL CATCH YOU!
TEE HEE HEE!
HA-HAHA! THIS IS FUN!
ZA—SSH
BY THE WAY, KUNO...

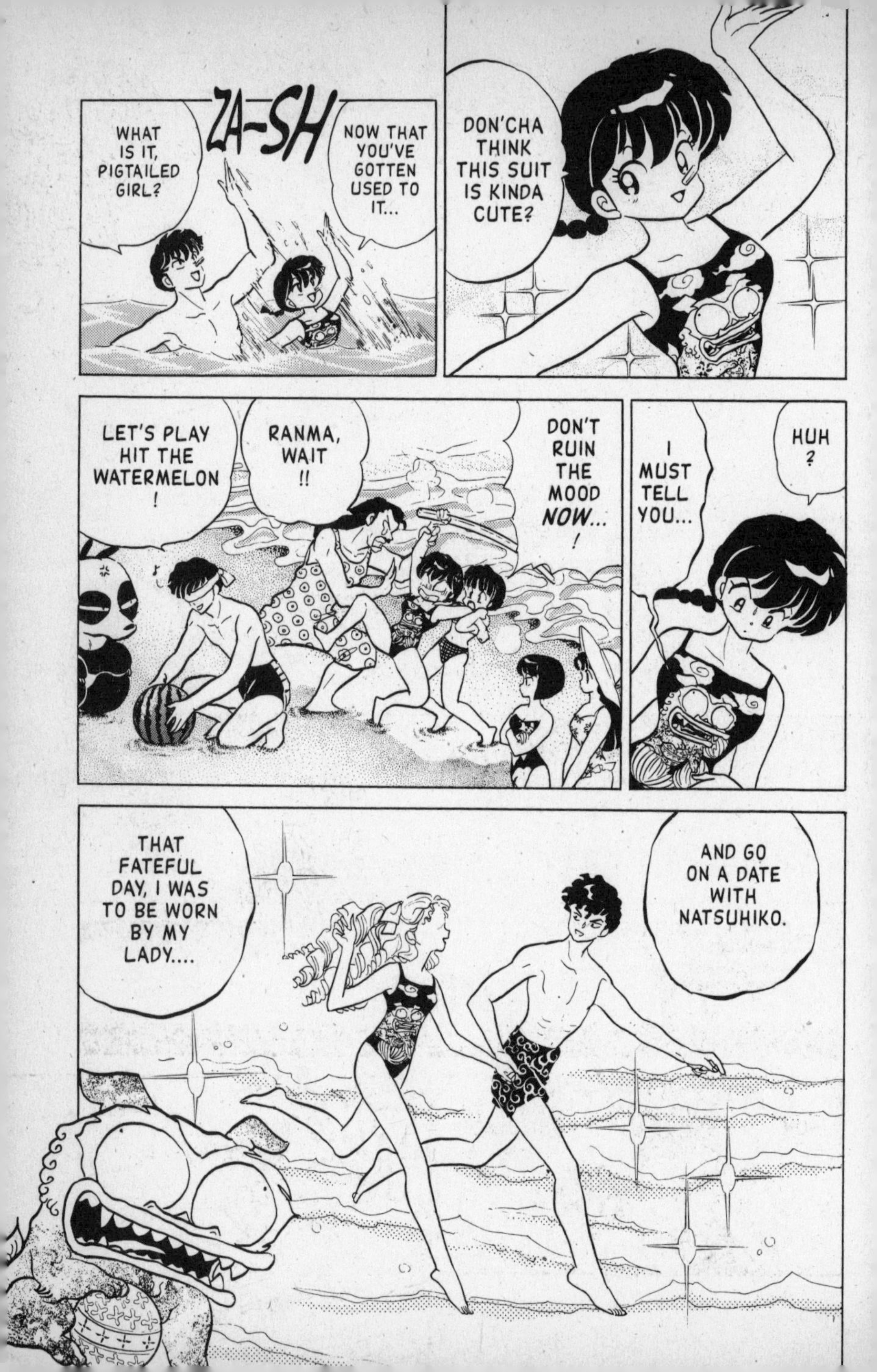
WHAT IS IT, PIGTAILED GIRL?
ZA-SH
NOW THAT YOU'VE GOTTEN USED TO IT...
DON'CHA THINK THIS SUIT IS KINDA CUTE?
LET'S PLAY HIT THE WATERMELON!
RANMA, WAIT!!
DON'T RUIN THE MOOD NOW...!
HUH?
I MUST TELL YOU...
THAT FATEFUL DAY, I WAS TO BE WORN BY MY LADY....
AND GO ON A DATE WITH NATSUHIKO.

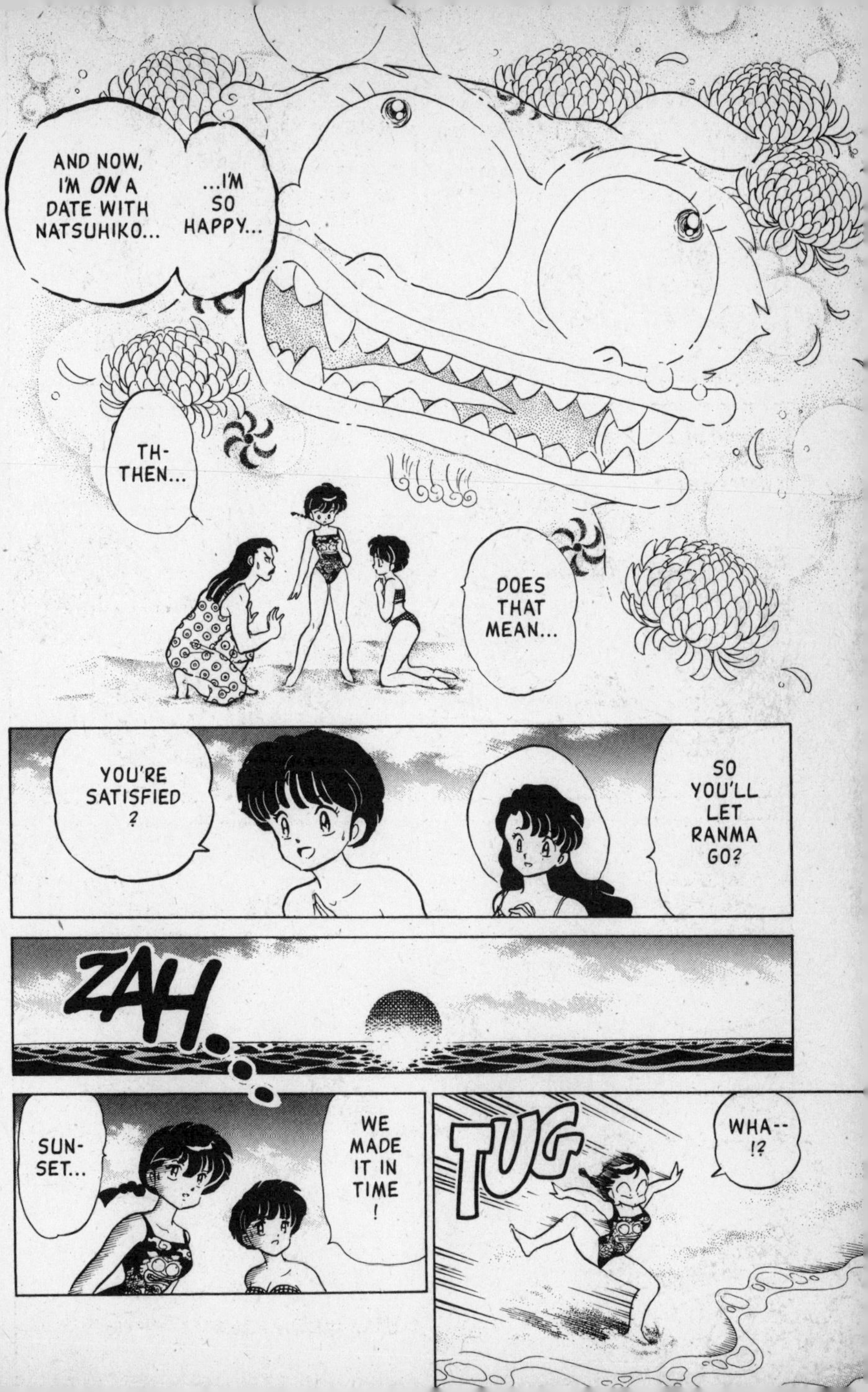
AND NOW, I'M *ON* A DATE WITH NATSUHIKO...
...I'M SO HAPPY...
TH- THEN...
DOES THAT MEAN...
YOU'RE SATISFIED ?
SO YOU'LL LET RANMA GO?
ZAH...
SUN- SET...
WE MADE IT IN TIME !
TUG
WHA-- !?

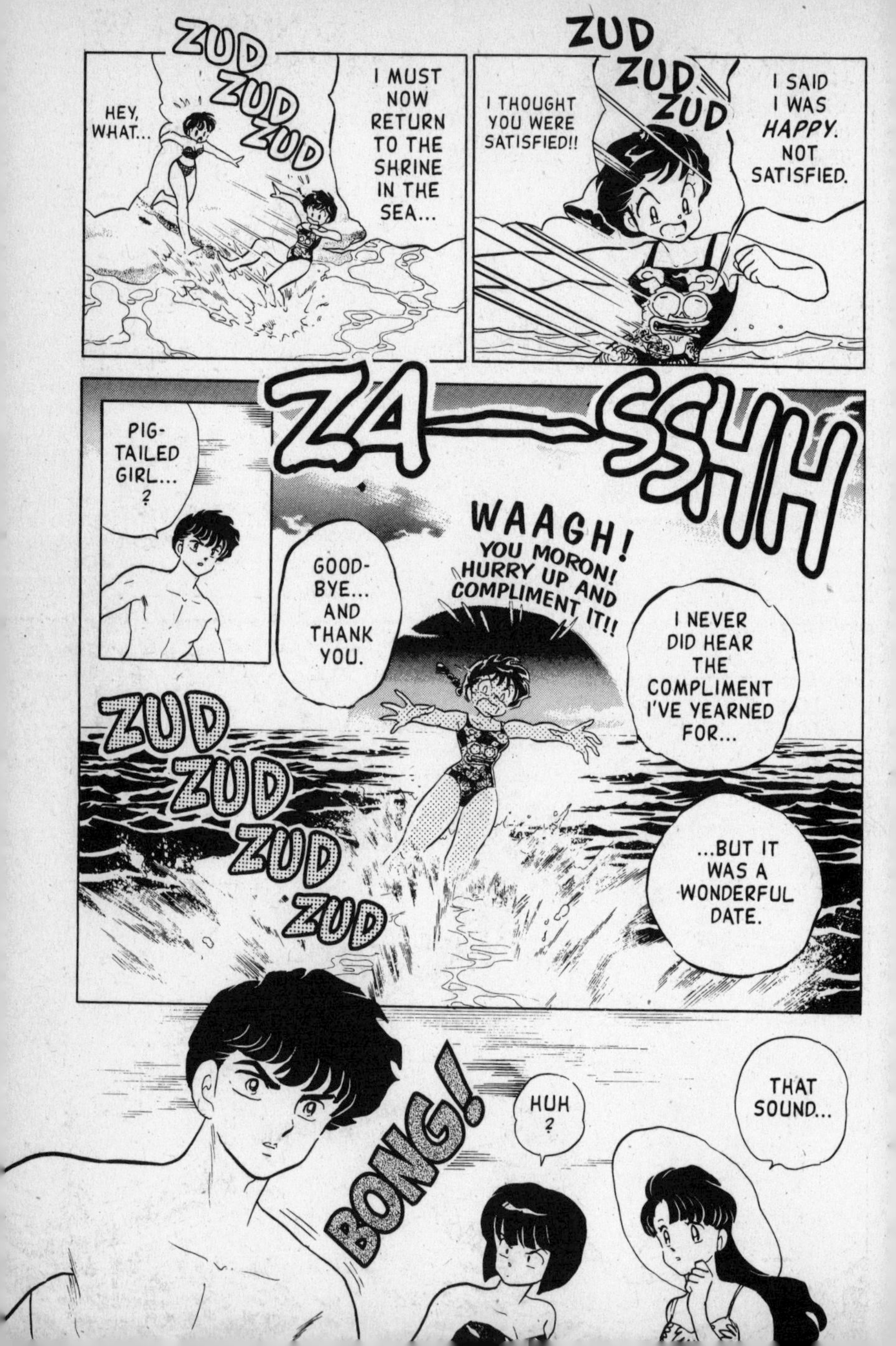
ZUD ZUD ZUD
HEY, WHAT...
I MUST NOW RETURN TO THE SHRINE IN THE SEA...
ZUD ZUD ZUD
I THOUGHT YOU WERE SATISFIED!!
I SAID I WAS *HAPPY*. NOT SATISFIED.
ZA—SSHH
PIG-TAILED GIRL...?
WAAGH! YOU MORON! HURRY UP AND COMPLIMENT IT!!
GOOD-BYE... AND THANK YOU.
I NEVER DID HEAR THE COMPLIMENT I'VE YEARNED FOR...
ZUD ZUD ZUD ZUD
...BUT IT WAS A WONDERFUL DATE.
BONG!
HUH?
THAT SOUND...

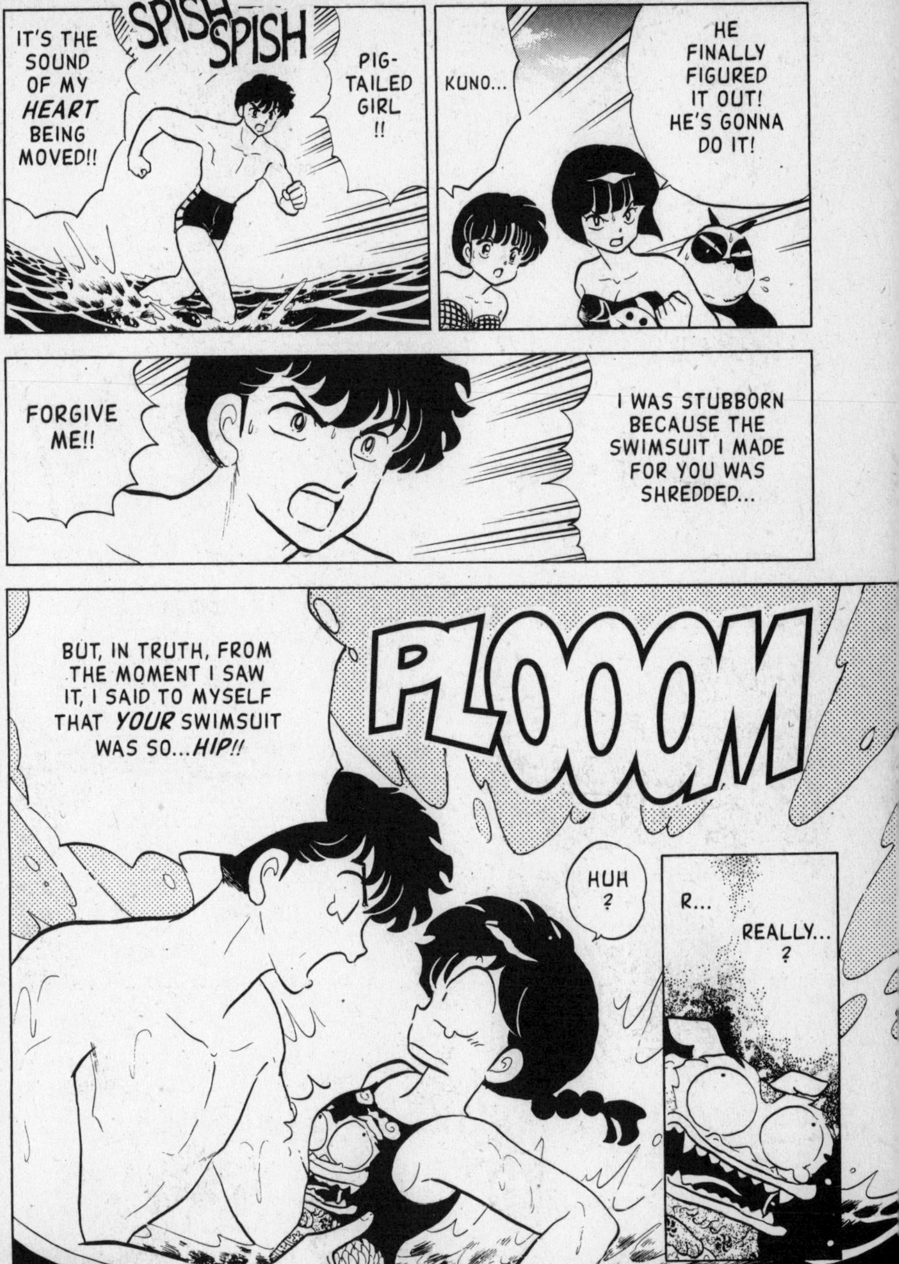
IT'S THE SOUND OF MY *HEART* BEING MOVED!!
SPISH SPISH
PIG-TAILED GIRL !!
KUNO...
HE FINALLY FIGURED IT OUT! HE'S GONNA DO IT!
FORGIVE ME!!
I WAS STUBBORN BECAUSE THE SWIMSUIT I MADE FOR YOU WAS SHREDDED...
BUT, IN TRUTH, FROM THE MOMENT I SAW IT, I SAID TO MYSELF THAT *YOUR* SWIMSUIT WAS SO...*HIP!!*
PLOOOM
HUH ?
R...
REALLY... ?

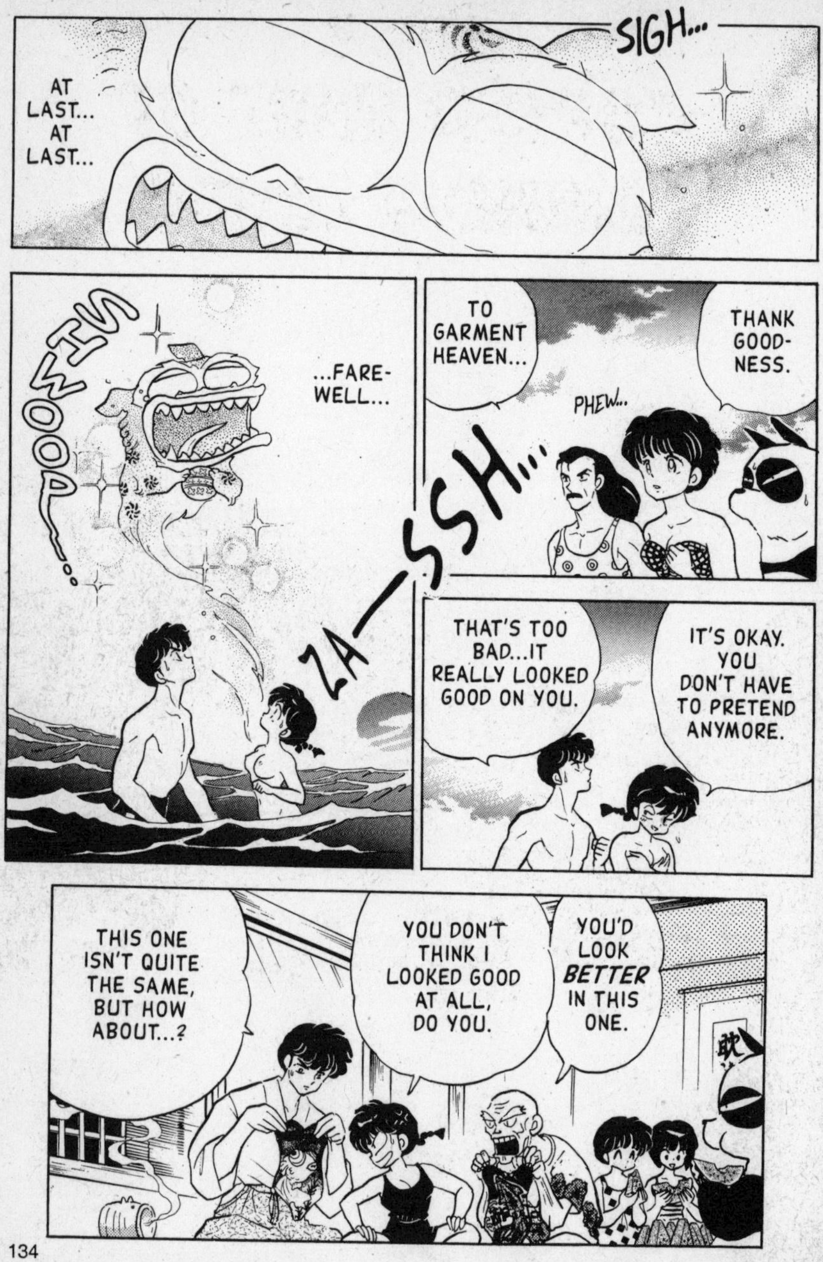
AT LAST... AT LAST...
SIGH...
SHWOOOP...
...FARE-WELL...
ZA—SSH...
TO GARMENT HEAVEN...
PHEW...
THANK GOOD-NESS.
THAT'S TOO BAD...IT REALLY LOOKED GOOD ON YOU.
IT'S OKAY. YOU DON'T HAVE TO PRETEND ANYMORE.
THIS ONE ISN'T QUITE THE SAME, BUT HOW ABOUT...?
YOU DON'T THINK I LOOKED GOOD AT ALL, DO YOU.
YOU'D LOOK *BETTER* IN THIS ONE.

Part 9

CURSÉD CAVE OF BROKEN LOVES

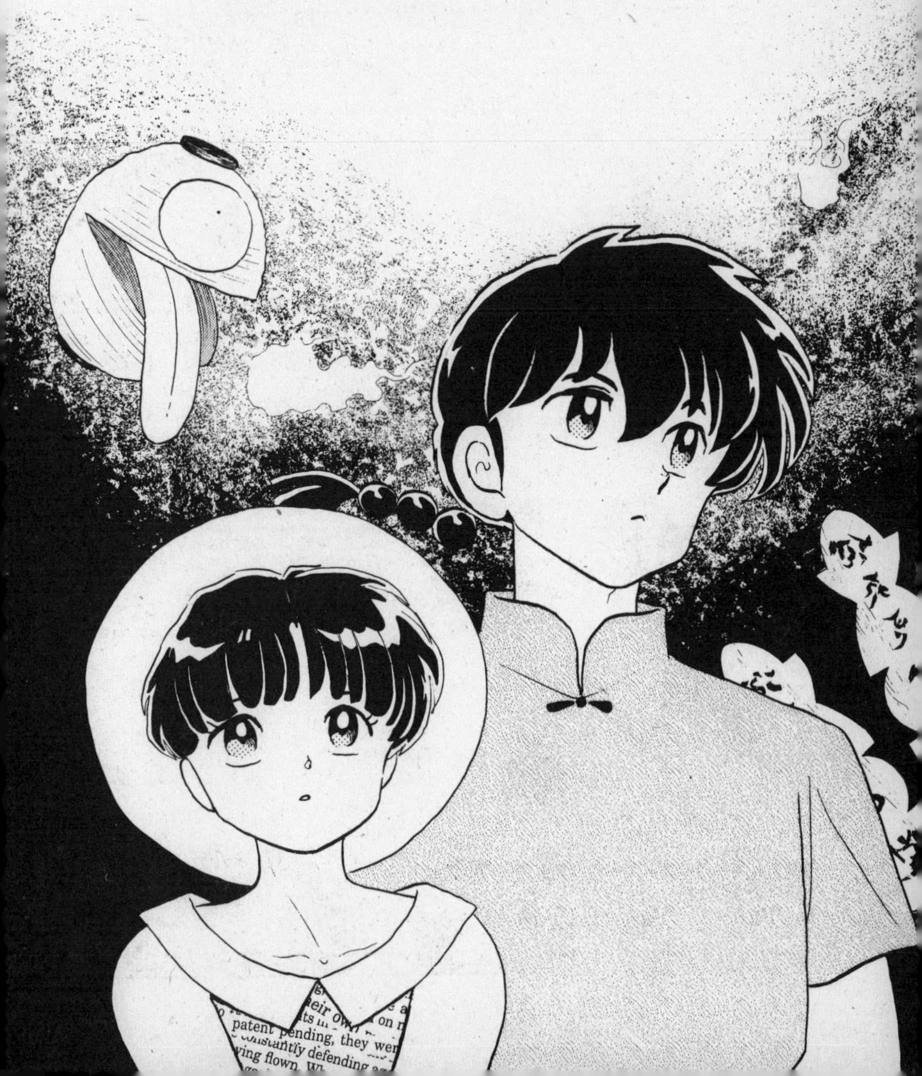

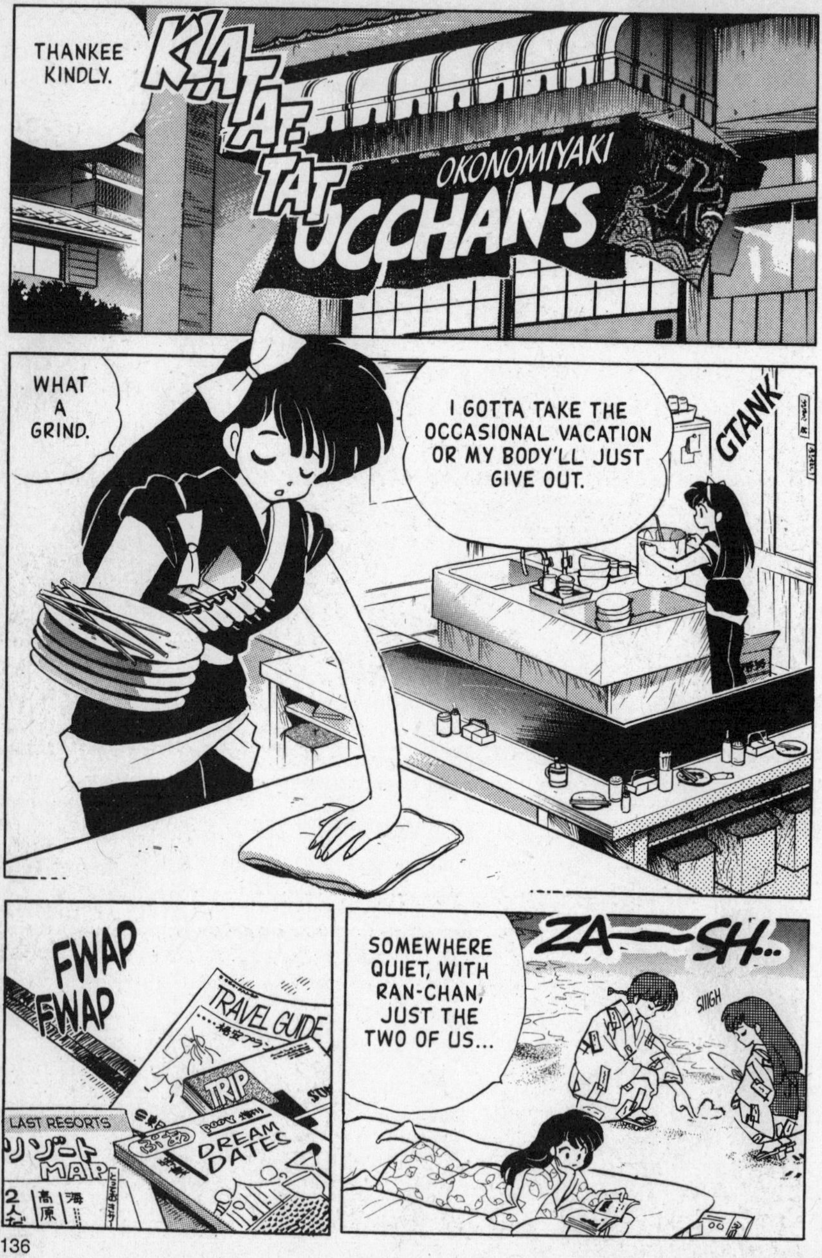
THANKEE KINDLY.
K'LATAT-TAT
OKONOMIYAKI
UCCHAN'S
WHAT A GRIND.
I GOTTA TAKE THE OCCASIONAL VACATION OR MY BODY'LL JUST GIVE OUT.
GTANK
FWAP FWAP
TRAVEL GUIDE
TRIP
LAST RESORTS
リゾート MAP
DREAM DATES
高原
海
ZA—SH..
SOMEWHERE QUIET, WITH RAN-CHAN, JUST THE TWO OF US...
SIIIGH

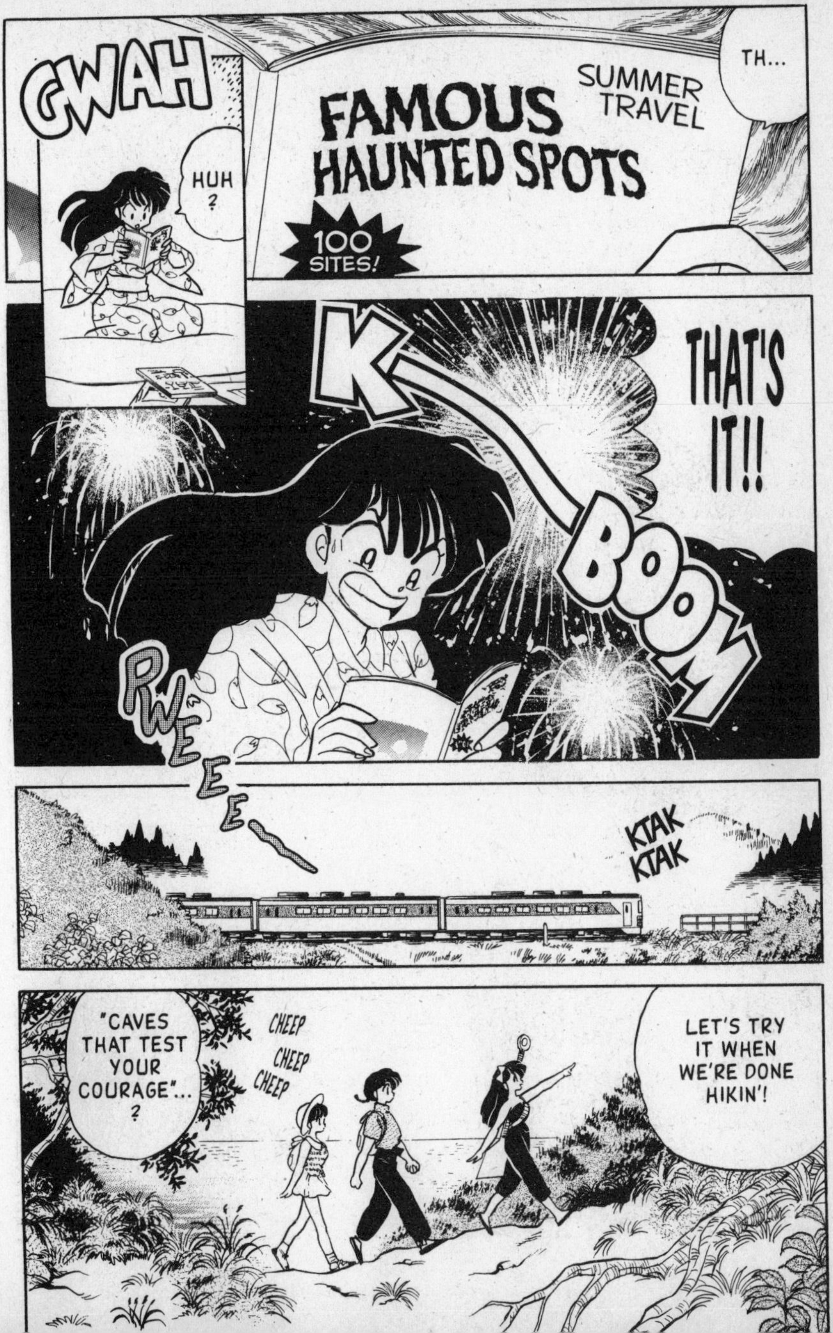
GWAH
HUH ?
FAMOUS HAUNTED SPOTS
SUMMER TRAVEL
100 SITES!
TH...
K
BOOM
THAT'S IT!!
PWEEEE
KTAK KTAK
"CAVES THAT TEST YOUR COURAGE"... ?
CHEEP CHEEP CHEEP
LET'S TRY IT WHEN WE'RE DONE HIKIN'!

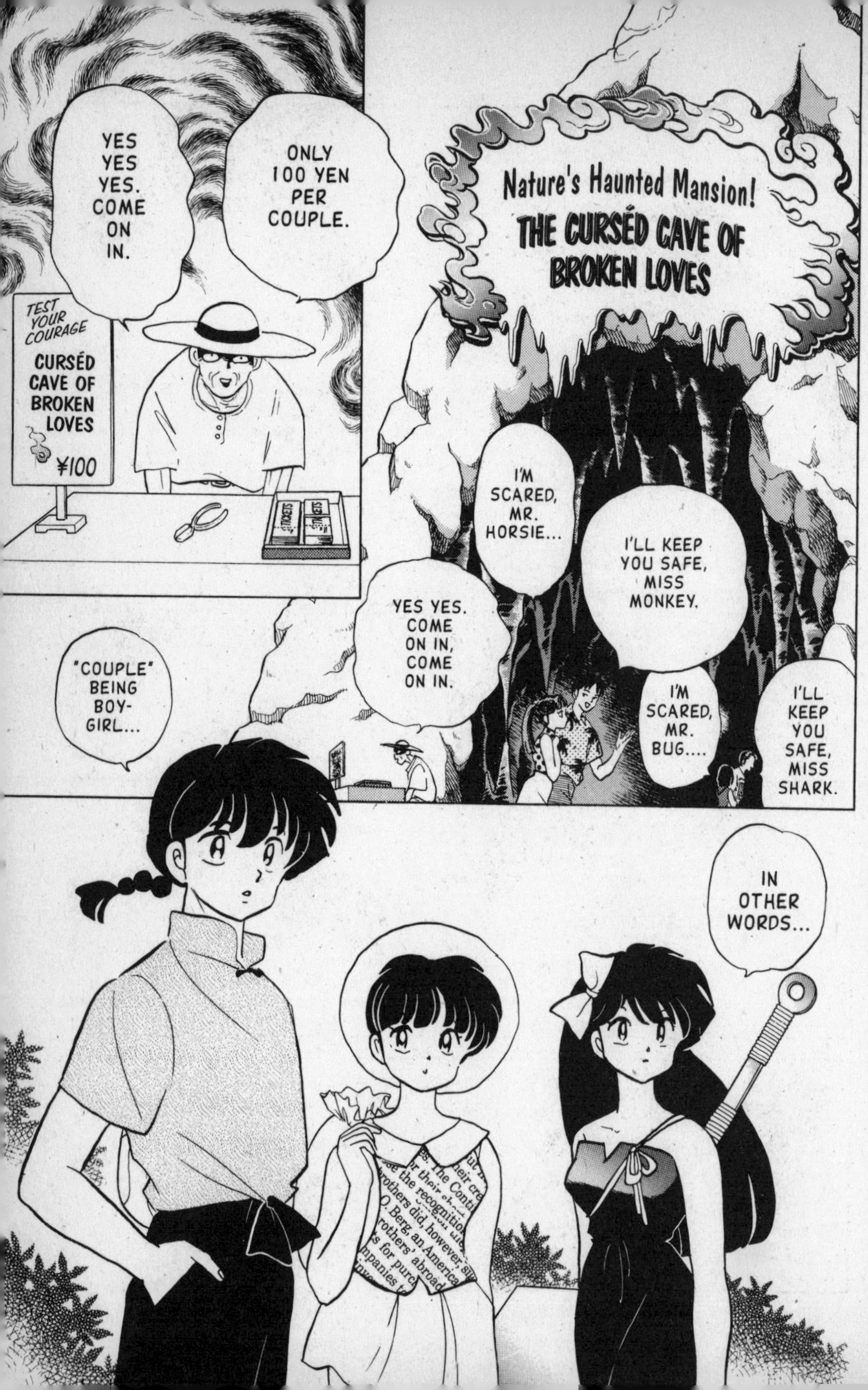
YES YES YES. COME ON IN.
ONLY 100 YEN PER COUPLE.
TEST YOUR COURAGE
CURSÉD CAVE OF BROKEN LOVES
¥100
TICKETS
Nature's Haunted Mansion!
THE CURSÉD CAVE OF BROKEN LOVES
I'M SCARED, MR. HORSIE...
I'LL KEEP YOU SAFE, MISS MONKEY.
"COUPLE" BEING BOY-GIRL...
YES YES. COME ON IN, COME ON IN.
I'M SCARED, MR. BUG....
I'LL KEEP YOU SAFE, MISS SHARK.
IN OTHER WORDS...

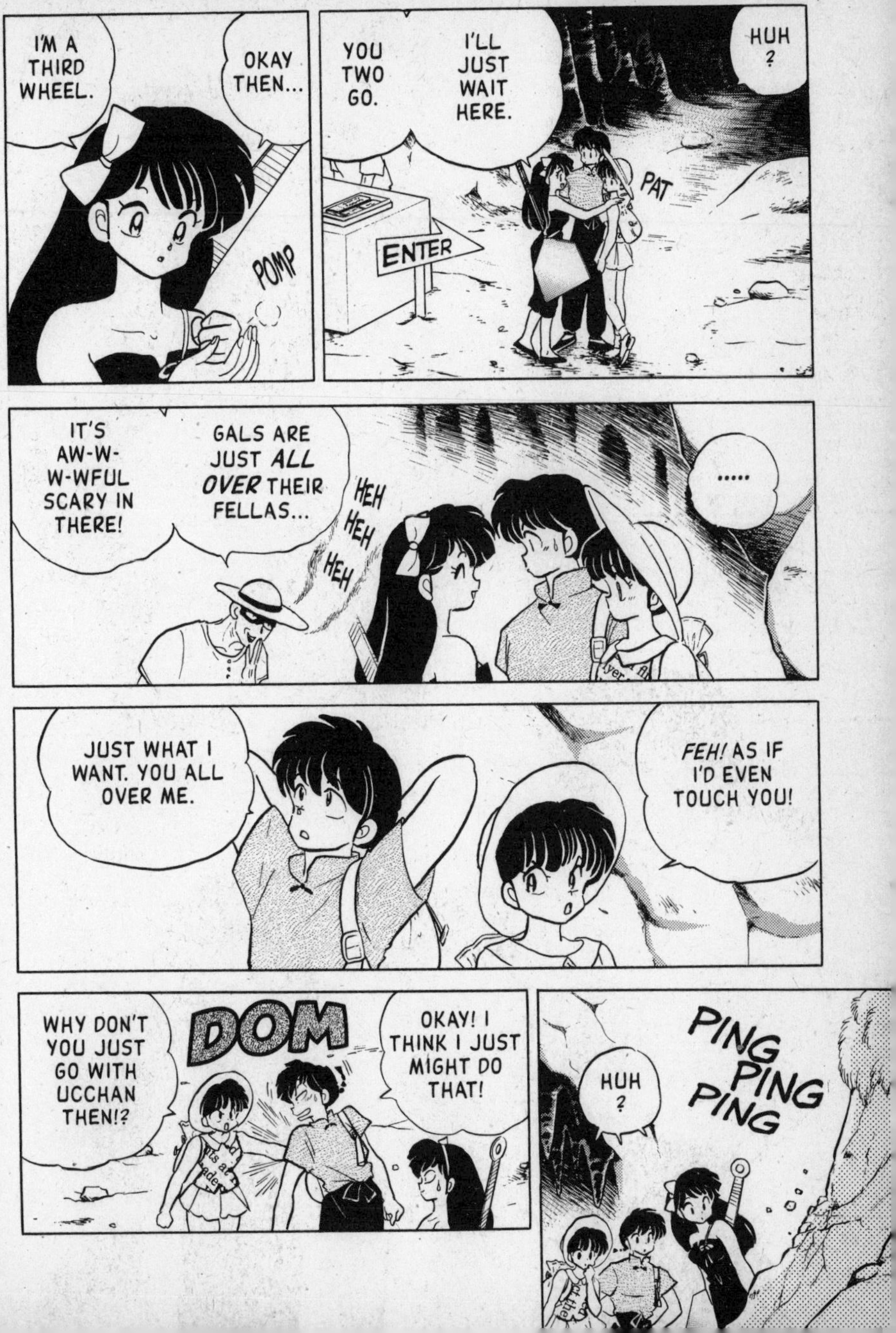
I'M A THIRD WHEEL.
OKAY THEN...
POMP
YOU TWO GO.
I'LL JUST WAIT HERE.
HUH?
ENTER
PAT
IT'S AW-W-W-WFUL SCARY IN THERE!
GALS ARE JUST *ALL OVER* THEIR FELLAS...
HEH HEH HEH
.....
JUST WHAT I WANT. YOU ALL OVER ME.
FEH! AS IF I'D EVEN TOUCH YOU!
WHY DON'T YOU JUST GO WITH UCCHAN THEN!?
DOM
OKAY! I THINK I JUST MIGHT DO THAT!
HUH?
PING PING PING

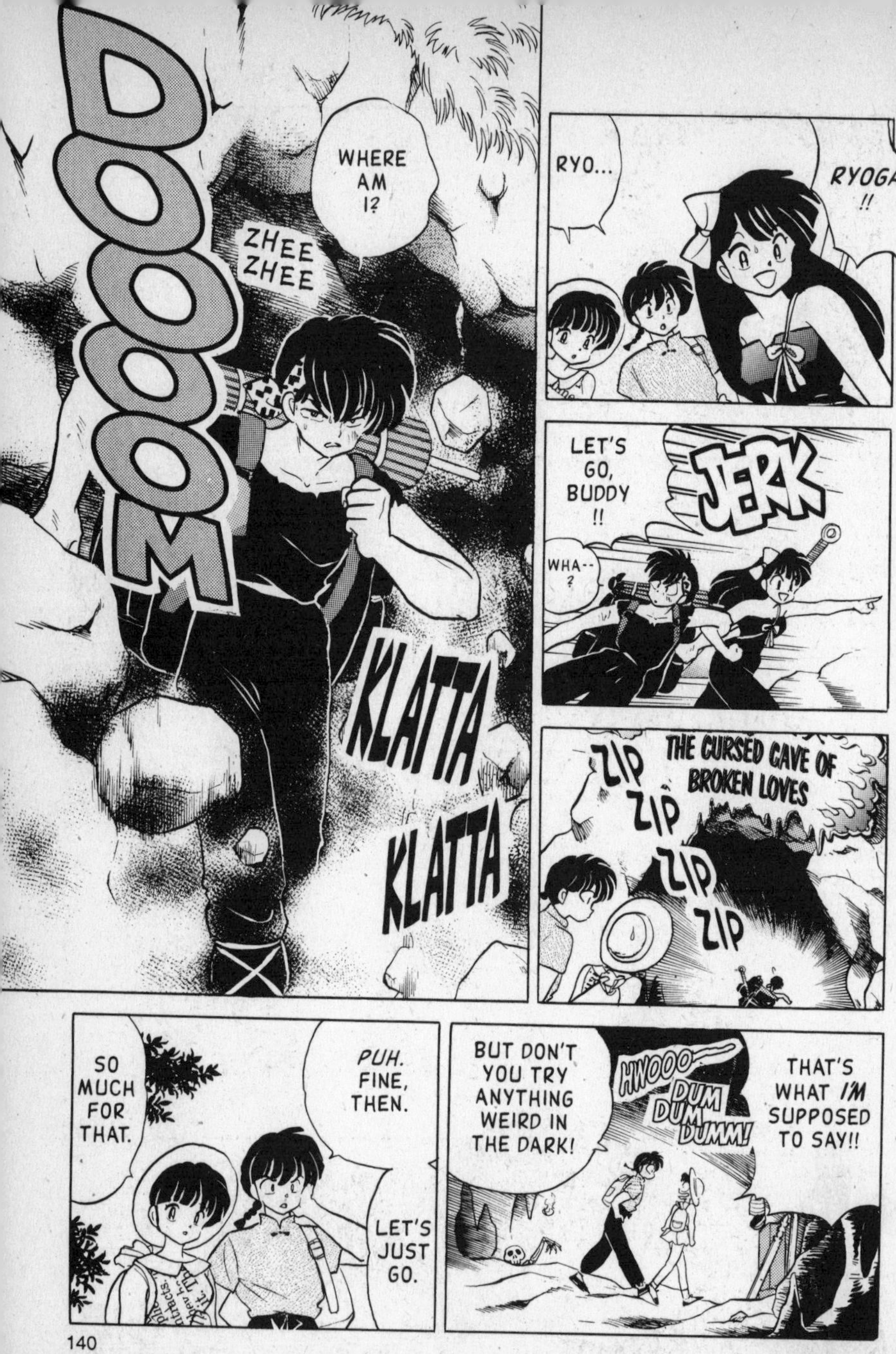
DOOOOOOM
WHERE AM I?
ZHEE ZHEE
KLATTA KLATTA
RYO...
RYOGA !!
LET'S GO, BUDDY !!
JERK
WHA-- ?
ZIP ZIP ZIP ZIP
THE CURSED CAVE OF BROKEN LOVES
SO MUCH FOR THAT.
PUH. FINE, THEN.
LET'S JUST GO.
BUT DON'T YOU TRY ANYTHING WEIRD IN THE DARK!
HWOOO
DUM DUM DUMM!
THAT'S WHAT I'M SUPPOSED TO SAY!!

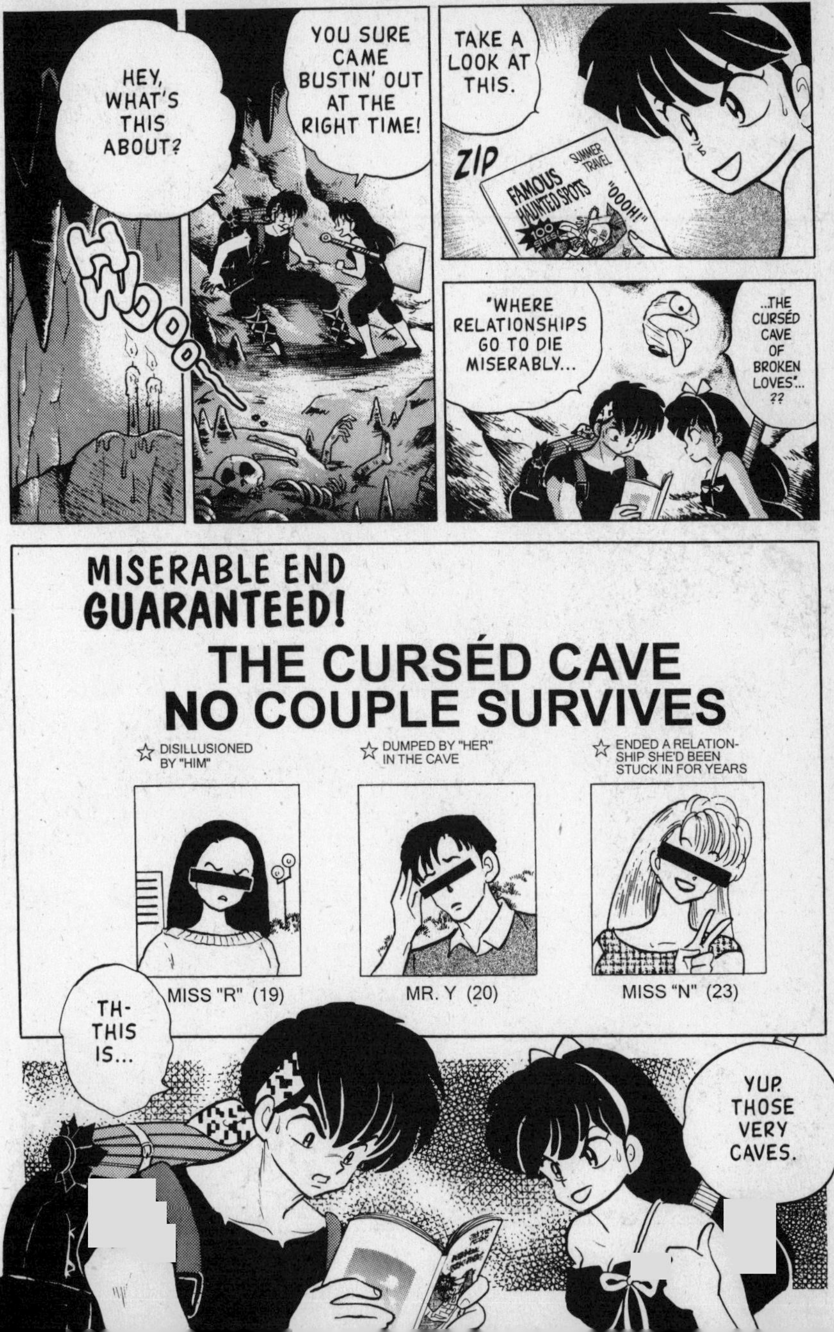
HEY, WHAT'S THIS ABOUT?
HWOOO—
YOU SURE CAME BUSTIN' OUT AT THE RIGHT TIME!
TAKE A LOOK AT THIS.
ZIP
SUMMER TRAVEL
FAMOUS HAUNTED SPOTS
100 SITES
"OOOH!"
"WHERE RELATIONSHIPS GO TO DIE MISERABLY...
...THE CURSÉD CAVE OF BROKEN LOVES"...??
MISERABLE END GUARANTEED!
THE CURSÉD CAVE NO COUPLE SURVIVES
☆ DISILLUSIONED BY "HIM"
☆ DUMPED BY "HER" IN THE CAVE
☆ ENDED A RELATIONSHIP SHE'D BEEN STUCK IN FOR YEARS
MISS "R" (19)
MR. Y (20)
MISS "N" (23)
TH-THIS IS...
YUP. THOSE VERY CAVES.

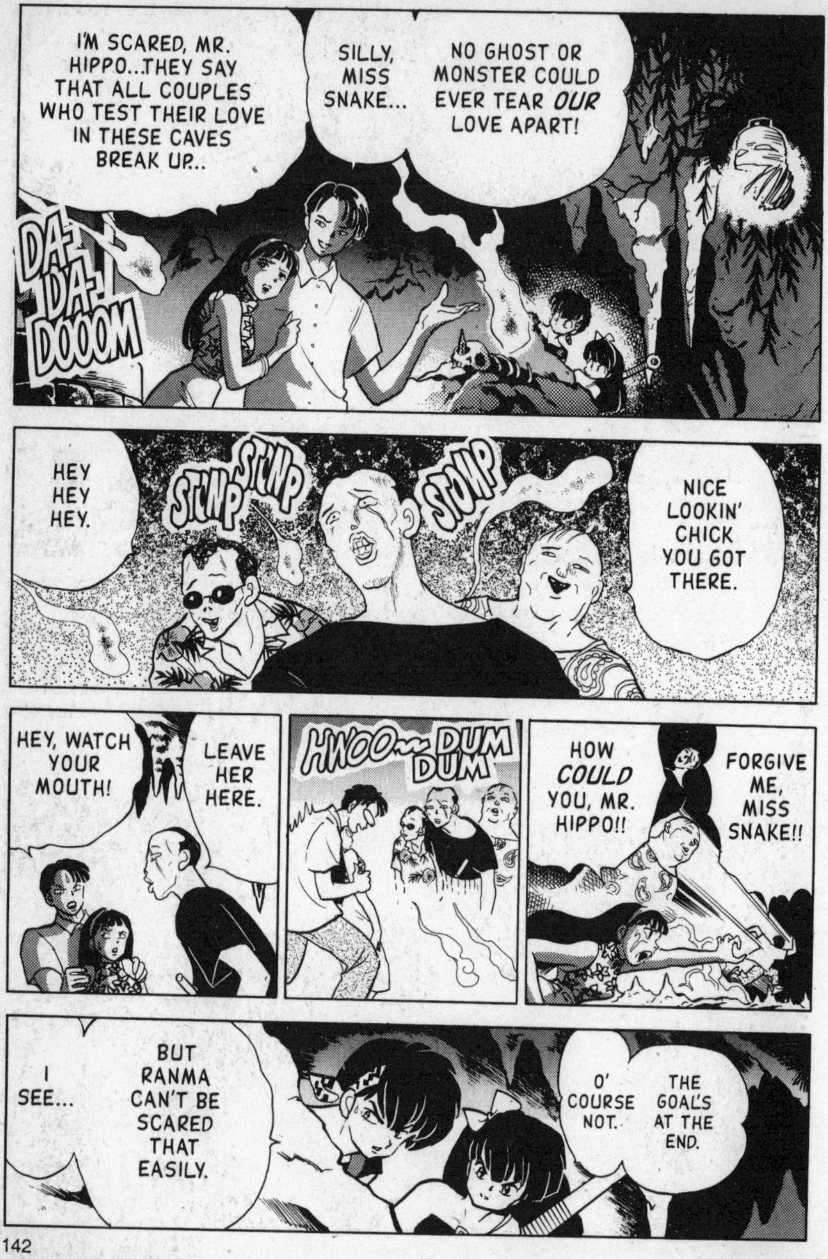
I'M SCARED, MR. HIPPO...THEY SAY THAT ALL COUPLES WHO TEST THEIR LOVE IN THESE CAVES BREAK UP..
SILLY, MISS SNAKE...
NO GHOST OR MONSTER COULD EVER TEAR *OUR* LOVE APART!
DA-DA-DOOOM
HEY HEY HEY.
STOMP
STOMP
STOMP
NICE LOOKIN' CHICK YOU GOT THERE.
HEY, WATCH YOUR MOUTH!
LEAVE HER HERE.
HWOO~ DUM DUM
HOW *COULD* YOU, MR. HIPPO!!
FORGIVE ME, MISS SNAKE!!
I SEE...
BUT RANMA CAN'T BE SCARED THAT EASILY.
O' COURSE NOT.
THE GOAL'S AT THE END.

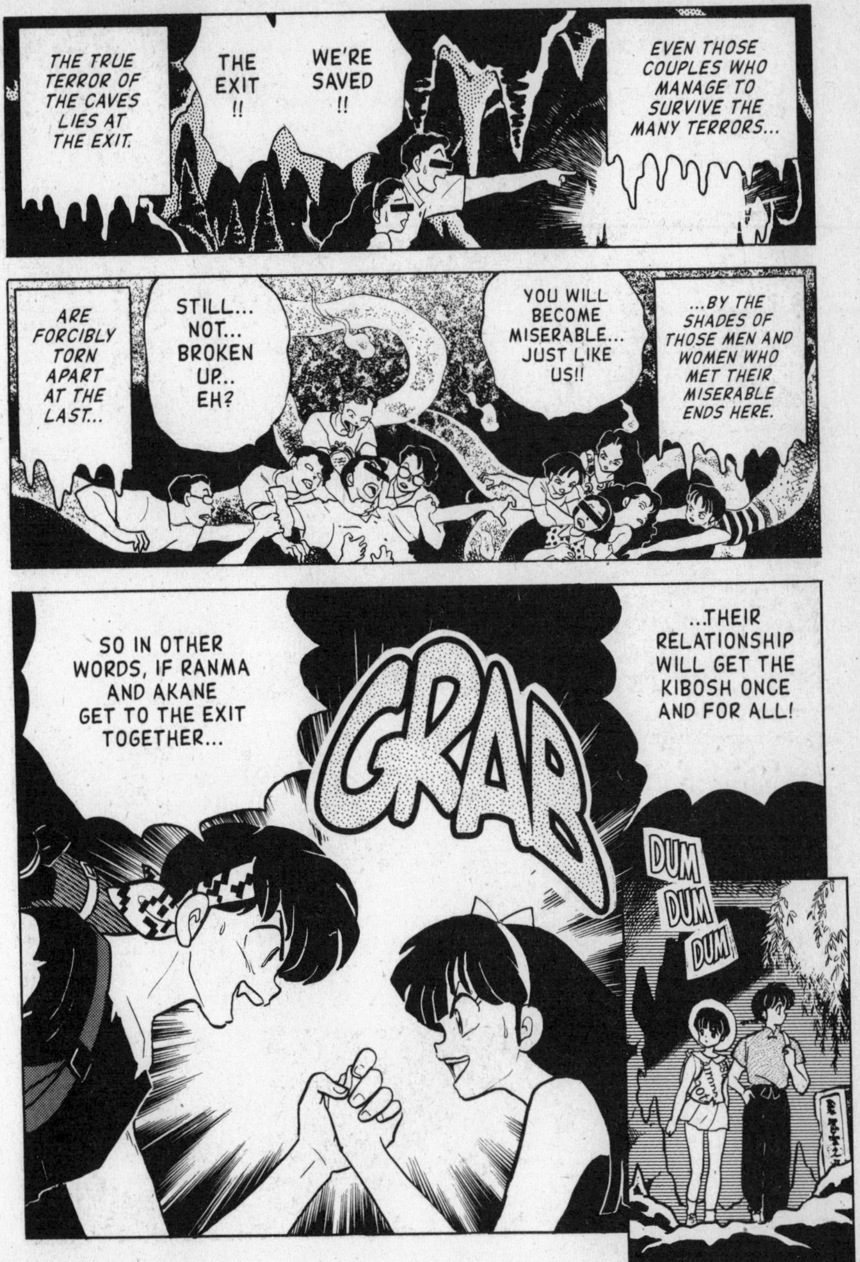
THE TRUE TERROR OF THE CAVES LIES AT THE EXIT.
THE EXIT !!
WE'RE SAVED !!
EVEN THOSE COUPLES WHO MANAGE TO SURVIVE THE MANY TERRORS...
ARE FORCIBLY TORN APART AT THE LAST...
STILL... NOT... BROKEN UP... EH?
YOU WILL BECOME MISERABLE... JUST LIKE US!!
...BY THE SHADES OF THOSE MEN AND WOMEN WHO MET THEIR MISERABLE ENDS HERE.
SO IN OTHER WORDS, IF RANMA AND AKANE GET TO THE EXIT TOGETHER...
GRAB
...THEIR RELATIONSHIP WILL GET THE KIBOSH ONCE AND FOR ALL!
DUM
DUM
DUM

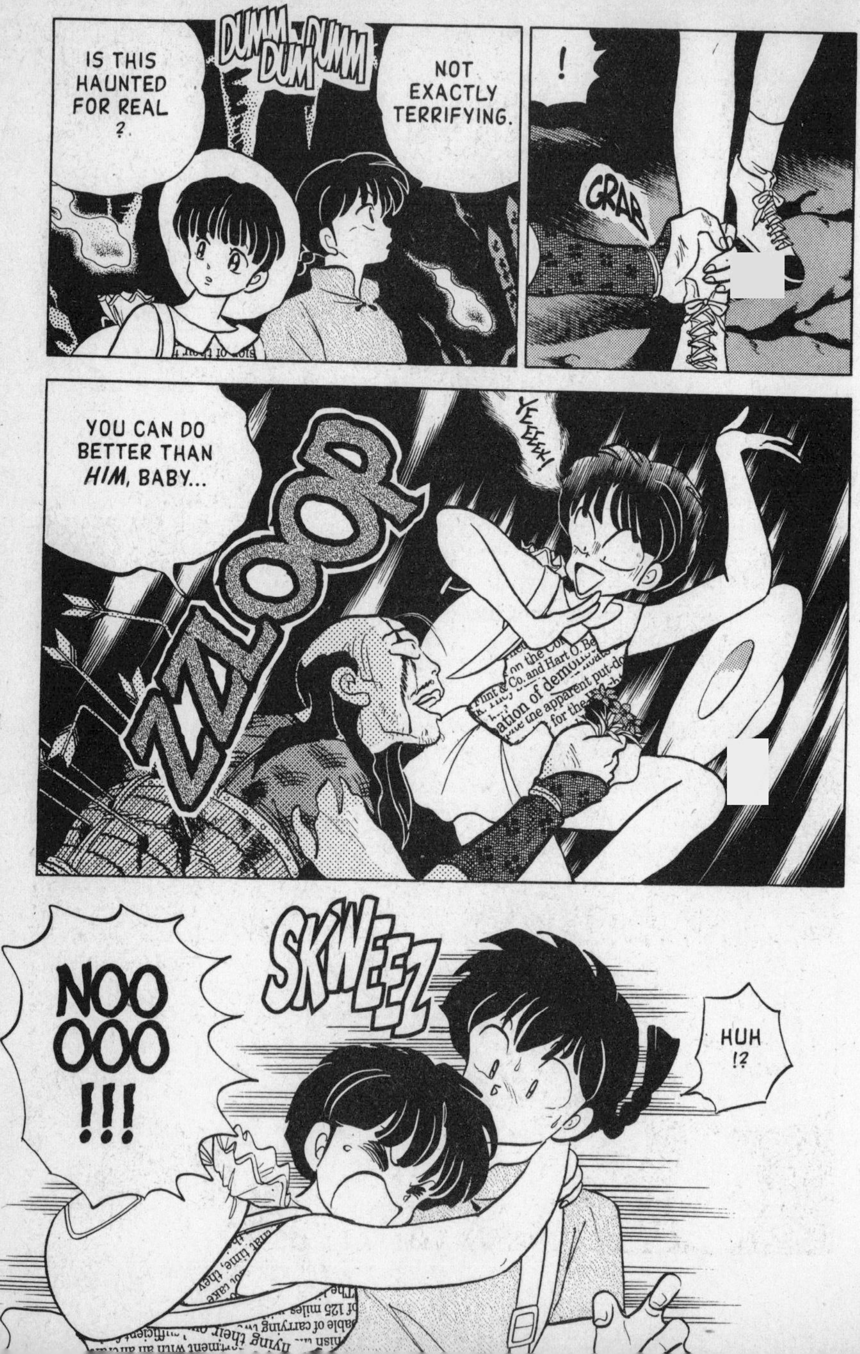
IS THIS HAUNTED FOR REAL ?
DUMM DUMM DUMM
NOT EXACTLY TERRIFYING.
!
GRAB
YOU CAN DO BETTER THAN *HIM*, BABY...
ZLOOP
NOO OOO !!!
SKWEEZ
HUH !?

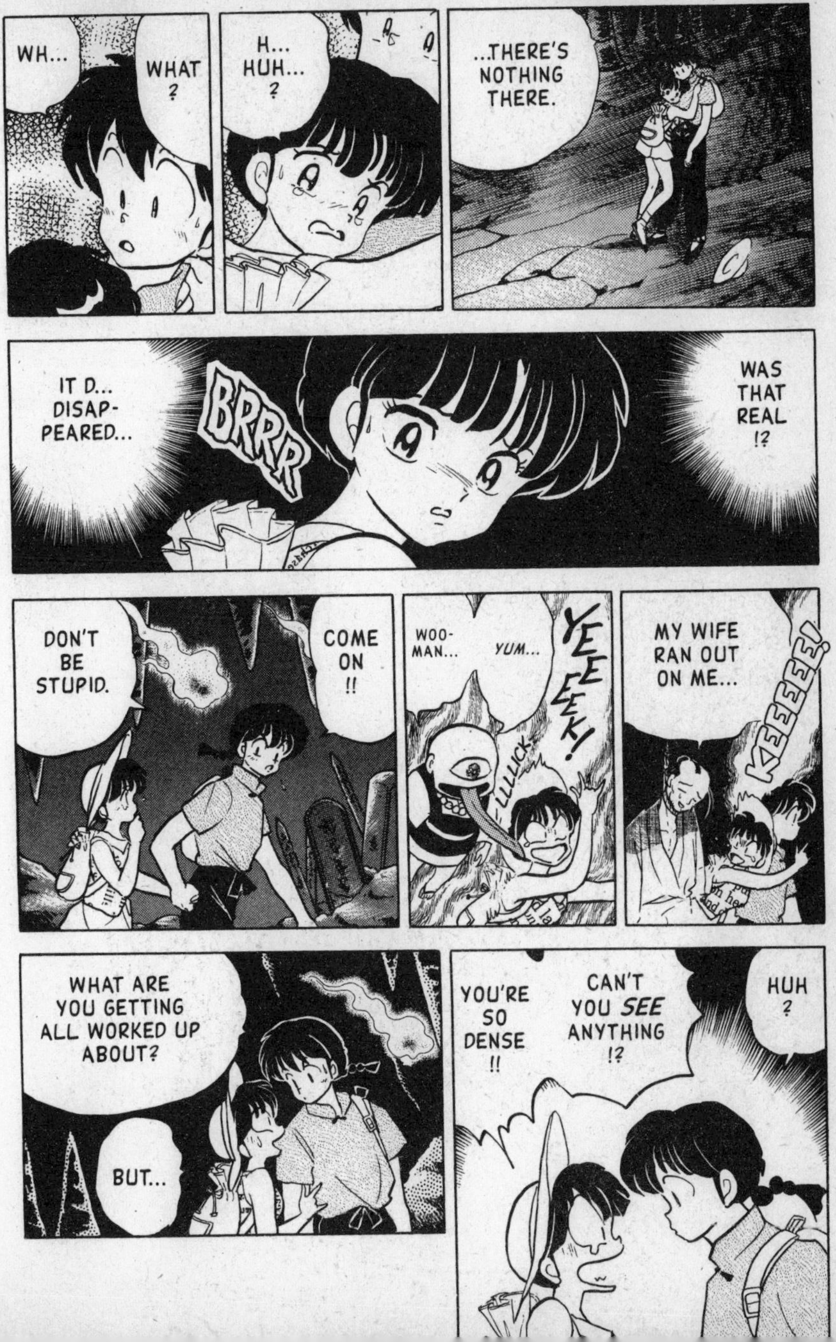
WH...
WHAT?
H... HUH...?
...THERE'S NOTHING THERE.
IT D... DISAP-PEARED...
BRRR
WAS THAT REAL!?
DON'T BE STUPID.
COME ON!!
WOO-MAN...
YUM...
LLLLICK
YEEEEK!
MY WIFE RAN OUT ON ME...
KEEEEEE!
WHAT ARE YOU GETTING ALL WORKED UP ABOUT?
BUT...
YOU'RE SO DENSE!!
CAN'T YOU *SEE* ANYTHING!?
HUH?

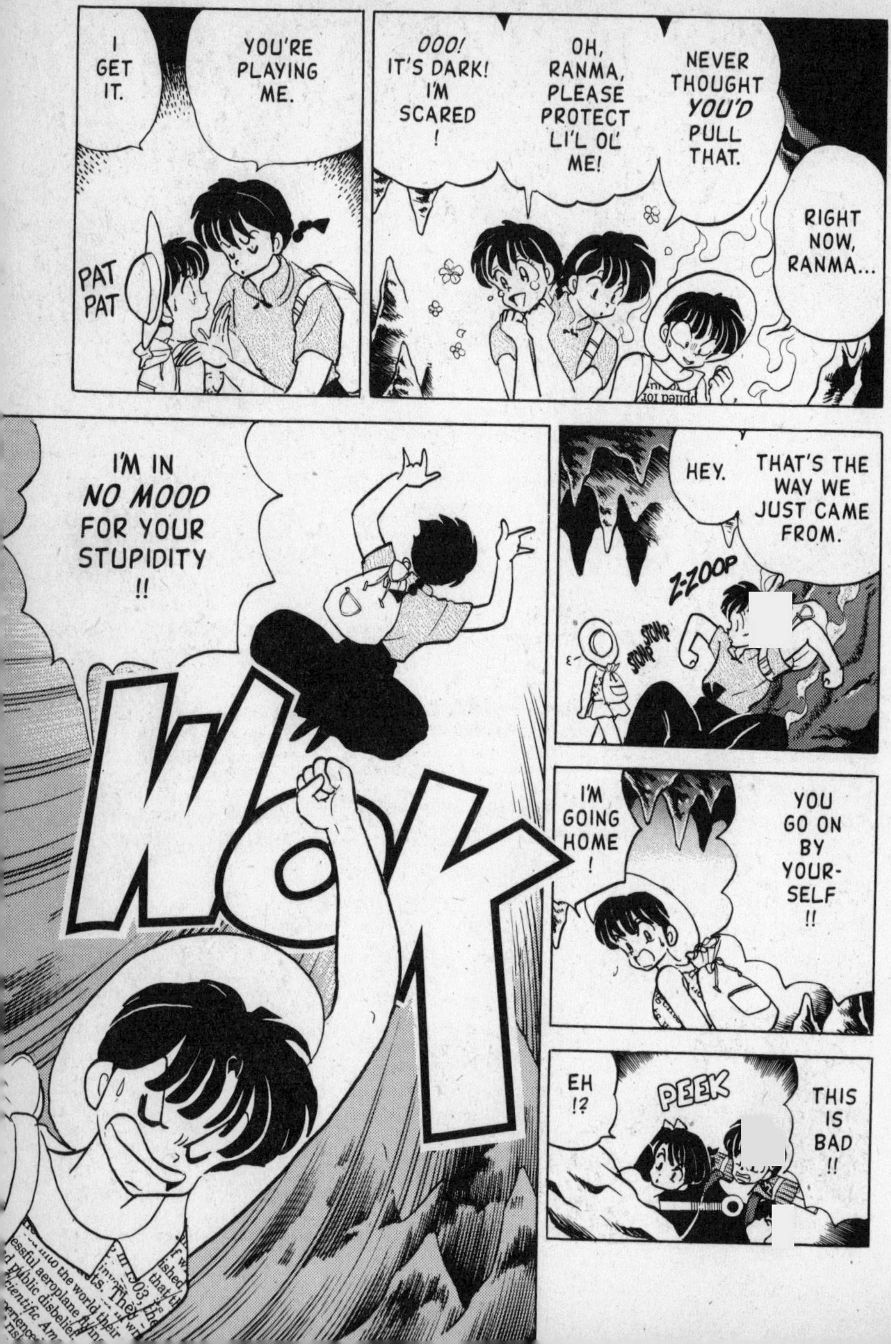
I GET IT.
YOU'RE PLAYING ME.
PAT PAT
OOO! IT'S DARK! I'M SCARED!
OH, RANMA, PLEASE PROTECT LI'L OL' ME!
NEVER THOUGHT YOU'D PULL THAT.
RIGHT NOW, RANMA...
I'M IN NO MOOD FOR YOUR STUPIDITY!!
WOK
HEY.
THAT'S THE WAY WE JUST CAME FROM.
Z-ZOOP
STOMP STOMP
I'M GOING HOME!
YOU GO ON BY YOURSELF!!
EH!?
PEEK
THIS IS BAD!!

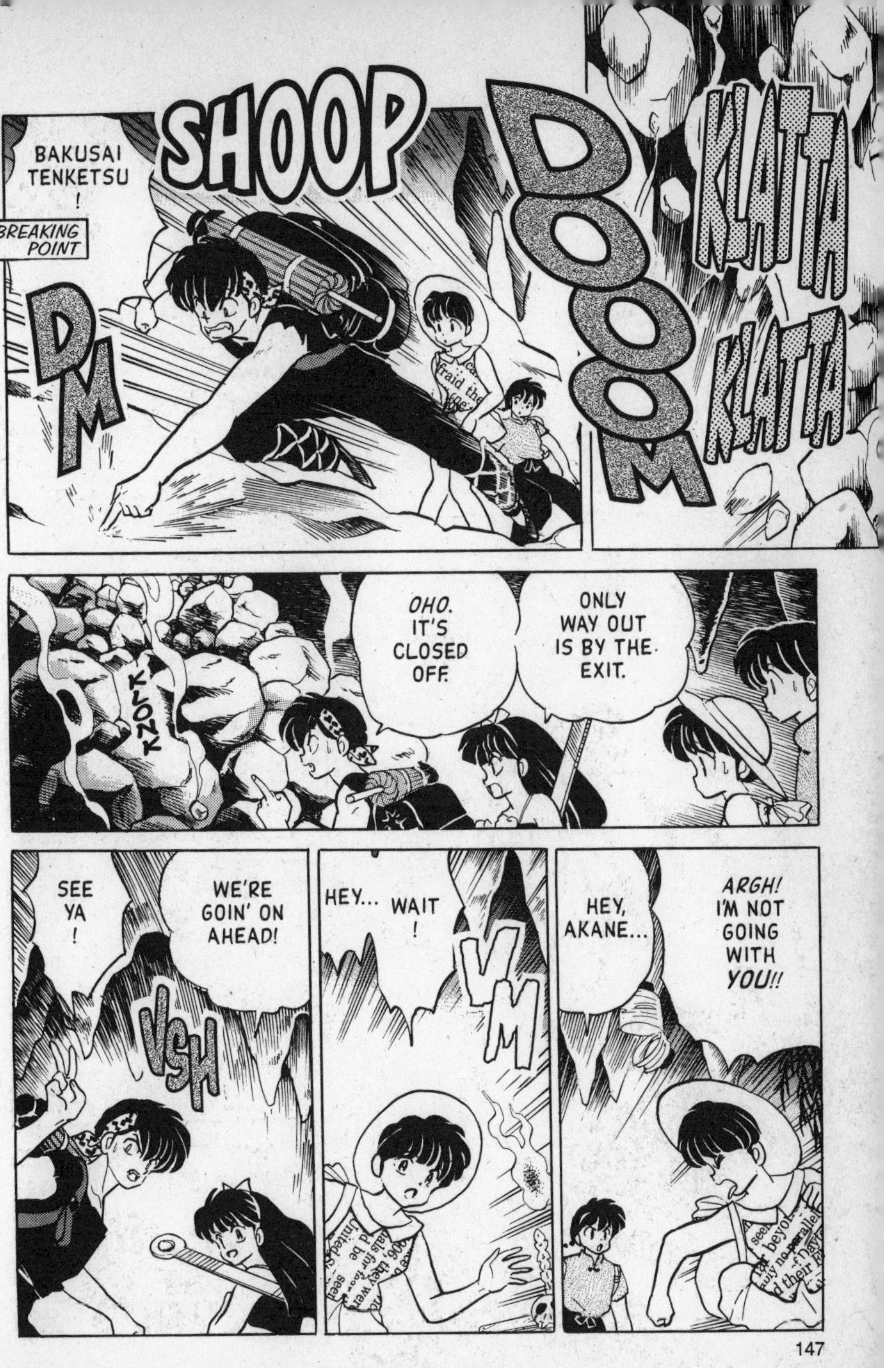
BAKUSAI TENKETSU !
BREAKING POINT
SHOOP
DM
DOOOM
KLATTA
KLATTA
KLONK
OHO. IT'S CLOSED OFF.
ONLY WAY OUT IS BY THE EXIT.
SEE YA !
WE'RE GOIN' ON AHEAD!
VSH
HEY...
WAIT !
VM
HEY, AKANE...
ARGH! I'M NOT GOING WITH YOU!!

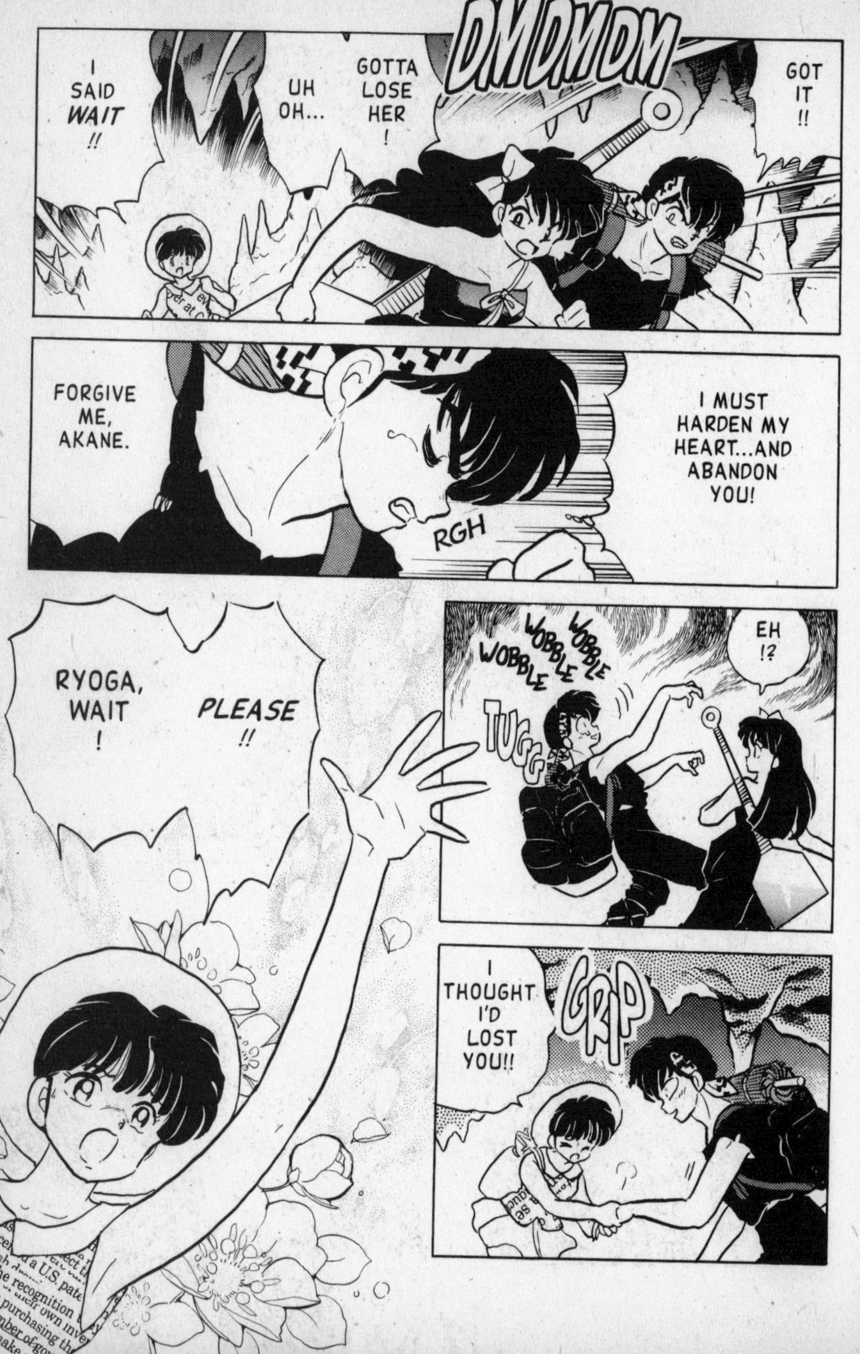
I SAID *WAIT* !!
UH OH...
GOTTA LOSE HER !
DMDMDM
GOT IT !!
FORGIVE ME, AKANE.
RGH
I MUST HARDEN MY HEART...AND ABANDON YOU!
RYOGA, WAIT !
PLEASE !!
WOBBLE WOBBLE
WOBBLE
TUGG
EH !?
I THOUGHT I'D LOST YOU!!
GRIP

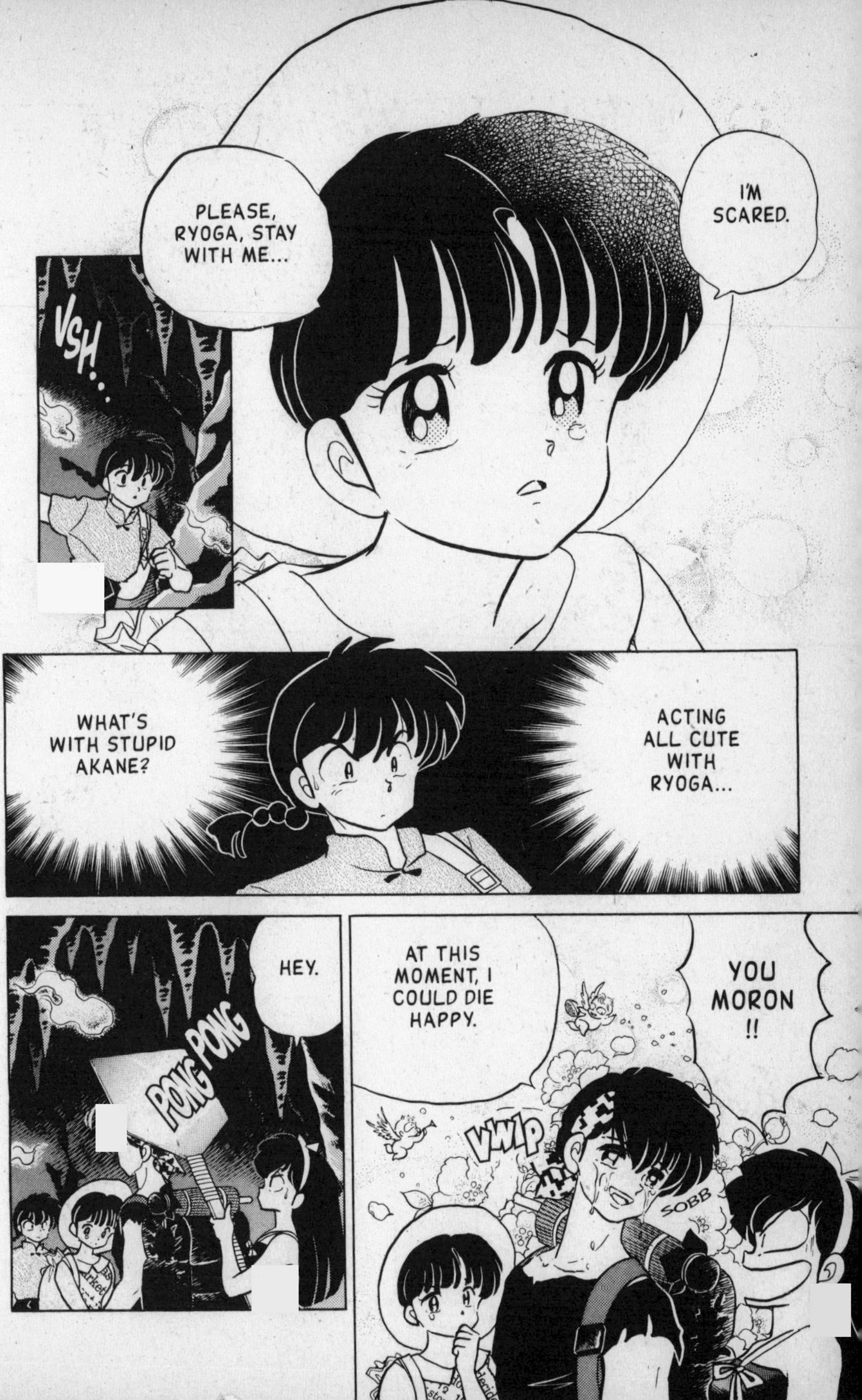
VSH...
PLEASE, RYOGA, STAY WITH ME...
I'M SCARED.
WHAT'S WITH STUPID AKANE?
ACTING ALL CUTE WITH RYOGA...
HEY.
PONG PONG
AT THIS MOMENT, I COULD DIE HAPPY.
YOU MORON !!
VWIP
SOBB

HUH, THIS IS STUPID.

LET'S GO, UCCHAN.

W-WAIT A SECOND, RAN-CHAN....

MOOSH!!

JERK

YOU. C'MERE.

YOU'RE NOT THINKING OF GOING THROUGH THE CURSED EXIT WITH AKANE?!

AUGH!!

THAT WOULD BE BAD!!

BETTER HURRY AND GET RAN-CHAN AND AKANE BACK ON GOOD TERMS...

ZIP ZIP ZIP

GRIP

NG!

OHH...

IF I COULD EXTEND THIS HAPPINESS EVEN A MOMENT LONGER...

BREAK UP~~~

BREAK UP-P-P-P-P~~~

Part 10

EXIT OF MISERY

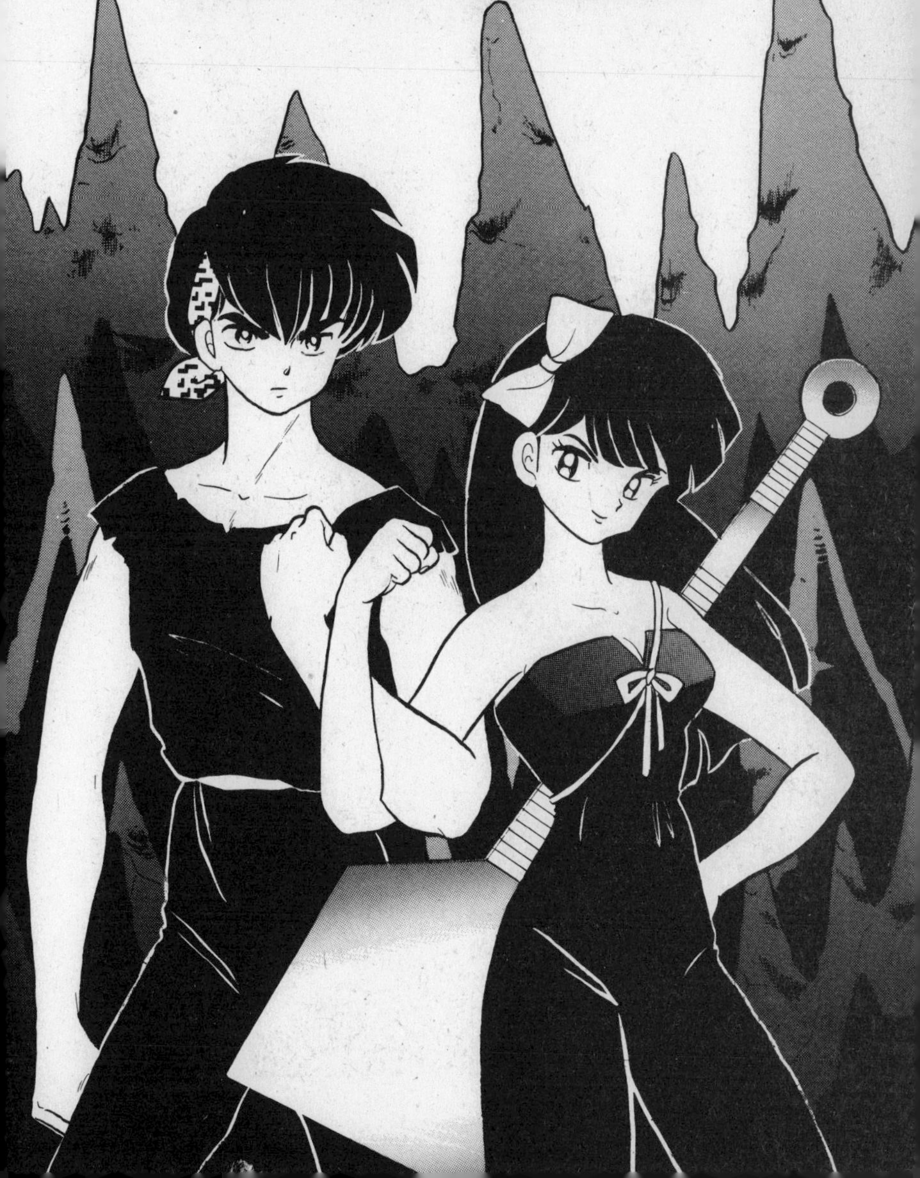

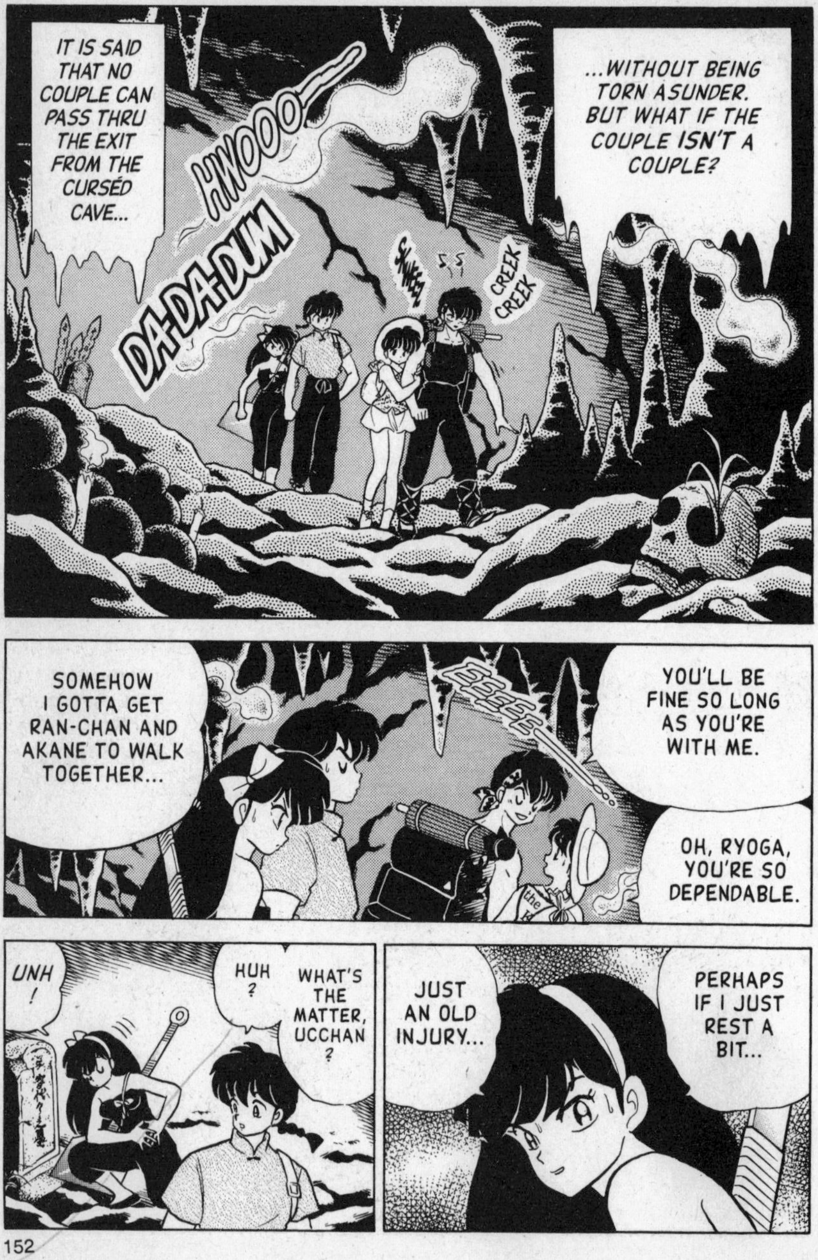

IT IS SAID THAT NO COUPLE CAN PASS THRU THE EXIT FROM THE CURSÉD CAVE...
HWOOO
DA-DA-DUM
CREEK CREEK
...WITHOUT BEING TORN ASUNDER. BUT WHAT IF THE COUPLE ISN'T A COUPLE?
SOMEHOW I GOTTA GET RAN-CHAN AND AKANE TO WALK TOGETHER...
YOU'LL BE FINE SO LONG AS YOU'RE WITH ME.
OH, RYOGA, YOU'RE SO DEPENDABLE.
UNH!
HUH?
WHAT'S THE MATTER, UCCHAN?
JUST AN OLD INJURY...
PERHAPS IF I JUST REST A BIT...

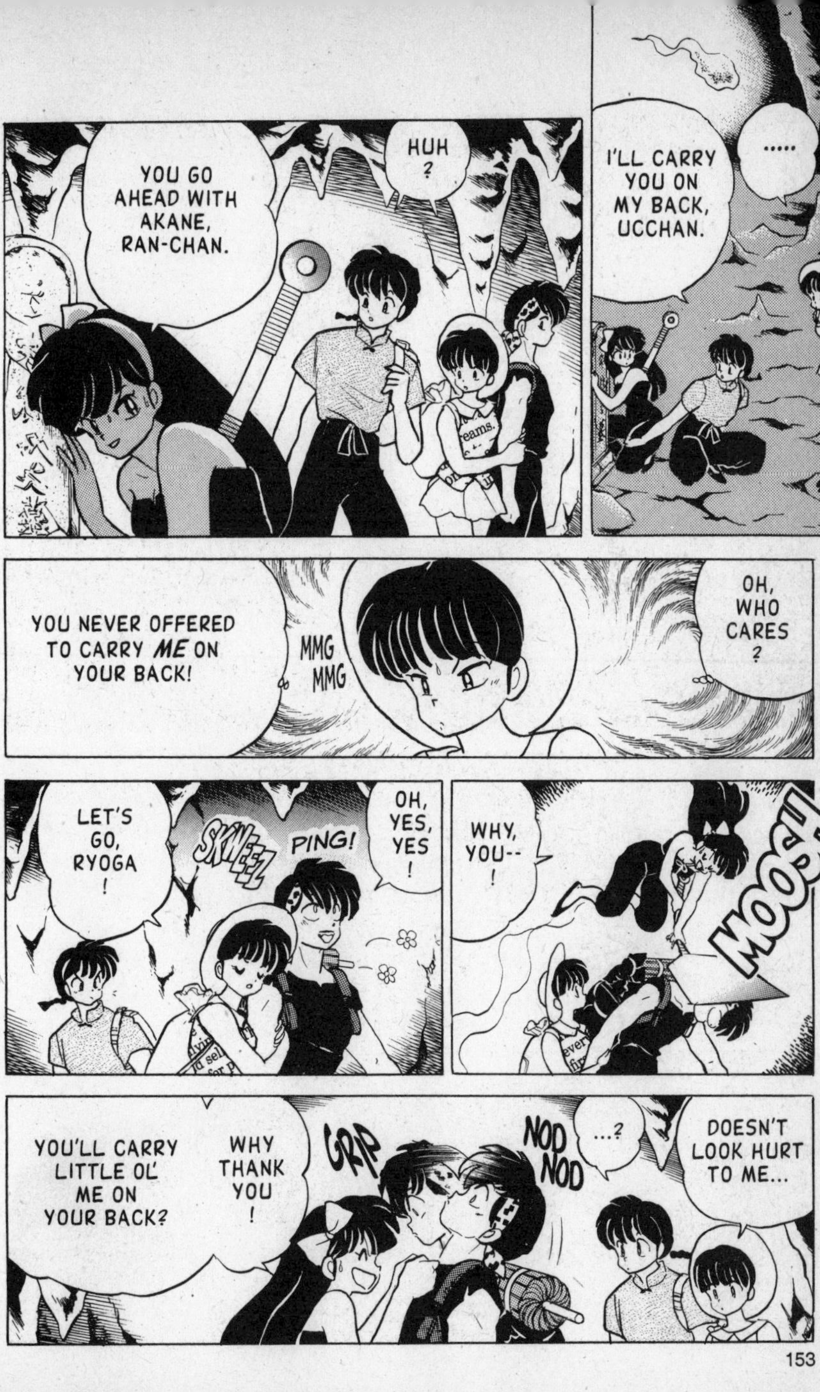
YOU GO AHEAD WITH AKANE, RAN-CHAN.
HUH?
I'LL CARRY YOU ON MY BACK, UCCHAN.
.....
YOU NEVER OFFERED TO CARRY *ME* ON YOUR BACK!
MMG MMG
OH, WHO CARES?
LET'S GO, RYOGA!
SKWEEZ
PING!
OH, YES, YES!
WHY, YOU--!
MOOSH
YOU'LL CARRY LITTLE OL' ME ON YOUR BACK?
WHY THANK YOU!
GRIP
NOD NOD
...?
DOESN'T LOOK HURT TO ME...

OUR OBJECT IS TO LEAD THEM TO THE CURSED EXIT.

HAVE YOU FORGOTTEN THAT!?

PSS·PSS· PSS

OF COURSE I HAVEN'T!!

LEAVE THE WOMAN AND RUN!!

YAAH YAAH

!

HEE!

AKANE, LOOK OUT!!

DOOM

FOMP

HUGS

RYOGA!!

OHHH...

NO "OHH." NO "OHH"--!!

SIGH

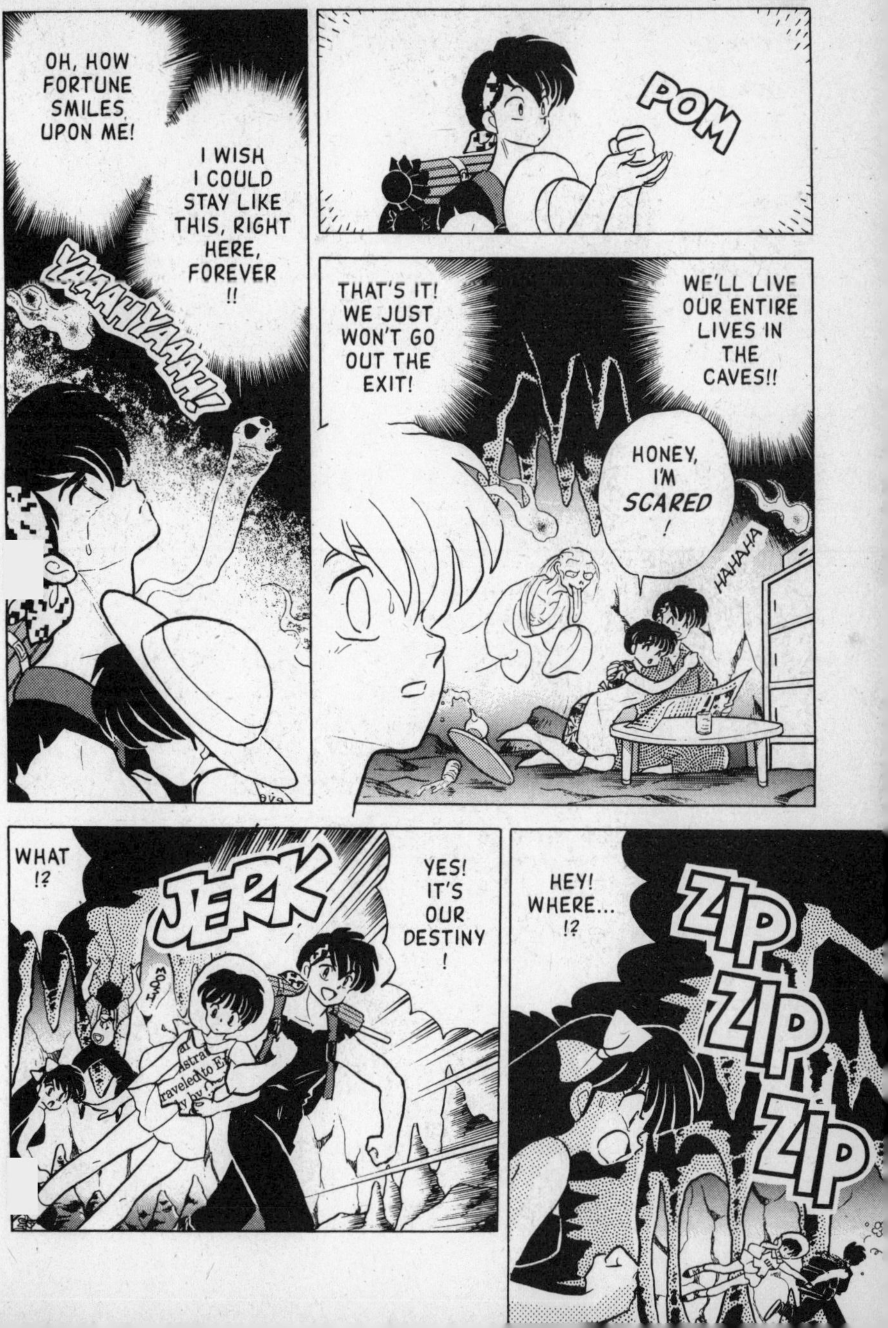
OH, HOW FORTUNE SMILES UPON ME!
I WISH I COULD STAY LIKE THIS, RIGHT HERE, FOREVER !!
YAAAHYAAAH!!
POM
THAT'S IT! WE JUST WON'T GO OUT THE EXIT!
WE'LL LIVE OUR ENTIRE LIVES IN THE CAVES!!
HONEY, I'M SCARED !
HAHAHA
WHAT !?
JERK
YES! IT'S OUR DESTINY !
HEY! WHERE... !?
ZIP ZIP ZIP

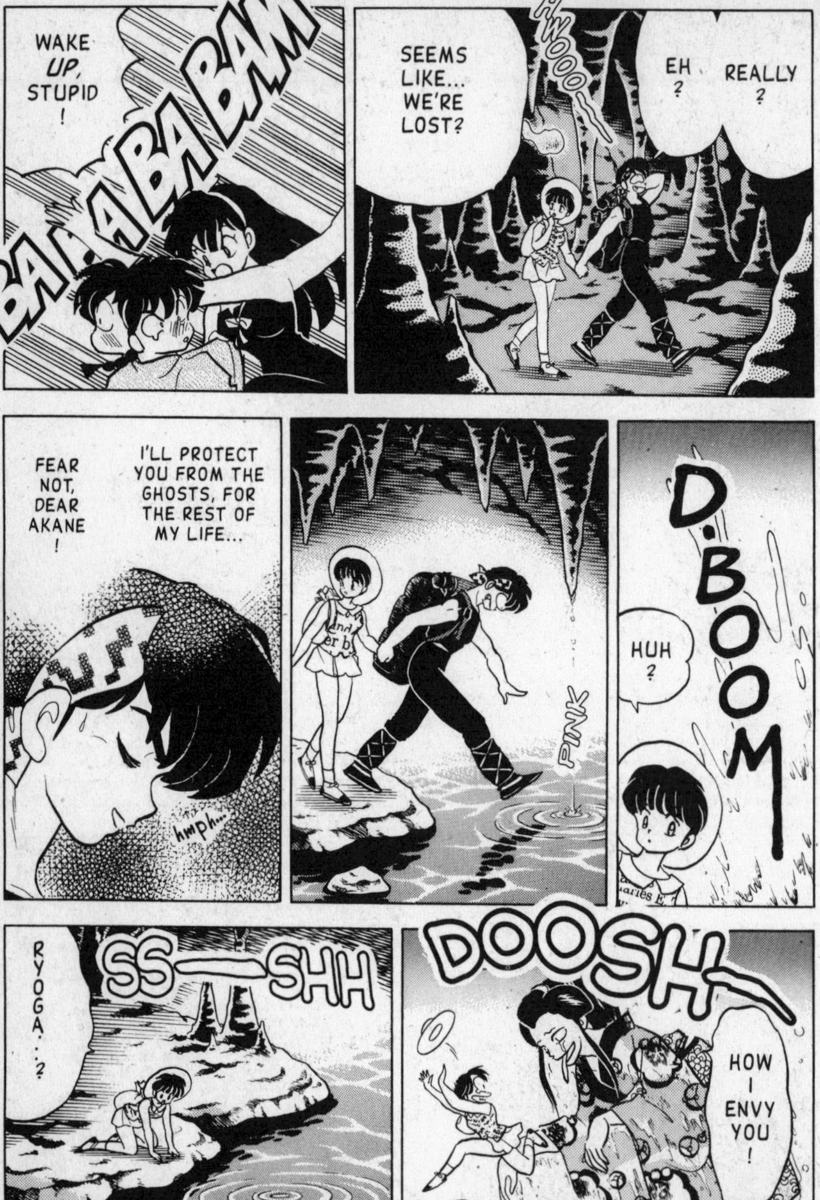
WAKE UP, STUPID!
BA BA BA BAM
HWOOO—
SEEMS LIKE... WE'RE LOST?
EH?
REALLY?
FEAR NOT, DEAR AKANE!
I'LL PROTECT YOU FROM THE GHOSTS, FOR THE REST OF MY LIFE...
hmph...
PINK
D.BOOM
HUH?
RYOGA...?
SS—SHH
DOOSH—
HOW I ENVY YOU!

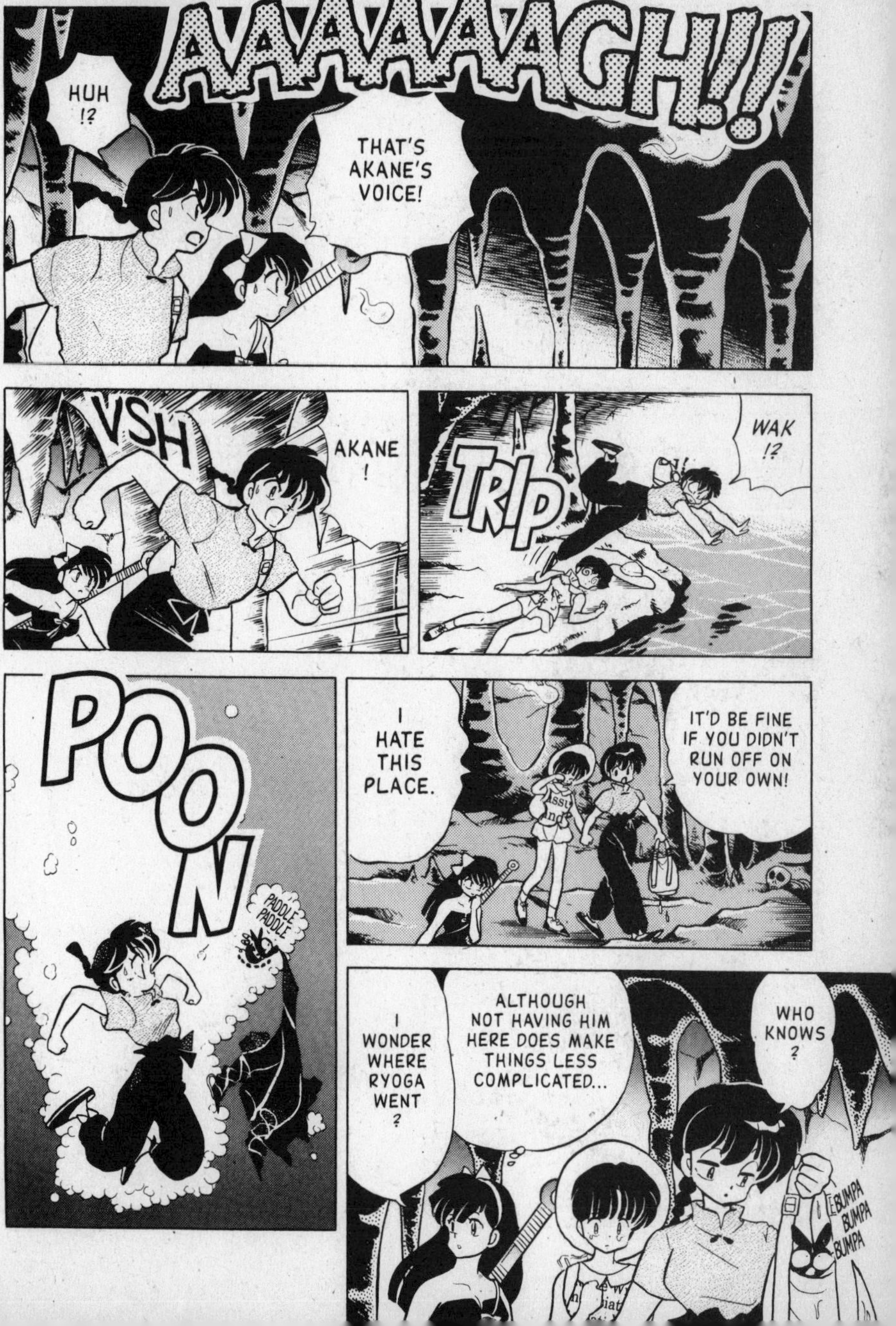
HUH !?
AAAAAAGH!!
THAT'S AKANE'S VOICE!
VSH
AKANE !
TRIP
WAK !?
POOON
PADDLE PADDLE
I HATE THIS PLACE.
IT'D BE FINE IF YOU DIDN'T RUN OFF ON YOUR OWN!
I WONDER WHERE RYOGA WENT ?
ALTHOUGH NOT HAVING HIM HERE DOES MAKE THINGS LESS COMPLICATED...
WHO KNOWS ?
BUMPA BUMPA BUMPA

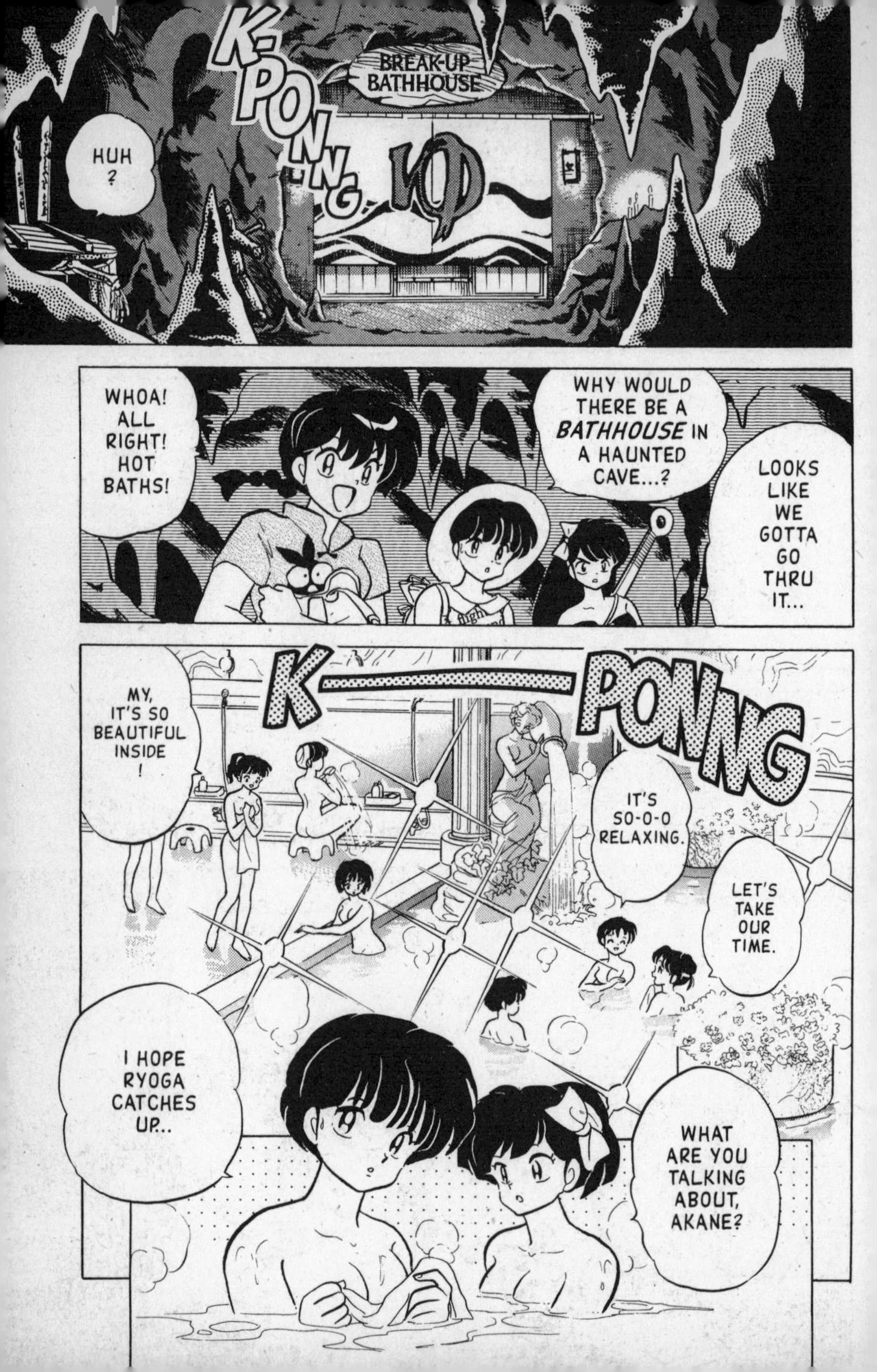

K-PONNNG
BREAK-UP BATHHOUSE
HUH ?
WHOA! ALL RIGHT! HOT BATHS!
WHY WOULD THERE BE A BATHHOUSE IN A HAUNTED CAVE...?
LOOKS LIKE WE GOTTA GO THRU IT...
MY, IT'S SO BEAUTIFUL INSIDE !
K——————PONNG
IT'S SO-O-O RELAXING.
LET'S TAKE OUR TIME.
I HOPE RYOGA CATCHES UP...
WHAT ARE YOU TALKING ABOUT, AKANE?

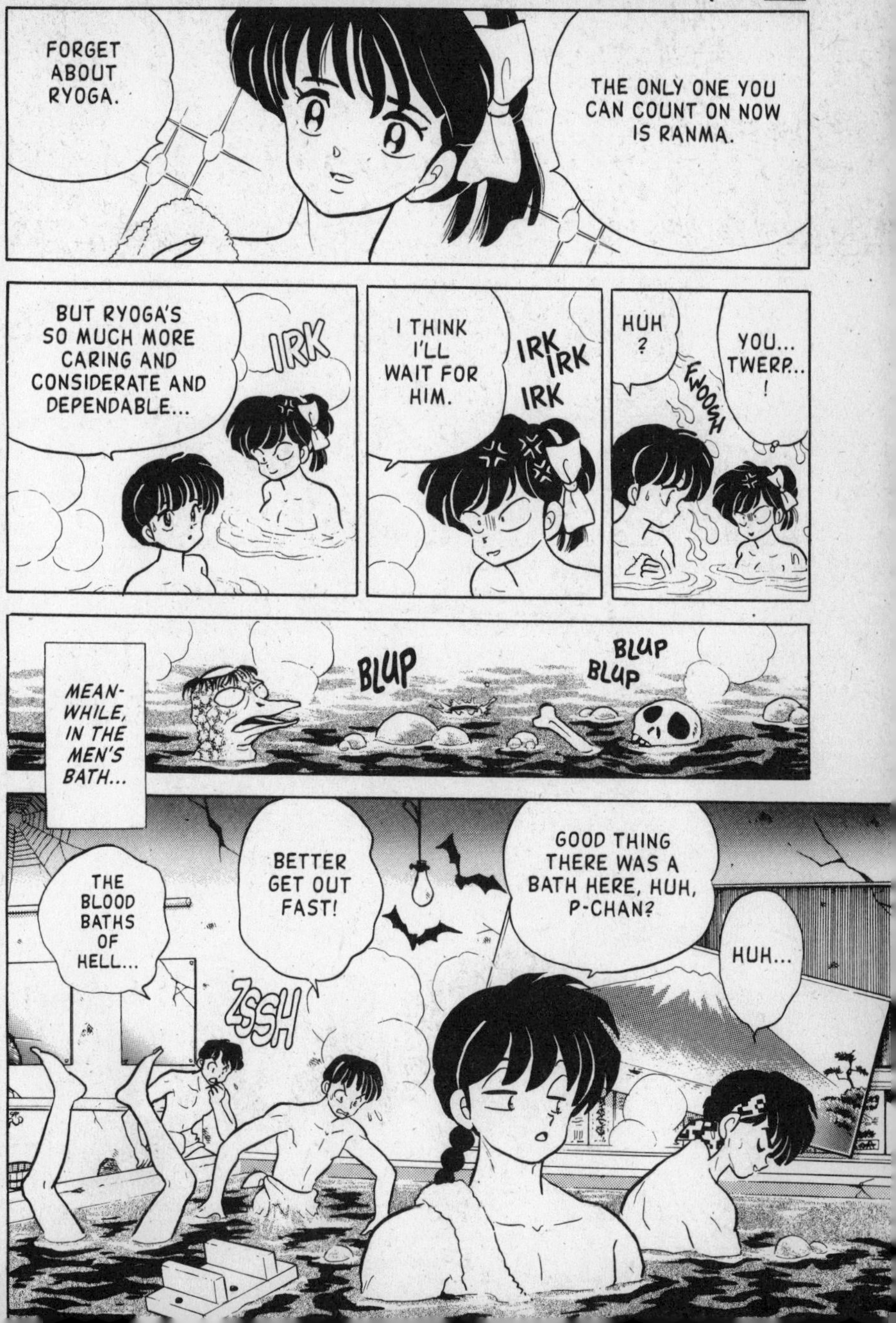
FORGET ABOUT RYOGA.
THE ONLY ONE YOU CAN COUNT ON NOW IS RANMA.
BUT RYOGA'S SO MUCH MORE CARING AND CONSIDERATE AND DEPENDABLE...
IRK
I THINK I'LL WAIT FOR HIM.
IRK IRK IRK
HUH ?
FWOOSH
YOU... TWERP... !
MEAN-WHILE, IN THE MEN'S BATH...
BLUP
BLUP BLUP
THE BLOOD BATHS OF HELL...
BETTER GET OUT FAST!
ZSSH
GOOD THING THERE WAS A BATH HERE, HUH, P-CHAN?
HUH...

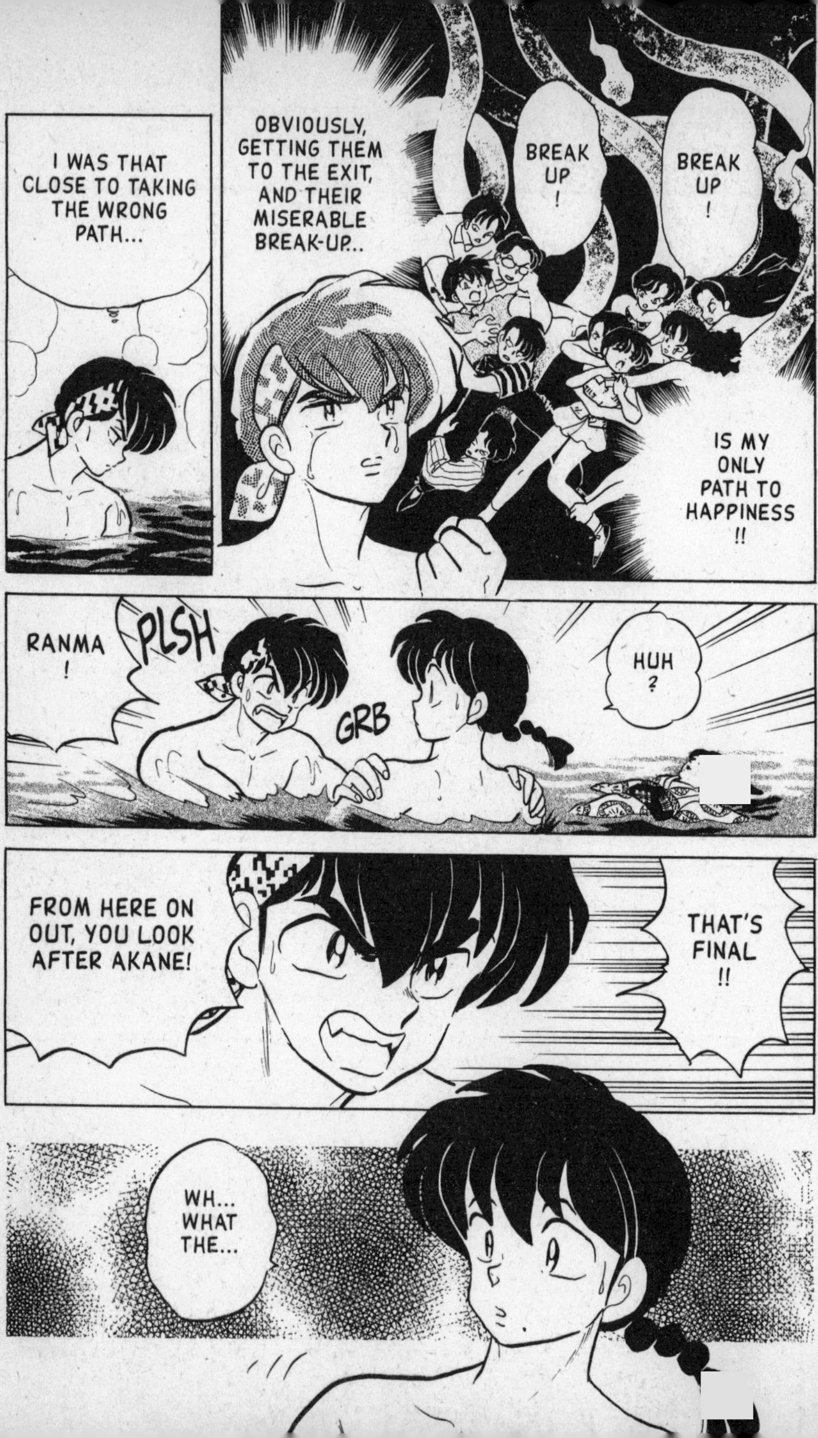
I WAS THAT CLOSE TO TAKING THE WRONG PATH...
OBVIOUSLY, GETTING THEM TO THE EXIT, AND THEIR MISERABLE BREAK-UP...
BREAK UP!
BREAK UP!
IS MY ONLY PATH TO HAPPINESS!!
RANMA!
PLSH
GRB
HUH?
FROM HERE ON OUT, YOU LOOK AFTER AKANE!
THAT'S FINAL!!
WH... WHAT THE...

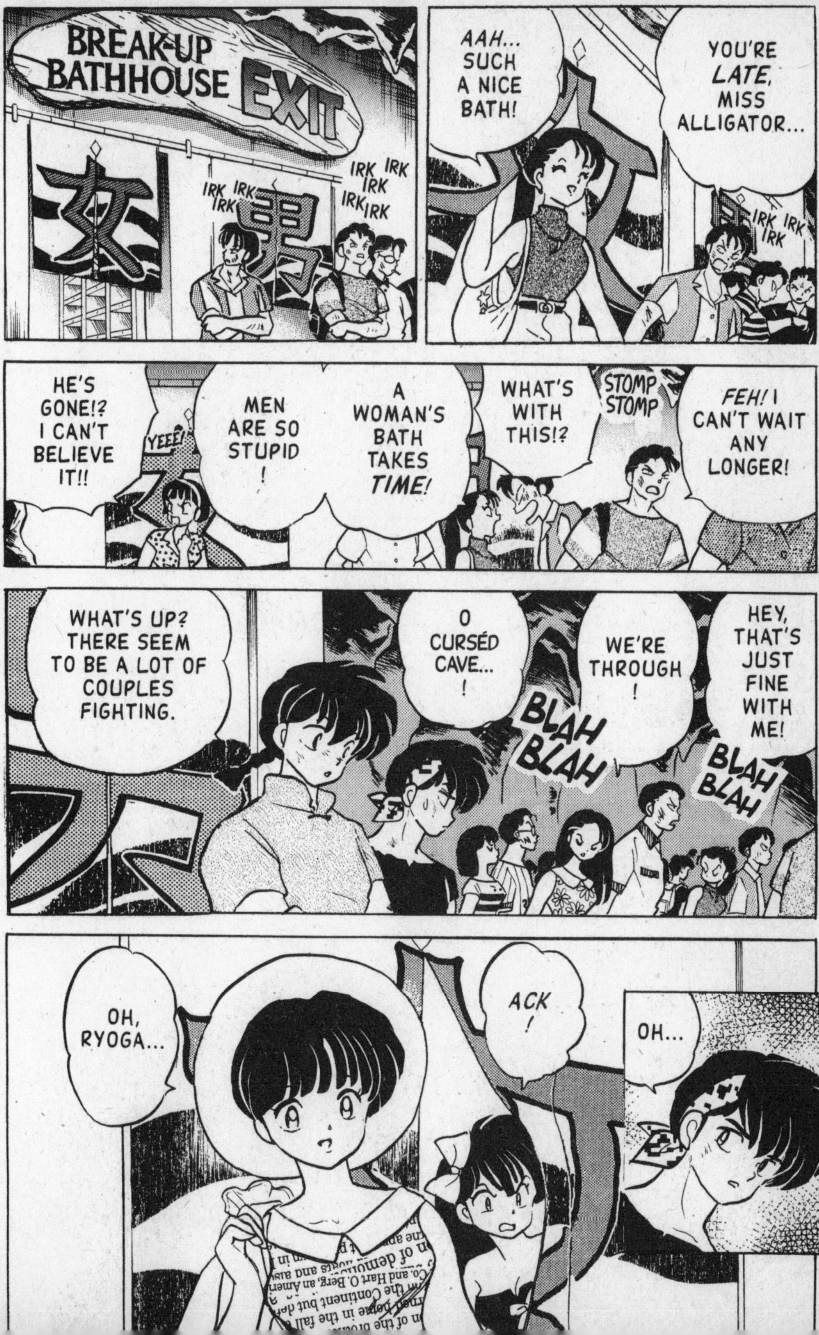
BREAK-UP BATHHOUSE EXIT
女
男
IRK IRK IRK
IRK IRK IRK IRK IRK
AAH... SUCH A NICE BATH!
YOU'RE LATE, MISS ALLIGATOR...
IRK IRK IRK
HE'S GONE!? I CAN'T BELIEVE IT!!
YEEE!
MEN ARE SO STUPID!
A WOMAN'S BATH TAKES TIME!
WHAT'S WITH THIS!?
STOMP STOMP
FEH! I CAN'T WAIT ANY LONGER!
WHAT'S UP? THERE SEEM TO BE A LOT OF COUPLES FIGHTING.
O CURSÉD CAVE...!
BLAH BLAH
WE'RE THROUGH!
HEY, THAT'S JUST FINE WITH ME!
BLAH BLAH
OH, RYOGA...
ACK!
OH...

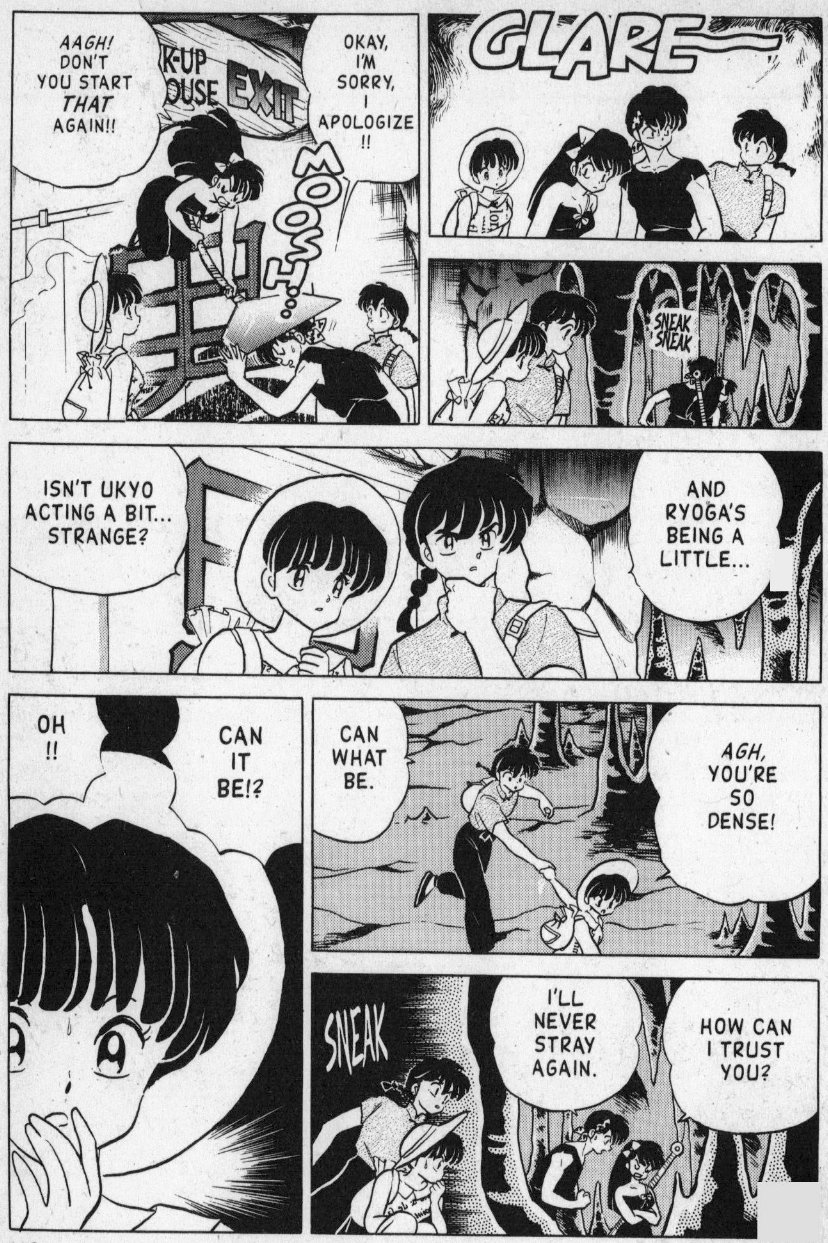
AAGH! DON'T YOU START *THAT* AGAIN!!
K-UP
OUSE
EXIT
OKAY, I'M SORRY, I APOLOGIZE !!
MOOSH...
GLARE—
SNEAK SNEAK
ISN'T UKYO ACTING A BIT... STRANGE?
AND RYOGA'S BEING A LITTLE...
OH !!
CAN IT BE!?
CAN WHAT BE.
AGH, YOU'RE SO DENSE!
SNEAK
I'LL NEVER STRAY AGAIN.
HOW CAN I TRUST YOU?

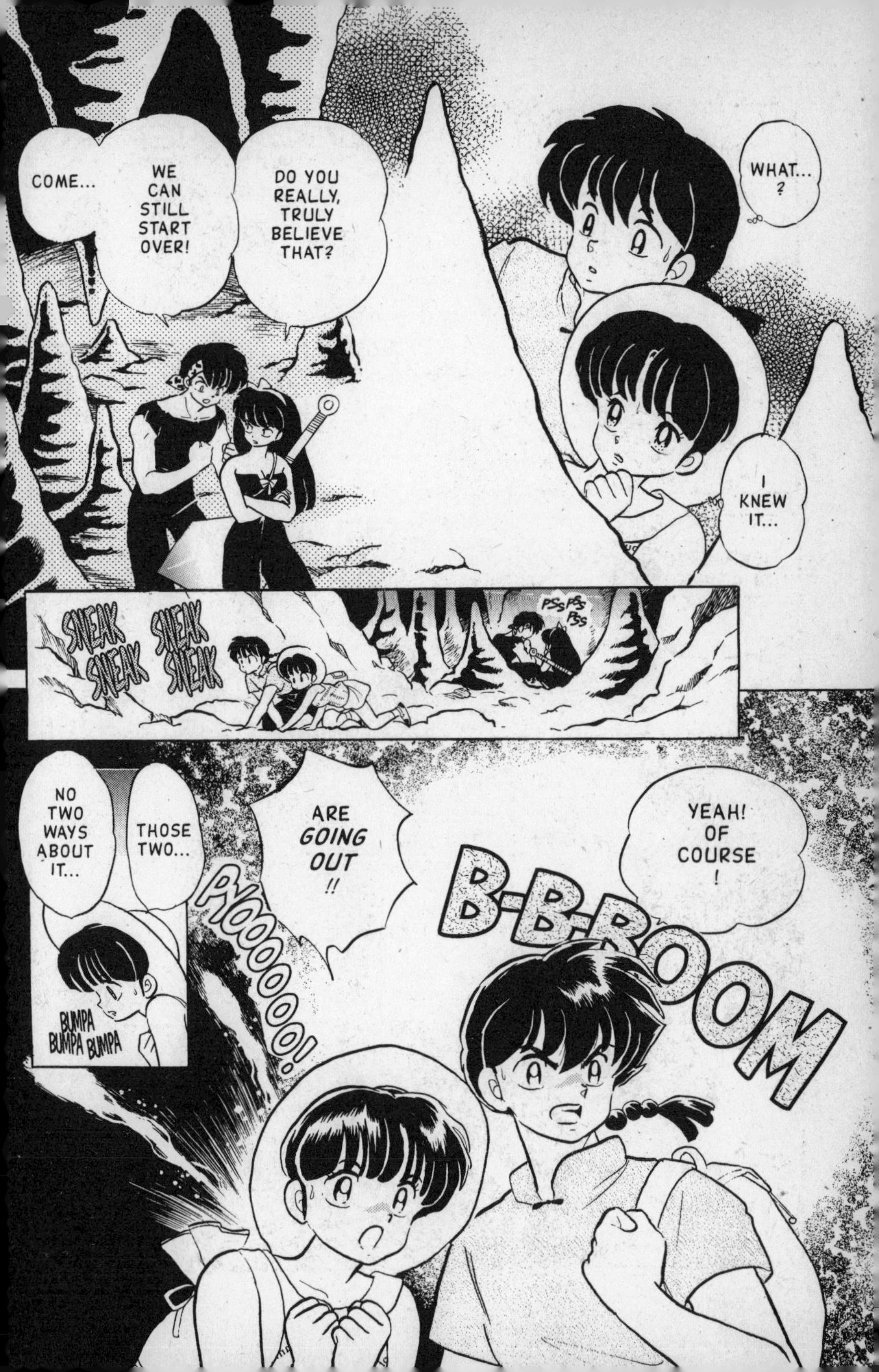

COME...
WE CAN STILL START OVER!
DO YOU REALLY, TRULY BELIEVE THAT?
WHAT...?
I KNEW IT...
SNEAK SNEAK
SNEAK SNEAK
PSS PSS PSS
NO TWO WAYS ABOUT IT...
THOSE TWO...
BUMPA BUMPA BUMPA
PYOOOOOO!
ARE *GOING OUT*!!
YEAH! OF COURSE!
B-B-BROOOM

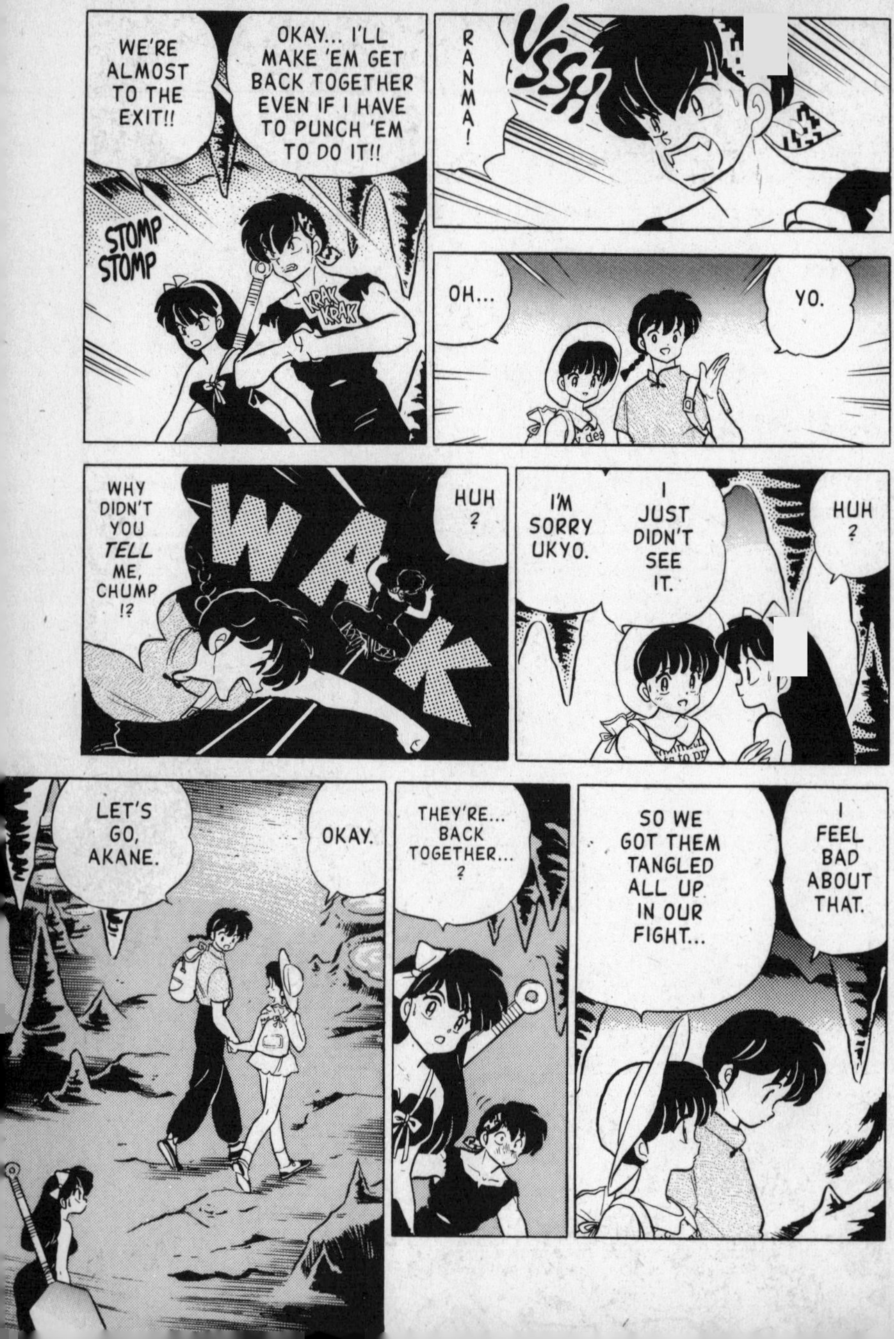
WE'RE ALMOST TO THE EXIT!!
OKAY... I'LL MAKE 'EM GET BACK TOGETHER EVEN IF I HAVE TO PUNCH 'EM TO DO IT!!
STOMP STOMP
KRAK KRAK
RANMA!
VSSH
OH...
YO.
WHY DIDN'T YOU *TELL* ME, CHUMP!?
WAK
HUH?
I'M SORRY UKYO.
I JUST DIDN'T SEE IT.
HUH?
LET'S GO, AKANE.
OKAY.
THEY'RE... BACK TOGETHER...?
SO WE GOT THEM TANGLED ALL UP IN OUR FIGHT...
I FEEL BAD ABOUT THAT.

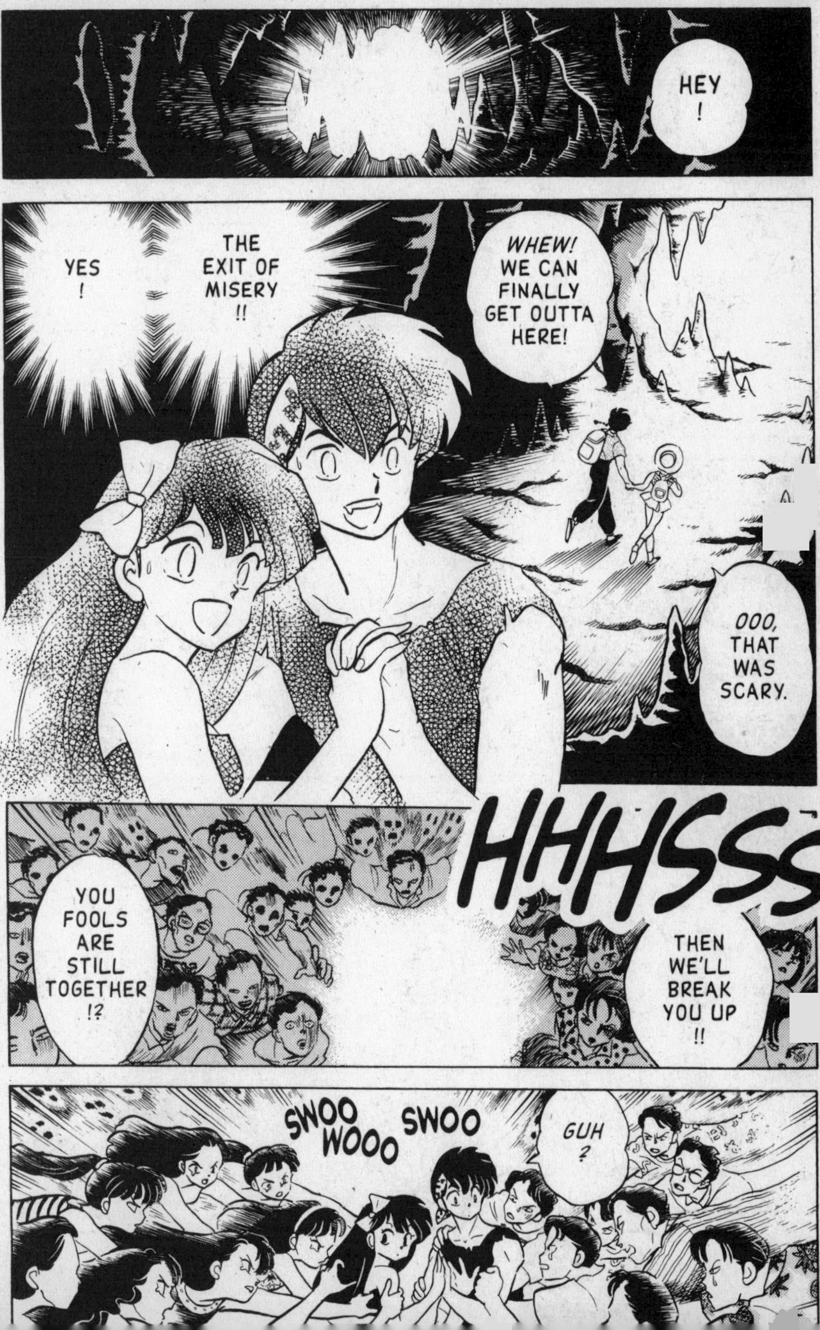
HEY!
YES!
THE EXIT OF MISERY!!
WHEW! WE CAN FINALLY GET OUTTA HERE!
OOO, THAT WAS SCARY.
YOU FOOLS ARE STILL TOGETHER!?
HHHSSS
THEN WE'LL BREAK YOU UP!!
SWOO WOOO SWOO
GUH?

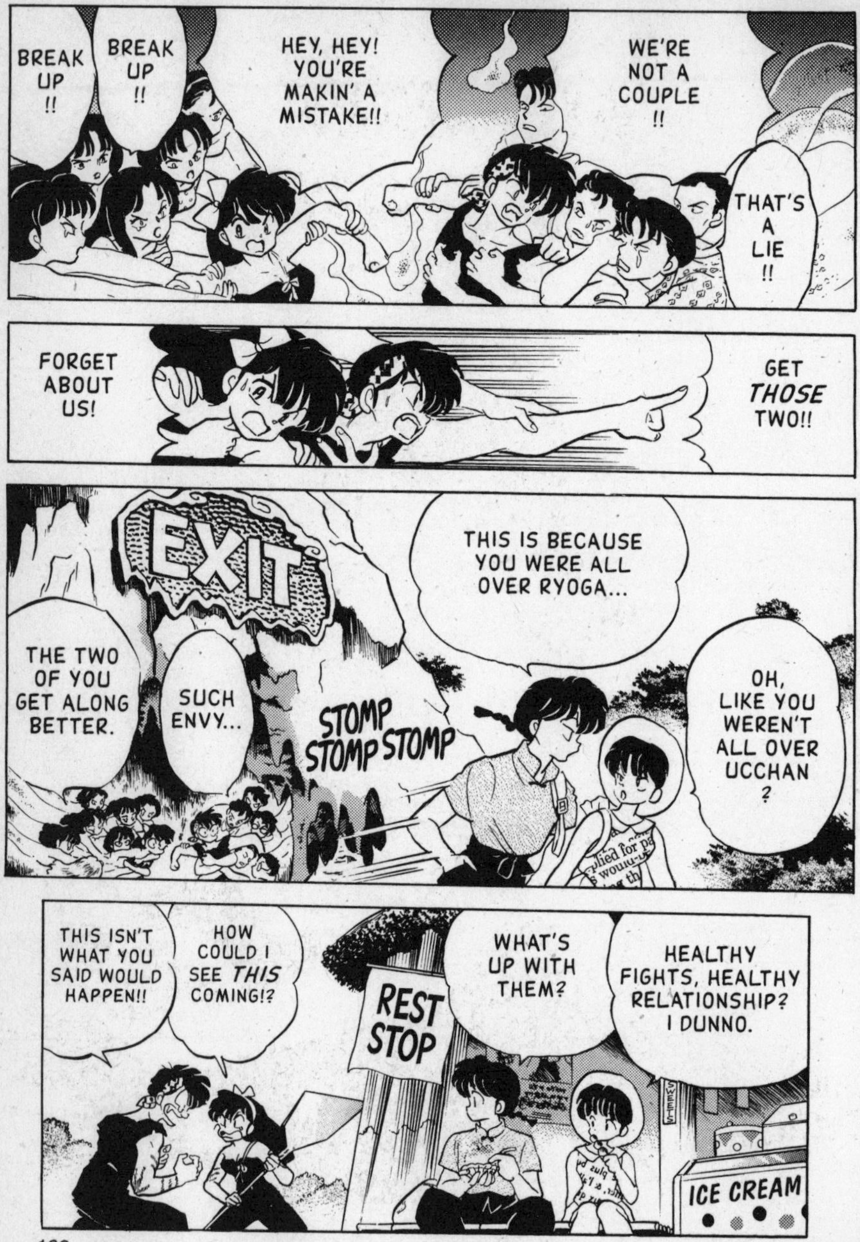
BREAK UP !!
BREAK UP !!
HEY, HEY! YOU'RE MAKIN' A MISTAKE!!
WE'RE NOT A COUPLE !!
THAT'S A LIE !!
FORGET ABOUT US!
GET *THOSE* TWO!!
EXIT
THIS IS BECAUSE YOU WERE ALL OVER RYOGA...
THE TWO OF YOU GET ALONG BETTER.
SUCH ENVY...
STOMP STOMP STOMP
OH, LIKE YOU WEREN'T ALL OVER UCCHAN ?
THIS ISN'T WHAT YOU SAID WOULD HAPPEN!!
HOW COULD I SEE *THIS* COMING!?
REST STOP
WHAT'S UP WITH THEM?
HEALTHY FIGHTS, HEALTHY RELATIONSHIP? I DUNNO.
SWEETS
ICE CREAM

Part 11

GIVE BACK THE TESTS!!

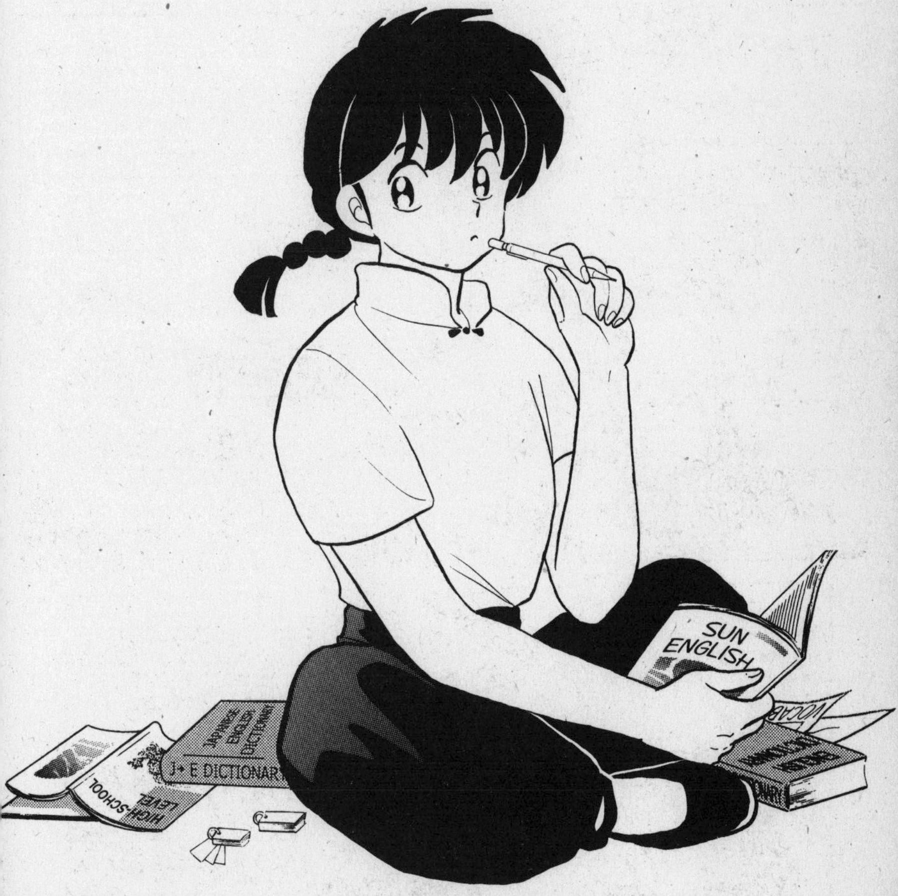
SUN ENGLISH
HIGH-SCHOOL LEVEL

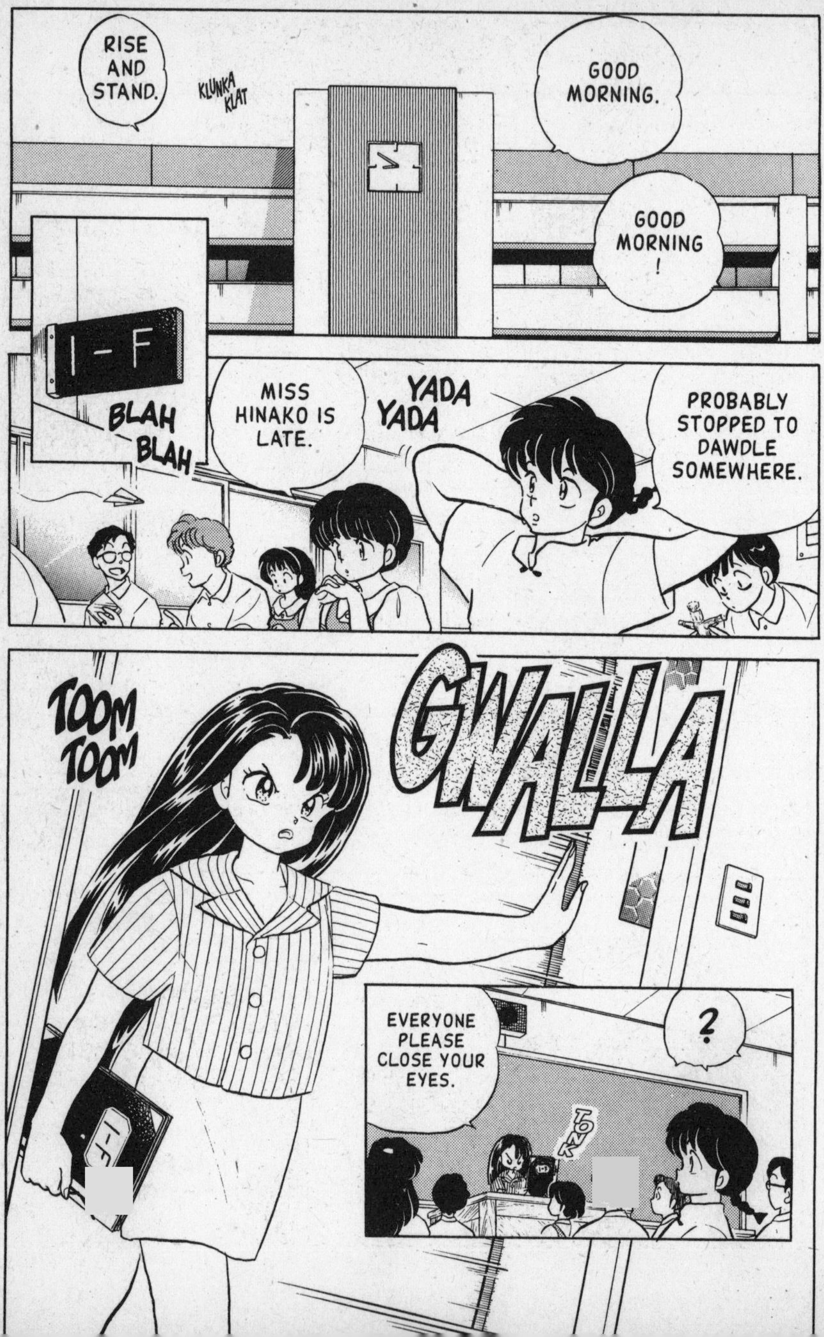
RISE AND STAND.
KLUNKA KLAT
GOOD MORNING.
GOOD MORNING!
1-F
BLAH BLAH
MISS HINAKO IS LATE.
YADA YADA
PROBABLY STOPPED TO DAWDLE SOMEWHERE.
TOOM TOOM
GWALLA
1-F
EVERYONE PLEASE CLOSE YOUR EYES.
TONK
?

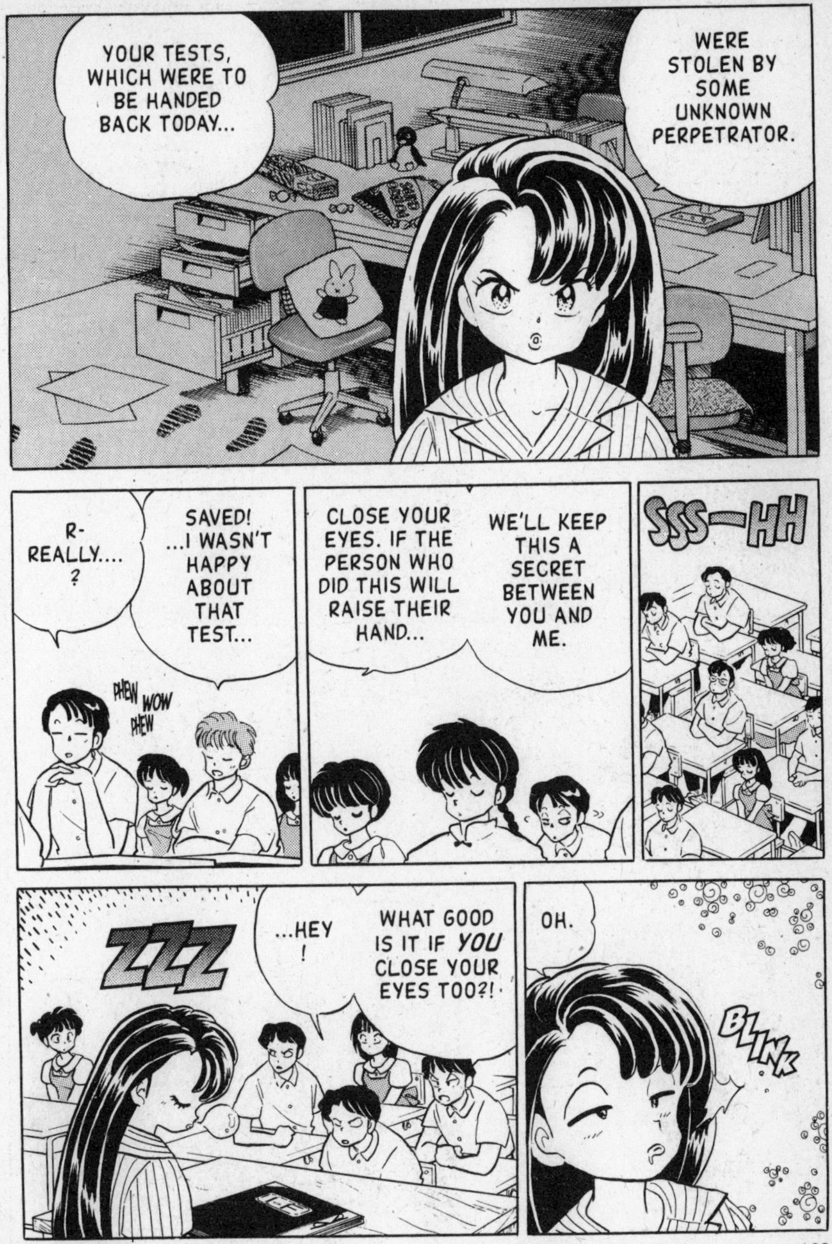
YOUR TESTS, WHICH WERE TO BE HANDED BACK TODAY...
WERE STOLEN BY SOME UNKNOWN PERPETRATOR.
R-REALLY....?
SAVED! ...I WASN'T HAPPY ABOUT THAT TEST...
PHEW WOW PHEW
CLOSE YOUR EYES. IF THE PERSON WHO DID THIS WILL RAISE THEIR HAND...
WE'LL KEEP THIS A SECRET BETWEEN YOU AND ME.
SSS—HH
ZZZ
...HEY!
WHAT GOOD IS IT IF *YOU* CLOSE YOUR EYES TOO?!
OH.
BLINK

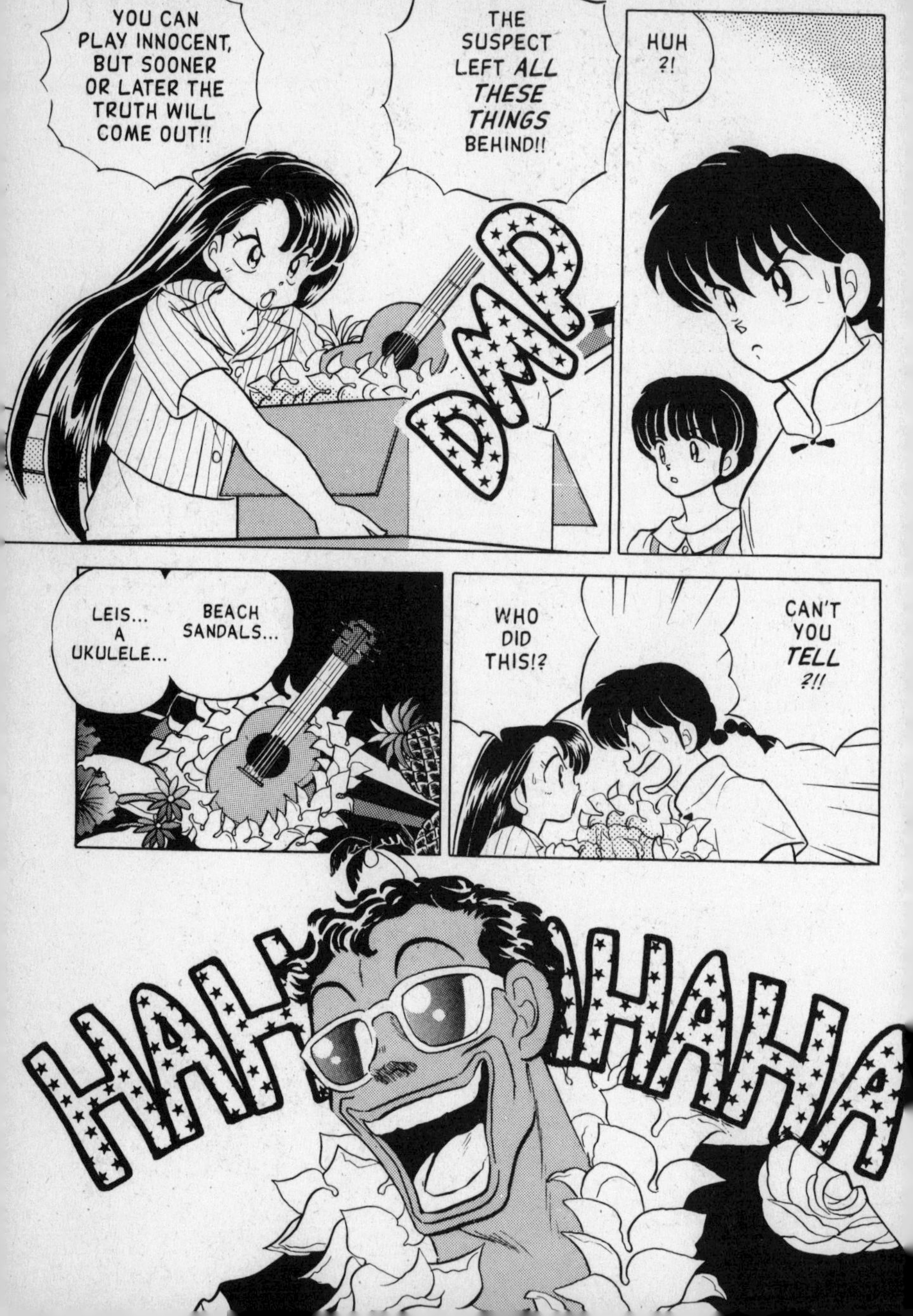
YOU CAN PLAY INNOCENT, BUT SOONER OR LATER THE TRUTH WILL COME OUT!!
THE SUSPECT LEFT ALL THESE THINGS BEHIND!!
DMP
HUH ?!
LEIS... A UKULELE...
BEACH SANDALS...
WHO DID THIS!?
CAN'T YOU TELL ?!!
HAHAHAHAHA

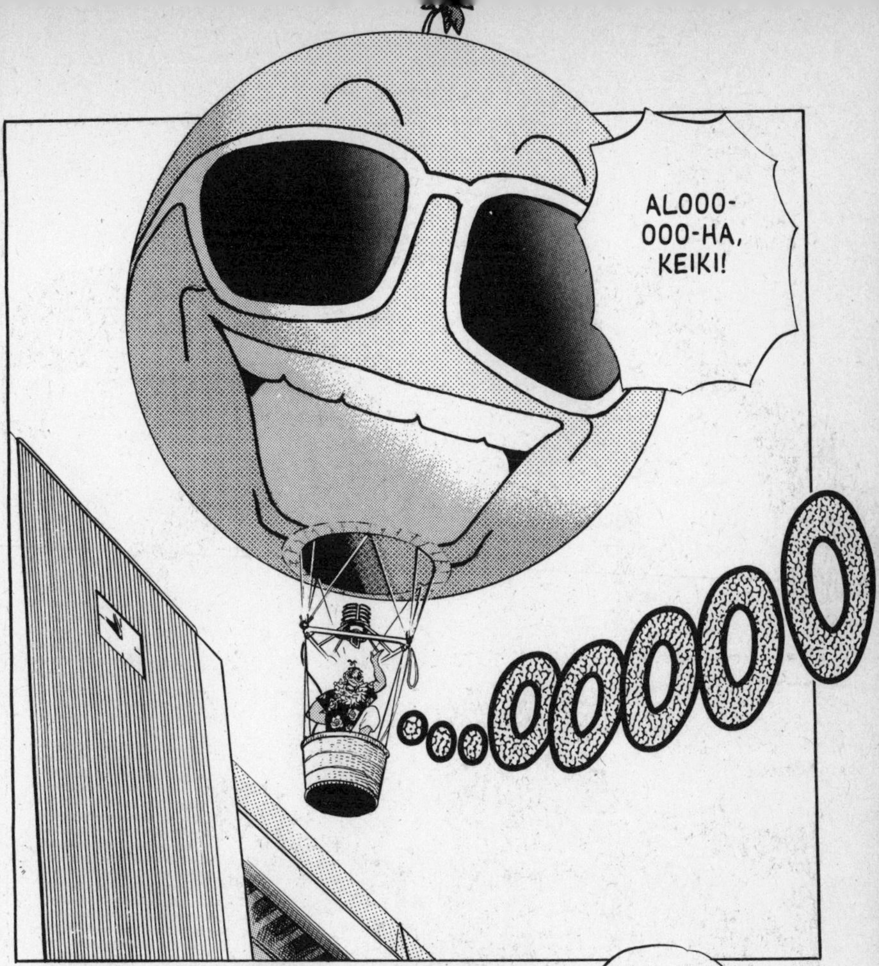
ALOOO-OOO-HA, KEIKI!
...OOOOOO
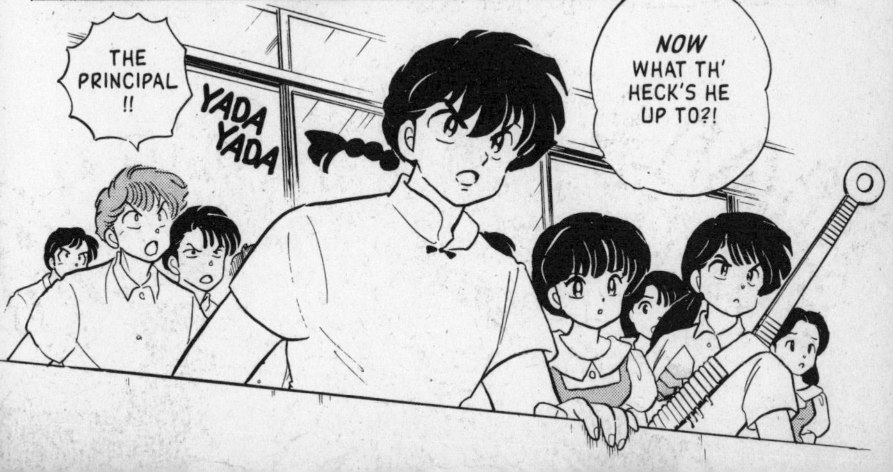
THE PRINCIPAL !!
YADA YADA
NOW WHAT TH' HECK'S HE UP TO?!

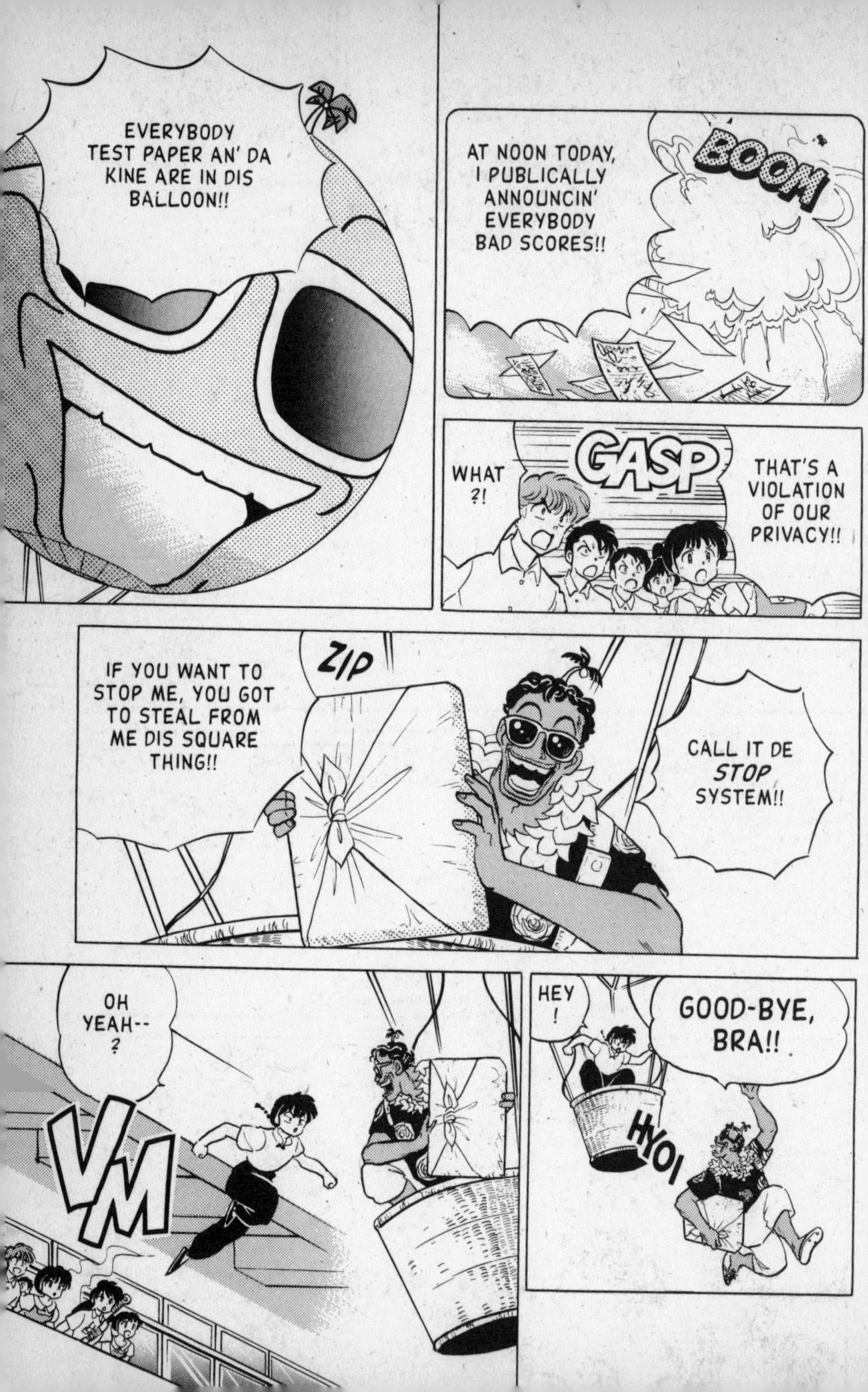
EVERYBODY TEST PAPER AN' DA KINE ARE IN DIS BALLOON!!
AT NOON TODAY, I PUBLICALLY ANNOUNCIN' EVERYBODY BAD SCORES!!
BOOM
WHAT ?!
GASP
THAT'S A VIOLATION OF OUR PRIVACY!!
IF YOU WANT TO STOP ME, YOU GOT TO STEAL FROM ME DIS SQUARE THING!!
ZIP
CALL IT DE *STOP* SYSTEM!!
OH YEAH-- ?
VM
HEY !
GOOD-BYE, BRA!!
HYOI

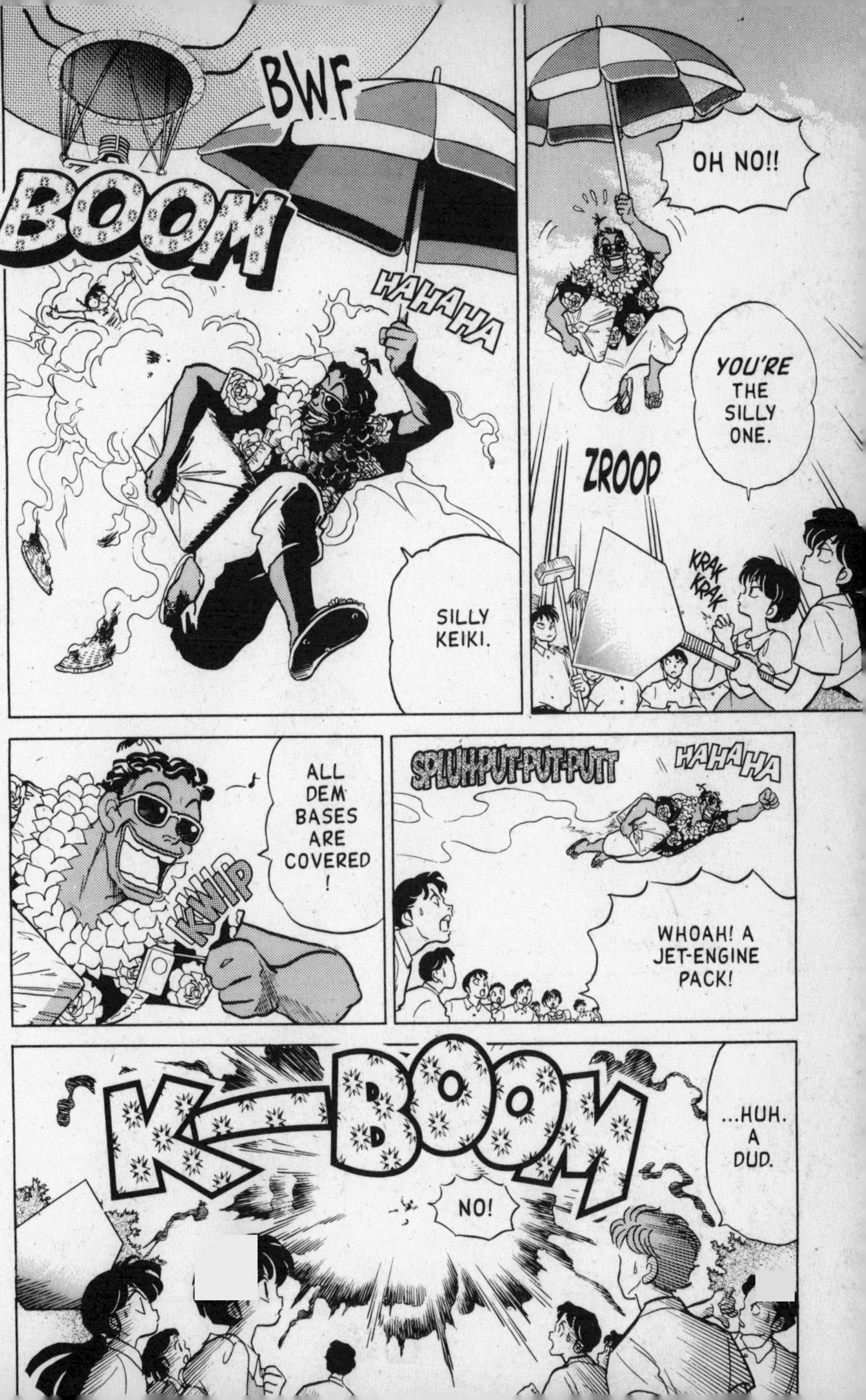
BWF
BOOM
HAHAHAHA
SILLY KEIKI.
OH NO!!
YOU'RE THE SILLY ONE.
ZROOP
KRAK KRAK
ALL DEM BASES ARE COVERED!
KWIP
SPLUHPUT-PUT-PUTT
HAHAHA
WHOAH! A JET-ENGINE PACK!
K-BOOM
NO!
...HUH. A DUD.

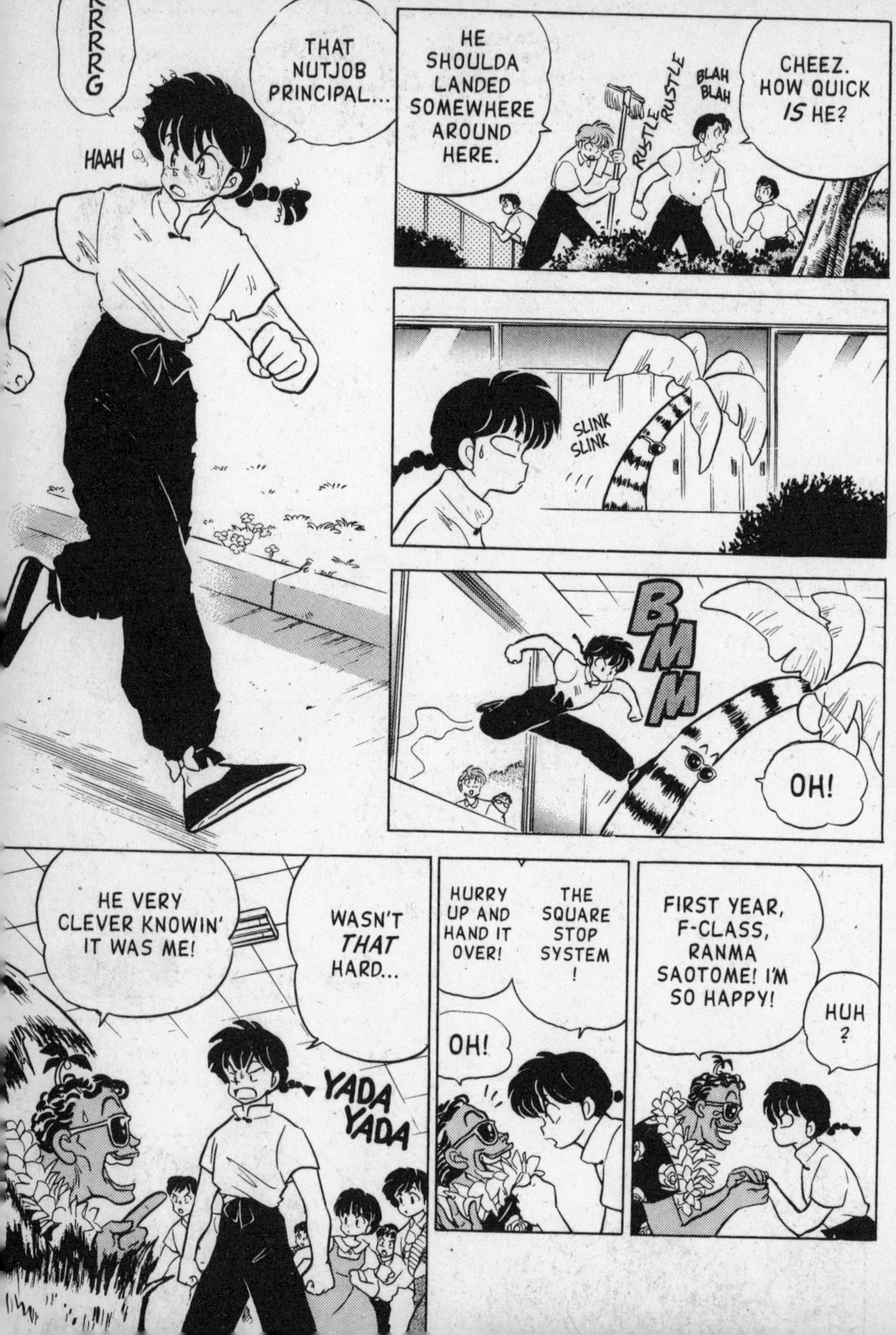
RRRRG
HAAH
THAT NUTJOB PRINCIPAL...
HE SHOULDA LANDED SOMEWHERE AROUND HERE.
RUSTLE RUSTLE
BLAH BLAH
CHEEZ. HOW QUICK IS HE?
SLINK SLINK
BMM
OH!
HE VERY CLEVER KNOWIN' IT WAS ME!
WASN'T THAT HARD...
YADA YADA
HURRY UP AND HAND IT OVER!
THE SQUARE STOP SYSTEM !
OH!
FIRST YEAR, F-CLASS, RANMA SAOTOME! I'M SO HAPPY!
HUH ?

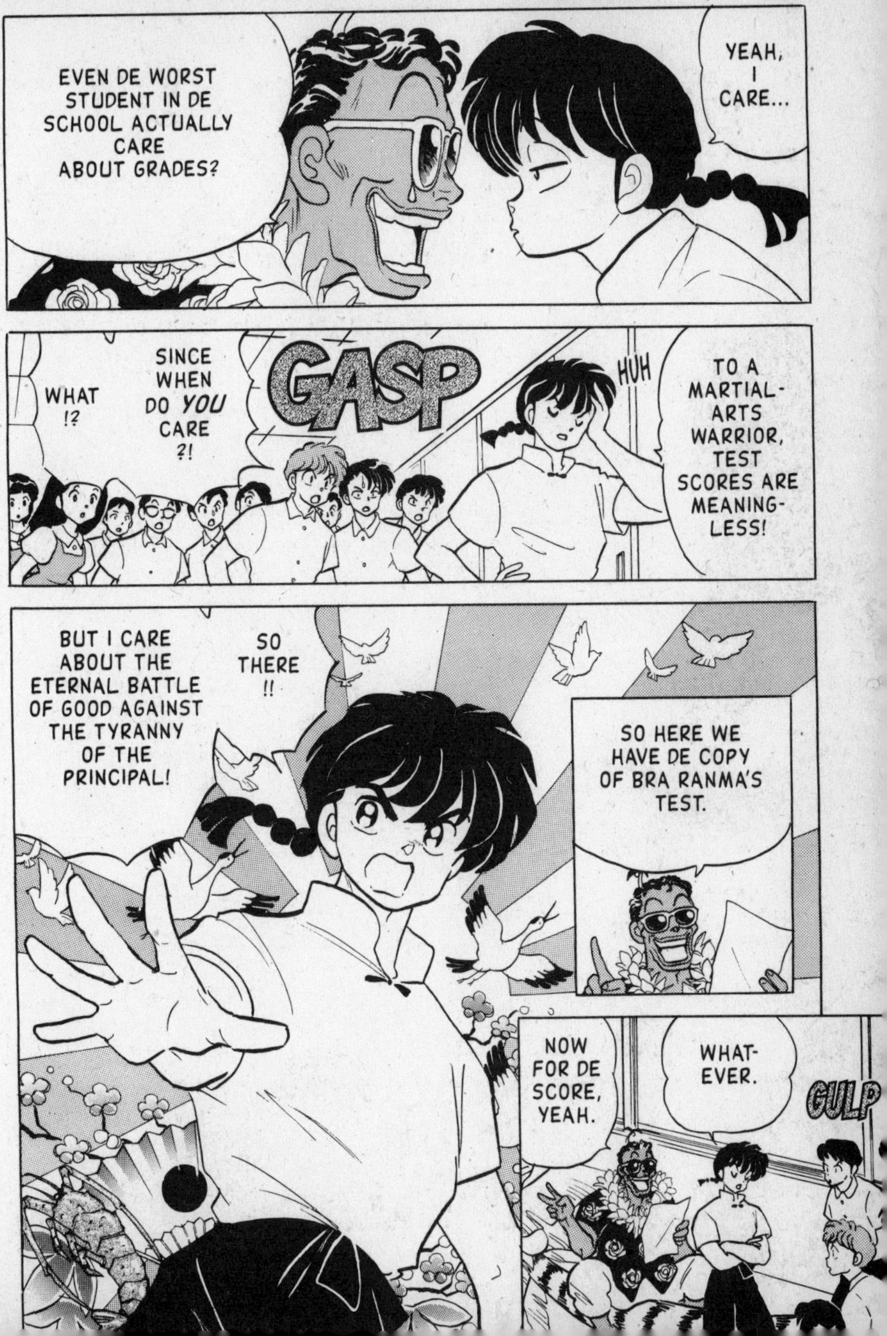
EVEN DE WORST STUDENT IN DE SCHOOL ACTUALLY CARE ABOUT GRADES?
YEAH, I CARE...
WHAT !?
SINCE WHEN DO *YOU* CARE ?!
GASP
HUH
TO A MARTIAL-ARTS WARRIOR, TEST SCORES ARE MEANING-LESS!
BUT I CARE ABOUT THE ETERNAL BATTLE OF GOOD AGAINST THE TYRANNY OF THE PRINCIPAL!
SO THERE !!
SO HERE WE HAVE DE COPY OF BRA RANMA'S TEST.
NOW FOR DE SCORE, YEAH.
WHAT-EVER.
GULP

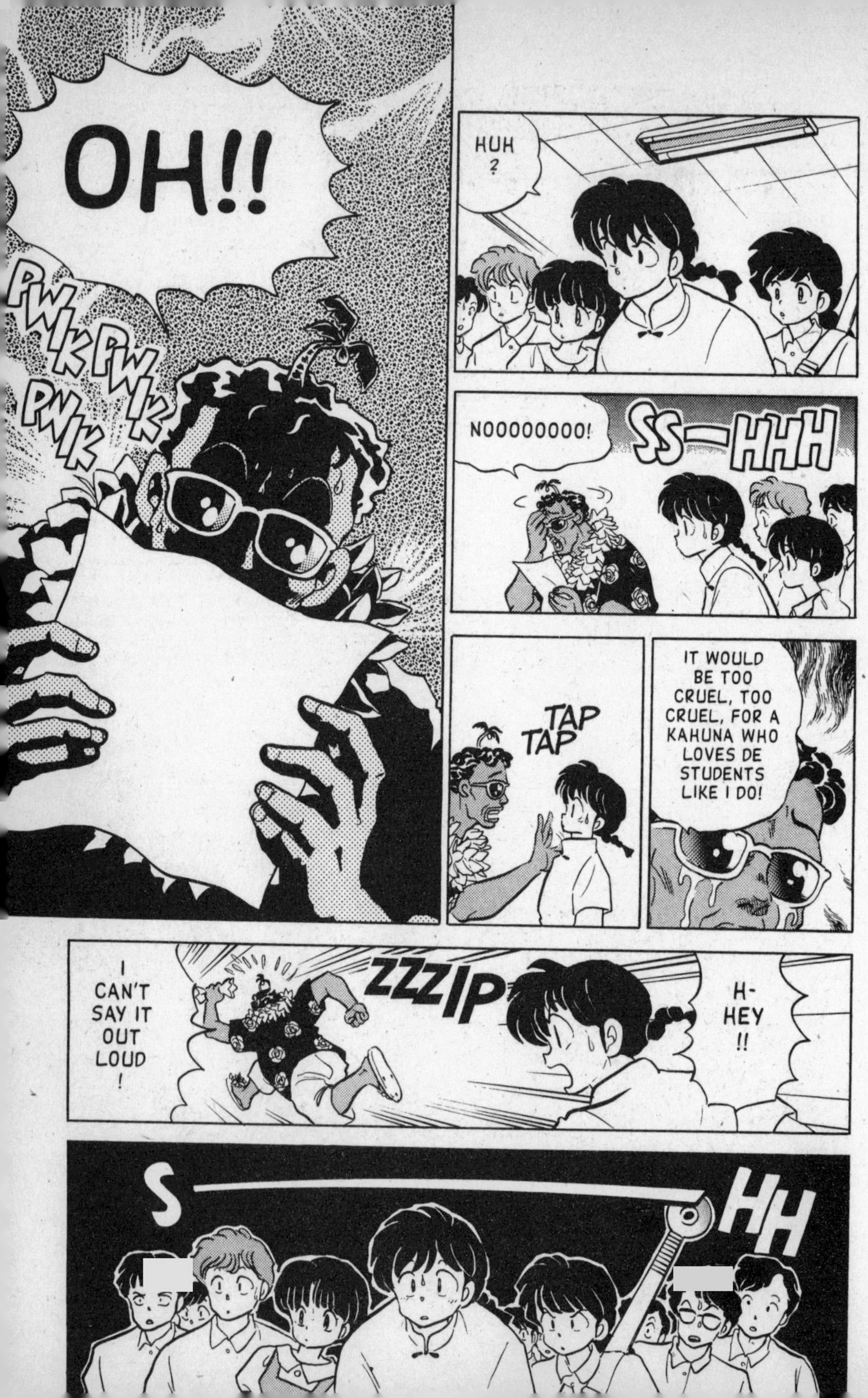

OH!!
PWIK PWIK PWIK
HUH?
NOOOOOOOO!
SS—HHH
TAP TAP
IT WOULD BE TOO CRUEL, TOO CRUEL, FOR A KAHUNA WHO LOVES DE STUDENTS LIKE I DO!
I CAN'T SAY IT OUT LOUD!
ZZZIP
H-HEY!!
S—HH

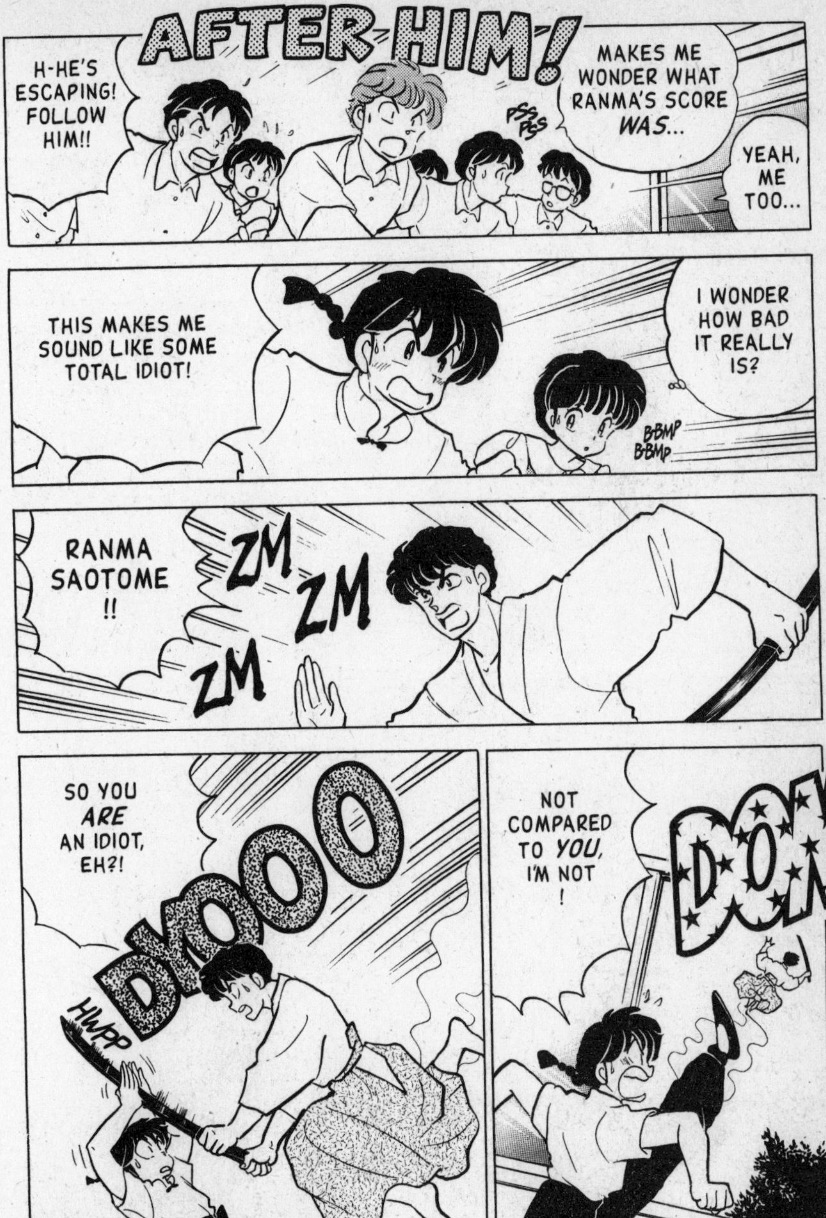
AFTER HIM!
H-HE'S ESCAPING! FOLLOW HIM!!
PSS PSS
MAKES ME WONDER WHAT RANMA'S SCORE WAS...
YEAH, ME TOO...
THIS MAKES ME SOUND LIKE SOME TOTAL IDIOT!
I WONDER HOW BAD IT REALLY IS?
B-BMP B-BMP
RANMA SAOTOME !!
ZM ZM ZM
SO YOU ARE AN IDIOT, EH?!
DOOOO
HWPP
NOT COMPARED TO YOU, I'M NOT !
DOM

EEEEEK! STUPID SAOTOME! STUPID, STUPID!

SHOOM

PONK PONK

I FEEL SO SAD! WAS YOUR GRADE THAT BAD?

YOU OUGHTTA KNOW!!

YOU GRADED ME! WHAT WAS MY SCORE?!

I FORGOT.

WHO'S THE IDIOT HERE?!

·CRACKLE·CRACKLE·

LISTEN UP, YEAH!!

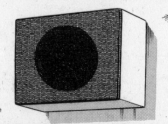

NOW DE BIG KAHUNA ANNOUNCE RANMA SAOTOME'S VERY BAD SCORE!

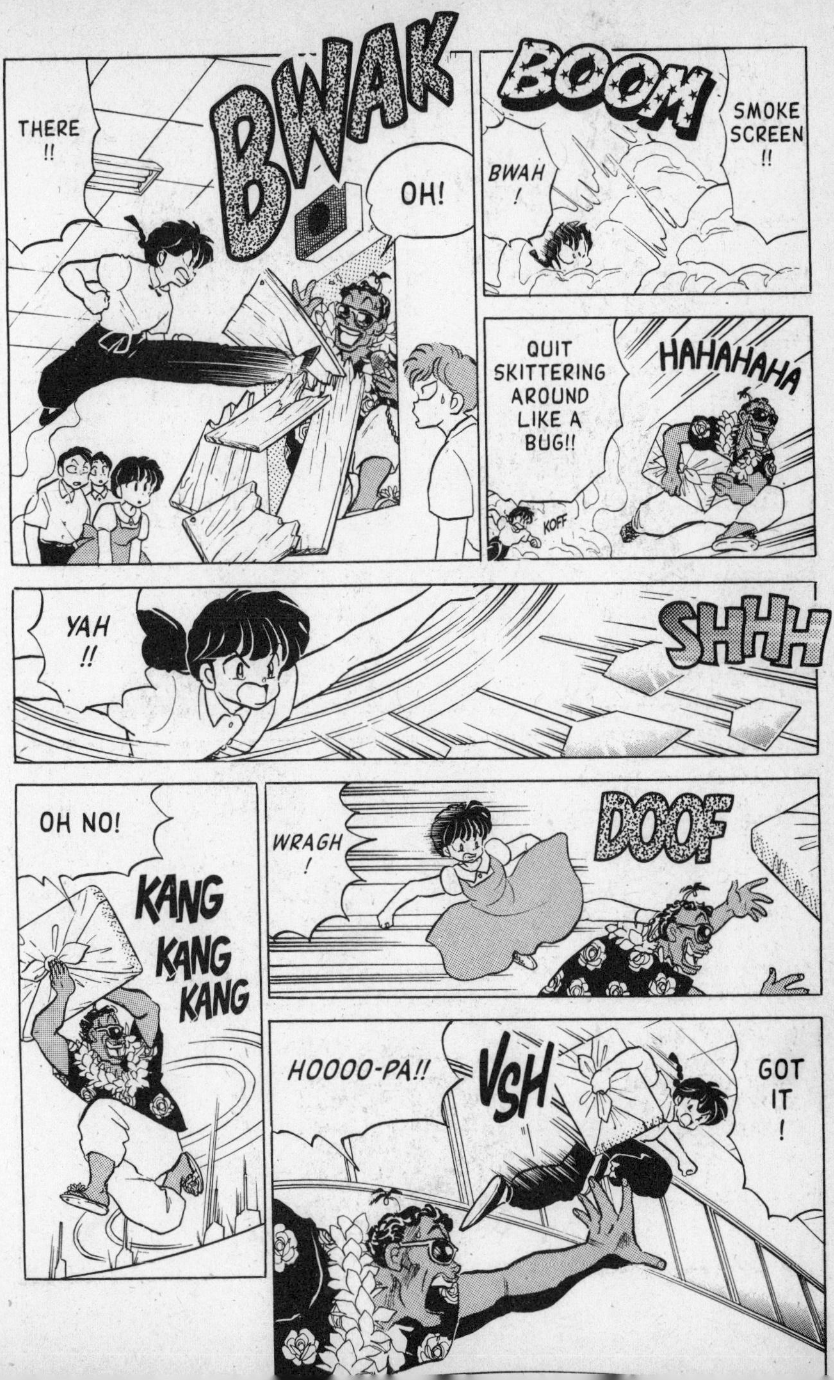
THERE !!
BWAK
OH!
BOOM
BWAH !
SMOKE SCREEN !!
QUIT SKITTERING AROUND LIKE A BUG!!
HAHAHAHA
KOFF
YAH !!
SHHH
OH NO!
KANG
KANG KANG
WRAGH !
DOOF
HOOOO-PA!!
VSH
GOT IT !

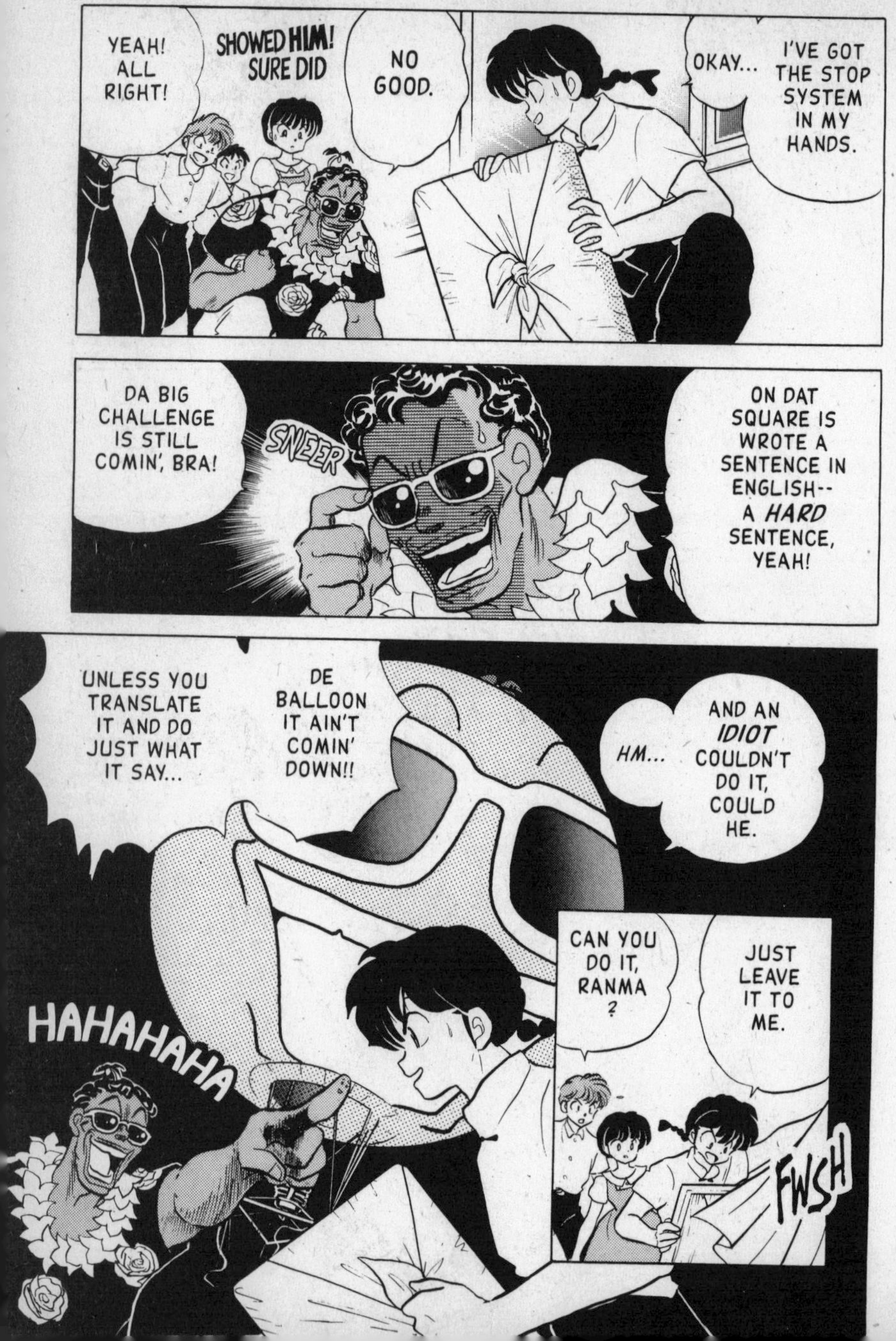
YEAH! ALL RIGHT!
SHOWED HIM! SURE DID
NO GOOD.
OKAY...
I'VE GOT THE STOP SYSTEM IN MY HANDS.
DA BIG CHALLENGE IS STILL COMIN', BRA!
SNEER
ON DAT SQUARE IS WROTE A SENTENCE IN ENGLISH-- A *HARD* SENTENCE, YEAH!
UNLESS YOU TRANSLATE IT AND DO JUST WHAT IT SAY...
DE BALLOON IT AIN'T COMIN' DOWN!!
HM...
AND AN *IDIOT* COULDN'T DO IT, COULD HE.
HAHAHAHA
CAN YOU DO IT, RANMA?
JUST LEAVE IT TO ME.
FWSH

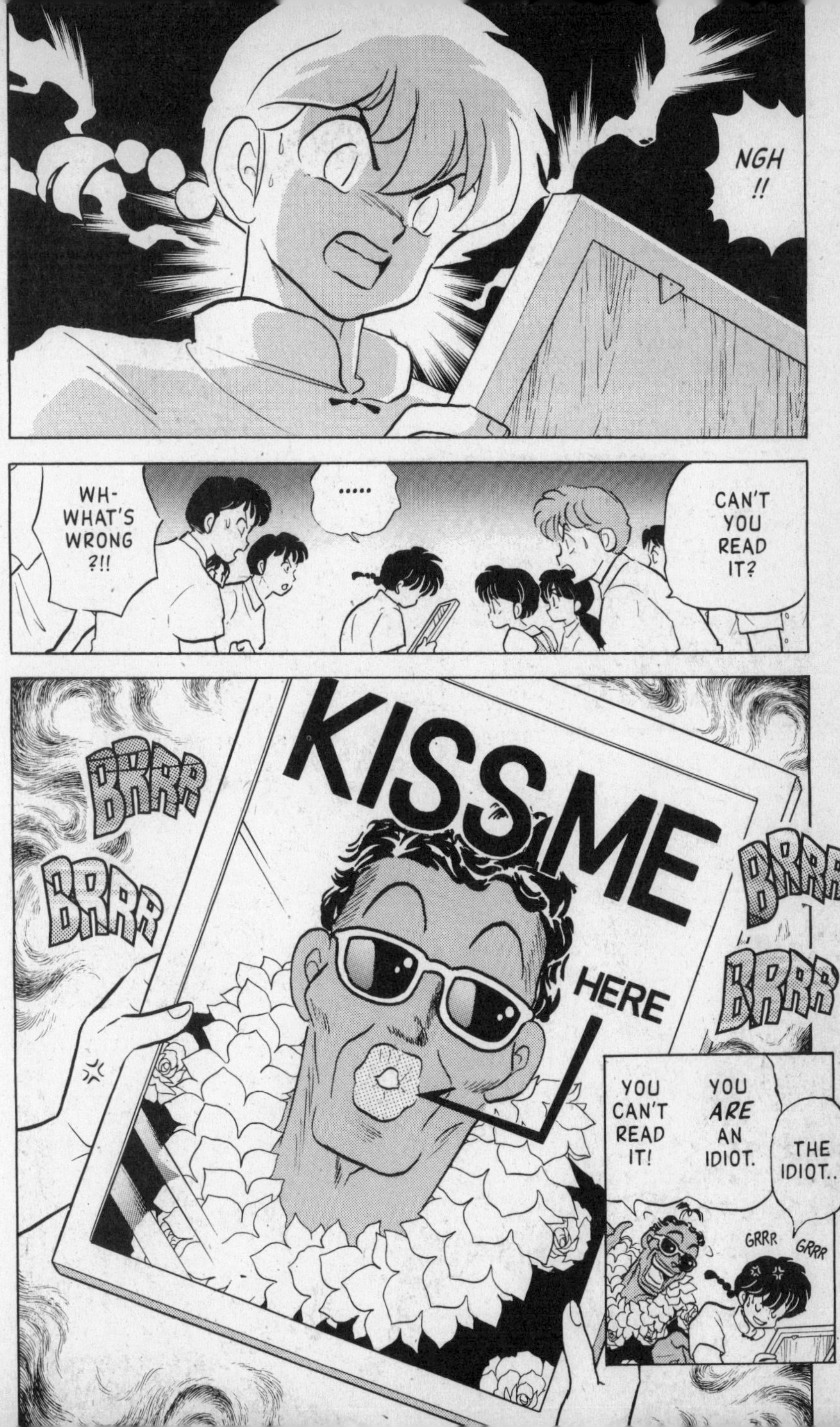
NGH !!
WH- WHAT'S WRONG ?!!
.....
CAN'T YOU READ IT?
BRRR
BRRR
KISS ME
HERE
BRRR
BRRR
YOU CAN'T READ IT!
YOU *ARE* AN IDIOT.
THE IDIOT...
GRRR
GRRR

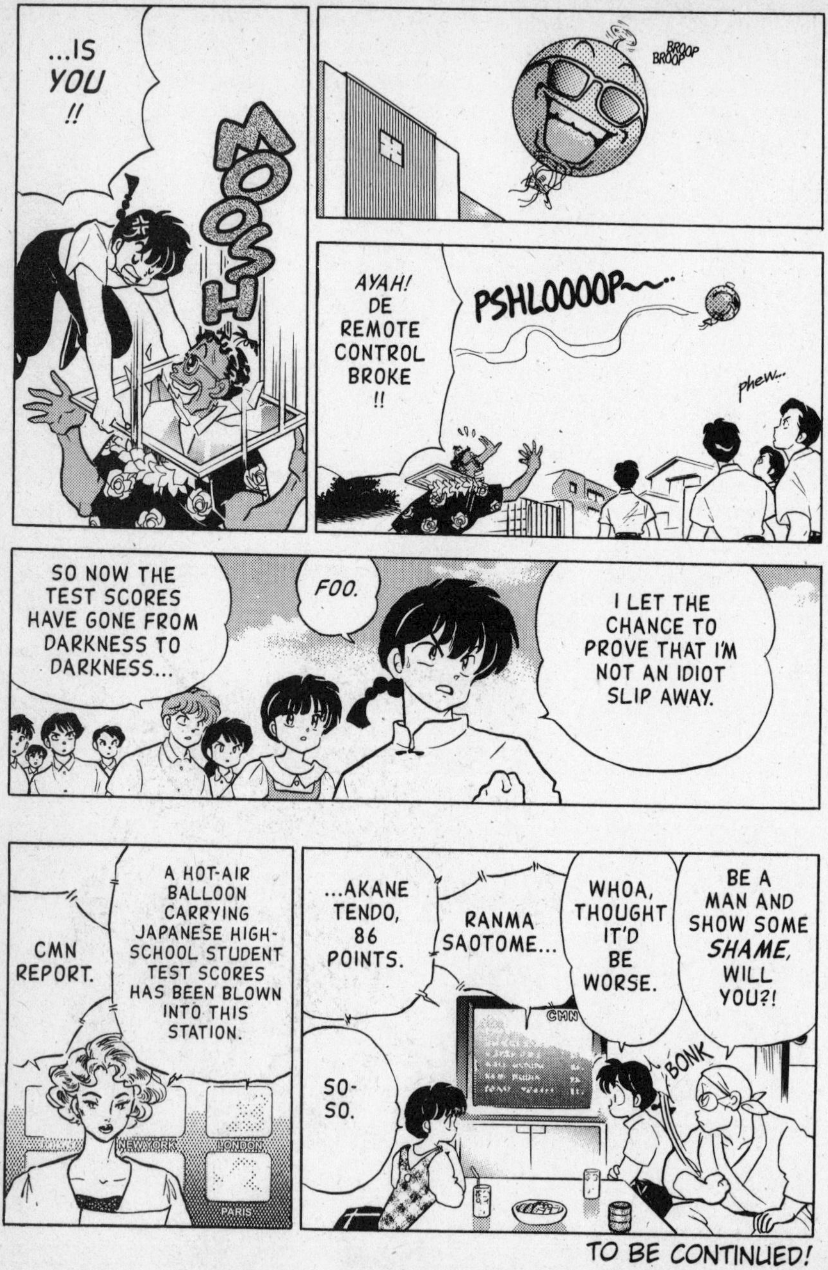
...IS YOU !!
WOOOSH
BROOP BROOP
AYAH! DE REMOTE CONTROL BROKE !!
PSHLOOOOP~~...
phew...
SO NOW THE TEST SCORES HAVE GONE FROM DARKNESS TO DARKNESS...
FOO.
I LET THE CHANCE TO PROVE THAT I'M NOT AN IDIOT SLIP AWAY.
CMN REPORT.
A HOT-AIR BALLOON CARRYING JAPANESE HIGH-SCHOOL STUDENT TEST SCORES HAS BEEN BLOWN INTO THIS STATION.
NEW YORK
LONDON
PARIS
...AKANE TENDO, 86 POINTS.
RANMA SAOTOME...
CMN
WHOA, THOUGHT IT'D BE WORSE.
BE A MAN AND SHOW SOME *SHAME*, WILL YOU?!
SO-SO.
BONK

TO BE CONTINUED!

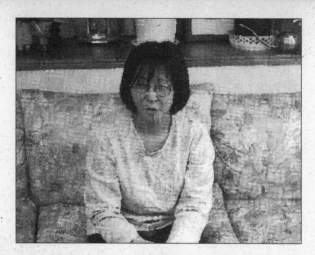

About Rumiko Takahashi

Born in 1957 in Niigata, Japan, Rumiko Takahashi attended women's college in Tokyo, where she began studying comics with Kazuo Koike, author of *CRYING FREEMAN*. She later became an assistant to horror-manga artist Kazuo Umezu (*OROCHI*). In 1978, she won a prize in Shogakukan's annual "New Comic Artist Contest," and in that same year her boy-meets-alien comedy series *URUSEI YATSURA* began appearing in the weekly manga magazine *SHÔNEN SUNDAY*. This phenomenally successful series ran for nine years and sold over 22 million copies. Takahashi's later *RANMA 1/2* series enjoyed even greater popularity.

Takahashi is considered by many to be one of the world's most popular manga artists. With the publication of Volume 34 of her *RANMA 1/2* series in Japan, Takahashi's total sales passed *one hundred million* copies of her compiled works.

Takahashi's serial titles include *URUSEI YATSURA, RANMA 1/2, ONE-POUND GOSPEL, MAISON IKKOKU* and *INUYASHA*. Additionally, Takahashi has drawn many short stories which have been published in America under the title "Rumic Theater," and several installments of a saga known as her "Mermaid" series. Most of Takahashi's major stories have also been animated, and are widely available in translation worldwide. *INUYASHA* is her most recent serial story, first published in *SHÔNEN SUNDAY* in 1996.